New Zealand
a travel survival kit

Tony Wheeler

New Zealand – a travel survival kit
5th Edition

Published by
Lonely Planet Publications
Head Office: PO Box 88, South Yarra, Victoria 3141, Australia
Branch Office: PO Box 2001A, Berkeley, CA 94702, USA

Printed by
Colorcraft, Hong Kong

Photographs by
Tony Wheeler (TW)
New Zealand Tourist and Publicity Travel Office (NZTP)
Mary Covernton (MC)
Vicki Beale (VB)
Lisa Smith (LS)
Veronica Curmi (VC)

Front cover
Mount Ngauruhoe during a minor eruption, Tongariro National Park (NZTP)
Back cover
Sheep grazing near Hinekura, Southern Wairarapa (NZTP)
Kiwi (NZTP)

Line illustrations
from *New Zealand: Its Physical Geography, Geology and Natural History* by Ferdinand von Hochstetter
(a German publication, 1863)

First published
December 1977

This edition
February 1988

National Library of Australia Cataloguing in Publication Data

Wheeler, Tony.
New Zealand, a travel survival kit.

5th ed.
Includes index.
ISBN 0 86442 020 X

1. New Zealand – Description and travel – 1981 –
Guide-books. I. Title.

919.31'0437

Tony Wheeler was born in England but spent most of his younger years overseas due to his father's occupation with British Airways. Those years included a lengthy spell in Pakistan, a shorter period in the West Indies and all his high school years in the USA. He returned to England and did a university degree in engineering, worked for a short time as an automotive design engineer, returned to university again and did an MBA. He then dropped out on the Asian trail with his wife Maureen. They've been travelling, writing and publishing travel guidebooks ever since. Now living in Melbourne, Australia, Tony has written a number of the Lonely Planet books including the popular *South-East Asia on a Shoestring*, and today divides his time between travel, writing and running Lonely Planet.

Lonely Planet Credits

Editor	Tony Wheeler
Maps	Vicki Beale
	Graham Imeson
Design &	Vicki Beale
Illustrations	Valerie Tellini
Typesetting	Debbie Lustig

Thanks also to: Lindy Cameron, Peter Turner and Sue Mitra for proof-reading and corrections; Ann Jeffree for additional typesetting and the title page illustration; and Debbie Lustig for map labels, index, contents and corrections.

Acknowledgements

Thanks must go to the NZTP for information and for the use of photographs. To Maui Campervans who lent us a campervan which we used for exploring the South Island. And to the many travellers who wrote to LP with suggestions, corrections and improvements. Thanks to:

Tom Agoston (USA), Helen Apouchtine (Can), Michael Arider (USA), Dr Trevor Avis (UK), Mrs Bain (NZ), Thomas Bäro, Sue Ball (Aus), Kaylene Blair (Aus), Anne Blair (NZ), June Bloom, Glen Brandenburg (USA), Mike Browne (NZ), Harriett Bryson (UK), Jane Burroughs (NZ), Candy Carosella (USA), Brian Carpenter (NZ), Lynda Chamberlain (NZ), Pam Cornell (NZ), Dick Coroone (USA), Harvey Currie (NZ), R & N Curtis (NZ), Eva S Dalix (NZ), Tom Difloure (USA), John Edwards (USA), Per Elvingson (Sw), Helen Fagerstrom (Sw), Rick Fehr (Can), Eric & Andy Foley (NZ), Patrick Frew (NZ), Peter Gassner (Aus), Susan & Frank Gilliland (USA), Graham Glen (NZ), Allen Gohbraun-Elwert Gottlieb (NZ), G A & C E Greenwood (NZ), Dave & Betsy Guyer (USA), Sue Hancock (Aus), Bill Harvey (NZ), Anne & Jack Hawthorn (NZ), Steve Hawthorn (Aus), David Hayen (USA), John & Mary Heaven (NZ), Nicole Heck (USA), Thomas & Annika Helin (Sw), Rick Hellriegel (NZ), Pamela Hinds (USA), Cedric Hockey (NZ), Ted Jimason (USA), Murray & Susan Johnson (Can), Jon Davies (Aus), Edward Day, Kathy & Gary Kurtz (USA), Ralph Levinstein (Can), Hans Lund (Sw), Vera Manther (Aus), Pam Matthews (NZ), Doug & Lorna Mettam (C), Mr Mcleay (NZ), Doug Mcleay (NZ), Jeanne Miche-Feldman (USA), Linda Montford (Can), Sandra Moorhouse (Aus), John Morrow (NZ), Wendy Mozenauer (NZ), Florence Murphy (NZ), Joachim Nölte (Dk), Paul & Pauline Pardy (Aus), R & M Perrin (Can), Stan Peyton (USA), Dorothy Preece (NZ), Bill Preis (NZ), Melissa Preston (NZ), Helen Quaife (NZ), Leslie Ransbottom (NZ), Simon Rea, Jane & Simon Robinson (NZ), Nigel Rushton (NZ),

John Schubert (Aus), Kim Skaya (NZ), Anette Sode & Paul-Erik Jensen (Dk), Michael Sorensen (Dk), John Stewart (Aus), Ralph Suters (Aus), Peter Swinhoe (Aus), Rosanne Tackaberry (Can), Wombat Tahanga (Aus), Deana Tesh (USA), I F Teding Van Berkhaut (NZ), Elly Van Ziel (Nl), Helen & Peter Warner (UK), J E Westmacott (Aus), Steven Wheeler (UK), R L White (NZ), Penny Williams (UK), Debra Kay & Edward Williams (NZ), Dick Williman (NZ), David Wise (USA), Ivan Young (Aus).

Aus – Australia, Can – Canada, Dk – Denmark, Nl – Netherlands, NZ – New Zealand, Sw – Sweden, UK – UK, USA – USA

This Edition

This book has had a varied history. I did the 1st edition back in 1977, the next two were updated by New Zealander Simon Hayman while the 4th edition was handled by Australian Mary Covernton. Robin Tinker wrote the tramping section, which has also been updated. This time I decided it was time I had another good look at the country and worked through New Zealand from north to south. The research was done in two trips, first of all a complete circuit of the North Island and a shorter visit to the South Island travelling solo. A two week intermission back in Australia was then followed by a circuit of the South Island in a Maui campervan, this time accompanied by Maureen and the children. Everybody had a great time and the campervan became something of a hitch-hikers special as we had plenty of room and picked up as many as four people at a time!

A Warning & a Request

Things change – prices go up, good places go bad and bad places go bankrupt – nothing stays the same. So if you find things better or worse, recently opened or long since closed, please write and tell us and help make the next edition better! In return for worthwhile information we'll send you a free copy of any Lonely Planet book you request.

To make this information available as soon as possible, extracts from the best letters are also included in the Lonely Planet Update. The Update is designed to provide an up-to-date 'noticeboard' for the invaluable information travellers contribute. It is published quarterly in paperback and is available from bookshops and by subscription. Turn to the back pages of this book for more information.

Contents

Introduction

Fresh open air, magnificent scenery and outdoor activities are the feature attractions of New Zealand. It's not a big country but for sheer variety it is hard to beat.

New Zealand's got everything, from sandy beaches and rugged coastlines to calm green meadows and ominously smoking volcanoes; from flat plains and placid lakes to high snow-capped mountains and bubbling hot mud pools. There are even icy glaciers that creep right down into sub-tropical rainforests.

There are cities too, but they pall beside the natural wonders. New Zealanders are friendly, easy going and helpful. Getting around is a breeze as there's lots of public transport and hitchhiking is reasonably easy. Finding places to stay is also no problem and generally won't empty your wallet too fast, although it's an idea to book ahead if you arrive somewhere in the high season. The food is fresh and there's plenty of it and these days even the wine can be excellent. It's a great country for travellers.

THE BIG 10

There are so many superb physical features in NZ that you find yourself taking the beauty of the country for granted after a while. But if I had to pick 10 'not to be missed sights or things to do in New Zealand' here's what they'd be:

1 – Bay of Islands and Waipoua Kauri Forest, Northland. This is the historic meeting point of New Zealand's European and Maori cultures and an area of great natural beauty.

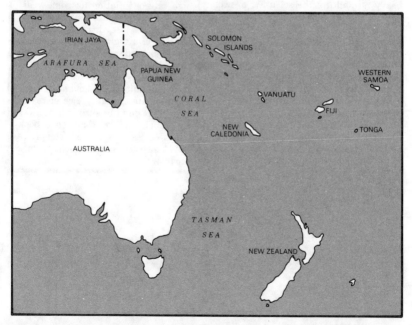

2 – Waitomo Caves, south of Hamilton. Limestone caverns with stalactites and stalagmites are obvious tourist attractions. There are a few of them scattered around both islands and one is much the same as another but how many have the unusual feature of a glow-worm grotto? See it on the way to Rotorua.

3 – Rotorua, central North Island. This is one of New Zealand's most interesting areas. Go there for the thermal activity (boiling water, hissing steam, bubbling mud pools) and the Maori culture (don't miss the night-time Maori concerts or a *hangi*).

4 – Tongariro National Park, central North Island. This park has some of the best mountain/volcano scenery in the country and excellent tramping tracks. It's a short run south of Rotorua.

5 – Fox and Franz Josef Glaciers, west coast of the South Island. Nowhere else do glaciers come so close to sea level so close to the equator. Steep mountains and heavy rainfall are the scientific answer but sitting in sub-tropical rainforest, looking at so much ice, drives the easy answers out of your head.

6 – Milford Sound, south-west coast of the South Island. This is Fiordland, just like the fiords of Norway, and Milford Sound is one of the most spectacular.

7 – Queenstown, South Island. This is a resort town which offers a whole host of activities including genteel boat trips on the lake, visits to sheep stations, shooting rapids upstream in jet-boats or downstream in inflatables, some excellent walking trips, plus skiing in the winter.

8 – Mt Cook, South Island. The highest mountain in New Zealand has fantastic scenery, good walking territory and the Tasman Glacier.

9 – A museum, in either Wellington, Auckland, Christchurch or Wanganui. While you're in one of the cities, go to a museum and get an insight into Maori culture. The four listed are amongst the best but New Zealand is well endowed with excellent museums.

10 – A walk. Somewhere along the line set a week aside and do one of the long walks for which New Zealand is justly famous. The Milford Track is the best known but others are equally rewarding.

Money Warnings

1. New Zealand has been suffering a high rate of inflation for some years and it shows no sign of abating. During the life of the last edition of this guide the cost of a night's stay at a Youth Hostel jumped from around $4 or $5 to around $10 to $12. Many other prices from bus fares to motel rooms zoomed up just as quickly. Although I've tried to anticipate as many price increases as possible don't be surprised if prices are much higher than this book indicates. Remember the cheap prices will still be cheap, the expensive ones expensive!

Facts about the Country

HISTORY

New Zealand's history has two distinct phases – the Maori part and the more recent history since the arrival of Europeans.

Maori History

The original inhabitants of New Zealand were known until fairly recently as Moriorisis. Recent evidence now indicates that the Maoris arrived in Aotearoa – the 'land of the long white cloud' as they called New Zealand – in a series of migrations and that the Moriorisis were in the first wave of Maori migration rather than being a separate and distinct race. It was these early settlers who hunted the huge flightless bird, the moa, both for food and its feathers until it became extinct. Today, the name Moriori refers to the original settlers of the Chatham Islands where the last full-blooded Moriori died in 1933.

Since the Maoris had no written language, their history and culture is recalled through story-telling and songs, which means it's probable that the saga of Kupe, Hawaiki and the 'great migration' has been embellished over the centuries. While it would be unwise to take the legend absolutely literally, there's obviously a good deal of truth in it. One of the heroes of the story, Kupe, obviously a particularly brilliant Polynesian navigator, is said to have set sail from Hawaiki in the 10th century for the 'great southern land, uninhabited and covered with mists' – and managed to return to tell the tale.

Centuries later, when things weren't going so well in Hawaiki – over-population, shortage of food and all those other familiar problems, the decision was made to follow Kupe's instructions and head south. Despite the similar names Hawaiki is not Hawaii; experts believe it was more likely to have been an island near Tahiti.

The similar spelling and pronunciation however, suggests that another party of emigrants from Hawaiki settled in Hawaii, naming it after their home island.

According to legend, 10 great canoes sailed to New Zealand in the 14th century, though historians now feel the great arrival may actually have been more than 1000 years ago. The names of the canoes are all remembered, and their landing points, crews and histories also recalled. Today, Maoris still trace their lineage back to one or other of the canoes of the great migration. Of course the 'moa hunters' were there and some other Maoris from an earlier, smaller migration, but the new immigrants from the great fleet soon established themselves in their adopted home.

Maori culture developed without hindrance from other cultures for hundreds of years but being warriors they engaged in numerous tribal battles in which the losers ended up as slaves or pot roast. Given the shortage of animal life in New Zealand, enemies must have been a useful source of protein. While they did not develop a written language the Maoris created a complex art form involving beautifully carved war canoes and meeting houses and intricate tattoos on both men and women. They were still stone age people (in New Zealand it would have been difficult to get beyond that stage since there are few metals apart from gold!) but they produced exquisite greenstone (jade) ornaments and war clubs. Expeditions were mounted to the South Island to find jade but otherwise they wisely stayed in the much warmer North Island.

European Exploration

In 1642 the Dutch explorer Abel Tasman, who had just sailed around Australia from Batavia (Jakarta), dropped by but didn't stay long after several of his crew were killed and cooked. His visit however, meant that Europeans now knew of New Zealand's existence and in those days of colonialism it also meant that they would eventually want it. The Dutch, after their first uncomfortable look, were none too keen on the place and it was left alone until Captain Cook sailed by in 1769, discovered that his Tahitian interpreter could communicate with the Maoris, claimed the whole place for Britain, sailed right round both islands mapping as he went, and split for Australia. The good captain made a number of friendly contacts with the Maoris and was impressed with their bravery and spirit and with the potential of this lightly populated land.

When the British started their antipodean colonising they opted for the even more lightly populated Australia so New Zealand's first European settlers were temporary ones – sealers (who soon reduced the seal population to nothing) and then whalers (who did the same with whales). They were hardly the cream of European society and they introduced diseases and prostitution, created such a demand for preserved heads that Maori chiefs started chopping off their slaves' heads to order (previously they'd only preserved the heads of warriors who had died in battle) and worst of all they brought in European arms. When they traded in greenstone *meres* for muskets, the Maoris soon embarked on wholesale slaughter of each other. By 1830 the Maori population was falling dramatically.

European Settlement

The arrival of Samuel Marsden, the first missionary, in 1841 righted the balance a little and by the middle of the 19th century warfare had been much reduced, cannibalism fairly well stamped out and the raging impact of *Pakeha* (white man's) diseases and his modern armoury were also curbed. But the unfortunate Maoris now found themselves spiritually assaulted and much of their traditions and culture were destroyed. Despite the missionary influence their numbers continued to decline.

During this time settlers were arriving in New Zealand and began to demand British protection from the Maoris and from other less savoury settlers. The Poms were not too keen on further colonising – what with burning their fingers in America, fighting in Canada, and generally messing around in other places, not to mention having Australia to worry about. But the threat of a French colonising effort stirred them to despatch James Busby to be the British Resident in 1833. The fact that this was a very low key effort is illustrated by poor Busby even having to pay his own fare from Australia and once he'd set up shop his efforts to protect the settlers and keep law and order were somewhat limited by the fact that he had no forces, no arms, no authority and was soon dubbed 'the man-of-war without guns'.

Clashes with the Maoris

In 1840 the British sent Captain William Hobson to replace Busby. Hobson was instructed to persuade the Maori chiefs to relinquish their sovereignty to the British Crown. In part this decision was made in the expectation that if the government didn't get in there and organise things every Tom, Dick and Harry settler would be buying land off the Maoris for two axes and a box of candles and chaos would soon result.

With a truly British display of pomp and circumstance, Hobson met with the Maori chiefs in front of Busby's residence at Waitangi at the Bay of Islands. It is now known as the Treaty House and the anniversary of 6 February 1840 is considered the birthday of modern New Zealand. Forty-five chiefs signed the treaty (or rather Hobson signed for them) and eventually 500 chiefs from around the country agreed to British rule.

This orderly state of affairs didn't last long. When settlers wanted to buy land and the Maoris didn't want to sell, conflict inevitably resulted. The admirable idea that the government should act as a go-between in all Maori-Pakeha deals to ensure fairness on both sides fell apart when the government was too tight-fisted to pay the price. The first visible revolt came when Hone Heke, the first chief to sign the Waitangi treaty, chopped down the flagpole at Kororareka (now known as Russell), across the bay. Despite new poles and more and more guards Heke or his followers managed to chop the pole down four times, and on the last occasion it was covered with iron to foil axe-wielding Maoris! After this final destruction of the pole he burnt down the town of Kororareka for good measure, an action which has since been acclaimed as a sign of his good taste because it was a pestilent place.

In the skirmishes that followed the British governor put a £100 reward on Heke's head, to which Heke brilliantly responded by offering a matching £100 for the governor's head. This was only one in a long series of skirmishes, battles, conflicts, disputes and arguments, which escalated between 1860 and 1865 into a more-or-less full-fledged war. The result was inconclusive, but the Maoris were effectively worn down by sheer weight of numbers and equipment.

Modern New Zealand

Things calmed down and New Zealand became an efficient agricultural country. Sheep farming, that backbone of modern New Zealand, took hold as refrigerated ships made it possible to sell New Zealand meat in Europe. Towards the end of the last century New Zealand went through a phase of sweeping social change that took it to the forefront of the world. Women were given the vote in 1893, 25 years before Britain or America and more like 75 years ahead of Switzerland. The range of far-sighted social reforms and pioneering legislation included old age pensions, minimum wage structures, the establishment of arbitration courts and the introduction of child health services. The latter included the foundation in 1907 of the Plunket Society, an organisation of nurses who care for expectant mothers and young babies.

Meanwhile the Maoris floundered. New Zealand grew through immigration (very selective immigration), but by 1900 the Maori population had dropped to about 42,000 and their numbers continued to decline. The Maoris were given the vote in 1867, but the continuing struggle to hold onto their culture and their ancestral

lands sapped their spirit and energy for some time. In the last few decades there has been a turn-around and the Maori population has started to increase, at a faster rate than the Pakehas. Today they number about 280,000.

New Zealanders are proud of their record of racial harmony, there has never been any racial separation and inter-marriage is common. In *Return to Paradise* James Michener tells of the outraged New Zealand reaction when WW II GIs stationed in New Zealand tried to treat Maoris like American blacks. Despite this the Maoris are a disadvantaged race sharing a less than proportional part of the nation's wealth and leadership. It's a problem New Zealanders are wrestling with but without great success as yet.

New Zealand Today

Today New Zealand is still predominantly an agricultural country but the '70s and '80s have been hard. The closure of much of its traditional European market for agricultural products combined with the oil crisis price hikes of many of its mineral and manufactured imports have done no good at all to the country's economic situation. Unlike Australia, New Zealand has little mineral wealth to supplement its agricultural efficiency. Furthermore the inefficiencies of small scale manu-facturing that afflict Australia are simply magnified by New Zealand's even tinier population. It's still an affluent, organised, tidy country but things simply aren't as rosy as they once were.

Internationally, however, New Zealand has become by far the most interesting and important country in the South Pacific region. It has taken a strong stand on nuclear issues, refusing entry to nuclear-equipped US warships and condemning French nuclear testing in the Pacific. This brave policy has caused more than a few problems for the Kiwis. The US has dumped them from the ANZUS treaty agreements and the French have even gone so far as to send government-

sponsored terrorists to sink the anti-nuclear Greenpeace ship the *Rainbow Warrior* in Auckland's harbour.

POPULATION

There are a little over three million people in New Zealand. About 280,000 are Maoris and New Zealand also has a large and growing population of Pacific Islanders. Many of the islands of the Pacific are currently experiencing a rapid population shift from remote and undeveloped islands to the 'big city' and Auckland is very much the big city of the South Pacific. It's causing a great deal of argument, discussion and tension and much of it is not between the recent Pacific immigrants and the Pakeha population but between the islanders and the Maoris.

If Pacific immigration were to continue unchecked and the Maori population also continued to grow faster than the population of European descent the Pakehas would eventually find themselves in the minority. Over the last 10 years the economic situation led to a mass exodus to Australia and further afield. In some years there was an actual population decline but recently the flow has started to slow.

New Zealand is lightly populated by European standards but much more densely populated than Australia with its forbidding stretches of empty country. The South Island once had a greater population than the North but now it's the place to go for wide open spaces. Its entire population is barely more than Auckland's. The capital is Wellington but Auckland is easily the largest city. The five largest cities are:

Auckland	815,000
Wellington	320,000
Christchurch	289,000
Dunedin	105,000
Hamilton	102,000

GOVERNMENT

The government of New Zealand is modelled on the British parliamentary system, elections being based on universal adult suffrage. The minimum voting age is 18 and candidates are elected by secret ballot. The maximum period between elections is three years but the interval can be shorter for various reasons, such as when the government of the day needs to seek the confidence of the people on a topic of particular national importance. Unlike in Australia voting in New Zealand is not compulsory, but on average more than 80% of those eligible to vote do so.

The difference between Britain's Westminster system and the New Zealand model is that New Zealand has abolished the upper house and governs solely through the lower house. Known as the House of Representatives, it has 92 member's seats, four of which are held by Maoris. Maoris were admitted to parliament in 1867. The House of Representatives functions primarily to legislate and review the actions of the government in power. No tax can be imposed, nor any money spent until the house has authorised such action. The procedure of legislature is similar to that of the British House of Commons with each bill being given three readings. The first reading introduces the bill; the second involves full-scale debate, followed by the committee stage – a clause-by-clause analysis of the proposed legislation; and the third is usually a formality unless a particular bill contains a contentious issue. Should this be the case, the opposition party can press for a full third reading debate, to place on record desired changes not achieved during the committee stage.

New Zealand follows a party system; the two main ones being the National (conservative) and Labour parties. Among the others is the Social Credit Party. The party that wins a majority of seats in an election automatically becomes the government and its leader, the Prime Minister. In July 1984 the Nationals, in office for three terms under the leadership of Sir Robert Muldoon, were bundled out unceremoniously by the landslide victory of the Labour Party led by David Lange. In August 1987 Lange won a second election, a mandate to continue his sweeping changes to the New Zealand economic system.

Like Britain, New Zealand is a constitutional monarchy; the traditional head of state, the reigning British king or queen, being represented by a resident governor-general, who is appointed for a five-year term. As well, an independent judiciary makes up another tier of government. The hierarchy of the courts comprises a Court of Appeal, High Court and District Courts. All three exercise both civil and criminal law jurisdiction, but as its name suggests, the Court of Appeal deals entirely with appellate cases, while the function of the High Court is concerned with major crimes, the more important civil claims, appeals and reviews. The District Courts have an extensive jurisdiction in civil and criminal cases and domestic proceedings. The Family Courts come within the division of the District Courts and have jurisdiction over most family matters including divorce.

GEOGRAPHY

New Zealand stretches 1600 km (992 miles) from north to south and consists of three large islands and a number of smaller islands scattered around the two main ones. The two major land masses are the 115,000 square km North Island and the 151,000 square km South Island. Stewart Island, which covers an area of 1700 square km, lies directly south of the South Island. The country is 10,400 km south-west of the US, 1700 km south of Fiji and 2250 km east of Australia. Its western coastline faces the Tasman Sea, the part of the Pacific Ocean which separates New Zealand and Australia.

New Zealand's territorial jurisdiction also extends to the islands of Chatham, Kermadec, Tokelau, Auckland, Antipodes, Snares, Solander and Bounty (most of them uninhabited) and the Ross Dependency in Antarctica.

FAUNA

When animal life is so common in New Zealand (the four-legged, off-white, woolly variety that is), it's kind of curious to discover that there are virtually no native mammals. The first Maori settlers brought some rats and the now extinct Maori dog with them but the only indigenous animals were bats. So you can imagine how surprised they were, the Maoris *and* the bats, when the Europeans turned up with sheep, cows, pigs and everything else old MacDonald's farm could offer. Today there are several species of deer, rabbits, possums – all introduced and many of them harmful to the environment – and, of course, sheep. In fact, there are so many sheep that after lambing time the sheep population can reach 100 million, 30 sheep for every man, woman and child.

Though New Zealand had few animals, it had plenty of birds – *had* being the operative word. Seven species of native birds are on the endangered list. Worst affected were the flightless birds like the kakapo and takahe which were easy prey for the introduced competitors and predators. In fact, the takahe was considered extinct until a small colony of them was discovered in the wild country of the southern fiords in 1948. Experts are having some success in breeding takahe in captivity and you can see them at a wildlife sanctuary in Te Anau. Other rare species are the crested grebe, the spotless crake, the black stilt, the fernbird and falcons. The rare brown teal's natural environment is the wetlands which have been affected by continued drainage and reclamation of swamps and the modification of rivers for irrigation and hydro-electricity.

The best known of New Zealand's birds is the kiwi which has become the symbol of New Zealanders. It's a small, tubby, flightless bird and, because it's nocturnal, is not easy to observe. There is a theory that the kiwi became so lazy it lost its ability to fly. But, although the short-sighted and sleepy kiwis may have no wings and feathers that are more like hair than real feathers, the All Blacks (New Zealand's champion rugby team) have nothing on

them when it comes to sheer leg power. The kiwi has one thing in common with Australia's usually quiet, cute and cuddly koala – a shocking temper! In the kiwi this is usually demonstrated by giving whatever or whoever it is upset with, a thumping big kick. Despite the fact that night time is when they are most active, they are still fairly lazy, sleeping as much as 20 hours a day. The rest of the time they spend poking around for worms which they sniff out with the nostrils on the end of their long bill.

The female is larger than the male and much fiercer. She lays an egg weighing up to half a kg, huge in relation to her size, but having performed that mighty feat leaves the male to hatch it while she guards the burrow. When kiwi junior hatches out it looks just like a mini version of its parents, not like a chick at all, and associates only with dad, completely ignoring mother kiwi. There are several 'nocturnal houses' in New Zealand where you can see kiwis in a good representation of their natural habitat. Although the kiwi is not endangered it is suffering from the destruction of native bush, pig-hunters' dogs and the use of opossum traps.

Other bird life includes the morepork (mopoke), a small spotted owl; and the kea, a large raucous parrot with drab green feathers and a most un-parrot-like preference for high altitudes and cold weather. The kea has a reputation for killing sheep which makes them unpopular with farmers but they may be just as unpopular with you since they like hanging around humans, tipping over garbage bins and sliding, noisily, down roofs at night. They're amusing, fearless, cheeky and inquisitive birds. Keep a close eye on your gear when they're around since they have incredibly strong beaks and will have a peck at anything, including pulling eyelets out of boots and ripping sleeping bags and tents.

Another amusing bird is the ducklike weka which hangs around campsites and rushes over to steal things when you turn your back. The weka will purloin anything it can carry in its bill – particularly if it's a nice, shiny object – so don't leave rings and watches lying around.

The New Zealand bird you won't see is the famous moa, a sort of oversized ostrich. Originally, there were numerous types and sizes, but the largest of them – the huge giant moas – were as high as four metres. They were well and truly extinct by the time the Europeans turned up but you can still see moa skeletons and reconstructions in many New Zealand museums. Surprisingly not extinct is the tuatara, the sole survivor of a group of ancient reptiles somewhat akin to the dinosaurs. Sometimes mistakenly referred to as a lizard it is now found only on a few offshore islands and is absolutely protected. New Zealand has no snakes and only one spider that is dangerous to humans, the rare katipo which is similar to the American black widow and the Australian redback.

THE MAORI LANGUAGE

Although the Maoris had a vividly chronicled history it was recorded in songs which dramatically recalled the great migration and other important events. It was the early missionaries who first recorded the language in a written form. They did this using only 15 letters of our alphabet and ending all syllables in a vowel.

The language is related to other Polynesian languages (including Tahitian and Hawaiian) and has some similarity to dialects found in Indonesia. It's a fluid, poetic language and actually surprisingly easy to pronounce if you just remember to say it phonetically and split each word (some can be amazingly long) into separate syllables. Few Maoris speak it in day-to-day life now; it is mainly used for ceremonial (and tourist) events, although it is a matter of some pride to have some fluency. Many places have delightful and descriptive Maori names – unfortunately some of the nicest are no longer used. Would you rather visit Mt Cook or *Aorangi* – the 'cloud piercer'?

When pronouncing Maori words the main thing is to master the five vowels:

a = ar, as the sound in f*ar*ther
e = air, as the sound in m*ea*sure
i = ee, as the sound in s*ee*m
o = or, as the sound in *or* or the long o in l*o*w
u = oo, as the sound in r*oo*m

In a Maori word each syllable ends in a vowel and there is never more than one vowel in a syllable. Thus Maori itself is pronounced Mar-or-ree. The only compound consonants are WH and NG. The nearest in English to WH is F, which is not quite the right sound, softening the F helps. NG is a nasal sound, but used at the beginning of a syllable, rather than the end of it as in English. Thus Ngaruawahia is pronounced Ngar-roo-ar-war-hee-ar, and Whangarei is pronounced Far-ngar-rair-ee. There are no silent letters and each syllable has equal stress.

You can find many Maori-English phrase books and dictionaries in New Zealand if you want to have a go. Recently interest in the Maori language has grown enormously in New Zealand and many *Pakeha* pronunciations of Maori words are suddenly reverting to their correct Maori pronunciation. The town of Whangarei has become something closer to 'Fangarei'! Meanwhile here are a few words to try out:

atua
    spirit or gods
haka
    war dance
hakari
    feast
hangi
    oven made by digging a hole and steaming food in baskets over embers in the hole
heitiki
    a carved, stylised neck ornament of green stone; often shortened to 'tiki'

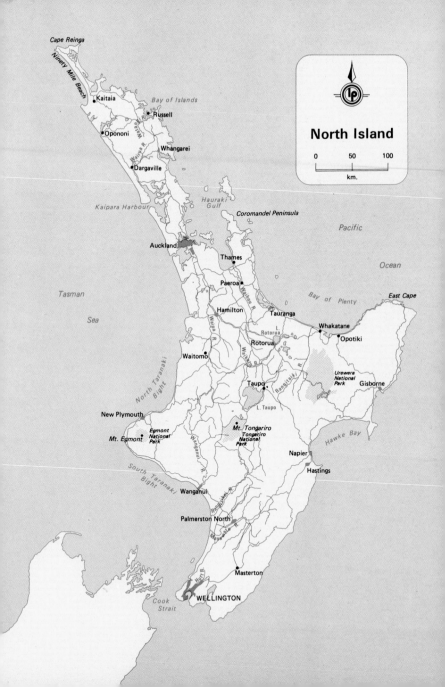

Cape Reinga

Ninety Mile Beach

•Kaitaia

Bay of Islands

•Russell

Opononi

Whangarei

Dargaville

Kaipara Harbour

Hauraki Gulf

Coromandel Peninsula

Pacific

Auckland

Thames

Ocean

Paeroa

Tasman

Hamilton

Waihou R.

Bay of Plenty

East Cape

Tauranga

Whakatane

Sea

Waipa R.

Rotorua

Opotiki

Waitomo

Rotorua

Waikato R.

Urewera National Park

Gisborne

Taupo

Rangitaiki R.

North Taranaki Bight

L. Taupo

New Plymouth

Egmont National Park

Mt. Tongariro

Tongariro National Park

Napier

Mt. Egmont

Wanganui R.

Hawke Bay

South Taranaki Bight

Hastings

Wanganui

Rangitikei R.

Palmerston North

Manawatu R.

Masterton

Hutt R.

WELLINGTON

Cook Strait

North Island

0   50   100

km.

South Island

kai
food, any word with kai in it will have some food connection

ka pai
good, excellent

kumara
sweet potatoes, a Maori staple food

mana
psychic power or influence

mere
flat, greenstone war club

moko
chin tattoo on women, not prevalent today but you may still see some old Maori women with them

pa
fortified village, usually on a hilltop

pakeha
whitey, European in general

tapu
taboo, forbidden

tiki
an amulet or figurine, often a carved representation of an ancestor

tohunga
priest, wizard or general expert

wai
water, place names with wai in them will often be on a river

whare
house; 'whare runanga' – meeting house, 'whare whakairo' – carved house

Greetings

haere-mai
welcome

haera-ra
goodbye, farewell

kia ora
good luck, good health

Place Names

Many place names have a clear Maori influence. Maori words you may come across incorporated in New Zealand place names include:

anatoki – axe or adze in a cave; cave or valley in the shape of an axe
awa – river or valley
ika – fish
iti – small
kahurangi – treasured possession, special greenstone
kai – food
kainga – village
kare – rippling
kotinga – cutting or massacre
koura – crayfish
manga – branch, stream or tributary
mangarakau – plenty of sticks, a great many trees
manu – bird
maunga – mountain
moana – sea or lake
moko – tattoo
motu – island
nui – big
one – beach, sand or mud
onekaka – red-hot or burning sand
pa – fortified village
papa – flat, broad slab
parapara – the soft mud used for dyeing flax
patarua – killed by the thousands, site of early tribal massacres
pohatu – stone
puke – hill
rangi – sky, heavens
rangiheata – absence of clouds, a range seen in the early morning
repo – swamp
roa – long
rua – two
roto – lake
rua – hole, two
takaka – killing stick for parrot, or bracken
tane – man
tapu – sacred or forbidden
tata – close to, dash against, twin islands
te – the
totaranui – place of big totara trees
uruwhenua – enchanted objects
wahine – woman
wai – water
waikaremumu – bubbling waters
waingaro – lost, waters that disappear in certain seasons

wainui – big bay or many rivers, the ocean
whanga – bay or inlet
whare – house
whenua – land or country

Try a few – Whanga-roa is long bay, Roto-rua is two lakes, Roto-roa is long lake, Wai-kare-iti is little rippling water. All those names with 'wai' in them – Waitomo, Waitara, Waioru, Wairoa, Waitoa, Waihi, and so on – all have something to do with water.

HOLIDAYS

People from the northern hemisphere never seem to become completely familiar with upside-down seasons. To them Christmas simply doesn't fall in the middle of summer and how is it possible to shiver in the mid-winter cold of August? But it's worth remembering since Christmas, in the middle of summer and in the middle of school holidays, means lots of vacationing New Zealanders, which in turn means crowds and higher prices. If you want to avoid the school-age hordes, they're out of captivity from mid-December until the end of January (the same as Aussie kids); then for a couple of weeks in May; and again in August.

Public holidays and special events around New Zealand include:

January
New Year's Day and the next day (2 January) – public holidays.
The Annual Yachting Regatta – Auckland.

6 February
New Zealand Day or Waitangi Day – public holiday; actively celebrated at Waitangi in the Bay of Islands.

March
Good Friday/Easter Monday (March or April) – public holidays.
Fiesta Week (mid-March) – Auckland; great fun with some terrific fireworks.
The Golden Shears Sheep Shearing Contest – Masterton (southern end of the North Island); a major event in this sheepish country!
The International Bill-fish Tournament – Bay of Islands.
The Ngaruawahia Regatta for Maori canoes – Hamilton.

April
Anzac Day – 25 April; public holiday.
The Highland Games – Hastings.

May
The National Woolcrafts Festival – Christchurch.

June
The Queen's Birthday, (1st Monday) – public holiday.
New Zealand Agricultural Field Days – a major agricultural show at Mystery Creek, Hamilton.

October
Labour Day (4th Monday) – public holiday.

November
Canterbury Show week – Christchurch.
An International Trout Fishing Contest – Rotorua.

December
Christmas Day and Boxing Day (25 and 26 December) – public holidays.

Each province also has its own anniversary day holiday. Local holidays include:

Wellington	22 January
Auckland	29 January
Northland	29 January
Nelson	1 February
Taranaki	31 March
Otago	23 March
Southland	23 March
Hawke's Bay	1 November
Marlborough	1 November
Westland	1 December
Canterbury	16 December

When these local holidays fall between Friday and Sunday, they are usually observed on the following Monday; if they fall between Tuesday and Thursday, they are held on the preceding Monday.

Facts for the Visitor

PASSPORTS & VISAS

Everyone needs a passport to enter New Zealand. Until recently Aussies coming direct from Australia technically didn't need their little blue book to enter, although they did need it to get home again! However, from November 1987, Australians also have to present their passports on entry. All passports must be valid for three months beyond the intended departure date.

Australians do not need visas and can stay indefinitely. British passport holders (who have UK residence rights) do not need visas and can stay up to six months. With certain exceptions if you're from a country of Western Europe, from Canada, Iceland, Japan, Singapore or the USA you do not need a visa for stays up to three months.

If you're from another country, or if you wish to stay for longer than those periods or to work or study then you must have a visa. Check with New Zealand consular offices for more visa information. As with almost anywhere in the world entry requirements are likely to change so always check the situation shortly before you depart. There's nothing worse than arriving at the airport when you leave home and finding you must have a visa, when you thought you didn't! All visitors must have onward or return ticketing and sufficient funds to maintain themselves for the duration of their stay without working.

CUSTOMS, ENTRY & EXIT

The usual sort of x cigarettes, y bottles of liquor regulations apply. Like Australia the customs people are very fussy about drugs. New Zealand has heavy duties on cameras, cars, televisions and other electronic equipment and you can expect customs to be finicky about these sort of consumer goods. Like Australia they are also fussy about animal products and the possibility of animal disease, which is not surprising when they've got 60 million sheep.

There's a $2 departure tax at the airport.

MONEY

A$1	=	NZ$1.15
C$1	=	NZ$1.25
DM1	=	NZ$0.90
S$1	=	NZ$0.80
UK£1	=	NZ$2.70
US$1	=	NZ$1.60
Y100	=	NZ$1.09

Unless otherwise noted all dollar prices quoted in this book are New Zealand dollars.

New Zealand currency is dollars and cents – there are 1, 2, 5, 10, 20 and 100 dollar notes and 1, 2, 5, 10, 20 and 50 cent coins very similar to Australia's. Yes their coins will fit Australian parking meters and pay phones! You can bring in as much of any currency as you like and unused foreign currency or travellers' cheques which you brought in with you may be exported without limitations. Unused NZ currency can be changed to foreign currency before you leave.

Banks are open Monday to Friday from 9.30 am to 4 pm. All the usual brands of travellers' cheques are accepted and they can be changed at banks or large city hotels. Australian Bankcards are widely accepted throughout New Zealand; as are Visa, Mastercard, American Express and Diners Club.

If you're intending a long stay it may be worth opening a Post Office Savings Bank account. You can withdraw money from this at any post office in New Zealand – very handy for travellers – and the Post Office Savings Bank is open for longer

hours than the other banks. Apart from saving on travellers' cheques you also get a free safe deposit envelope when you open the account. You can put airline tickets or other valuables in this envelope and deposit it with the bank while you travel around New Zealand. They'll even forward it on to your departure city if you don't leave from the same place as you arrive.

Inflation & GST

Inflation is hot and heavy in New Zealand. During the life of the last edition of this book prices virtually doubled and they're still galloping along. One recent cause for the rapid price hikes was the introduction in late '86 of GST – Goods & Services Tax. It's a European-style VAT (value added tax) which added 10% on to the price of just about everything. Most prices in New Zealand are quoted inclusive of GST but when you're paying for something beware of any small print announcing that the price is GST exclusive; you'll be hit for the extra 10% on top of the stated cost. GST has been such a wonderful money spinner for the government that there are strong rumours that it will be increased, possibly to 15%.

Tipping

New Zealanders do not believe in it – they have an even greater aversion to tipping than Australians. The first sign you see on arriving in New Zealand is likely to advise you that 'tipping is not a New Zealand custom'. So don't!

CLIMATE

It's upside down compared to the northern hemisphere and similar, though a little colder, to southern Australia. The North Island has an average rainfall of around 130 cm, with average maximum daily temperatures from around 10°C to 25°C. Generally, it doesn't get as cold in Northland as it does further south.

Auckland is more-or-less like Sydney, but not so hot in summer, with average temperatures around 23°C and average rainfall about 130 cm.

Generally snow is only seen on the mountains (Egmont, Ruapehu, Ngauruhoe and Tongariro), though there are sometimes snowfalls in the high country in winter.

The South Island tends to have more extremes in climate, though at any one time there's really not a great difference in the temperature or rainfall throughout the country.

Generally the west of the South Island is wetter than the east. The west can have an annual rainfall of 700 cm or so, while not far away in Central Otago the rainfall is only 30 cm. Even in the middle of summer it can be cold and rainy in the West Coast area of the South Island, although when the sun comes out it's as pleasant as you could ask. In the south of the South Island it can get quite cold in the winter (June, July and August), but not as cold as it does in the northern USA.

Central Otago has both New Zealand's coldest winter days and hottest summer days. Snow is common in the hills in the South Island in winter, especially in the very south where it occasionally even snows at sea level.

Prevailing winds tend to be westerlies of one sort or another. This explains the rainfall pattern in the South Island, where the 'nor-westers' dump their rain in the west as they hit the Southern Alps, continuing across the Canterbury Plains as hot dry winds, often of gale force.

INFORMATION

The NZTP (New Zealand Tourist &

Publicity Office) has overseas travel offices in the following locations:

Argentina
   10th floor, Marcelo T Alvear 590, Buenos Aires (tel 066 4143)
Australia
   Watkins Place, 288 Edward St, Brisbane Qld 4000 (tel (04) 221 3722)
   270 Flinders St, Melbourne Vic 3000 (tel (03) 67 6621)
   16 St George's Terrace, Perth WA 6000 (tel (09) 325 7055)
   115 Pitt St, Sydney NSW 2000 (tel (02) 233 6633)
Canada
   Suite 1260, IBM Tower, 701 West Georgia St, Vancouver BC V7Y IB6 (tel (604) 684 2117)
West Germany
   Kaiserhofstrasse 7, 6000 Frankfurt am Main (tel (0169) 28 8189)
Japan
   Kokusai Building, 30 2-Chome, Azachimachi, Higashi-ku, Osaka 541 (tel (06) 271 2415)
   Toho Twin Tower Building, 2F 1-5-2 Yurakucho, Chiyoda-ku, Tokyo 100 (tel (03) 508 9981)
Singapore
   13 Nassim Rd, Singapore 10 25 (tel 235 9966)
UK
   New Zealand House, Haymarket, London SW1Y 4TQ (tel (01) 930 9422)
USA
   Suite 1530, 10960 Wilshire Boulevard, Los Angeles CA 90024 (tel (213) 477 8241)
   Suite 530, 630 Fifth Avenue, New York NY 10111 (tel (212) 586 0060)
   Citicorp Center, 1 Sansome St, San Francisco CA 94104 (tel (415) 788 7404)

They have information on all aspects of a visit to New Zealand available for potential visitors. They can also offer advice and in many cases they can book tours, accommodation and travel within New Zealand.

There are also NZTP offices in New Zealand where they perform much the same function as straightforward travel agents. These offices actually in New Zealand are not as useful for general information as the local Public Relations Offices, of which there is one in nearly every city or town. Almost any town big enough to have a pub and a corner shop seems to have a PR office. They're usually mines of information on local activities and attractions and have plenty of brochures and maps. Make use of them.

The Automobile Association is a very useful organisation to join. Benefits of membership (many of them free) include detailed info on accommodation, guides, maps and services for motorists including breakdown services and technical advice and vehicle inspections. If you are a member of an overseas auto association bring along proof of membership because you're then eligible for reciprocal rights. If you're not a member you may find it worthwhile to take out temporary six month membership which is available to overseas visitors only. There are AA offices in all major towns with agents in the smaller ones. The main offices are:

33 Wyndham St (PO Box 5), Auckland (tel 774-660)
324 Lambton Quay (PO Box 1053), Wellington (tel 738-738)
210 Hereford St (PO Box 994), Christchurch (tel 791-280)

GENERAL INFORMATION
Post
Post offices are generally open weekdays from 8.30 am to 5 pm; and to 8 pm on Fridays. You can have mail addressed to you care of 'Poste Restante, CPO' in whatever town you require. CPO stands for Chief Post Office. Telephone facilities are also available at post offices.

Telephone
From private phones local calls are free, from phone boxes they cost 20c. Although new electronic phones are now being introduced, pay phones have generally lagged far behind inflation. Most of them are the old fashioned button A and button B type. When the call is answered you press the button on the front and your money is swallowed up. If there's no answer press the button on the side and your money is returned. They have coin slots for 1c, 2c (both blanked off) and 10c. So even the cheapest local call requires two coins!

Conceivably you could make a three minute call to Australia from a pay phone – as long as you had 55 10c coins ready to feed into the phone! Actually what you do is make your call through a post office – you go in, pay a deposit, they connect you and afterwards you collect the change or pay the excess. You can even do this for after hours phone calls – pay now and when you want to make the call the operator should have a record of your deposit on hand.

For emergencies in the major centres dial 111 and say whether you want the police, fire or ambulance authorities.

Electricity
Electricity is 230 volts AC, 50 cycle.

Time

Being close to the international date line, New Zealand is one of the first places in the world to start a new day. New Zealand is 12 hours ahead of Greenwich Mean Time and two hours ahead of Australian Eastern Standard Time. In summer New Zealand observes Daylight Saving Time, an advance of one hour per day, which comes into effect on the last Sunday in October and lasts to the first Sunday of the following March. Usually when it's 12 noon in New Zealand it's 10 am in Sydney or Melbourne, 2 am in London, 5 pm the previous day in San Francisco or Los Angeles.

Business Hours

Office hours are generally 9 am to 5 pm Monday to Friday. Shops are usually open weekdays 9 am to 5.30 pm, to 9 pm on Fridays. In most places shops are also open on Saturday mornings. Additionally there are now many convenience stores open much longer hours. This is a considerable improvement on just a few years ago when the doors clanged shut at 5 pm Friday and absolutely everything was closed up like Fort Knox until 9 am on Monday.

Media

There is no real national paper although the *New Zealand Herald* (Auckland) and the *Dominion* (Wellington) both have wide circulations. Backing up the city newspapers are numerous local dailies: some OK, some not. The closest to a national weekly newsmag is the *Listener*, an excellent publication which provides lots of info on radio and TV programmes, a weekly guide, plus in-depth articles on the arts, social issues and politics. *Time* and *Newsweek* are available almost anywhere.

There are two national non-commercial radio stations and lots of regional or local commercial stations, broadcasting on the AM and FM bands. There are also two state-owned TV stations, although both have commercials. Although New Zealand's film industry is even smaller than Australia's, it has recently produced some highly acclaimed films like *Quiet Earth, Utu, Mr Wrong* and *Smash Palace*.

BOOKS

New Zealanders have the same self-fascination as Australians – there are plenty of books about the country's history, prospects, activities and pretty views. Particularly the latter. Almost any bookshop will have a section specialising in books on New Zealand. The book which has had the most attention and interest in New Zealand over the past couple of years is *The Bone People* by Keri Hulme, winner of the British Booker Prize for fiction in 1985, which made it an international bestseller. It's a book people either love or hate, I'm on the hate side!

HEALTH

There are no vaccination requirements. New Zealand is a healthy, disease-free country. Medical attention is high quality and reasonably priced but you should have medical insurance. If you suffer personal injury by accident in New Zealand you are entitled to compensation as a right – irrespective of fault – and may no longer sue in the courts for damages. This covers such things as medical expenses and payments for permanent incapacity but note that it covers only accidents, not illnesses. If you simply get ill and require medical attention you'll have to pay for it.

FILM & PHOTOGRAPHY

Photographic supplies, equipment and maintenance are all readily available.

ACCOMMODATION

New Zealand has a wide range of accommodation and places to stay but to all of it there is one catch: the Kiwis are great travellers. Even Australians fall behind the New Zealanders when it comes to hitting the road – a greater proportion of New Zealanders have passports than in any other country and when they are not jaunting around overseas they'll be jaunting around at home. So during the holiday season you may well find a long queue at popular places. This applies particularly to Youth Hostels and almost any cheap accommodation in major holiday areas. The answer is to book ahead if you are going to be arriving in tricky places on popular occasions.

Accommodation has been bracketed into several categories. First of all there are hostels – both Youth Hostel Association (YHA) hostels, YWCA and YMCA hostels and private hostels. Then there are campsites and cabins. Followed by guest houses or bed & breakfasts, hotels and motels. There is considerable overlap between these various groups. Some hostels may be straightforward bunkroom style while others may have double or even single rooms. One establishment may have both guest house accommodation and motel rooms. Hotels and motels are often very similar and at some campsites you may find not only areas for camping but also cabins, motel units and perhaps even a hostel-style bunkroom.

Accommodation Information

To find your way around New Zealand's campsites, cabins, motels, motel flats and so on you need three books put out by the Automobile Association. An *Accommodation & Camping Guide* covers the South Island, while the North Island is split into two separate publications. The *Accommodation Guide* is for hotels, guest houses and motels; and the *Outdoor Guide* lists tourist flats, cabins and camps. They are revised every year and are available from any AA office. They're not a complete listing but most places are included. Copies are available free to members of the AA or to overseas visitors who belong to an automobile

association enjoying reciprocal rights with the AA.

Jason's accommodation directories are very similar commercially produced guides and there's also an NZTP *New Zealand Accommodation Guide*.

Hostels

Hostels offer cheap accommodation in locations all over New Zealand. At a hostel you basically rent a bed, usually for around $10 to $12 a night. Some hostels have male and female bunkrooms for 10 or more people. Others have smaller bunk-rooms or even double or single rooms. You usually have to provide your own bedding although sometimes this can be rented. There's usually a communal kitchen, a lounge and probably a dining area.

To an even greater extent than Australia the hostel scene has gone through a real revolution in the past few years. It's a combination of strong growth, more liberal attitudes and a new commercial approach.

Hostels have always been popular in New Zealand, after all it's a good country for backpackers. But the recent growth in demand has been phenomenal as there are now a lot more travellers. So many more in fact, that hostels have frequently been booked out far in advance which has, of course, created the need for more hostels – both YHA and private.

The second factor affecting the hostel scene has been a change in the general attitude towards hostelling. The old, strict segregation by sex, lights out early, stay away all day policies have taken a considerable battering. In part it's been because people staying at the hostels have been demanding a more easy going approach, but also because younger-minded people have been running the hostels. The old hostel 'wardens' have even metamorphosed into 'managers'!

A major factor, of course, has been the growth in private hostels. Attitudes are much more liberal at these new hostels, forcing the YHA hostels to catch up.

Finally both these factors – growth in demand and the need for more liberal attitudes – have come together in a new more commercial approach. Getting people to stay in hostels has become a commercial decision just like other businesses. If hostel A is better equipped, cheaper or a more pleasant place than hostel B then people will stay in A rather than in B. And running a hostel, many people have suddenly realised, is just as good a way of making a living as running a motel. What's the difference between a motel room for $48 with two people in it and a bunkroom for four at $12 each? Well with the bunkroom you don't have to provide a TV, telephone or attached bathroom, or launder bedding for starters!

So today hostels, YHA or private, are much more attractive places to stay. If you're a couple you can often manage to get a room to yourself rather than have to separate into male and female bunkrooms. You can often arrive rather later at night, you're much less likely to be locked out if you get back from the pub late at night (but be quiet!) and if it's pouring down with rain you're much less likely to be pushed out the door because 'the hostel is closed from 10 am to 4 pm'.

Apart from being just about the most economical form of accommodation, particularly if you're travelling solo, hostels are also a great place for meeting people and making friends. They're also wonderful information sources – almost every hostel has a noticeboard smothered in notes, advice and warning and the hostel managers are also often a great mine of local information. Hostels, both private and YHA, often negotiate special discounts and deals for their hostellers with local businesses and tour operators.

YHA Hostels The New Zealand YHA produce a very useful annual *YHA Handbook* which, along with general information, also lists all their hostels with a description of their facilities, prices, phone numbers, other information and a location map. You may be able to get a copy from your own national YHA but if not you can write to the New Zealand association. Their national head office address is PO Box 436, Christchurch, New Zealand.

YHA hostels are only open to members of the Youth Hostel Association. You can either join the YHA in your home country (don't forget to bring your membership card) or in New Zealand either at the Auckland or Christchurch office, at any YHA hostel or at Westpac banks. There's a joining fee of $10 and annual membership is then $27.50. Membership of the New Zealand YHA also allows you to use YHA hostels anywhere else in the world. Your YHA membership also entitles you to a host of discounts in New Zealand; the *YHA Handbook* details them. A recent innovation is a one-night temporary membership charge of $6 for non-members who just want to spend one night in a hostel.

You must have sheets or, much better, a sheet sleeping bag when you stay at YHA hostels. A regular sleeping bag is not good enough – it has to go in a sheet sleeping bag or a regular sheet must be used to separate your bag from the mattress. Blankets and sheets or sheet sleeping bags are available for hire at some hostels but you're better off having your own. The YHA handbook shows the approved dimensions if you want to make one from a couple of sheets or you can buy ready made new ones at the YHA shops in Auckland or Christchurch for $14 or from the YHA in your home country.

New Zealand YHA hostels have considerably relaxed their rules in the last few years and they've never had the 'thou shalt not arrive by car' attitude that some European hostels have. There's usually a time bracket during which you can book in and you're expected to do a duty every morning. At most hostels there's a three night stay limit but this is only likely to be enforced when the hostel is crowded. Some of the smaller and more remote

hostels have a very relaxed and easy going atmosphere.

During the summer extra hostels open up to cater for some of the demand. A higher overnight fee may be payable at these. Some of the major and very busy hostels have overflow facilities which they can call on when they get very crowded. There are also a few Associate Hostels – privately owned premises approved by the YHA as suitable for members' use.

Particularly during school holidays and at popular hostels it is a wise idea to book ahead. You can do this either directly with the hostel in question, through the New Zealand offices or one hostel can make a reservation for you at another hostel. Reservations have to be paid for in advance and again the handbook has full details on what to do.

Finally if you want to make a lengthy stay in New Zealand think about being a hostel manager, they often need temporary or long term managers, particularly in the off-season. The pay may be very little but you get free accommodation, plenty of spare time and you'll meet lots of people. Write to the YHA for info.

Christchurch National Office
   28 Worcester St (PO Box 436) (tel 799-970)
Auckland Office
   Australis House, 36 Customs St East (PO Box 1687) (tel 794-224)

Wellington Office
40 Tinakori Rd (tel 736-271)

Private Hostels The numerous new private hostels not only provide many of the additional hostel beds but they've also been a principal cause of the changing policies at YHA hostels. Although there is no formal association between the private hostels they do produce a useful *Budget Accommodation in New Zealand* leaflet which covers a number of private hostels around the country. Like YHA hostels nightly costs are typically around $10 to $12.

Many of the private hostels operate just like regular YHA hostels with bunkrooms, kitchen and lounge facilities and so on. Some of them are operated by ex-YHA managers so they're fully aware of all the plus and minus points about YHA hostel operations. Some of the private hostel operations are just camp ground bunkrooms or farm hostels but one of the most interesting aspects of private hostels has been the new-from-the-ground-up hostels which have opened recently. The *Rainbow Lodge* in Taupo, *Thermal Lodge* in Rotorua and *Tasman Towers* in Nelson are three examples of brand new, purpose-built hostels.

YMCA & YWCA Hostels There are YMCA and YWCA hostels in several larger towns which offer straightforward, no frills accommodation and are generally reasonably priced. A few of them are single-sex only but most of them take men and women. Although the emphasis is on 'permanent' accommodation – providing a place to stay for young people coming to work in the 'big city' – they are increasingly going after the 'transient trade'.

Accommodation in these hostels is almost always in single rooms. They've got one extra plus point – they are often less crowded during the holiday seasons, when every other place is likely to be short of space.

Camping
If you plan to camp, New Zealand is a great place for it. If you've ever been camping in Australia or Europe you'll know that the former is OK but would be better if the sites weren't aimed so much at the caravanners, and that the latter is very good but increasingly expensive and crowded. Well, New Zealand is simply better; for the tent camper the Kiwi campsites are the best in the world. This doesn't mean caravanners aren't catered for, just that people with tents get a fair go for once.

If you are driving, biking or hiking around with a tent and sleeping bag everything will be fine – there are a lot of sites, particularly in touristy places, and they are very well equipped. Many of them have kitchens and dining areas where the cooker, hot plates and often kettles and toasters are provided; all you need to bring is the utensils, plates, bowls, etc and the food. This has a secondary benefit that they're great places to meet people – you talk with other people while you're fixing your food, you carry on when you share a table to eat it. There are also laundry facilities and often TV rooms too.

How the sites are charged varies fairly widely. Sometimes there's a site charge and then an additional cost per person. Sometimes it's just a straight site charge. But most of the time it's a straight per person charge and that's typically around $5 to $8 per adult, half price for children. Most sites charge a dollar or two more per person if you want a powered site for a caravan or campervan as opposed to a tent site without power.

At most sites the kitchen and showers are free but at a very few sites there are coin-in-the-slot operated hot plates and/or hot showers. At most sites laundry facilities are coin operated.

If you intend to camp round New Zealand but haven't got any equipment consider buying it there. Good, high quality tents and sleeping bags are amongst the best buys to be found in

Kiwiland, though prices have leapt up in recent years. A really good tent or top-of-the-line down sleeping bag won't be cheap but it will be excellent quality. Remember it gets cool in New Zealand in the winter, so camping becomes a lot less practical then, especially in the south. If you're well enough equipped it's not quite so bad in the north, although New Zealand's weather is very changeable.

Sites in the Parks There are Department of Conservation camping sites in reserves and national, maritime and farm parks. Most of these camping grounds have minimal facilities – fresh water, toilets, fireplaces and not much else – but they also have minimal charges, often $5 or less. They include sites on islands in the Hauraki Gulf off Auckland, up towards Cape Reinga, on islands in the Bay of Islands, on the Coromandel Peninsula, on the Marlborough Sounds and at numerous other locations.

Check with the appropriate regional offices of the Department of Conservation for details on what you need to take with you, facilities and whether you should book in advance. There are also some free campsites, particularly in the North Island, that although often difficult to get to are worth the walk if you're geared for camping.

Each national park also has huts which can only be reached on foot. Once again there are basic facilities only – pit toilets, fresh water and bunks. Cooking has to be done on open fires or gas or wood stoves. The fee for a bed in these huts can vary from a minimal dollar or two up towards $10 although with the new commercial attitude of government departments the costs are likely to rise.

In the remoter areas of the park, trampers must be self-sufficient. You need a tent and a portable stove. Huts are about four or five hours walking distance apart on the more accessible tracks. Contact specific national parks for more details.

Cabins & Tourist Flats

Many of the campsites will also have cabins, which are simply equipped rooms where you have to provide your own sleeping gear (a sleeping bag is fine) and towels; unlike a hotel where all that stuff is there. Cabins can be very cheap, often less than $20 for two which makes them even cheaper than hostels. They generally charge per two adults, plus so much for each additional person, but some charge per cabin and some per person. We did one trip round New Zealand on a motorcycle where we generally camped but if it was a chilly night (or a wet one) opted for the comforts of a cabin. Usually you can rent sheets and blankets if you come unequipped.

These days the standards of cabins seems to be rising – the prices too. Often the cabins become 'tourist flats' which seems to mean they're equipped closer to motel standard with kitchens and/or attached bathrooms. You will still be left to yourself to clean up and you will have to provide bedding, towels and so on. On-site caravans (trailer homes in US parlance) are another campsite possibility. Many campsites have regular motel rooms or an associated motel complex and hostel-style bunkrooms are another possibility.

Guest Houses & Bed & Breakfasts

There's a wide variation in types and standards in this category. Some guest houses are spartan, cheap, ultra basic accommodation in some cases defined as 'private' (unlicensed) hotels. Others are comfortable, relaxed but low key places, patronised by people who don't enjoy the impersonal atmosphere of many motels. Others are very fancy indeed and try to give their guests a feeling for life with a New Zealand family. Because they tend to get lumped into this one category the 'bed & breakfast' places at the top of the heap try hard to dissociate themselves from the rock bottom guest houses at the other end of the strata.

Bed & breakfast accommodation in

private homes has recently become a fashionable concept in the US and there are now many New Zealanders offering family run enterprises of that type. Get a copy of *The New Zealand Bed & Breakfast Book* by J & J Thomas from Moonshine Press, 27 Marine Drive, Mahina Bay, Eastbourne, Wellington, New Zealand for suggestions about bed & breakfast accommodation all over the country.

Although breakfast is definitely on the agenda at the real bed & breakfast places it may or may not feature at other places in this category. Where it does it's likely to be a pretty substantial meal – fruit, eggs, bacon, toast, coffee or tea are all likely to make an appearance. Many guest houses seem to really pride themselves on the size, quality and 'traditional value' of their breakfasts. If you like to start the day heartily it's worth considering this when comparing prices. There are several co-operatively produced lists of bed & breakfast accommodation. They're usually available from guest houses which appear on the list. A list produced from the *Aspen Lodge* in Auckland lists only places that guarantee to provide a good breakfast!

Also guest houses can be particularly good value if you're travelling on your own. Most motels, hotels, cabins and so on are priced on a 'per room' basis whereas guest houses usually charge 'per person'. Typically bed & breakfast singles cost $25 to $40 but in some of the more spartan breakfastless guest houses the price can drop to $20 or less. A double in some of the country's best bed & breakfasts can cost $100 or more. Except at the most expensive bed & breakfast guest houses, rooms generally do not have attached bathrooms.

Hotels

As in Australia a hotel essentially has to be licensed to serve alcohol. So at one end of the scale the hotel category can include traditional older-style hotels where the emphasis is mainly on the bar and the

rooms are pretty much a sideline. At the other end it includes all the brand new five star hotels in the big cities, hotels which are pretty much like their relations elsewhere in the world in facilities and in their high prices. In between, many places that are essentially motels can call themselves hotels because they have a bar and liquor licence. At the cheapest old-style hotels singles might cost down toward $20 while at the most luxurious new establishments a room could be $200 or more.

THC Hotels Scattered around New Zealand are a number of THC (Tourist Hotel Corporation) hotels. The THC is a government-run organisation whose intention is to operate hotels in tourist areas where it would be difficult for privately run hotels to charge reasonable rates and make a profit. Actually some of the THC places are so expensive it would be difficult to make a loss!

You'll find THC hotels at some of the most scenic spots in the country and two of them, the *Hermitage* at Mt Cook and the *Chateau* at Tongariro, are the most famous hotels in New Zealand. You won't find budget travellers staying at these places (they're expensive) but they're often worth a look. The hotels themselves may be rather attractive (the Chateau), have a bit of history to them (the Hermitage) or have other attractions. They may also serve as the focal point for the area and you'll find their bars crowded and friendly. If the idea of a public-service-run hotel is pretty horrible you're in for a surprise, as they're interesting, well run places.

Motels

Motels are pretty much like motels anywhere else in the world although New Zealand motels are notably well equipped. They always have tea and coffee making equipment and supplies, a fridge and there's often a toaster and electric frypan which is handy if you feel like whipping yourself up scrambled eggs. Even a real kitchen is not at all unusual, complete with utensils, plates and cutlery. Although long life milk for your coffee or tea is starting to take over, at a great many traditional motels you'll still find a small bottle of fresh milk by your door every morning

Sometimes there's a distinction drawn between 'serviced motels' and 'motel flats'. Essentially the difference is that a motel flat has more equipment and less service. You don't get people rushing around pulling the sheets straight everytime you turn round – which is just fine with me and probably with you too. They're a sort of indicator of the basic rightness of the New Zealand way of life – for how long would all that kitchen equipment last in a motel in the US? Someone would cart the lot out on the second night, right!

A motel room typically costs around $55 to $65. Sometimes you can find them cheaper, even as low as $40, and there are lots of more luxurious new motels where $70 to $100 is the usual range. There's usually only a small difference in price, if any, between a single or double motel room.

Farm Holidays

New Zealand has been called the world's most efficient farm so a visit to a farm is an interesting way of getting to grips with the real New Zealand. Farm holidays are a very popular activity as many farms take guests who can 'have a go' at all the typical farm activities and be treated as one of the household into the bargain. If you want to know more about it contact the NZTP who can make recommendations or provide names and addresses of organisations that specialise in booking farm stays. Their *New Zealand Accommodation Guide* lists individual farms and also umbrella organisations that list farms in specific locales or all over the country.

There are all sorts of farms you can

choose from – dairy farms, sheep farms, high country farms, cattle farms, mixed farming farms. If you're staying in the homestead typical daily costs are in the $60 to $120 range including meals. Some farms have separate cottages where you fix your own food and have to supply your own bedding; these usually charge by the week. You'll probably find that the cheapest farm holidays are booked when you're actually in New Zealand, only the more expensive places go looking for customers abroad.

A very economical way to stay on a farm and actually do some work there is to join Willing Workers on Organic Farms (WWOOF), based in Nelson in the South Island. Membership of WWOOF provides you with a list of farms in both islands where in exchange for your 'conscientious work' the farm owner will provide food, accommodation and some hands-on experience in organic farming. Once you've made a decision about which farm you'd like to visit you have to contact the farm owner or manager directly by telephone or letter. They emphasise that you cannot simply turn up cold. Write to Tony West, WWOOF, 188 Collingwood St, Nelson for full details. Enclose at least three postal reply coupons for information. Membership costs vary with the airmail cost to where you live but they're typically about £3 or US$6.

FOOD & DRINK

If you're expecting any sort of gastronomic highlights in New Zealand you may be in for a bit of a disappointment. Nowhere does New Zealand's solid English ancestry show through clearer than on the dining table. New Zealand has not had the wide variety of immigrants that has given Australians a healthy liking for spicy tucker. But if straightforward, solid, honest fare like steak & chips, fish & chips, roast lamb and the like suit your taste, then you won't be unhappy.

Having said that let me immediately add that it wouldn't be possible for the

Kiwis to be the keen travellers they are without bringing some of it back from abroad. The choice of restaurants is a lot more cosmopolitan than it was just a few years ago although Chinese restaurants still predominate over any other sort of overseas eateries. Everything from Middle Eastern food to Vietnamese food can be found but curiously, despite the proliferation of international restaurants, there is nothing to be seen from the Pacific Islands, the source of New Zealand's largest number of immigrants.

There's not much of a New Zealand national cuisine – no moa & chips or Auckland fried kiwi. They're big meat eaters though and a NZ steak is generally every bit as good as an Aussie one. With all that coastline it's also not surprising that seafood is pretty popular and there are some fine local varieties of oyster and the now rare and expensive *toheroa* or slightly less pricey *tuatuas*. New Zealand is renowned for its dairy products and the milk and the ice-cream are excellent.

Fast Food & Takeaways

Starting from the bottom there are plenty of fast food joints along with those symbols of American culinary imperialism Colonel Sanders, Pizza Hut and McDonald's. I developed a theory on my last visit that the more prominent the big fast food operators were the worse the local alternatives were likely to be. Wanganui, with what must be the poorest selection of sandwiches of any comparable town in the country, is a wonderful example.

Of course there is fish & chips. Unlike in Australia, where frying up good English fish & chips seems to be an Italian or Greek occupation, in New Zealand it's very often a Chinese one. New Zealanders are just about as tied to the meat pie as Australians but they probably do make a better job of them. To any Americans or Poms out there, the meat pie has as great a cultural significance to Australians as the hot dog does to a Noo Yorker – and is as

frequently reviled for not being what it once was or currently should be.

Pub Food

If you move up a notch and into the pubs you'll probably find, as in Australia, the best value for money. Counter meals (pie & chips, stews, etc, very cheap) have more or less died out, though some bars still sell pies from a pie warmer. A lot of pubs now have bistro meals – simple but good food like schnitzel, steak, fish or the like with chips (French fries), and a good fresh salad or coleslaw. Average main course price is $8 to $12 and they are usually excellent value. Cobb & Co restaurants are a chain offering pub-style food in locations all over New Zealand. They're safe, sound and consistent and also open commendably generous hours seven days a week.

Restaurants

Up another jump and into the restaurants. As in Australia there's the BYO-licensed restaurant split. BYO (bring your own booze) aren't as clearly defined as in Australia but the same basic story applies – you can bring your own bottle of wine or whatever along with you and the food prices are generally a notch lower than in licensed restaurants. Check before you arrive if it is BYO or not. If you like reading about restaurants before you try them *Michael Guy's Eating Out* is an interesting guide to restaurants all over both islands of New Zealand.

One of the real pleasures of my most recent visit to New Zealand was the proliferation of excellent vegetarian restaurants. *Gopals*, the Hare Krishna run places, can be found in several locations while in Auckland there are a number of cheap and excellent vegetarian places including *Dominoes* and *Simple Cottage*. In Christchurch *Mainstreet Cafe* is more expensive but the food, especially the desserts, is superb. The best meal, vegetarian or non-vegetarian, I had in either island however, was in the wonderful *Te Kano* restaurant in Te Anau – definitely worth a detour.

Preparing your own Food

Buying your own food to cook yourself is generally far cheaper, of course, and with most camps and all hostels and motels having cooking facilities it's a relatively easy alternative. Shops are open Monday to Friday, 9 am to 5 pm, and Saturday mornings; supermarkets, of course, tend to be cheapest. In the evenings, early mornings, and weekends the good old corner dairy is the place to go. A dairy is a small shop found on many street corners throughout New Zealand, which sells milk, food, the local newspaper, chocolate and sweets, milkshakes – in fact a bit of everything, but mostly food lines. They're open for longer hours than other shops, are far more widespread, but their selection is usually not as good as a larger shop, and their prices tend to be higher.

Beer

New Zealanders are great drinkers and the beer and pubs are pretty good. Almost all the beer is now brewed by only two companies but down in the deep south you'll see some different labels – Speights, Southland Bitter, Bavarian. Bavarian used to be brewed by a private company, as was much of New Zealand's beer, before it was taken over by one of the two giants. Many a true Bavarian drinker will tell you it's not the same as in the good old days.

Cans aren't very popular and most beer is sold in bottles anyway as they're refundable and cheaper than cans. In a pub the cheapest beer is on tap. You can ask for: a '7', originally seven fluid ounces but now a 200 ml glass – the nearest metric equivalent (old ways die hard!); a 'handle' which is a half litre or litre mug with a handle; or a jug, which is just that.

Public bars are the cheapest while lounge or other bars tend to mark their drinks up more but prices vary very widely. I noted half handle prices of $1.20, $1.25, $1.50, $1.70 and $2.30 in various bars around the country. In public bars you can pretty much wear anything, but lounge bars have a lot of 'neat dress required' signs around. You sometimes get the feeling they are determined that New Zealand should be the last home of the necktie. The bars with entertainment are normally lounge bars, which can sometimes make things a bit awkward for the traveller with his jeans, sandals and T-shirt.

A New Zealand invention is the Trust-operated pub which started in Invercargill. For some time that stout town was 'dry' and when the prohibition was repealed they decided that pubs should be publicly owned and the profits go to the community. It worked so well that many other pubs around the country are also Trust operated.

Wine & Other Intoxicants

New Zealand also has a thriving wine producing industry. Never thought about the Auckland vineyards did you? Like Australian wine, the local product once had a terrible reputation but it has improved so much in recent years that today there are some wines (particularly the whites) of excellent international standard. In fact in 1985 and 1986 the UK magazine *Business Traveller* recommended that if you chose your airline on the basis of the wine they served then Air New Zealand was the best in the world! In 1987 Air New Zealand was pipped for 1st place by the Australian wines served by Qantas and British Airways came from nowhere to 3rd place by dropping French wines in favour of Australian ones too! Poor old Air France had done so poorly in previous years they wouldn't even enter.

An unusual local nectar is kiwifruit wine. There are lots of different types including still and bubbly or sweet and dry, and there's even a liqueur. You may not like it, but NZ's the best place to try it. It's also an interesting way to while away a few hours – taking a look at a kiwifruit winery and

Top: One that didn't get away, fishing at Tongariro River (NZTP)
Left: Skiing at the Cardrona Ski Field, Otago (NZTP)
Right: Appletree Bay, Abel Tasman National Park (NZTP)

Top: Detail of Maori war canoe, Waitangi (MC)
Left: Carved Posts at Whaka Village, Whakarewarewa Thermal Reserve (NZTP)
Right: Intricately carved gateway to Whaka Village, Rotorua (MC)

having a free tasting in pleasant surroundings. The ever resourceful Kiwis even grow a little dope, which may not rival Acapulco Gold but is still very pleasant stuff.

THINGS TO BUY

You don't go to New Zealand intending to come back with a backpack full of souvenirs (a photograph of some flawless moment may be your best reminder) but there are some things worth checking out.

Greenstone

Greenstone or jade is made into ornaments, brooches, earrings, cufflinks and *tikis*. The latter are tiny, stylised figures (usually depicted with their tongue stuck out in a warlike *haka* challenge), worn on a thong or necklace around the neck. They've got great *mana*, or power, and they also serve as fertility symbols.

Arts & Crafts

Maori wood carvings are worth checking out, particularly in Rotorua. New Zealanders have a reputation as great do-it-yourselfers and there are a lot of excellent handicraft shops. The quality of the pottery and weaving is particularly fine: they make good presents to take back home and don't take up much room in your pack. Nelson in particular is noted for its excellent pottery, the quality of the local clay has attracted many potters there.

Other

If you're planning a camping trip around New Zealand you can buy top quality sleeping bags, tents, clothes and other bush gear. Unfortunately these days the prices are also in the top bracket. You can also buy stunning woollen gear, particularly jumpers (sweaters) made from hand-spun, hand-dyed wool. Sheepskins are also popular buys. Fashion clothing has also become very competitive and the Canterbury sports clothing label is internationally known.

WHAT TO BRING

The main thing to remember about New Zealand is that while it may be a small compact country it has widely varying and very changeable weather. A T-shirt and shorts day at the Bay of Islands can also bring snow and sleet to a high pass in the Southern Alps. In fact on those southern mountains you can often meet T-shirt and snow-gear weather on the same day. So come prepared for widely varying climatic conditions and if you're planning on tramping come prepared for anything!

Come prepared for New Zealand 'dress standards' too. An amazing number of restaurants, bars, clubs and pubs have signs proclaiming their equally amazingly varied dress rules. I sometimes have the feelings that if you combined all of the rules together (one place proclaims no denim, the next no leather, the next no shirts without collars, the next no sandals, etc) the only thing you'd be permitted to wear was your birthday suit!

So, apart from clothes, there aren't any great preparations to make. New Zealand is a modern, well organised country and you should be able to find most requirements from film to pharmaceuticals. Although laundromats don't seem to be as prevalent as in many other countries nearly every motel, campsite or hostel will have a laundry. The cheaper the accommodation the more they seem to charge for using their laundry machines!

Tramping & Skiing

Tramping

Tramping, or hiking/walking/bushwalking/
trekking as it is known in various
countries, is the best way of coming to
grips with New Zealand's natural beauty.
It gives the traveller the greater satisfaction
of being a participant rather than just a
spectator.

The country has literally thousands of
km of tracks, many well marked, some
only a line on the maps. What makes
tramping especially attractive is the
hundreds of huts available, allowing
trampers to avoid the weight of tents and
cooking gear. Many tracks are graded so
that they are easily covered by those with
only a moderate amount of fitness and
little or no experience. Many travellers,
once having tried a track, then gear the
rest of their trip in New Zealand to
travelling from one track to another, with
side trips to see the 'in' sights. This section
should open your eyes to the possibilities
of tramping but before attempting any
track consult the appropriate authority
for the latest info.

Tracks, Huts & Wardens
The following notes on tracks, huts and
wardens apply only to the popular
'tourist' tracks. If you venture off these on
to any of the other alternatives, things will
be quite different. For example on some it
may take you an hour to cover one km,
huts may be eight hours or so apart, there
won't be any wardens and you have to be
much better prepared.

When walking allow about four km per
  hour on easy ground.
Huts are usually placed three to four
  hours apart.
Huts usually have beds for up to 24 with
  thick foam mattresses on bunks.

Huts on the more popular tracks usually
  have wood stoves with gas burners.
There is a two night limit on huts, if they
  are full.
Camping on tracks is, in theory, banned
  because of the effect on the environment.
  In practice, if the hut is packed,
  wardens will turn a blind eye. Check
  with the warden. The main point is to
  leave the site cleaner than when you
  arrived – washing dishes in lakes is a
  strict no-no.
Always leave firewood in huts for the next
  group; in case they arrive in heavy rain
  or the dark.
Tracks are administered by rangers and
  wardens; the former are permanent
  staff, normally well trained and very
  knowledgeable. The wardens are
  temporary; usually employed for the
  summer season to keep an eye on huts
  and maintain the track for a km in each
  direction. In some cases wardens spend
  long periods in the bush becoming a
  little peculiar and should be treated
  with some consideration.
Wardens in the national parks collect hut
  fees, when they're on duty. When they
  leave, at the end of February or March,
  payment is up to the conscience of
  trampers. Fees vary, depending on the
  park, but with the recent rationalisation
  they're tending to go up.
Check with wardens for weather forecasts
  and information about the track.
  Unfortunately many wardens have
  been helicoptered in and don't have a
  chance to do the track and therefore
  are unable to give precise facts.
Getting into and out of tracks can be a
  problem. Having a vehicle simplifies
  getting in, but not the problem of getting
  out again. Having two vehicles allows the
  positioning of one at either end of the
  track. If you have no vehicle then you have
  to take public transport of hitch in. If

the track starts or ends at the end of a dead end road, hitching will be difficult. Fortunately with the far greater number of trampers now walking New Zealand's tracks there is also far more transport available.

Leave excess luggage behind or send it on to a point near the end of the track. Camping grounds will often hold luggage for free. Bus companies will carry excess luggage at a very reasonable price and will hold it in their offices until it is picked up.

Surprisingly most people on the tracks are from outside NZ. It's quite common to have only 10% Kiwis in a hut although on the Milford Track, of course, it can reach 50%. Kiwis do tramp, but they tend to avoid the more popular tracks, seeking the really wild and untouched regions. To most New Zealanders tramping is still considered to be blazing trails through deep snow over 4000-metre passes. Sleeping out in the open during blizzards then fording rivers neck deep, ducking to avoid the blocks of ice, all done in shorts and T-shirt. In the last 10 years there has been an amazing improvement in the conditions of tracks and huts.

Citizens of Oz should note that it isn't necessary to carry drinking water in rainforest!

Once on the track be careful. In good weather most of the tracks are safer than walking around town but what makes them dangerous is New Zealand's contrary weather. A glorious walk in perfect conditions suddenly becomes a fight for survival in a blizzard. An easy two-hour walk to the next hut turns into a grim struggle against wind, wet and cold over a washed-out track and swollen rivers. Hopefully this won't happen but it has often, and will again, so be prepared and be careful. Weather forecasts should be watched but taken with a grain of salt. NZ's prevailing weather comes from the south-west, an area which does not have any inhabited land and very little sea or air traffic, making accurate reporting difficult. In Fiordland it is considered that the forecasted weather hits the area a day before it is forecast.

The 'season' for tracks is approximately the same as the Christmas school holidays – from one to two weeks before Christmas to the end of January. The couple of weeks before school breaks up in December can also be bad as many school groups are on the trails. December-January on the main trails is a good period to avoid. The best weather is January to March inclusive. June and July are considered the middle of winter and not the time to be out on the tracks. It's best to time your walks so that the most southerly are done in the middle of summer.

For an enjoyable tramp the primary consideration is your feet and shoulders. Make sure your footwear is adequate and that your pack is not too heavy.

Fauna

New Zealand has a great range of birdlife although their numbers have been seriously depleted by introduced cats, rats and dogs which kill flightless birds and raid the nests for eggs. Recently, stoats have become a serious problem especially in Westland.

The chances of seeing kiwis are very slim as they are nocturnal and very shy. Look in thick bush, after 11 pm and after rain, around areas which have just been dug up, usually along the track. Check with the hut warden if there is one.

In the South Island hill country the friendly brown wood hen is a weka; the green parrot with bright red underwings is a kea; the small green bird with a beautiful call is a bellbird; the more shy and larger black bird with a white crop under its throat and pure call is a tui. All over the country you'll see the friendly little fantail which will flit almost within reach, but not quite.

There are no poisonous animals in New

Zealand, however there are sandflies and mosquitoes throughout the country. They are at their almost unbearable worst on the West Coast of the South Island and in Fiordland. The mosquitoes pale into insignificance compared to the sandflies. In many areas the sandflies are a curse. Don't start out on any South Island track without some repellent. Mosquitoes breed in stagnant water, the sandflies are thickest around moving water; both prefer low altitudes.

Books

Each of the National Parks produces very good books on their park, giving detailed info on fauna and flora, geology and history. *Tramping in New Zealand*, by Jim DuFresne, is another Lonely Planet guide. It has descriptions of a variety of walks, of various lengths and degree of difficulty, in all parts of the country. The tramps range from an easy walk in the North Island's Coromandel Forest Park to a strenuous hike through the muddy bogs of Stewart Island. Detailed routes are given for each day's tramping with approximate times and the availability of

huts, as well as access information for getting to and from each track.
Moir's Guide Book (two volumes) put out by the NZ Alpine Club is the definitive work on tracks in the south of the South Island.

Maps

The Lands & Survey maps are the best, though stationery shops tend to have a very poor selection of them for sale. The L&S department has good map sales offices in the North Island in Auckland, Hamilton, Gisborne, Napier, Rotorua, New Plymouth, Wellington and Whangarei; and in the South Island in Blenheim, Christchurch, Dunedin, Hokitika, Invercargill and Nelson.

They have Tourist Maps (numbers are the NZMS reference number) for: Rotorua-Taupo Thermal Region 50, Tararua Mountains (for trampers) 57, Lake Taupo 116, Bay of Islands 151, Rotorua Lakes 152, Lake Te Anau 155, Lake Wakatipu 156, Stewart Island 219, Marlborough Sounds 236, Waiheke Islands 249.

Various parks also have special maps: Fiordland NP 122, Tongariro NP 150, Nelson Lakes NP 164, Egmont NP 169, Urewera NP 170, Westland & Mt Cook NPs 180, Abel Tasman NP 183. Walks in the Chateau area of Tongariro NP 186, Heaphy Track 245, Arthurs Pass NP 194, Ruapehu Skifields 221, Wangapeka Track 235, Lake Waikaremoana 239. The maps currently cost $5.50. The best maps that L&S produce are the inch to the mile series, now being changed to a metric series. They have the best details, but the problem is you may need two or three maps to cover one track.

The Authorities

The authorities and organisations who look after parks, tracks, huts and general tramping facilities have been going through a major revamp during 1987. Previously there were several different organisations trampers had to deal with, but these are now being amalgamated into one Department of Conservation. It is likely to be some time, however, before the reorganisation is complete.

Previously there was a National Parks Authority, a National Parks Board, the New Zealand Forest Service and the Department of Lands & Survey. The Lands & Survey people were the most visible because they actually administered the national parks and also produced most of the maps and tramping information. They form the core of the new organisation. The New Zealand Forest Service had two hats to wear as they handled both commercial forestry work in the State Forests and also walks in those forests. The disadvantage of this arrangement was that commercial interests sometimes overpowered conservationist ideals. On the other hand they usually had greater funds to maintain tracks and huts. Their huts were often free.

With the new organisation this is all changing and the walking part of the Forest Service is being hived off from the commercial part. Unfortunately this is also means that 'user pays' rules are being applied to the ex-Forest Service huts which, as a consequence, are becoming more expensive.

Seal Colony, Kaikoura Coastline, Marlborough

The Parks
Information centres for the various National Parks and Maritime Parks are found at:

Egmont – Dawson Falls and North Egmont on Mt Egmont
Urewera – Aniwaniwa, half-way along Lake Waikaremoana
Tongariro – Whakapapa on Mt Ruapehu
Abel Tasman – Totaranui at the northern end of the park
Nelson Lakes – St Arnaud
Westland – Franz Josef and Fox
Arthurs Pass – Arthurs Pass village
Mt Cook – near the Hermitage Hotel
Fiordland – Te Anau
Aspiring – Wanaka
Hauraki Gulf Maritime Park – Auckland
Marlborough Sounds Maritime Park – Blenheim
Bay of Islands Maritime & Historic Park – Russell

It is sometimes necessary to push some info offices hard to get the facts you require. Towards the end of summer they frequently run out of info sheets; as a precaution collect what you can at any National Park you visit. Park Rangers can be very knowledgeable and helpful. As well as the National Parks there are State Forest areas covering 11,850 square km.

Walkways
Walkways are a new idea, similar to the American National Trails. The New Zealand Walkways Commission, appointed in 1976, is establishing walkways close to urban centres which are suitable for families, with the intention of eventually linking them into a nationwide network. There are already many walkways open, and many more being planned. They are all one-day walks and good practice for the real thing. Info is available from the Walkways Commission, Charles Ferguson Building, Bowen St, Wellington (Private Bag), or from Department of Conservation offices.

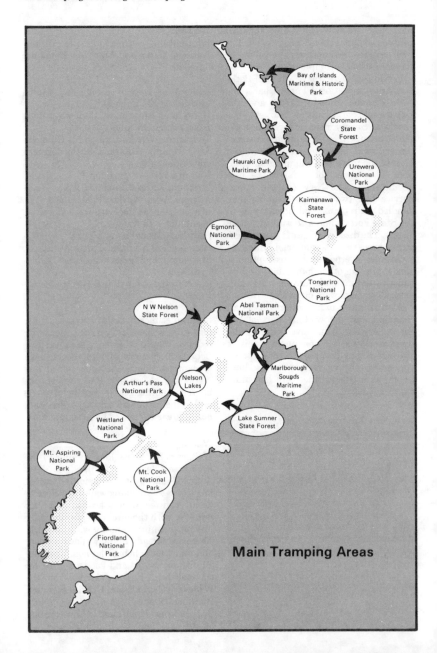

Main Tramping Areas

What to Take

Equipment This list is for someone who will be sticking to the main tracks, staying in huts and tramping during the summer months. It is inadequate for snow country or winter.

Boots – light to medium is sufficient; it is possible to get through in tennis/running shoes or street shoes, but they make the going much harder and the risk of injury much greater and are not recommended. The boots should be broken-in or you'll get painful blisters. Cover your heels with band-aids before you start if you think there is any chance of blisters. Feet are the greatest source of discomfort when tramping so they should be given the most care.

Alternate footwear – thongs/sandals, running/tennis shoes for strolling around the huts and if the boots become just too painful to wear.

Socks – three heavy woollen pairs; two to be worn at once to reduce the chance of blisters. Frequent changes of socks during the day also reduces the chance of blisters but isn't too practical.

Shorts, light shirt – for everyday wear, swimsuits for the immodest.

Woollen sweater/jersey, woollen trousers – essential in case of cold weather. Wool is the only thing to have when it's wet.

Raincoat – must be waterproof, although it is unlikely such a thing has yet been made. A combination of wet and cold can be fatal.

Knife, fork & spoon, cup, plate, soup bowl. (You can cut this back to knife, spoon and bowl – a bowl is multi-purpose; you can eat or drink out of it, and mix things in it.)

Pot/billy (one) – 1½ to two litres capacity is sufficient.

Pans (two) – 15 cm across and five cm deep is plenty. The pot and pans are adequate for two to three course meals for two people. Preferably they should fit into each other and be made of aluminium for lightness.

Camping stove – not essential, but can be handy when huts are full, or the gas runs out.

Matches/lighter – for cooking and lighting candles. Matches are a bit of a bind as it is difficult to keep them dry.

Candle – half to one candle per day, depending on how many are sharing the hut. Some huts have lanterns supplied.

Torch (flashlight) – for nocturnal toilet visits and late arrival at the hut.

Toilet paper.

Insect repellent – try Dimp or ask a chemist for the active ingredient of Dimp, then water it down. Some people suggest you start taking vitamin B a couple of weeks before you hit sandfly country as it's supposed to sweat out through your pores and put the sandflies off.

First-aid kit – nothing fancy, but band-aids are a must.

Small bath towel – should dry quickly.

Sleeping bag – light to medium weight; plus light stuff bag for easy packing.

Pack of cards – to play crib, 500, euchre . . .

Pen/pencil & paper

Pot scrubber & tea towel – the scrubber makes washing up in cold water easier and the towel is for drying dishes and wiping things down.

Food It should be nourishing, tasty and lightweight:

Breakfast – the most important meal of the day.
Muesli/porridge (quick cooking) – good with sultanas.
Bacon & eggs – bacon in vacuum pack will last days.
Bread, butter/margarine, Vegemite/honey.
Tea/coffee, sugar, instant milk.

Lunch – it's normally eaten between huts so it shouldn't require too much preparation.

Bread/crackers, butter/margarine. (There are some nice wholemeal crackers available, but 'Cabin Bread' is larger and stronger and so will stand up to being crammed in a pack better.)

Cheese – tasty, not bland.

Dinner – must be hot and substantial

Instant soups – help to whet the biggest appetites.

Fresh meat – good for the first two days.

Dehydrated meals – Alliance excellent, Vesta OK, TVP bad.

Dehydrated vegetables, instant mash potatoes – check the preparation time; 20 minutes is the limit.

Rice – goes with everything.

Dessert – easy to cook, instant such as tapioca or custard.

Snacks – important as a source of energy while tramping

Chocolate – 100 gm per person per day.

Raisins, sultanas, dried fruit.

Scroggin – combination of all the above; make it yourself.

Glucose – in the form of barley sugar, glucose tablets or powder from chemists; it gives almost instant energy.

Biscuits – great before bed with tea.

Cordial concentrate – powder; great thirst quencher, adds extra excitement to the fresh water of waterfalls and streams.

As all rubbish should be burnt or carried out, ensure that all your stuff is in suitable containers. Extra lightweight metal or plastic containers are available from supermarkets and some chemists. Avoid taking bottles and things in plastic or paper wrappers; transfer the ingredients, such as coffee, Vegemite and biscuits etc, into light containers.

This list of equipment is by no means complete but it should get you through the first tramp without suffering from withdrawal symptoms. For a three day tramp, one loaf of bread, 200 to 300 gm of butter/margarine and 200 gm of instant dried milk is sufficient. As so many dishes require milk it is important not to underestimate your requirements.

Everything should be in plastic bags, preferably two, to protect them from the elements. Clothes must be kept dry under all circumstances. The green rubbish/garbage bags are the best available. Put the whole schemozzle into a lightweight, waterproof backpack. The total weight should not exceed 14 kg for a three-day tramp.

The Tracks

Only brief descriptions of the most popular tracks are given and pointers to other possibilities. My personal preferences are the Abel Tasman track for coastal/bush scenery, the Routeburn for sub-alpine scenery and the Tongariro

National Park (Ketetahi-Mangatepopo) for thermal/volcano activity.

MILFORD TRACK (4 days)

'The finest walk in the world' is a special track, unique in New Zealand. It is by far the country's best known track and one which most Kiwis dream of doing, even if it's the *only* track they ever walk. Many overseas visitors also make a special effort to do the track, sometimes planning years in advance, though sadly they often leave New Zealand without realising that other tracks even exist.

For most walkers who have done other tracks, Milford generates a lot of bitterness because of how it is run. It is interesting that a lot of trampers doing the Routeburn, only a few km away, move on to other tracks and refuse to do the Milford because they feel they will be ripped-off.

Hassles aside, the highlights of Milford are the beautiful views from the MacKinnon Pass; the 630-metre Sutherland Falls; the rainforest; and the crystal clear streams, swarming with clever, fat trout and eels.

The track can only be done in one direction, from Lake Te Anau to Milford and you need a permit from the Park Headquarters in Te Anau. This allows you to enter the track on a particular day and no other. Bookings can be very heavy so it's a good idea to book at least several days in advance during December and January. The track is open from early November to early April although heavy rain can close it sooner. As a party of trampers usually leaves every day during the season, it's only possible to stay extra nights in huts if the following party does not fill the hut. As it is necessary to enter and leave the track by boat, the tight control is necessary to handle the large numbers.

For independent walkers the cost of doing the walk is made up of $8 a night for the three nights in huts, the bus to Te Anau Downs, the boat from there to the track, the boat from the track end to

Milford, the hostel at Milford if you stay there and the bus back to Te Anau. Plus food of course, particularly at Milford.

THC's stranglehold over Milford and the Milford Track has been a source of bitterness over the years. There was a stage when 'freedom walkers' were not allowed on the track, and you had to go on a THC tour. Until fairly recently the THC ran the boat from the track end to Milford so that it missed the bus back to Te Anau forcing trampers to stay overnight in the THC hotel or hostel; the nearest campground is conveniently several km out of town. The only meals available are those supplied by the THC or a THC snack bar which is only open limited hours. The public bar, however, is very popular with trampers in the evening!

In & Out

Te Anau End NZRRS has a bus from Te Anau to Te Anau Downs to connect with the boat to Glade House at the head of Lake Te Anau. There is a route, very difficult to follow and only for those with climbing experience, over the Dore Pass east of Glade House, cutting out the boat trip.

Milford End The ferry goes from Sandfly Point at the end of the track in the afternoon for Milford. Buses from Milford take about 2½ hours to Te Anau and there are connections to Queenstown. There's also a Magic Bus between Te Anau, the Divide and Milford. Hitching out is possible but requires patience.

Walking Times

Boat landing to Clinton Forks hut: two hours, Clinton to Mintaro hut: 3½ hours, Mintaro to Dumpling hut: five hours, Dumpling to Sandfly Point: 5½ hours.

The track follows the fairly flat valley of the Clinton River up to the Mintaro hut, passing through rainforest. From Mintaro the track passes over the Mackinnon Pass and down to the THC Quinton hut and

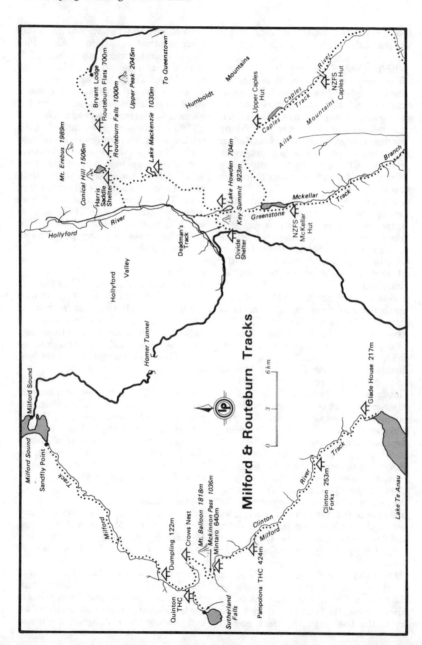

Milford & Routeburn Tracks

through the rainforest in the valley of the Arthur River to Milford Sound. If the pass appears clear on arrival at Mintaro hut make the effort to climb it, after a hot drink, as it may not be clear the next day. The view from Mackinnon is the exceptional feature of the track.

Milford is synonymous with rain: 5½ metres (over 200 inches) of it a year is only average. However, the number of rainy days is not exceptionally high, so when it does rain in this country of granite the effect is an experience not to be missed. Water cascades *everywhere* and small streams become raging torrents within minutes. A few years ago large sections of the track were washed away, as were several bridges which only hours previously had been standing several metres above the surface. The level of Lake Te Anau rose half a metre in less than eight hours. Imagine the state of any hapless trampers making their way to the next hut - and remember your raincoat! You should also pack your belongings in an extra plastic bag and send any excess luggage to Milford or leave it in Te Anau.

In addition to 'freedom walkers', organised parties are taken through by the THC guides staying at a different chain of huts. The THC huts are usually an hour before the 'freedom walkers' huts so there is little mingling of the two. The THC walk - five days and four nights - costs around $700 or $500 for children 10 to 15 years of age. Children under 10 are not accepted.

KEPLER TRACK (3 days)

This new track is due to open in early '88 although it could actually be walked even earlier. The track was cut in '86-87 to give access to the Kepler Mountains at the southern end of Lake Te Anau. Like any Fiordland track the walk depends on the weather; when it's wet it's very, very wet.

In & Out

The track is a loop, starting from the flood

control gates at the south end of the lake, within walking distance of the town, and finishing only about eight km down the road towards Manapouri at the Rainbow Reach Swingbridge.

Walking Times

The walk can be done over three days via Mt Luxmore Hut, Iris Burn Hut and Shallow Bay Hut. The three large huts are well equipped and the track is top quality, well graded and gravelled. The alpine stretch between Iris Burn hut and Mt Luxmore hut goes along a high ridge line, well above the bush with fantastic views when it's clear.

ROUTEBURN (3-4 days)

The variety of country and scenery makes the Routeburn the best rainforest/sub-alpine track in the country and only the Abel Tasman National Park coastal track rivals it for sheer beauty.

The track can be started from either end, but it's probably best to approach it from the Queenstown side because the bus service is irregular from this end and it's much better to come out on the Milford road where there are regular buses and good opportunities for hitching. You don't want to have to hang around for hours waiting for transport after a walk like that. It's easier to plan the date you go in, than the date you'll get out.

Many people travelling from the Queenstown end attempt to reach the Divide in time to catch the bus to Milford, connecting with the launch trip across Milford Sound. The highlight of the track is the view from the Harris Saddle especially from the top of Conical Hill. It is recommended that you stay an extra night at the Falls hut, if the saddle is clouded over, in the hope of better weather the next day. Almost as good is the view from Key Summit which offers a panorama not only of the Hollyford Valley but also of the Eglington Valley and the Greenstone River Valley.

Trampers starting from Queenstown

can return by the easy, flat Greenstone track (two days or one very long day) to Elfin Bay on Lake Wakatipu. You can then walk the 10 km up the road to the bus at Kinloch (the same service that you use for the Routeburn), or charter a jet boat back to Queenstown.

In & Out

Queenstown End It's possible, but difficult, to hitch-hike. The Magic Bus service up to the start of the walk is probably the most popular way of getting to the trailhead. See the Queenstown section for more information.

Up at the northern end of Lake Wakatipu, Glenorchy is a convenient base – it now has excellent facilities – to do the Routeburn, Rees-Dart or Greenstone-Caples tramps. You can stay at the *Glenorchy Camping Ground* and they offer special packages from Queenstown which include transport to Glenorchy, overnight accommodation and then transport to the trailhead in the morning. Again see the Queenstown section for information. You can also organise to be collected from the trailheads if you do the walks in the opposite direction. The cost of transport to or from the trailheads may seem expensive but they're good value considering the state of the roads.

The store at Glenorchy has a reasonable selection of tramping supplies – freeze-dried food, basic trampers' stodge, grains, cereals, dried fruit, a selection of fresh vegetables and fruit, eggs, frozen foods and gear like candles, pots, pans and toiletries, as well as ice-cream, milkshakes and pies. There's also a pub, post office – no bank so take enough cash with you – and a new information centre.

Divide/Te Anau End It's possible to hitch-hike from Te Anau (you must leave in the morning), or Milford (leave early morning or mid-afternoon). Hitching out is much easier, early morning to Milford, mid-afternoon to Te Anau; the problem is to connect with people driving

up to Milford from Te Anau for the day. There are also NZRRS buses from Te Anau via the Divide to Milford and back every day. Check the latest schedule details so you know what time to expect the bus.

Walking Times

Bryants Lodge/Routeburn Shelter to Flats hut: 2½ hours, Flats to Falls hut: ¾ hour, Falls to Harris Saddle: 1½ hours, Harris Saddle to Lake MacKenzie hut: 3½ hours, Lake MacKenzie to Howden hut: three hours, Lake Howden to Divide: one hour.

There are guided four-day walks on the Routeburn which include transport between Queenstown and Routeburn Valley and between the Divide and Queenstown, accommodation, meals and guiding.

ROUTEBURN-CAPLES

An alternative to the Routeburn trek is to combine it with the Caples walk and make a round trip. Access at the Caples end is at Greenstone Wharf. There is now a road from Kinloch to Greenstone Wharf which is OK, though fairly rough in spots as there are some fords to cross.

Walking Times

Greenstone Wharf to Caples hut: three hours, Caples hut to Upper Caples hut: 2½ hours, Upper Caples hut to McKellar Saddle: three hours, McKellar Saddle to Howden hut: three hours, Howden hut to Lake MacKenzie hut: three hours, Lake MacKenzie to Routeburn Falls or Flats hut – Falls is usually very crowded as most people do the Routeburn from the other way – six hours.

Alternatively, Mid Greenstone to McKellar: six hours, McKellar to Howden hut: two hours.

Most huts have four bunks with gas stoves at higher altitudes, wood stoves elsewhere. Those at Lakes Howden and McKenzie

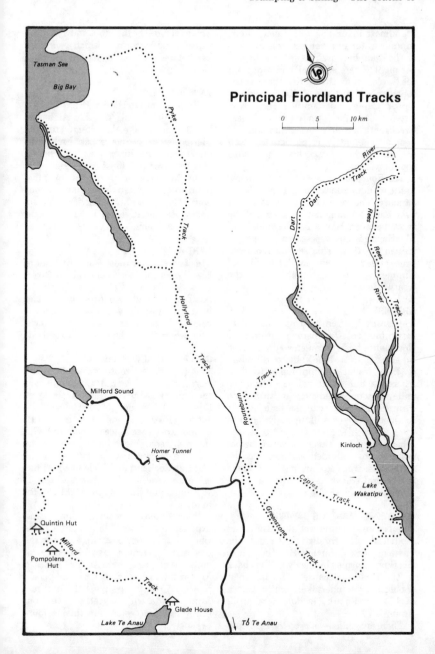

Principal Fiordland Tracks

0   5   10 km

Tasman Sea

Big Bay

Pyke

Track

Dart

River

Track

Rees

Rees

River

Track

Hollyford

Track

Milford Sound

Routeburn

Track

Homer Tunnel

Kinloch

Quintin Hut

Caples

Track

Lake
Wakatipu

Milford

Greenstone

Pompolena
Hut

Track

Track

Glade House

Lake Te Anau

To Te Anau

are almost luxurious, with flush toilets, running water and even gas cookers. Huts on the Routeburn track cost $7 per person per night. There are some newer huts on the Caples route: the McKellar hut at the southern end of Lake McKellar and the Upper Caples hut, upriver from Kay Creek and not far down river from Fraser Creek, both of which can accommodate 20 people. The latter is particularly well designed and has a good wood stove with coal provided.

The Routeburn track is closed by snow in the winter and is extremely popular in January. The record for one night was 44 people in a 20-bunk hut! A stretch of the track between Harris Saddle and Lake MacKenzie is very exposed and dangerous in bad weather. This section has even been closed by snow in the middle of summer, so check with the warden if the weather looks dicey.

GREENSTONE

This track is often used as a means of returning to Queenstown from the Routeburn. It is a nine hour walk down the broad easy Greenstone Valley to Elfin Bay on Lake Wakatipu, from Lake Howden. There's a hut about halfway down the valley but only a shelter at Elfin Bay. From Elfin Bay you can charter a jet boat to Queenstown or walk up to Kinloch to meet up with the bus to the Routeburn (check what days this is operating before you set out). Guided walks along the Greenstone track cost around $400. There are several tracks in the adjacent more attractive Caples valley.

HOLLYFORD-MARTIN'S BAY-PYKE

This is a well known track along the broad Hollyford valley through rainforest to the Tasman Sea at Martin's Bay then on to Big Bay, returning by the Pyke River back to the Divide. Because of its length it should not be undertaken lightly. Check at Fiordland Park Headquarters in Te Anau.

There are guided walks on the Hollyford

which include the flight out and a jet-boat trip on Lake McKerrow, which avoids the hardest and most boring part of the walk, Demon Trail.

Walking Times

Hollyford camp to Hidden Falls hut: four hours, Hidden Falls to Lake Alabaster hut: 3½ hours, Lake Alabaster hut to Lake McKerrow hut: two hours, Lake McKerrow hut to Hokuri River hut: five hours, Hokuri River hut to Martin's Bay: two hours, Martin's Bay to Big Bay hut: five hours, Big Bay hut to Upper Pike hut: four hours, Upper Pike hut to Barrier River: six hours, Barrier River to Lake Alabaster hut: seven hours.

DART-REES

This is a circular route from the head of Lake Wakatipu by way of the Dart River, Rees Saddle and Rees River, with the possibility of a side trip to the Dart Glacier if you're suitably equipped. Access by vehicle is possible as far as Muddy Creek, from where it's 2½ hours to 25 Mile Hut.

COPLAND TRACK (3-4 days)

This well known route crosses from the Hermitage Hotel near Mt Cook right over the southern Alps and down to the West Coast road, just south of Fox Glacier. The actual crossing is only for those with alpine experience in ice or snow and with the right equipment but once over the pass the descent down to the road by the Douglas Rock hut and Welcome Flat hut is quite simple. The hot springs at Welcome Flat hut is the highlight for many.

If you do not have the equipment and experience it is possible to take a guide who will take your party up and over the pass and then leave you to follow the trail down to the coast. From Alpine Guides in Mt Cook this costs $300 for a one person party, $375 for two people, $410 for three. Alpine Guides will also lead you over from the West Coast side but this is more expensive.

Walking Times

From the Hermitage it's an easy day walk to the Hooker Hut, from where it takes about half a day over the pass to Douglas Rock hut. Douglas Rock to Welcome Flat hut: 2½ hours, Welcome Flat to West Coast road: 5½ hours.

ABEL TASMAN NATIONAL PARK COASTAL TRACK (3-4 days)

This track is little known outside the Golden Bay/Nelson district but is probably the most beautiful in the country. The track passes through pleasant bush overlooking beaches of golden sand lapped by bright blue water. The numerous bays, small and large, make it like a travel brochure come to life.

In & Out

There are regular buses on weekdays from Nelson to Motueka, one of which continues on to Takaka. Additional services run during the summer high season. From the north end at Totaranui you have the choice of hitch-hiking from Takaka, or travelling from Motueka to Kaiteriteri and chartering a boat from there.

If you hitch in via the south end at Marahau, there's more traffic on the road from Kaiteriteri, even though it looks longer on the map. Neither end is easy for hitching. In fact getting back to civilisation from Totaranui by any method of transport is a major problem. If you're with a group of people it's probably cheaper – and certainly more convenient – to arrange for a taxi to drive out empty from Motueka to pick you up in Totaranui. There's a telephone at Marahau parking area to phone for a taxi if you miss the mail run. An enterprising individual has set up a food stand at the Marahau end with all sorts of delicious goodies waiting for hungry trampers.

In the summer there's a boat service from Kaiteriteri to Torrent Bay, Bark Bay, Tonga, Awaroa and Totaranui. If you want to stop the boat elsewhere there are red flags at several points, you set one up on the beach to signal the boat to stop for you.

Walking Times

South to north, road end to the start of track: one hour, track start to Anchorage hut: three hours, Bark Bay to Awaroa hut: three hours, Awaroa to Totaranui: two hours.

Huts have bunks for a minimum of 16 and are equipped with wood stoves. The coastal track huts cost $7 per person per night, the inland track huts are cheaper. Several sections of the main track are tidal with long deviations during high tides. As the tidal stretches are all just on the north side of huts it is important to do the track in a southerly direction if the low tides are in the afternoons and from south to north if they are in the mornings. Check the newspaper, subtracting 20 minutes from the Nelson tidal times.

If you have the time take additional food so that you can stay longer should you have the inclination. Bays around all the huts are very nice but the sandflies are a problem, except at the tiny, picturesque

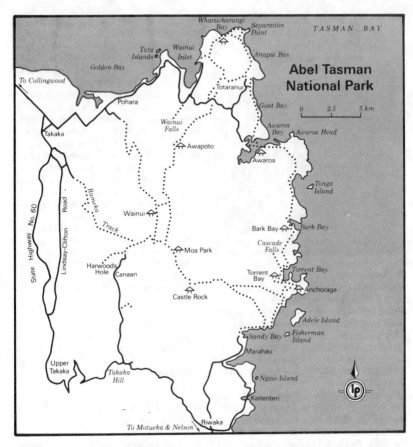

beach of Te Puketea near the Anchorage hut. There are some Maori rock carvings on the coast track between the Bark Bay and Awaroa huts. They're in a cave at the extreme north end of Onetahuti Beach, just north of the Tonga Quarry. You have to ford a small stream to reach the two caves and the spiral, abstract carvings are in the left cave, not the one half filled with water.

There is a big information centre at Totaranui and information is also available at Takaka. Kaiteriteri and Totaranui have large campgrounds; there is a

smaller one at Pohara Beach, 10 km east of Takaka on the road to Totaranui. Excess luggage can be sent very cheaply by Newmans bus between Motueka and Takaka. There are four-day guided walks on the track for around $450.

HEAPHY TRACK (4-6 days)

The Heaphy is one of the best known tracks in New Zealand (second only to the Milford), which is due to a great extent to the controversy over attempts to convert it into a road. The road has been shelved for the present for economic reasons. The track hasn't got the spectacular scenery of something like the Routeburn, but it still has its own beauty. Some people find it a disappointment if done immediately after the nearby Abel Tasman National Park coastal track.

The track lies almost entirely within the North-West Nelson State Forest Park. Highlights are the view from the summit of Mt Perry (two hour walk, return, from Perry Saddle hut) and the coast, especially around the Heaphy hut. It's worth spending a day or two resting at the Heaphy hut; this is particularly advisable for those travelling south from Collingwood. It is possible to cross the Heaphy River at its mouth at low tide, but with caution, scramble through a hole in the cliffs and come out to a wrecked Japanese squid boat.

Alternatively, take the very badly marked track (check with wardens carefully) over the hill to the coast then walk south along the beach. Almost an hour up the coast is a seal colony. Take matches and a billy and have a meal of delicious mussels; only available at low tide of course. To find the best mussels turn over all the large rocks – you'll see them hiding on the underside, and they're often as big as 15 cm. You're only allowed 40 mussels a day per person.

It is possible to return to the Nelson/Golden Bay region by the more scenic, if harder, Wangapeka Track (five to seven days) starting just south of Karamea. The track now has km markers its full length; zero marker is at the start of the track at the Kohaihai River near Karamea and the total length is 76 km.

In & Out

Collingwood End Hitch-hiking in either direction is very difficult. There's a bus service from Nelson to Takaka with a connecting bus from there to Collingwood. From Collingwood you can charter the minibus to take you to the trailhead. See the Nelson and Collingwood sections for details. There's a phone at the trailhead so

you can call for the bus. There's also an airstrip nearby and it's possible to fly back from there to Karamea.

Karamea End Hitching is very difficult. You can take a taxi between Karamea and the start of the track – it can be called from the end of the track. A bus is also available and it's possible to charter a plane back to the Collingwood end of the track. There is a bus service to Westport from Karamea. See the Westport section for details. There is a rather primitive camping ground at the Karamea end of the track

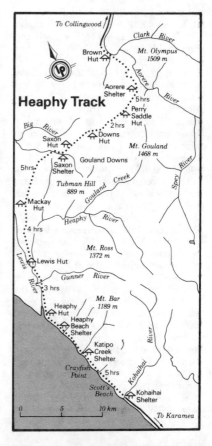

and Karamea has a very popular hostel during the busy season.

There's an Info Centre at Kohaihai, at the Karamea end of the track, and at the Collingwood end you can get info from the ranger at Browns hut.

Walking Times

Browns hut to Perry Saddle hut: five hours, Perry Saddle to Downs hut: two hours, Downs to Mackay hut: five hours, Mackay to Lewis hut: four hours, Lewis to Heaphy hut: three hours, Heaphy to Kohaihai River (track start): five hours.

Km Markers Browns 76, Perry Saddle hut 61, Downs 49, Blue Duck Shelter turn-off 47, Mackay 36.5, Lewis 24, Heaphy 17 and Kohaihai River 0.

Huts are geared to handle 16 people. They have wood stoves, except Perry Saddle and Mackay which have gas. The great majority of people travel west from Collingwood to Karamea. Downs hut is not recommended as it is smaller and in poor shape but bypassing it means a seven-hour walk between Perry Saddle and Mackay. From Browns hut the track passes through beech forest to Perry Saddle (but don't take the shortcut going uphill, unless you are fit). The country then opens up to the swampy Gouland Downs then closes in with sparse bush all the way to Mackay. The bush becomes more dense towards the Heaphy hut with the beautiful nikau palm at low levels.

The final section is along the coast through heavy bush and partly along the beach. Unfortunately the sandflies are unbearable along this, the most beautiful part of the track. The climate here is surprisingly mild but do not swim in the sea as the undertows and currents are vicious. The lagoon at Heaphy hut is good for swimming though and fishing is possible in the Heaphy river.

Send excess luggage by Newmans bus between Westport and Nelson/Takaka/Collingwood/Motueka.

WANGAPEKA

Although not as well known as the Heaphy Track in the same park, it is a more enjoyable walk. The track starts some 25 km south of Karamea on the West Coast and runs 56 km east to the Rolling River. It takes about five days and there is a good chain of huts.

STEWART ISLAND

The northern portion of the island has a circular track but unfortunately it is long, some seven days, and uninteresting for stretches with many patches of muddy bog. However, the section from Oban to Christmas Village Bay contains some very attractive, sheltered bays and bush, ideal for relaxing. The drawback is having to return along the same track. Recently a new track has been opened between Port William hut and North Arm, making an interesting circular route near Oban.

In & Out

See the Stewart Island section for details. There are no roads on the island outside the immediate vicinity of Oban.

Walking Times

Ferry terminal to track start: one hour, track start to Port William hut: three hours, Port William to Big Bungaree Beach hut: three hours, Big Bungaree to Christmas Village Bay hut: three hours. Mud can lengthen these times.

More details and a map of the walking trail can be found in the section on Stewart Island on page 339.

Huts range from the smallish smoke-filled Big Bungaree Beach hut to the relatively new and well-located Port William hut with 24 bunks. The Port William hut is frequently used by school parties who are expected to take tents and use them if others require the bunks. Huts are free and have wood stoves. From Christmas Village Bay hut it's a 3½ hour climb to the summit of Mt Anglem (1070 metres) and an outstanding view of part of the South Island and most of Stewart Island. An excursion can be made to Yankee River (four hours one way) but the track is very boggy. An old boiler at Maori Bay is a reminder of the timber milling days.

Due west of Oban is the attractive and wild Masons Bay with its extensive sand dunes. The walk between Oban and Freshwater hut is not particularly pleasant though and tends to be boggy. It's possible to hire a small boat to North Arm hut, cutting out the first day. From Freshwater to Masons Bay you're walking on a tractor track, firmer under foot, but it may be under water.

Walking Times

Oban to North Arm hut: four hours, North Arm to Freshwater River hut: four hours, Freshwater River to Big Sandhill hut (Mason's Bay): three hours. The first two times are subject to mud.

KETETAHI TRACK (2-3 days)

The Tongariro National Park has a long, circular track embracing the three mountains and requiring some 10 days. Regrettably, for the most part it is hard, unrewarding walking.

One exception is the Ketetahi Track, running from Highway 47 near Lake Rotaira to the Mangatepopo hut, in the far northern part of the park. Highlights of the track are the hot springs at Ketetahi and the view over hundreds of square km to the north, including the whole of Lake Taupo. It's an eerie feeling looking over the dormant craters, the beautiful colours of the crater lakes and the smoky majesty of Mt Ngauruhoe. The track is very accessible, as it's only a few km off National Highway 1, but unfortunately several reports indicate that the track is overused and badly maintained.

In & Out

Transport is available from Turangi to the trail head, which is eight km off the road from the Te Ponanga Saddle road and Highway 47 junction. See the Turangi section for details. Previously it was difficult to get to the trailhead as buses to the junction were generally at inconvenient times and traffic for hitching was light. And you still had that eight km walk.

Walking Times

Ketetahi Springs to Ketetahi hut to Mangatepopo hut: five hours, Mangatepopo to Chateau: two hours, Mangatepopo to Highway 47: 1½ hours.

Refer to the section on Tongariro National Park (page 182) for a map of this trail and information about other walks in this area. Both huts have bunks for 24 with wood stoves, not noted for the heat they generate. The track is subject to wild storms but is well marked with poles. The atmosphere around both huts, especially Ketetahi, can be very peaceful if it's uncrowded – consider taking extra food for a leisurely stay. If a big crowd turns up it's anything but peaceful.

If the weather is fine, try climbing Mt Ngauruhoe from the Mangatepopo hut. The climb is demanding, the track partly marked (but the route is fairly obvious), and the scoria makes it a hard slog. If people are coming up when you descend move to the right (east) of the tracks into the softest scoria but be very careful not to dislodge rocks on to those below you. One little piece of scoria dislodged can collect material until it becomes a huge slide further down. Try to keep control as you descend – the scoria can rip you to shreds.

Walking Time

Mangatepopo hut to the saddle near Tongariro's South Crater: 1½ hours, the saddle to the summit: two hours, summit to the saddle: half an hour!

Starting from the northern end, the track passes through beautiful bush for an hour, then tussock up to the springs and rock and

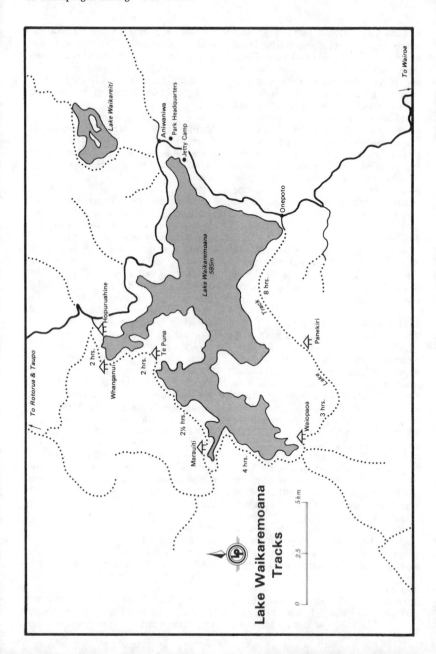

Lake Waikaremoana Tracks

scoria to Mangatepopo. You pass vast panoramas that look amazingly like moon-scapes, with awesome craters and steam oozing out of the ground. Take your pick between walking by track and road out to Highway 47, or by the Park Headquarters' track to the Chateau; both through tussock. There isn't a hut at the Chateau but there is a campsite and more expensive accommodation. See the Tongariro section for details.

WAIKAREMOANA TRACK (Lake Track, 3-4 days)
A very attractive walk through beech forest with vast panoramas and beautiful views of the lake. The track, entirely within Urewera National Park, can be rather difficult to get to since it is well off most travel routes on the North Island. Many travellers rate Urewera Park as one of the most attractive in New Zealand.

In & Out
NZRRS has a twice weekly bus service between Rotorua and Wairoa from where you can continue to Gisborne or Napier. See the Gisborne section for more details.

Walking Times
Onepoto to Panekiri hut: eight hours, Panekiri to Waiopaoa hut: three hours, Waiopaoa to Marauiti hut: four hours, Marauiti to Te Puna hut: 2½ hours, Te Puna to Whanganui hut: two hours, Whanganui to Hopuruahine Stream: two hours.

The track can be done from either end. Starting from Onepoto all the climbing is done in the first few hours. There is a motor camp with cabins at Waikaremoana, and a campsite at Mokau Landing. You could probably pitch a tent at Onepoto or Hopuruahine too.

OTHER TRACKS
In addition to these specific tracks there are numerous possibilities in all State and National Parks, especially Arthur's Pass, the Nelson Lakes, Coromandel and of course Mt Egmont – an easy climb in good weather. See *Tramping in New Zealand* for more details.

Skiing

Skiing is still in its infancy in New Zealand but its popularity is growing fast. For Australians it's got a number of big attractions, not the least of which is that it's more reliable and cheaper than in Oz. Australia's relatively low mountains mean the snow cover is unpredictable and the season is short, so the costs of skiing have to be high to cover the limited season. The lower lift, parking and hiring costs in New Zealand however, balance out the extra cost of getting there.

For Europeans and Americans the attraction is skiing 'down under', skiing in the middle of the northern summer, not to mention some unique attractions such as skiing on the slopes of a volcano or the long Tasman glacier runs. Heli-skiing is another attraction of New Zealand skiing. New Zealand seems to have more helicopters than it knows what to do with and in winter many of them are used to lift skiers up to the top of long stretches of snow. These flights are surprisingly reasonable.

New Zealand's ski fields are generally not very well endowed with on-field chalets, lodges or hotels. The places to stay are usually some distance from the slopes, so it's a bit of a drag going back and forth every day. This does however mean that the accommo-dation, when you get to it, is fairly cheap.

At the major ski fields, lifts cost about $35 to $40 a day and lessons are around $25. You may as well bring your own equipment if you have it, although all the usual stuff can be bought or hired in New Zealand. The ski season is generally from June to October, although it varies considerably from one ski field to another.

There are plenty of ski-package tours

both from Australia and within New Zealand. The NZTP has a host of brochures on the various packages and can make bookings.

NORTH ISLAND
Chateau (Whakapapa)
The Chateau or Whakapapa Skifield is seven km above the Chateau Hotel on Mt Ruapehu in Tongariro National Park. It's the end of the road – known as the Top of the Bruce. They are the most popular ski slopes in New Zealand and include a downhill course dropping nearly 1000 metres over five km. The normal season is mid-June to November.

There are chairlifts, T-bars and ropetows. If you drive yourself up to the slopes there's a parking charge or you can take the 'Mountain Goat' bus-truck up from the Chateau. There's an expensive hotel, cheaper motel and a campsite with cabins at Whakapapa Village around the Chateau (see the Tongariro section for details – bookings are very heavy during the ski season). There are also ski club lodges at Iwikau Village on the slopes but these are generally available only to members and friends.

During the ski season there are bus services to the Chateau from Auckland and Wellington.

Turoa
The Turoa Skifield, on the south-west side of Mt Ruapehu, was opened in 1979. Chairlifts, T-bars and ropetows take you up to the start of a four-km run. There's also a beginner's lift. The season lasts from June to November. There is no road toll or parking fee and daily uphill transport to the ski field is available from Ohakune, 17 km away. At present skis must be hired at Ohakune – they're not available on the slopes. Accommodation is also available at Ohakune; see that section for information.

Egmont
There's more volcano-slope skiing on the eastern slopes of Mt Egmont. This is a club-operated ski field near Stratford with a T-bar and several ropetows. The season is July to September and accommodation is available in New Plymouth or closer to the snow in Stratford.

SOUTH ISLAND
Coronet Peak
New Zealand's southernmost slopes, near Queenstown, are rated the best in New Zealand and comparable to any in the world. There's even talk of running a future winter Olympics here. The season is comparatively short – July to September. Access to the ski field is from Queenstown, 38 km away, and there's a bus service in the ski season. You can hitch it if you leave early in the morning and depart before 4 pm to come down again.

There are chairlifts, T-bars and beginners tows to take you up the slopes. The Coronet Peak chairlifts run to altitudes of 1585 and 1650 metres. The treeless slopes and good snow provide excellent skiing.

The ski field is operated by Mt Cook and it has a licensed restaurant, overnight ski storage, ski repair shop, creche and pre-school ski lessons. For accommodation see the Queenstown section, there are active apres-ski possibilities.

Mt Cook
Although it is not strictly necessary to fly up to the Tasman Glacier (people have been known to walk!) this is really a ski-resort for the skiing jetsetter only. You need to be a fairly competent skier, as well as a rich one, to savour this unique experience as skiing down from the upper reaches of the Tasman Glacier usually requires a flight up from the Hermitage in a ski-plane. The lower reaches of the glacier are almost dead flat and are usually covered in surface moraine so you must either walk out – or fly once again. In exceptional circumstances the run down the glacier can be 20 km in length although it's usually less than 10 km. Quite an experience.

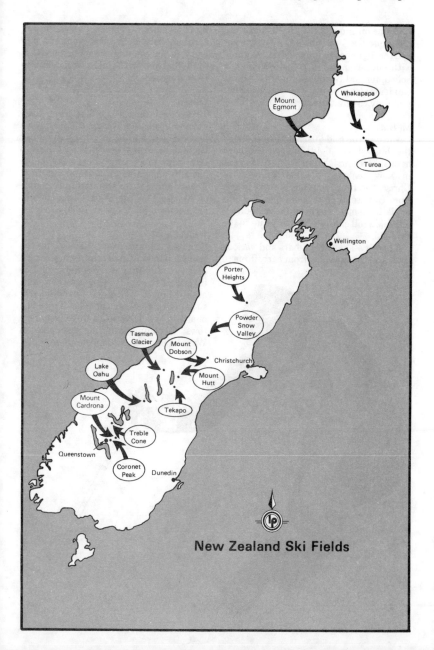

New Zealand Ski Fields

Count on around $350 for a flight up, the guide fee, two runs down the glacier and the flight back. You must have a guide with you. You can also 'heliski' from a helicopter and Nordic skiing with Alpine Guides is also possible. The season is from mid-July to late October.

Mt Hutt

Opened in the mid-70s, Mt Hutt is one of the highest ski fields in the southern hemisphere and is rated as one of the best in New Zealand. It's 104 km west of Christchurch and you can get there by bus from Christchurch or from local accommodation centres Methven and Ashburton. There's a toll charge if you drive up to the ski field.

There's a chairlift, T-bars and various tows and the season is from early June to mid-November. There's a variety of accommodation in Methven (24 km away) or you can stay at Ashburton, 34 km from Methven on the main Christchurch-Dunedin road.

Tekapo

Tekapo ski field is 33 km from Lake Tekapo in the MacKenzie country. It's a less developed field, but a good one for beginners. Normal season is mid-June to late September and there's a double chairlift and three tows. Buses run from Tekapo where there's a camp and a couple of hotels. The Mt Cook Christchurch-Queenstown bus stops at Tekapo.

Treble Cone

Situated 29 km from Wanaka in the Southern Lake District the normal season here is mid-June to September. The highest of the fields in the southern lake area, Treble Cone is spectacularly situated overlooking the lake. There is a chairlift, two T-bars and three beginners tows. Accommodation is available in Wanaka and buses run from there.

Cardrona

Wanaka's other ski field, Cardrona is 30 km out and is open from June-July through September. It's a relatively new ski field with three chairlifts and a couple of rope tows. Buses run to the snow from Wanaka. If you want to try heli-skiing this is a great place to do so. You don't have to be a star as there are numerous runs to choose from over variable terrain that are suitable for intermediate and advanced level skiers.

Porter Heights

The closest commercial ski field to Christchurch, Porter Heights is 22 km from Springfield (the nearest town) and about 100 km from Christchurch on the Arthurs Pass road. The snowfield offers a 700-metre run and the normal season runs from late June to early October. There are three T-bars and two beginners tows. You can stay on the field but accommodation is limited in neighbouring Springfield.

Other

There are lots of other slopes in the South Island, many of them club operated including a whole collection of club ski fields off the Arthurs Pass road, some offering all-inclusive ski weeks. In the north there's a club field at St Arnaud in Nelson Lakes National Park.

Scuba Diving

Of course tramping and skiing aren't the only popular outdoor activities in New Zealand. Scuba diving also has its devotees and while the Bay of Islands and other areas in the North Island are obvious attractions there are diving possibilities around both islands. Even Invercargill has a club!

Fiordland in the extreme south is a surprisingly interesting place for diving. The diving here is most unusual because the extremely heavy rainfall leaves an actual layer of freshwater, often peaty brown, over the saltwater. You descend through this murky and cold freshwater into amazingly clear and warmer saltwater.

The freshwater cuts out light which discourages the growth of seaweed and this provides ideal conditions for the growth of black coral which can be found much closer to the surface than is common elsewhere in the world. Leave it there, though. It's 100% protected in New Zealand. The Fiordland sounds also have plenty of crayfish and amazing shoals of dolphins who display great interest in the relatively rare appearance of scuba divers.

Getting There

AIR

The overwhelming majority of visitors to New Zealand fly there. There are three airports that handle international flights – Auckland, Wellington and Christchurch. Most international flights go through Auckland; certainly if you're flying from the US you're going to arrive in Auckland. Wellington airport has limited runway capacity and international flights are all to and from Australia. Flights to and from Christchurch are also mainly with Australia although there are also some connections with other countries.

There are some special ticket types and definitions which may be of interest to visitors to New Zealand:

Circle Pacific Fares

Circle Pacific tickets let you circle the Pacific using a combination of airlines. You can start and finish the circle at any point and it goes from the US west coast, via various islands in the Pacific to New Zealand, on to Australia, to Asia and back to the west coast. Typically the fare for a Circle Pacific ticket is around A$2200 or US$1600.

A Circle Pacific route offered by Air New Zealand in conjunction with Singapore Airlines or Cathay Pacific allows you to start in Los Angeles, with Air New Zealand and fly to Honolulu, then on to Auckland and later continue to Sydney. From Sydney you could switch to Singapore Airlines to fly back to LA via Singapore. There are countless CP alternatives.

Circle Pacific tickets usually have some sort of advance purchase requirement and there will probably be restrictions on changing your route once you've bought the ticket. Typically you're allowed four stopovers but additional stopovers can be included at extra cost. You will probably have to complete the circuit within a certain period of time.

Round the World Fares

Round the World or RTW fares can be a very useful way of visiting New Zealand in combination with other destinations. They work particularly well from Europe – having come half way round the world to New Zealand in one direction you might just as well continue the same way!

These fares usually offer a round the world ticket using the combined routes of two airlines. Air New Zealand offer RTW tickets in combination with Singapore Airlines, British Airways, Cathay Pacific, Lufthansa, Thai International and various other airlines. As with Circle Pacific tickets you can join the loop at various places round the world. They typically cost around A$2500, US$1800 or £1200 and you could use a RTW ticket to make stops in Australia, New Zealand, the USA and Europe.

Apart from the official airline RTW tickets there are also RTW combinations put together by travel agents. Out of London, for example, they might put together a combination such as a cheap flight to Asia, hooking up with the popular and heavily discounted UTA trans-Pacific route and then another cheap fare back to London from the US.

Apex Fares

Many low fare tickets are Apex or Advance Purchase Excursion tickets. Basically this means that the ticket must be booked and paid for a certain period in advance (usually 21 days) and once you've entered that advance purchase period you're locked in to your outward and return dates and can only make changes at additional cost. It is possible to insure against some eventualities so that if, for example, you're suddenly taken ill and cannot take your flight you don't lose your fare. Check the small print carefully on Apex fares.

Bucket Shops

Particularly in Europe special deals on air fares are often found through travel agents known as 'bucket shops'. A bucket shop is an agent specialising in discounted tickets. These tickets are usually quite legitimate, they're tickets which the airline is unable to sell at the full listed fare. Since a normal travel agent cannot sell tickets to some customers at one price and to others at another the airline releases some tickets at a special lower price through selected agents.

The more obscure the airline or the

more inconvenient the route the bigger the discount is likely to be. Although it's really only in Europe that ticket discounters are known as bucket shops similar operations can also be found in the US, in Australia, in Hong Kong and in many other places. To find a ticket discounter simply scan the travel ads in the travel pages of newspapers.

FROM AUSTRALIA

The number of air routes between Australia and New Zealand has proliferated in the last few years. New Zealand cities with flights to or from Australia are Auckland, Christchurch and Wellington. Australian cities with flights to or from New Zealand are Adelaide, Brisbane, Hobart, Melbourne, Perth, Sydney and Townsville. Examples of regular one-way economy fares are from Sydney to Auckland, Christchurch or Wellington A$333; from Melbourne to Christchurch A$367, to Auckland or Wellington A$386. Fares from Brisbane or Hobart are similar, from Adelaide to Auckland is slightly more.

It's much cheaper to take an advance purchase fare which can get you to New Zealand and back for little more than a regular one-way fare. With these fares you must book and pay for your ticket at least seven days prior to departure and once the tickets are issued cancellation charges apply should you wish to change your reservation or if you fail to fly. Insurance is available to protect against the advance purchase cancellation fees. You must stay in New Zealand for at least six days but at most 120.

The fare depends on the day you fly out as well as where you fly to and from. The year is divided up into peak, shoulder and off-peak times. If you fly out during the off-peak (June and July) the return fare can be as low as A$394 from Sydney, A$433 from Melbourne. If you want to go out during peak season (mid-December to mid-January) the fare from Sydney will be A$522, from Melbourne A$577 or A$602. At other times of year the fare falls between these high and low rates.

It pays to plan your flight dates carefully – if you were planning to visit New Zealand in the summer, leaving just a few days earlier in December or later in January could save you about A$70.

If you're travelling from Australia to the US west coast via New Zealand the one-way fare from Sydney or Brisbane is A$949, from Melbourne A$1105. Return fares vary with the season and vary from A$1448 to A$2016 out of Sydney, from

A$1574 to A$2144 out of Melbourne. Circle Pacific Fares ex-Australia are A$2185. Round-the-World fares are A$2499.

FROM THE USA

Regular economy return fares from the US west coast are US$2126 to New Zealand or US$2576 to New Zealand and on to Australia. There are two cheaper excursion fares available, the lower priced of the two has more restrictions and advance purchase requirements. To New Zealand the cheaper excursion fare is US$946 in the low season, US$1260 in the high season. The more expensive excursion fare is US$1096 and US$1460. The same excursion fares to Australia are all US$100 more expensive.

You can do better than these straight-forward fares with travel agents. The Sunday travel sections of papers like the *New York Times*, the *Los Angeles Times* or the *San Francisco Examiner* always have plenty of ads for cheap airline tickets and there are always good deals on flights across the Pacific. Council Travel and STA, the two student travel specialists, both have good fares on offer.

Examples of discounted trans-Pacific fares are west coast-Auckland-west coast for about US$750. Using the UTA Pacific island hopping fare you can do a multi-stop trip across to Auckland, Sydney and back again to the west coast for about US$800.

FROM EUROPE

There has always been cut throat competition between London's many 'bucket shops' and with the weaker pound London is once again the European centre for cheap fares. There are plenty of bucket shops in London and although there are always some untrustworthy operators most of them are fine. You'll find advertisements from agents and examples of their fares in give-away papers like the *TNT (The News & Travel) Magazine* or *LAM*. The weekly magazine *Time Out*

has plenty of travel ads and they also give some useful advice on precautions to take when dealing with bucket shops. The magazine *Business Traveller* is another good source of information and advice on discount fares. Two good low-fare specialists are Trailfinders at 46 Earls Court Rd, London W8 and STA Travel at 74 Old Brompton Rd, London W7.

Return tickets London-Auckland can be found in London bucket shops for around £800 to £1000. Some stopovers are permitted on this sort of ticket. Since New Zealand is about as far from Europe as you can get it's not that much more to fly right on round the world rather than back-tracking. Round-the-World tickets that go through the South Pacific generally cost around £1200 to £1500.

FROM ASIA

There are far more flights to New Zealand from Asia than there were only a few years ago. From Tokyo, Japan Apex return fares vary from around 290,000 to 360,000 yen depending on the season. From Kuala Lumpur, Malaysia you can get return fares of around M$2400 and Malaysia is a very popular place for fare discounting. From Singapore return fares go from around S$2100. Hong Kong is another popular fare discounting centre and discounted return tickets to New Zealand cost around HK$5700.

SEA

Cruise ships apart there are no longer any regular passenger ship services to New Zealand and these days arriving on some romantic tramp steamer (something you can still do in various Pacific Island nations) is pretty much a thing of the past. Ditto for the idea of working your passage. But if you're adventurous, flexible and persistent finding a berth on a yacht is a real possibility. Refer to the following section on yachting for more details.

Yachts

New Zealand is one of the most

enthusiastic yachting nations on earth (look at how they did when they first had a go at the America's Cup) and it's also a very popular destination for yachts cruising the South Pacific. So finding a berth on a yacht to or from New Zealand is a real possibility.

There are lots of yachts cruising back and forth in the Pacific and they're very often looking for crew. After all sailing along with just a couple of people soon gets to be boring and hard work, much better to take somebody on in port A drop them off in port B and recruit somebody else to give a hand from port B to C. Of course yachties would like to have somebody fully skilled in ocean sailing but since those sort of people aren't always waiting round looking for boats quite often the requirements are simply that you're an easy going, hard working, non-complaining type and that you're willing to chip in money for the food you eat.

To find a yacht you have to go to the appropriate port at the appropriate time. There are lots of favourite islands, ports and harbours where you're likely to find yachts. Examples are Sydney and Cairns in Australia; Bali in Indonesia, various ports in Fiji or Tahiti; Hawaii, San Diego or San Francisco in the US. In New Zealand popular yachting harbours are the Bay of Islands and Whangarei (both in Northlands), Auckland and Wellington.

Yachts tend to move around the Pacific with the calendar – they sail with the prevailing winds, they stay out of the typhoon areas when it's cyclone season so there are certain times when you're more likely to find yachts. From Fiji October-November is a peak departure season as cyclones are on their way. March-April is the main departure season for yachts heading to Australia. Be prepared for rough seas and storms crossing the Tasman Sea.

To find a yacht looking for crew simply scan noticeboards in popular ports, ask at yacht clubs, actually ask around the yachts at their anchorages or check newspaper ads. In Auckland try the *New Zealand Herald* personal columns under 'crew'.

LEAVING NEW ZEALAND

As from other countries scan the travel small ads for air fare bargains. Typical fares offered from Auckland include London NZ$850 one-way (NZ$1650 return), US west coast NZ$600 (NZ$1060), Singapore NZ$600, Hong Kong NZ$800 and Tokyo NZ$650.

Getting Around

AIR

Air travel within New Zealand went through quite a revolution in 1987. Once upon a time the government-owned Air New Zealand had more-or-less a monopoly on the major routes around the country. The only competition was Mt Cook Airlines who basically flew between major tourist destinations like Mt Cook, Queenstown and Rotorua. Then Australia's Ansett Airlines, partly owned by expansion-minded media mogul Rupert Murdoch, took a large interest in Newmans Air and created a new airline called Ansett New Zealand. At first it operated a network very similar to Mt Cook but in mid-87 a batch of Boeing 737s were added to the fleet and Ansett New Zealand started head-on competition with Air New Zealand.

Having things all to themselves had made Air New Zealand rather complacent and the high standards of service passengers enjoy on their international routes certainly didn't apply to domestic passengers. Ansett started up with economy and 1st class service and in reply Air New Zealand quickly added an upper class to their previously all-economy operation and also a price cutting low-service 'City Saver' operation. The City Saver flights operate to six major airports including Auckland, Christchurch and Wellington and undercut regular economy fares by 25%. There are no advance purchase restrictions or other complications on these tickets. The Domestic Air Fares chart shows regular economy fares in New Zealand dollars on some of the main routes.

For visitors from overseas Air New Zealand has a special Visit New Zealand Fare which can only be purchased prior to arrival and in conjunction with your international flight. The ticket allows either four flights for $320 or six flights for $440. Mt Cook has a Kiwi Air Pass which gives you 30 days unlimited travel on Mt Cook Airline services for $599. Again it must be bought before you arrive in NZ. The Student Travel section at the end of the chapter has info on student discounts.

Although New Zealand is a compact country and ground transport is generally quite good there are still places where flying can make a lot of sense, particularly if you've already done the same journey by land. Travellers have quoted examples of trips between the North and South Islands where a long bus trip is followed by the inter-island ferry and another bus trip, taking a couple of days altogether. By air the same trip could be done in an hour or two and actually cost less. There are also great views to be enjoyed, particularly if your flight takes you over the mountains or volcanoes.

Local Air Services

Apart from the three major operators there are also a host of local and feeder airlines. Services that may interest travellers include Southern Air's hop between Invercargill and Stewart Island, a favourite with trampers. Or there's Sea Bee Air's amphibious services from Auckland to Waiheke or the Bay of Island's. Flights between the two islands are also a popular alternative to the ferry services, you can hop across from Wellington to Picton for little more than the ferry fare.

Flightseeing

At some point in their travels most visitors also do a little flightseeing. New Zealand has plenty of attractions which are simply wonderful to fly over and there are an enormous number of local operators ready and waiting to fly you over them. In particular there must be more helicopters per capita than anywhere else on earth.

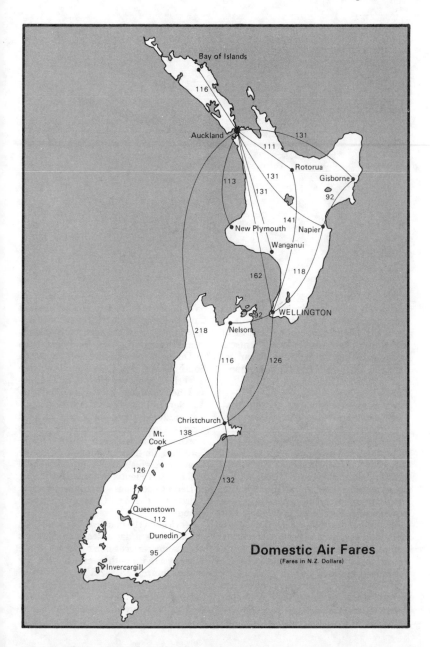

Domestic Air Fares
(Fares in N.Z. Dollars)

Particular favourites include the trips over the glaciers, mountains or fiords of the South Island. Rotorua on the North Island also has a host of local flights to enjoy including my personal favourite, flights in a vintage Tiger Moth biplane.

BUS

There is an extensive bus network that supplements and extends the rail services. The main operator is New Zealand Railways Road Services who are known by all sorts of abbreviations such as 'Road Services', 'the Railways' bus', 'Railways', 'NZR' – but more often NZRRS. With a few exceptions there is an NZRRS bus to almost any town of reasonable size in New Zealand and they often operate to and from railway stations where they share facilities. New Zealand passenger railway services are contracted year by year, so it's a good job they have an alternative use for the railway stations!

The two other major bus operators are Newmans and Mt Cook/H&H. Although these companies have much less extensive route networks than NZRRS they also have interests in numerous other areas of tourism including local tours. Newmans operate services through both islands from Whangarei in Northland right down to Dunedin towards the bottom of the South Island. Mt Cook Landline have recently taken over H&H Travel Lines and their combined networks extend from Auckland all the way to Invercargill.

In addition there are a host of local operators including companies like Clarks Northliner which operate between Auckland and the Bay of Islands; Mainline Coachways which operate from Auckland to the Bay of Plenty, Rotorua and Taupo; or Delta Coachlines who connect Picton, Nelson and the West Coast on the South Island.

Services on the main routes usually run at least once a day, except on Sundays when some services don't operate at all. Where there is another service operating on the same route as NZRRS, the NZRRS buses will usually operate more often. The Getting There & Away section of each chapter has more information on buses. Although bus travel is relatively easy and well organised it can be expensive and time consuming. Bus fares, like everything else in New Zealand, have jumped considerably in recent years and these days it pays to consider the alternatives carefully. Sometimes buying a car can actually work out cheaper than travelling by bus (see the Driving section). Bus trips can also be slow and time consuming. This problem seems particularly prevalent on the once-a-day NZRRS services where the bus also operates as a means of local communication, by picking up and dropping off mail at every little town along the way. Frequent stops at small cafes for cups of tea also slow things down, so it can take a long time to get anywhere.

Although fares do vary from company to company they are generally fairly close and seem to play leapfrog with one another. The fares on the Bus Routes & Fares map are indicative of the fares on these routes. NZRRS offer some off peak or advance purchase discount fares and they also have a New Zealand Travelpass. Travelpasses give you unlimited travel on any NZR bus, rail or inter-island ferry service. The passes cost approximately $300 for eight days, $400 for 15 days or $500 for 22 days and any of these passes can be extended for a further six days.

As with any unlimited travel pass of this type you have to do lots of travelling to make it pay off – they're best for people whose time is limited and want to see a lot in a short time. If you do feel a Travelpass is for you be prepared to do a lot of pre-planning to work out an itinerary you can stick to. Also it's often necessary to book ahead on the buses to be sure of a seat. The pass can be used on certain Mt Cook and Newmans services but it cannot be used on NZRRS tours in Rotorua. It can be used on the day tours to Waitomo from Rotorua or the day tours to Milford Sound in the South Island. There are some restrictions on Travelpasses during the mid-December to end of January peak summer season when the passes are only available to overseas visitors.

Kiwi Coach Passes are another travelpass possibility. These allow travel on Mt Cook Landline, NZRRS and Newmans bus services but must be purchased before you arrive in New Zealand. Newmans offer a 10/30 Pass exclusively to YHA members – it allows unlimited travel on Newmans services on any 10 days out of 30.

Off Peak Saver fares are available on NZRRS services and give a 25% discount on trips over 100 km so long as you travel at off peak times and get your tickets a week in advance. They don't apply during the summer peak period or during school holidays.

DRIVING

Driving yourself around New Zealand is no problem – the roads are generally good and very well signposted. Traffic is light, distances short. Petrol is expensive – at around a dollar a litre, that's about US$2.50 for a US gallon. Curiously petrol is price controlled in New Zealand and it costs precisely the same at every station throughout the country. This is a great contrast with Australia where prices vary enormously from big city price cutters to distant outback stations where they charge whatever they can get.

Kiwis drive on the left, as in the UK, Australia, Japan and most of South-East Asia, and there's a 'give way to the right' rule, similar to that in Australia. This is interpreted in a rather strange fashion when you want to turn left and an oncoming vehicle is turning right into the same street. Since the oncoming vehicle is then on your right you have to give way to them. Ask a New Zealander to explain it to you before setting off! This rule is interpreted the same way in some states of Australia, notably Victoria. Some visitors have commented that New Zealand driving is terrible but I think most people find the driving in other countries terrible in one way or another.

To drive in NZ you need an international driving permit, though ordinary licences from some countries are also acceptable.

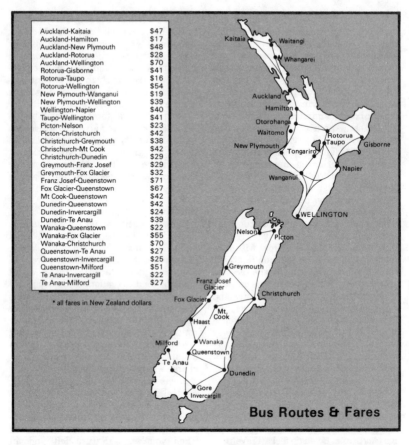

Auckland-Kaitaia	$47
Auckland-Hamilton	$17
Auckland-New Plymouth	$48
Auckland-Rotorua	$28
Auckland-Wellington	$70
Rotorua-Gisborne	$41
Rotorua-Taupo	$16
Rotorua-Wellington	$54
New Plymouth-Wanganui	$19
New Plymouth-Wellington	$39
Wellington-Napier	$40
Taupo-Wellington	$41
Picton-Nelson	$23
Picton-Christchurch	$42
Christchurch-Greymouth	$38
Chrischurch-Mt Cook	$42
Christchurch-Dunedin	$29
Greymouth-Franz Josef	$29
Greymouth-Fox Glacier	$32
Franz Josef-Queenstown	$71
Fox Glacier-Queenstown	$67
Mt Cook-Queenstown	$42
Dunedin-Queenstown	$42
Dunedin-Invercargill	$24
Dunedin-Te Anau	$39
Wanaka-Queenstown	$22
Wanaka-Fox Glacier	$55
Wanaka-Christchurch	$70
Queenstown-Te Anau	$27
Queenstown-Invercargill	$25
Queenstown-Milford	$51
Te Anau-Invercargill	$22
Te Anau-Milford	$27

* all fares in New Zealand dollars

Bus Routes & Fares

Speed limits on the open road are generally 100 kph, in built up areas the limit is usually 50 kph although in some smaller towns you may see a sign announcing LSZ. This means Limited Speed Zone and the rule is that although there is no stated limit (except for the overall 100 kph limit) if anything happens you better have a good excuse for going as fast as you were!

Car Rental

The major operators – Avis, Budget, Hertz – have extensive fleets of cars in New Zealand with offices in almost every town of any size. Typical costs for unlimited distance rental of a small car (Toyota Corolla, Mitsubishi Mirage) are around $80 per day with a minimum rental of three days. Medium size cars (Toyota Corona, Ford Telstar) are typically around $100 to $110 per day with unlimited km. In addition there's a daily insurance charge which varies from around $8 to $12 a day, depending on the company. All sorts of special deals are available including long weekends, extended hire periods and discounts for using certain credit cards.

Apart from the three major international operators there are also a number of other large operators like Thrifty, Dollar or Southern Cross. Plus there are numerous purely local rental operators, found only in certain cities. Their rates often undercut the major operators but there may be more restrictions on use and one-way rentals may not always be possible. Always compare all the costs – one operator's daily charge may be $5 less than another's but their daily insurance might be $5 more. Be careful when comparing daily rates plus a km distance charge with a straight unlimited km charge.

Sometimes you may find special one-way rentals available when the company ends up with too many cars banked up at one place and too few at another. Operators always want cars to be shifted from Wellington to Auckland and from Christchurch to Picton – most renters travel in the opposite directions. Avis, for example, will give you a $20 discount if you collect and drop in that direction. Usually you must be at least 21 years old in order to rent a car in New Zealand and sometimes there will be an insurance excess if you're under 25.

Campervan Rental

Renting a campervan (also known as mobile homes, motor homes or, in US parlance, RVs) has become an enormously popular way of getting around New Zealand. In some touristically popular, but out-of-the-way areas of the South Island almost every other vehicle seems to be a campervan.

There are numerous companies renting campervans and their costs vary with the type of vehicle and the time of year. Unlike rental cars, which are used for business as well as pleasure, campervans are strictly a pleasure business so demand, and hence costs, depend heavily on the tourist seasons.

Campervans are typically Japanese light commercial vehicles modified locally

and equipped with beds, a dining area, cooking facilities, a fridge, a sink with foot operated water system and storage space. Usually the table in the dining area folds down and the seatback cushions rearrange to make a couple of beds at night, one or two more are accommodated in a compartment above the driving cabin. They usually come well-equipped – there'll be towels, bedding, cooking utensils, plates, bowls, knives and forks and so on.

With a campervan you have your transport and accommodation all in one neat package. At night you just find one of New Zealand's excellent campsites, connect up to the campsite power system, put a bucket under the drain from the sink and you're at home. Of course you don't even have to find a campsite, you can simply find a quiet place off the road almost anywhere. Apart from transport and accommodation you've also got your own kitchen on wheels – the cooking facilities are sufficient to fix most simple meals so you don't have to worry about finding a restaurant or affording their costs.

Maui Campas are one of the larger campervan operators and their choice of vehicles and rentals costs are fairly typical. As with the other operators their costs vary with the season. Costs drop to their lowest level in the mid-May to mid-October winter season, climb up in spring (mid-October to mid-December) or the autumn (mid-January to mid-May). The summer plus school holiday plus Christmas period from mid-December to mid-January is the worst time of the year when costs can be two to three times the winter rate.

Starting at the bottom the typical costs for a Maui Hi-Top, going by the seasons, are $60, $80 or $120. This vehicle is a Toyota Hi-ace with a raised roof area. It's really only large enough for two, although you might squeeze a third, small person in. A Maui Mini-Campa is a Mitsubishi L300 which costs $70, $100 or $140. This one is billed as a two plus two but the plus two should be very small children as you'll be cramped with two larger children and four adults would find it impossible. Both these smaller vehicles are powered by petrol engines.

The Maui Campa, a diesel-powered Mitsubishi FB100, costs $80, $110 or $170. This is fine for a couple with two children or even for four adults. Finally there's the Maui Travel Deluxe which not only can accommodate six people but also has a shower, a chemical toilet, a water heater and a gas oven. The vehicle is a Mitsubishi FE 100 and costs are $90, $140 or $200.

While researching the South Island section of this book I used a Maui Campa and it worked just fine. The four of us, two adults, a six year old and four year old, had plenty of room, day or night. In fact we had so much room that several times along the West Coast we could pick up all a town's hitch-hikers in one go!

Other campervan operators include Newmans, Endeavour, Blue Sky, Adventure Vans, Mt Cook Line and Horizon. There's some variance in vehicle types and costs but each operator has colour brochures which explain all about their campervans and what they have to offer. Although they're good fun and a pleasant way of seeing New Zealand, measured strictly on a cost basis they're not the cheapest way of getting around with a rental vehicle. You could rent a car and spend the night in campsite cabins – even in motels at the high season when campervans are expensive – at comparable or lower costs.

Whether you rent a campervan or not watch out for the colourful and exotic house-trucks you see around New Zealand. These individually built constructions often look like a collision between an elderly truck and a timber cottage, sometimes complete with shingle roof and bay windows! Many of these uniquely Kiwi contraptions look far too fragile for road use but they seem to travel all over the country.

Buying a Car

If you're planning a longer stay and/or if there are a group of you, buying a car and then selling it again at the end of your travels can be one of the cheapest ways of seeing New Zealand. You're not tied to the often inconvenient and expensive bus schedules nor do you find yourself waiting by the roadside with your thumb out looking for a ride.

You can find cars in the Saturday newspaper small ads just like anywhere else in the world. In Auckland a Danish couple recommended the Saturday morning car fair at Newmarket on the corner of Khyber Pass Rd and Broadway where lots of cars are available from around $500 to $4000. Come early, though, between 8 and 9.30 am for the best choice of cheaper cars. A German traveller recommended Christchurch as there are lots of cars, it's a popular arrival and departure point and the dry climate keeps them fairly rust free.

You'll often see ads at youth hostels from other travellers keen to sell their cars and move on. I even saw two travellers standing in the arrivals lounge at Auckland airport holding a sign saying 'buy our car'! Make sure any car you buy has a WOF or Warrant of Fitness and that the registration lasts for a reasonable period. You have to have the WOF certificate proving that the car is roadworthy in order to register it.

CYCLING

With sky-rocketing petrol prices and public transport also becoming increasingly costly, there has been a marked increase in the number of cyclists touring New Zealand. You seem to see touring bicycles almost everywhere, particularly with Canadians aboard! There are lots of hills in New Zealand, so it's hard going at times, but it's a compact country and there's always plenty of variety.

Apart from giving you independence from public transport or hitching, cycling also gives you the ideal means of getting around once you get to your destination. If you do get fed up with cycling you can easily take your bike by train or, with some packing, by bus. Coming to New Zealand many airlines will carry your bicycle at no additional cost as 'sporting equipment'. There are guidebooks about bicycle riding in both islands and Bicycle Tours of New Zealand (tel 591-961), PO Box 11-296, Auckland 5 operates guided bicycle tours ranging from a six day tour of the Coromandel Peninsula from around $400 to two to three week tours for over $1000. Pedaltours (tel 674-905), PO Box 49-039, Roskill South, Auckland 4 also have a variety of cycle tours from around $350 to $4000 if you wanted to do their grand circuit of both islands, combining all their tours together.

HITCHING

Overall, New Zealand is a great place for hitch-hiking and most travellers rate it highly. It's basically safe and although the roads are not crowded, there are just enough cars to make things fairly easy. The Kiwis are also well-disposed towards hitch-hikers.

The usual hitching rules apply. If you're standing in one spot, pick your location so that drivers can see you easily and stop safely. In larger towns it usually pays to get out of town before starting to hitch, either by local bus or walking. You may even pick up a lift on the way out, but don't count on it, it's much harder to get a ride in town with a pack. On the other hand on the open road, it's a lot easier to get a lift if you're wearing a pack. Learn which rides not to take – not just crazy drivers but also rides that leave you at inconvenient locations; wait for the right one.

Dress for the occasion – not in your fancy clothes ('they can afford to take the bus') or too shabbily ('don't want them in my car'). If someone else is already hitching on the same stretch of road remember to walk ahead of them so they get the first ride, or leave the road until

they get a ride. Most important be cautious and careful – there are some unpleasant people on the road in New Zealand just like anywhere else in the world. During my last visit two Swedish hitch-hikers tossed their backpacks in the back of a car which stopped for them, and the car immediately drove off leaving them standing by the roadside, totally ripped off.

Generally hitching on the main routes in the North Island is good. In the South Island hitching down the east coast from Picton through Christchurch to Invercargill is mostly good. Elsewhere in the South Island there are hundreds of km of main roads with very little traffic. Expect long waits – even days – in some places. It's a good idea to have the Mt Cook, Newmans and NZRRS timetables with you so you can flag a bus down if you're tired of hitching. Make sure you show the driver the colour of your money. Quite a few drivers have been stopped by hitch-hikers who have then decided they can't afford the fare so some busdrivers are wary about stopping unless they know you're prepared to pay.

It's easier hitching alone if you are male but, unfortunately, even though New Zealand is a safe country for hitching, a woman on her own may experience some tricky – if not dangerous – situations. Better to travel with someone else if possible. Many hostels have local hints for hitching (such as what bus to get out of town, where to hitch from) on their noticeboards.

RAIL

Railways in New Zealand are operated by a government body, New Zealand Railways (NZR for short). Their main aim appears to be to close down as many branch lines as possible and to dissuade people from using trains. For example the suburban train services in Auckland operate to a timetable which is a closely guarded secret. The contraction of rail services continued in 1987 as more minor halts were deleted from the main routes. This does make getting from the starting to the finishing point faster but tough luck if you wanted to go somewhere in between.

New Zealand has a reasonable rail network but like the Australian equivalent it's no great shakes for speed. Fortunately the much shorter distances make rail travel feasible and the trains are quite comfortable. The main routes are Auckland to Wellington, Wellington to Napier, Picton to Christchurch, Christchurch to Invercargill, and Christchurch to Greymouth. See the relevant city sections for details. On a map you'll notice quite a number of other branch railways, but don't be deceived – most of them no longer have any passenger trains.

The Travelpass, described in the section on buses, also provides unlimited use of the country's railway services. The Off Peak Saver fares can also be used on New Zealand trains.

INTER-ISLAND FERRIES

Between Wellington and Picton there are at least four services daily in each direction, sometimes more at peak seasons. The ferries are the *Aratika* and the newer *Arahura*. They handle passengers and vehicles and the crossing takes about three hours. It can get pretty rough so if you're prone to seasickness come prepared. Watch out for dolphins during the crossing.

Fares vary with the seasons, see the Wellington section for details. If it's not too crowded or the sea too rough the crossing can be quite comfortable. It's best to do the trip in daylight, if the weather's good, to see Wellington Harbour and the Marlborough Sounds.

If you going to arrive in Picton late at night make sure you have some sort of accommodation arranged or you may be in for a cold and uncomfortable night as they push everybody off the ferry and close the terminal building.

A number of travellers have made

recommendations about what to do with your baggage and how to make a quick exit after the ferry docks. 'Don't put your pack in the luggage vans if you can avoid it,' wrote one traveller. Because, 'if you are able to hang on to your pack, you can get off the other end without delays – no waiting around for hours until the luggage is unloaded.' Other travellers have reported that the luggage vans are off very quickly, however.

Another traveller warned that cars start driving off almost the second the ferry docks so if you're hitching and have not pre-arranged a ride all the cars will be on the road out of Picton by the time your feet hit dry land. More seriously there have been reports of backpacks being gone through and valuables stolen during the crossing. Don't leave your camera or other important items in your pack.

The Wellington Ferry Terminal is about 20 minutes' walk from Wellington Railway Station or there's a connecting bus service to the ferry. In Picton the terminal is right in town.

LOCAL TRANSPORT
Bus

There are bus services in most larger cities but with a few honourable exceptions they are mainly weekday operations. On weekends and particularly on Sundays buses can be very difficult to find.

Rail

The only city with a good suburban train service is Wellington which has regular trains up the main corridors to the north. It is the only electrified railway in New Zealand.

Auckland has the crumbling remains of a suburban passenger service which, despite considerable pressure for it to be rejuvenated and improved, the government is promising to axe.

Taxis

Although there are plenty of taxis in the major towns they rarely 'cruise'. If you want a taxi you usually either have to phone for one or go to a taxi rank.

Bicycles

Bicycles can be rented by the hour or day in most major cities and in some smaller locales.

STUDENT TRAVEL OFFICES

Student Travel Services NZ have offices at the universities at Auckland, Christchurch, Dunedin, Hamilton and Palmerston North. The head office of Student Travel (tel 850-561) is on the 1st floor of the Hope Gibbons Building, 11-15 Dixon St, Wellington. There's also an off-campus office (tel 399-191) at 64 High St, corner of the High & Victoria St Carpark, Auckland.

As well as issuing ISIC cards (International Student Identity Cards) they have information on a wide variety of student travel concessions plus they book flights overseas. The main concession is a 50% discount on a standby basis on flights with Air New Zealand and other domestic airlines. To get this concession you must not only have an ISIC card but you must also have it stamped by the office in Auckland or Wellington.

NORTH ISLAND

Auckland

Population 815,000

The city of Auckland, surrounded by water and volcanic hills, sprawls across a fairly narrow stretch of land between two large harbours. The beautiful Waitemata Harbour, on one side, is part of the Hauraki Gulf which flows into the South Pacific; and Manukau Harbour, on the other side, joins the Tasman Sea.

Auckland is New Zealand's largest city and is also the main entry point for overseas visitors. There are plenty of things to see, a wide choice of accommodation, lots of restaurants and some good places for night time entertainment.

Auckland has a lot of enthusiastic yachties who sail back, forth and around Waitemata Harbour on weekends, making it look very picturesque. Like Sydney, however, Auckland also has a harbour bridge which is every bit as unattractive as the 'coathanger'. It was opened in 1959 with due pomp and ceremony – but only four traffic lanes. Not surprisingly, it was soon discovered that the reason why not many people lived on the North Shore was because there was no bridge; as soon as there was, so many people moved there that the bridge wasn't big enough. Fortunately the Japanese came to the rescue and 'clipped' two more lanes (known locally as the 'Nippon Clippons') on each side.

In recent years Auckland has become the 'big city' for the Polynesian islands of the South Pacific. So many islanders from New Zealand's Pacific neighbours have moved to Auckland that it now has the largest concentration of Polynesians in the world. This helps to give it a much more cosmopolitan atmosphere than other cities in New Zealand.

Information & Orientation

Auckland's main drag is Queen St, which runs from the waterfront, by the CPO and up (literally) to Karangahape Rd. The downtown Airline Terminal is also by the waterfront, 1½ blocks from the CPO.

Information The NZTP (New Zealand Tourist & Publicity office) (tel 798-180) is at 99 Queen St. They're open 8.30 am to 5 pm on weekdays, 9.30 am to 12 noon on Saturdays.

The Auckland Visitors Bureau (tel 31-889) is more useful for local information. It's on Aotea Square, at 299 Queen St just below the Town Hall. The centre has all sorts of local information and can supply the answers to most visitors' questions. It's open 8.30 am to 5 pm on weekdays, 9 am to 3 pm on weekends.

Auckland Tourist Times is a useful free weekly newspaper of events and activities in Auckland. The Automobile Association office is at 33 Wyndham St. If you're a member of an equivalent overseas auto club you can use their services. The AA have accommodation and campsite directories for both islands and excellent regional maps. The Auckland YHA office (tel 794-224) is at 36 Customs St East which is very close to the Downtown Bus Terminal, not far from the Airline Terminal. The office is open from 8.30 am to 4.30 pm weekdays.

Books, Maps & Newspapers The Book Corner, upstairs at the Queen St and Victoria St West corner, has lots of books. Or try Bloomsbury Books on Lorne St for a wide selection of secondhand books. At 283 Karangahape Rd the Polynesian Bookshop has an excellent selection of books on the South Pacific islands.

The mini-map series is handy for finding your way around Auckland – small enough for a pocket, yet detailed enough to show everything. The *New Zealand Herald* is Auckland's morning daily, the *Auckland Star* is the evening paper.

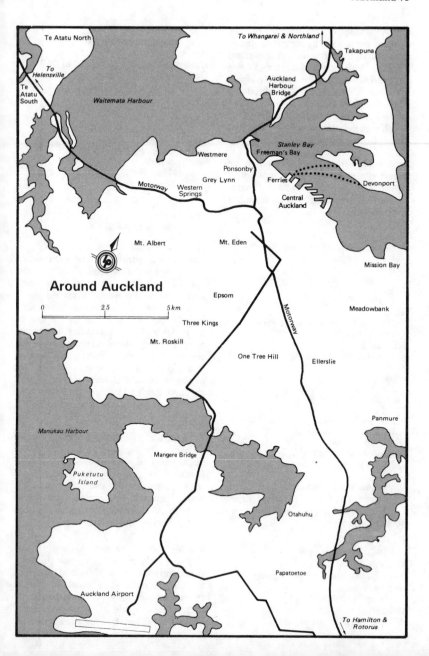

Around Auckland

Money Changing The Bank of New Zealand branch at the airport is open for all international arrivals and departures. Thomas Cook have a Bureau de Change on the corner of Customs St and Queen St. It's open 8.30 am to 5 pm Monday to Thursday, 8.30 am to 8 pm on Friday, 9 am to 1 pm on Saturday. Otherwise you can change money at any bank Monday to Friday from 9 am to 4.30 pm.

Consulates Although Auckland is the largest city in New Zealand it is not the capital; that honour goes to Wellington. There are, however, a number of consulates in Auckland.

Australia
    Union House, 32-38 Quay St, City (32-429)
Canada
    61 Wakefield St, City (tel 398-516)
Germany
    17 Albert St, City (tel 773-460)
Japan
    National Mutual Centre, 41 Shortland St, City (tel 34-106)
Netherlands
    Cromwell Building, 30 Quay St, City (tel 795-399)
Sweden
    NZ Dairy Board Building, Dominion Rd, Mt Eden (tel 689-986)
UK
    Norwich Insurance House, corner Queen & Durham Sts, City (tel 32-973)
USA
    corner Shortland & O'Connell Sts, City (tel 32-724)

Airlines Auckland is the main arrival and departure point for international airlines flying to New Zealand. Airlines serving Auckland include:

Aerolineas Argentinas
    1 Queen St (tel 793-675)
Air Nauru
    309 Karangahape Rd (tel 789-113)
Air New Zealand
    1 Queen St (tel 793-510)
Air Pacific
    43 Shortland St (tel 792-404)

Ansett New Zealand
    50 Grafton Rd (tel 376-950)
British Airways
    corner Queen & Customs St (tel 771-379)
Canadian Airlines International
    45 Queen St (tel 390-735)
Cathay Pacific
    29-31 Shortland St (tel 33-681)
Continental Airlines
    7-9 Albert St (tel 795-861)
Japan Airlines
    29 Customs St West (tel 793-202)
Singapore Airlines
    West Plaza Building, Customs St West (tel 793-209)
UTA
    11 Commerce St (tel 31-229)
United Airlines
    3 Shortland St (tel 33-249)

Central Auckland

The spine of central Auckland is Queen St, which starts at the busy waterfront and runs uphill (gently at first and taking a slight kink on the way) to Karangahape Rd which is the centre for Auckland's Maori and Islander population. To the east of Queen St is Albert Park, a popular lunchtime haven for city workers and students and the venue for free rock concerts on Sunday afternoons in summertime. Beyond the park is Auckland University, the largest in New Zealand, where outsiders are welcome to most activities.

The Domain

Covering about 80 hectares near the centre of the city, the Auckland Domain is a lovely public park that's worth wandering through to take a look at the Winter Gardens and the war museum. It's also a pleasant walk down through the Domain and back through the University grounds and Albert Park to Queen St.

War Memorial Museum

If you're only going to see one thing in Auckland see the War Memorial Museum on the Domain. The museum has a tremendous display of Maori artefacts and culture: pride of place goes to a magnificent 25-metre long war canoe, but there are many other examples of the Maoris' arts and lifestyle. The museum also houses a fine display of South Pacific items and New Zealand wildlife, including a giant moa model.

Admission is free and it is open from 10 am to 5 pm daily (closes 45 minutes earlier in winter) and 11 am to 5 pm on Sundays. A number 635 bus from the Downtown Bus Terminal will take you out to it.

Auckland City Art Gallery

On Wellesley St East in the city the gallery has New Zealand and European art. It's open 10 am to 4.30 pm daily and admission is free.

Museum of Transport & Technology

The Museum of Transport & Technology (Motat) is out at Western Springs, which is also the venue for big rock concerts. The most interesting exhibit here is concerned with pioneer aviator Richard Pearse. It's quite possible that this eccentric South Island farmer actually flew before the Wright brothers but to Pearse a mere hop off the ground wasn't flying and he made no personal claims. During his life he produced a steady stream of inventions and devices, though not surprisingly he was a lousy farmer!

A new section of Motat, known as the Sir Keith Park Memorial Airfield, has opened a km away on the Meola Rd (call at the main museum first). The featured aviation displays are basically just a few aircraft sitting in a hangar or out in the open. Hardly anybody visits it on the weekends and the hangar may not even be open. If you really want to, you can get to the airfield from the main museum area by walking through the park and by the zoo or you can take the regular free tram service to the zoo and walk from there.

Motat is open from 9 am to 5 pm on weekdays, from 10 am to 5 pm on weekends and holidays. Admission is $7 (children $3.50). Get there on an 045 bus from the city.

Parnell

Parnell is an old inner suburb, only a km or two from the centre, where there was a concerted effort to stave off the office developers and restore the old houses and shops, many of them with a decidedly eccentric touch. Parnell now has one of the most appealing streets in New Zealand with lots of arty-crafty shops, good (and expensive) restaurants, galleries and trendy Kiwis. It's a good place to have a snack in one of the open-air cafes and people watch.

Historic Buildings

There are a number of restored and preserved historic buildings around the city, including Ewelme Cottage at 14 Ayr St, Parnell, and Kinder House (1819) nearby at 2 Ayr St (corner of Parnell Rd). Highwic is at 40 Gillies Avenue and the big (18 rooms), old (1862) Alberton House is at 100 Mt Albert Rd. All these places are open from 10.30 am to 12 noon and 1 to 4.30 pm, and each charge $2 or $2.50 admission.

Mt Wellington Stone Cottage is at the Shopping Centre in Panmure. There are several of the early 'Fencible Cottages' including one from the 1840s at Jellicoe Park, Quadrant Rd, Onehunga. It's open 1.30 to 4.30 pm on weekends. In Howick the Howick Colonial Village in Lloyd Elsmore Park, Pakuranga has 20 restored colonial buildings and is open 10 am to 4 pm daily.

Auckland Zoo

The Auckland Zoo is in the same area as Motat and is connected to it by a tram service. It has a nocturnal house (day is night) where you can see kiwis foraging for worms. Kiwis are not in fact rare, it's just that they are rarely seen in their natural setting because of their nocturnal habits. Amongst the real New Zealand rarities in the zoo are the tuataras, the prehistoric New Zealand lizards. The usual lions, hippos, rhinos and so on can also be seen.

The zoo is open from 9.30 am to 5.30 pm daily (last admission 4.15 pm) and entry is $6 (children $3). The 045 bus from Customs St will get you to both Motat and the zoo.

Underwater World

New York may have mythical crocodiles in its sewers but Auckland has real live sharks in its stormwater tanks. Underwater World, at Orakei Wharf on Tamaki Drive, is a unique aquarium housed in old stormwater holding tanks. An acrylic tunnel leads through the aquarium and you travel through the tunnel on a moving footpath, while the fish swim all around you. The aquarium is divided into two sections, a reef fish area and a sharks and stingrays area. Underwater World was devised and developed by New Zealand diver Kelly Tarlton who unfortunately died in 1985, only seven weeks after his aquarium opened.

You can get to Underwater World on a 1A or 1B bus from the Downtown Terminal. It's open from 9 am to 9 pm daily and entry costs $6.50 (children $3).

Beaches & Pools

Beaches are another Auckland attraction, dotted all around the harbours and up and down both coasts. You can run around them each March with 80,000 fit New Zealanders in the 'Round the Bays' run, one of the largest fun runs in the world.

East coast beaches include Judges Bay, Kohimarama, Mission Bay, Okahu Bay and St Heliers Bay, all accessible from Tamaki Drive. With most east coast and harbour beaches swimming is better at high tide. Popular north shore beaches include Takapuna and Milford.

There's good surf on west coast beaches within an hour's drive of the city. Try Bethells where the water is often very rough, Karekare, Muriwai, Piha with a

KELLY TARLTON'S underwater world

sheltered lagoon and Whatipu with good day walks in the area. These beaches are all less than 50 km from the centre. *Whatipu Lodge* (tel 811-8860) at Whatipu has hostel-style accommodation from $10.

There are swimming pools in the city and various swimming centres outside. At Parakai (45 km north west, bus 069 from the Downtown Bus Terminal) the Aquatic Park has hot mineral pools and various waterslides. The centre is open 10 am to 10 pm. You can stay there at *Craigwell House* (tel Helensville 8277) where there are rooms and also dorm beds.

Waiwera (48 km, bus 895 from Auckland) also has thermal pools which are also open 10 am to 10 pm. Within walking distance of Waiwera is the Wenderholm Regional Park with a good beach, estuary, grass, trees and bushwalks.

One Tree Hill

One Tree Hill is a small (183 metres high) extinct volcano cone which was used by the Maoris as a fortified 'pa'. You get an excellent wide-angle view of the city from here. One Tree Hill has an observatory with a bookshop and office which is open 9 am to 3 pm on weekdays. There's night telescope viewing on Tuesdays if it's clear.

Not much further away is the similar Mt Eden (13 metres higher) which is also a good vantage spot. You can get there on a 274 or 275 bus.

Other City Attractions

Microworld is on the corner of Halsey and Madden Sts at Freemans Bay Lighter Basin, two blocks from Victoria Park Market. It has microscanners to look at things up to 500 times actual size. Microworld is open 9 am to 11 pm daily and admission is $7.50 (children $3.50). Victoria Park Market on Victoria St West is opposite Victoria Park and operates every day of the week. Get there on a 005 bus from the corner of Queen and Customs St.

Heritage Park

New Zealand Heritage Park is an all-New-Zealand-in-one-place package – ideal if you've only got one day for the whole country. You'll see everything from kiwis, farm shows and a small museum to a Maori concert. It sounds a bit of a come on but some travellers reckon it's good value since $12 gets you a whole bunch of things you'll pay separately for elsewhere around the country.

It's open 9.30 am to 5.30 pm daily and a bus 522, 523, 584, 585 or 586 will get you there. It's on Harrison Rd off the Ellerslie-Panmure Highway.

Out-of-the-City Attractions

The Auckland Lion Safari is on Redhills Rd at Massey, 16 km from town. As well as wild animals there's a 100-metre corkscrew water ride, and other attractions. At weekends admission is $14 (children $7) including all rides. During the week it's $7 for adults or children but the rides are extra.

Another nearby attraction is the Clevedon Woolshed, 35 km south-east of the city. Two Auckland amusement parks are The Footrot Flats Fun Park, at Te Atatu, and the Rainbow's End Adventure park, on the Great South Road at Manukau.

Tours

A Gray Line morning tour of Auckland costs $25 (children $12.50), there's another afternoon tour which covers different attractions. A lunchtime harbour cruise on the *Tiger Lily* costs $15 (children $7.50) but you can combine the two bus tours and the cruise for $57 (children $28.50) and 'do' all of Auckland in a day. There are also discounts on two-tour combinations.

Various other operators also have bus tours of the city and further afield. AGM Productions (tel 398-670) have vineyard tours and farm tours ($53). Pounamu Ventures (tel 836-7876) have free guided tours of the Maori exhibits at the War Memorial Museum followed by a Maori cultural programme ($3.50). Bush & Beach (tel 779-029) have a volcano tour ($35), a Waitakere Ranges tour ($45) and an evening visit to a gannet colony on the west coast followed by a swim in a thermal mineral pool and a barbecue (all for $65).

On weekdays there's a 1½ hour walking tour of inner-city Auckland which costs $15. Phone Alice or Dean (tel 790-031) for more information.

Harbour Cruises

See the following section on Hauraki Gulf islands for more information on boats out of Auckland.

A ferry across the harbour to Devonport makes an interesting trip. Departures are generally every half hour to an hour and the fare is $4 return ($2.50 one-way) for the short trip. Children cost $2 and $1.30 respectively. North Head in Devonport is a reserve riddled with old tunnels originally built due to fears of a Russian invasion at the end of the last century. The same Russian fears also convulsed Australia at that time. The fortifications were extended and enlarged during WW I and WW II but dismantled after the last war. There are fine views of the harbour and city from the top of extinct Mt Victoria at Devonport. The Devonport ferry leaves from the wharf on Quay St.

Blue Boats have a Birkenhead ferry service during the morning and afternoon rush hours. It takes 15 minutes each way and leaves from opposite the Downtown Airline Terminal. Blue Boats also have services to Rakino, Home Bay, Motuihe, Islington Bay and Rangitoto but not every day. Phone 394-901 for details. Mt Cook run various cruises on the *Tiger Lily*. A lunch cruise lasting 1½ hours costs $15 (children $7.50). Fullers also have cruises and there are a host of other cruise and charter operators in everything from small speedboats to large yachts. You can even take a trip around the harbour on the tug *William C Daldy* on summer Sundays.

Quick Cat, the catamaran which serves Waiheke and Pakatoa Islands, does Hauraki Gulf cruises on its normal island services. The fare is the same whether you simply go out there and back or stop off for a few hours or the whole day. The return fare to Waiheke is $19 (children $9.50), to Pakatoa $25 ($12.50). Straight out to Waiheke and back on the 8 am or 5.30 pm service costs $15 ($7.50). On Fridays there's a night cruise to Pakatoa with dinner at the resort for $45. Phone Gulf Ferries (tel 790-092, 393-918 & 9) for details. Departures are from opposite the Downtown Airline Terminal.

Auckland makes good use of its fine harbour, particularly on the annual Anniversary Regatta in late January of each year. The waters are dotted with more boats than you'd believe possible and if it's a good windy day, there'll be a fair number of dunkings!

Flights

There are scenic flights over Auckland and the islands of the Hauraki Gulf. Check with Sea Bee Air (tel 774-406) about their amphibious aircraft flights over the gulf from around $30 to $50 (less for children). They also have helicopter flights from around $35 to $80. Other flightseeing operators include Ardmore Air, Air North Shore, Capt Al's Fantasy Flights and others.

Places to Stay

Hostels Auckland has had something of a hostel explosion and there are now a number of hostel-style places apart from the YHA hostels. The Percy Shieff YHA Hostel is very central and conveniently located while the Mt Eden Hostel is four km out. During this edition, however, the Percy Shieff Hostel building is probably going to be redeveloped and the hostel will shift to a new location in Churton St at the city end of Parnell. Check with the Auckland YHA office (tel 794-224).

Meanwhile the *Percy Shieff Youth Hostel* (tel 790-258) is right in the centre

Top: Northland tree ferns (NZTP)
Left: Kiwi (NZTP)
Right: Tuatara (NZTP)

Top: Auckland, city centre (TW)
Bottom: The marina, Auckland (MC)

at 7 Princes St, only a short walk from Queen St. Coming from the airport on the airport bus service get off at the Hyatt Hotel, the hostel is right across the road. There are 74 beds in the 11 dormitories and they cost $13 a night. There's a free direct phone line to the hostel from the airport. This is New Zealand's busiest youth hostel.

The *Mt Eden Youth Hostel* (tel 603-975), is four km out at 5A Oaklands Rd, Mt Eden. It costs $11 a night and has room for 46 people. You can get there on a 273, 274 or 275 Three Kings bus from the station behind the CPO. You can also ask the airport bus driver to drop you at Gillies Avenue. It's a 1.5 km walk from there to Mt Eden Rd, where you turn right and then first right again into Oaklands Rd. If that's all too much, get the driver to drop you at a Three Kings bus stop and catch another bus from there to Eden Village.

The *YMCA* (tel 32-068) is in a modern building close to the city centre at the corner of Pitt St and Grays Avenue. It takes men or women, segregated by floors, in single rooms which cost $30 on day one, $27 thereafter or $140 a week, all including breakfast and dinner. On weekends lunch is included as well and on weekdays you can fix yourself lunch to take with you at breakfast time. Breakfast is available only from 6.30 to 7.45 am (8 to 9 am on weekends), dinner from 5 to 6 pm. Although it is aimed more at long term residents than casual visitors rooms are usually available.

The *YWCA* (tel 794-912) has hostel accommodation for men and women at 10 Carlton Gore Rd, Grafton. That's an easy stroll from the Queen St-Karangahape Rd intersection. From the centre take a Hospital Bus 283 from downtown to Auckland Hospital, walk up Seaview Park Rd and turn right. Or take a 274 or 275 bus from Customs St to Grafton Bridge. From the airport get off the airport bus at the Sheraton Hotel which is near to Grafton Bridge. Dorm beds at the Y are $9 a night plus a $10 key bond. You

can hire sheets and blankets if you don't have them but the office is only open from 8.30 am to 5 pm and from 6.30 to 9 pm on weekdays. On weekends it's open 8.30 am to 9 pm. This is a very small but very pleasant little hostel.

A little further up Carlton Gore Rd is the *Georgia Hostel* (tel 399-560) at the corner at 189 Park Rd. Dorm beds here cost from $11 and there are also double rooms from $13 per person. There are kitchen, dining and laundry facilities in this big, busy and rather crowded hostel. To get there follow the same instructions as for the YWCA. It's about a km walk from the Sheraton Hotel (airport bus stop), from the city centre it's two km (take a 31 or 31 bus from Victoria St East).

Ivanhoe Traveller's Lodge (tel 862-800) is a long running private hostel at 14 Shirley Rd, Western Springs. It had become rather run down but in '87 was going through some major renovations. Costs depend on what you get and how long you stay – there are dorm beds and also singles and doubles and self-contained rooms. Costs range from $10 for a bed, $12 each in a double or twin room, $15 for a single. Serviced doubles are $27. Stay a week and you get one day free. Get there by taking an 045 bus to Grey Lynn Springs

"GEORGIA"

WELCOME TO
GEORGIA
189 Park Rd, Grafton,
Auckland, New Zealand.
Phone 399 560

Travellers backpackers & hikers hostel

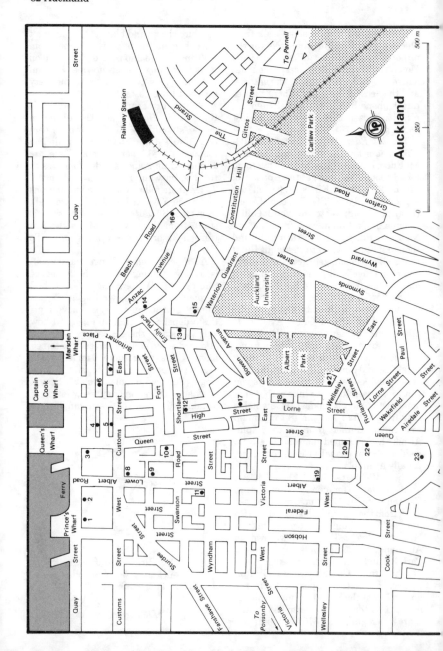

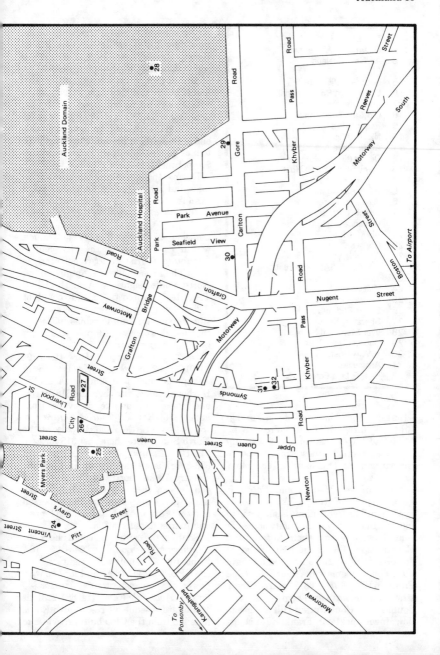

1	Travelodge
2	Downtown Air Terminal
3	Air New Zealand
4	CPO
5	South Pacific Hotel
6	Downtown Bus Terminal
7	YHA Office
8	Old Customs House
9	Regent Hotel
10	NZTP Office
11	Automobile Association
12	De Brett's Hotel
13	Percy Shieff Youth Hostel
14	Aspen Lodge
15	Hyatt Kingsgate
16	Farthings Hotel
17	Simple Cottage
18	Dominoes Cafe
19	Abby's Hotel
20	Gopal's
21	Art Gallery
22	Auckland Visitor's Bureau
23	Town Hall
24	YMCA
25	Railton Hotel
26	Smart Budget Hotel
27	Sheraton Hotel
28	War Memorial Museum
29	Georgia Hostel
30	YWCA Hostel
31	Armadillo
32	First & Last Cafe

– the fare's 90c – then walk down Turangi Rd to 14 Shirley Rd. Or if you're arriving by air late, they will arrange to pick you up from the airport. The hostel is very close to the Museum of Transport & Technology and the Zoo.

International Hostels and *Cotels* is another part of the Auckland hostel explosion. The 'cotel' name is supposed to indicate that they're 'community hotels', or something. Anyway their *Cotels* at 6 Constitution Hill (tel 34-768) and at 82 Jervois Rd (tel 767-211) are smaller and have more double rooms while their *Hostel* at 2 Franklin Rd (tel 780-168) is a larger, more strictly bunkroom place. Dorm beds are $11, doubles $30. Constitution Hill is close to downtown Auckland; Franklin Rd is just

off Ponsonby Rd, and if you continue up Ponsonby Rd it crosses Jervois Rd in Herne Bay. There have been some complaints that these hostels are something of an attempt to cash in cheaply on the hostel boom and that they're somewhat spartan and poorly equipped.

Holiday Hostels (tel 760-989) is at 39 Hamilton Rd, Herne Bay, near the south end of the harbour bridge. They'll arrange to pick you up downtown and cost is from $10 per night.

During the university vacations you may find some student accommodation available to visitors. Try phoning *Student Accommodation* on 737-691 or 737-686.

Camping & Cabins There's not much within easy reach of the city centre. *Takapuna Tourist Court* (tel 497-909) is at 22 The Promenade, Takapuna, on the North Shore, eight km from the CPO. Tent sites for two costs $16, add a couple of dollars for sites with power. There are on-site caravans for $36 and cabins at $25. It's the usual story – supply your own bedding, cutlery, etc.

North Shore Caravan Park (tel 419-1320) at 52 Northcote Rd is also in Takapuna, just four km north of the Harbour Bridge. Sites here are $18 for two and there are on-site caravans from about $36. *Kontiki Tourist Centre* (tel 487-644) is at Little Shoal Bay, also on the North Shore. Sites here cost $15 for two. *Tui Glen Camping Park* (tel Henderson 836-8978) is at Henderson, in the wine country 13 km north-west of Auckland centre. Get there on the north-western motorway. Camp sites are $6 per person and there are also cabins from $25 for two and tourist flats from $38.

South of the centre you could check out *Remuera Motor Lodge* (tel 545-126), 16A Minto Rd, off Remuera Rd, eight km from the CPO. Cost is $18 a night for two with power, or you can get tourist flats for $46 for two. *Avondale Camp* (tel 887-228), at 46 Bollard Avenue off New North Rd, is nine km from the CPO but fairly close to

Motat and the zoo. Sites are $15 for two, tourist flats cost from $32 for one, $37 for two or there are on-site caravans for a couple of dollars more.

Finally *South Auckland Caravan & Camping Park* (tel Papakura 294-8520) is on the Great South Rd at Ramarama. Camping cost is $8.50 per person.

Hotels & Guest Houses Right behind the Sheraton Hotel, get off there if you're coming in on the airport bus, the *Smart Budget Hotel* (tel 392-800) is on the corner of City Rd and Liverpool St. It's squeaky clean and new and has 80 rooms – all *without* private facilities. Toilets and showers are by the lift and stairs on each floor. The rooms – singles, doubles and twins – are functional, modern, small and rather student-like. At around $50 for singles, $64 for doubles, they're not terrific value although there is a TV lounge, laundry and *Bytes Cafe* where you can get breakfast from 7 to 9 am, lunch and dinner later in the day. The same company is planning the *Park Towers Hotel* (tel 392-800), across Queen St from Smart Budget. Here there will also be some rooms with attached bathroom for $80.

The nearby *Railton Private Hotel*, 411 Queen St (tel 796-487), is well kept and popular. Singles/doubles cost $46/66 with attached bathrooms, or $33/50 for rooms with only a sink. There are also some fully self-contained suites at $72/102. All these costs include breakfast and a newspaper at your door in the morning. Dinner is available in the restaurant here from 5.15 to 7 pm and costs $11, on Sunday it's a smorgasbord at $12. *Manor House* at 363 Queen St has rooms at $35/40 and up.

Very centrally located *Abby's Hotel* (tel 34-799) is at the corner of Wellesley and Albert Sts and has rooms, all with attached bathrooms, at $50 for singles, $60 for doubles, including breakfast. There's a good selection of bars and restaurants here and the only real drawback is that some of the singles are extremely compact, postage-stamp size.

There are a couple of cheaper places down towards the waterfront, both very close to the Hyatt Hotel, another airport bus stopping point. At 62 Emily Place the *Aspen Lodge* (tel 796-698) is a straightforward place but clean, tidy and well organised. Rooms here are $36/50 including breakfast for singles/doubles, all without private facilities. The *Grand Vue Private Hotel* (tel 793-965) is at 3 Princes St, right across from the Hyatt and right next to the Percy Shieff Youth Hostel. Rooms have washbasins and tea and coffee making equipment and cost $35 for singles, $50 to $55 for doubles. There are some rooms with private facilities at $65. Breakfast is an additional $5. It's possible that this hotel may be facing the same redevelopment threat as the youth hostel.

Other small private hotels and guest houses include the *Rosana Travel Hotel* (tel 766-603) at 217 Ponsonby Rd, Ponsonby. Rooms here are $30/48 including a 'homestyle' breakfast. The rooms all have washbasins and there are tea and coffee making facilities for the guests. Rooms with attached bathroom are $40/60. *Aachen House* (tel 502-329) is at 39 Market Rd, Remuera with rooms, again including breakfast, at $40/55.

Across from the railway station at 131 Beach Rd *Farthings Hotel* (tel 390-629) has singles from $40/55 without private facilities or from $55/70 with attached bathrooms. The cheaper rooms include breakfast if that makes any sense! In Parnell the *Ascot Parnell* (tel 399-012) at 36 St Stephens Avenue, off Parnell Rd at the top, is a small hotel in a restored old home. Rooms, with attached bathroom and including breakfast, cost from around $55/70 for singles/doubles.

If you want Auckland's best you can try the recently refurbished *Hotel De Brett* or move right up into the *Hyatt, Regent, Sheraton* bracket. At the Regent a single is over $200 and you can pay $1000 a night for their best suite.

Motels Auckland has over 100 motels, so it's hard to make any particular recommendations. Generally costs start from around $50 for singles, $60 for doubles or twin. Some of the camping grounds mentioned above have tourist flats or motel units. Try the *Remuera Motor Lodge* or the *Kontiki* camp for example.

There are several areas reasonably close to the city with a selection of motels. Try along Parnell Rd in Parnell. At the corner of St Stephens Avenue and Parnell Rd the *Casa Nova Motor Lodge* (tel 771-463) has rooms in an older building and in a newer extension from $50/60 and up. Some of them are very spacious with fully equipped kitchens. Going down Parnell Rd towards the city the *James Cook Motel* (tel 33-426) at number 320 is another reasonably priced motel with some budget rooms at around $40/48, plus more expensive rooms.

Another alternative is Jervois Rd in Herne Bay from the junction with Ponsonby Rd. There are a number of places along here or off Jervois Rd along Shelly Beach Rd. This is close to the south end of the Harbour Bridge and at 6 Tweed St, which in turn is off Shelly Beach Rd, the *Harbour Bridge Motel* (tel 763-489) has singles from as low as $35 to $45, doubles from $45 to $55. This is another older buildings with a new extension added on.

Continue across the bridge and there are more reasonably priced motels in Takapuna or Birkenhead. If you have an early flight to catch and want to stay out near the airport there are lots of motels in Mangere, particularly along Kirkbride Rd and McKenzie Rd. Almost every one of them manages to get the word 'airport' into their names and most of them are from around $70 a night. The *Auckland Airport Skyway Lodge* (tel 275-4443) at 28-30 Kirkbride Rd has straightforward rooms from $35/44, a couple of motel units from $60 and a bunkroom at $24.

Places to Eat
Auckland, once the home of overwhelming blandness, has undergone something of a culinary revolution in the last decade. There are now all sorts of dining possibilities but, unlike some cities, there are no distinct ethnic areas. You can find almost anything almost anywhere.

City - Cheap Eats There are numerous places in the city ready to turn out a good sandwich for you. Try *Matthew Mulvaney* at 18 Lorne St. Nearby on High St, almost at the corner with Victoria St West, you'll find *Crumbs* which has a particularly good local reputation. Actually on the High St/Victoria St West corner is *Boulangerie Croix du Sud* with a good selection of croissants, French-style bread and lunchtime snacks.

In the small shopping centre by the Downtown Bus Terminal *Peppercorns* has all sorts of ready-to-go sandwiches and rolls - well made and cheap as well. On the corner of Customs St West and Albert St there's the pleasant little *Corner Cafe* sandwich shop in the old Customs House.

Don't forget the *University Cafeteria* as another city cheap eats possibility. The cheap eats and late nights quandry can be solved by the *The White Lady* mobile hamburger stand on Shortland St off Queen St. It's open 6 pm to 2.30 am Monday to Thursday; 24 hours on weekends and holidays. Burgers are in the $2.50 to $4 range.

City - Vegetarian The High St/Lorne St area is a great place for vegetarians who are fairly well catered for in Auckland. The very popular *Dominoes' Cafe* at 4 Lorne St has a wide assortment of meals from around $3.50 to $6 plus good fruit juices, lassis, desserts and a mouth watering selection of cakes from around $1 to $2. There's also a pleasant courtyard but best of all it's open for breakfast, lunch, dinner and even Sunday evenings when Auckland tends to be a bit quiet.

At 50 High St *Simple Cottage* is another popular vegetarian place with good food from around $4.50 and more fine desserts. Vegetarian places really seem to turn out great desserts! Right across the road is *Badgers* at number 47. This is more a lunch time snack place with salads and other healthy light meals at around $5, delicious although expensive fruit juices at $2.25 to $2.75 and an amazingly eclectic selection of chairs.

Not far away, opposite the Theatre Centre at 291 Queen St on the 1st floor, is *Gopals* which is run by the Hare Krishnas. It's essentially a lunchtime place, open 12 to 2.30 pm from Monday to Thursday and 12 to 8.30 pm on Friday. At this relaxed, comfortable place vegetarian-Indian-type food is served and you can get snacks (pizza slices at $1.80 for example) or a combination plate which includes a bit of everything and dessert for $4.50.

City - Fast Food & Pubs Yes, Auckland has *McDonald's*, quite a number of them in fact. You'll find one of them about halfway up Queen St and another just around the corner on Karangahape Rd. There's also a *Wendy's* more or less opposite the Queen St McDonald's and upstairs. In the same vicinity you'll find a *Pizza Hut*, downstairs in the Strand Arcade.

Also downstairs is *Ziggies*, a clean and glossy up-a-notch fast foodery out of the Denny's mould. Main courses are around $7.50 to $11. The various city pubs are another economical possibility, particularly at lunchtime. Try the relaxed and pleasant *Alexandra Hotel* on the Federal St/Kingston St corner in the centre. They have a great selection of hot sandwiches priced from $1.80 to $3. By the Downtown Airline Terminal on Lower Albert St the *Akarana Tavern* has meals for $6 to $8 at lunch time.

City - Restaurants The *Middle East* at 23A Wellesley St is a tiny place and usually a pretty crowded tiny place at that, and deservedly so as the food is excellent and economical. There's the usual Lebanese specialties (shawerma, kebabs, felafel) for about $3.50 to $5.50 for snacks, or $9.50 to $11 for full meals with salad and pita bread. Check out their great camel collection in the display case on the bar.

Round the corner at 295 Queen St the *Mekong* has been consistently voted the 'best ethnic restaurant in Auckland' by all and sundry. It's got a varied collection of Vietnamese specialities with prices for main courses around $13 to $16. At lunchtime they're around $9 to $10.

A number of places in the city provide Italian food including *Pisani's* at 43 Victoria St West where you can get good pizzas or pasta. The *Hard to Find Cafe* at 47 High St is a small Mexican restaurant, tucked away back from the street in an arcade. Main courses are mostly around $12 or $13. The *Tony's* most be doing something right because they've been carrying on unchanged while plenty of other places have come and gone. They have a basically similar steakhouse-style menu which also features New Zealand lamb dishes and pastas. Find them at 32 Lorne St and 39 Victoria St West.

There are plenty of foreign dining possibilities in Auckland these days. You could try a Sri Lankan curry at *Palmyrah* upstairs at the Mid-City Centre on Queen St, head back to the Lebanon at *Baalbeck* at 58 Wellesley St, sample Indian curry at several places including the glossier *Shahi Tandoor* at 41 Wellesley St or go Chinese at anything from cheap takeaways to flashy restaurants. Surprisingly, despite the big Polynesian population there's no Polynesian restaurant as yet.

Several glossy places provide drinks and meals with a stylish air. Try the Wine Bar in the *Hotel De Brett* on the corner of High St and Shortland St or *Cheers* at 12 Wyndham St, just off Queen St. Or moving a little up market there's French provincial cooking at the pleasant *Le Brie* at the corner of Chancery and Warspite Sts. Starters are $5 to $7, main courses $13 to $17.

Symonds St There's a string of restaurants up Symonds St from the university – not too far from the centre. At 178 Symonds St the extremely popular *Armadillo* is a greatly enlarged version of the restaurant of the same name in Wellington. It's a cavernous and noisy place done up in John-Wayne-western style. 'Born to grill' the sign over the kitchen announces and the menu features burgers and similar straightforward 'western' food at $15 for main courses. Desserts are all $5. It's not cheap but you won't leave hungry.

A couple of doors down at number 192 is the very smooth *Last & First Cafe*. It's much quieter than Armadillo but equally popular and features starters at $6, main course pastas at $13, other main courses at $15 or $16, desserts at $6.

Other places in the same area include the *Front Page Cafe* at number 163 – straightforward but well prepared food and a newspaper decor. *Ali Baba* at 181 is a good Middle Eastern place with takeaway or eat there facilities and prices around $5 to $6. There are a number of other restaurants and cafes in the vicinity.

ARMADILLO
129 WILLIS STREET, WELLINGTON
GST NO. 43-891-030
178 SYMONDS STREET, AUCKLAND
GST NO. 49-311-575

Parnell There are all sorts of restaurants along Parnell Rd in Parnell. They range from pizzerias to pub food specialists to Chinese takeaways and a whole host of Italian restaurants apart from the fancier places. Lots of places have tables outside so you can enjoy the fresh air. Try the popular *Alexandra Tavern* which has good value and straightforward pub food and live music in the evenings. Other pubs along Parnell Rd also have food.

For sandwiches or snacks there's *Toute de Suite*. *La Trattoria Cafe*, next to the Alexandra Tavern, has pastas dishes from $8 or there's *Valerio* for fancier Italian meals around $12 to $15 plus the *Italian Cafe*.

Ponsonby There are numerous eating places along Ponsonby Rd, again offering all sorts of cuisines. Don't miss *Fed Up* at number 244. It's kind of shabbily kitsch but there's real art on the walls and real food at reasonable prices as well. The dishes are imaginative, well prepared and great value. Anyway, a restaurant playing Derek and the Dominoes' *Layla* as you step through the door can't be bad!

Other Ponsonby Rd possibilities include *Ivan's* on the corner of Anglesea St. It's cheap eats here of the sausage and chips variety. Across the road at 134A Ponsonby Rd is the *Open Late Cafe* with straightforward food, good desserts and coffee and it is indeed open late.

Further down towards the bay you come to *Espresso Love* with good food but lunchtimes only. Round the corner from Ponsonby Rd on College Hill is *Java Jive*, very popular but closed on Sunday and Monday nights. Curiously there's nothing Indonesian about it at all. Main courses, from around $9, are an Indian-Lebanese-Mexican mix! Turning the other way from Ponsonby Rd the *Ponsonby*, right on the Ponsonby/Jervois Rd corner, has reasonable pub food in their *Three Lamps* bar.

Entertainment
Whatever you're doing late at night in Auckland keep your eye on the time if you're dependent on public transport – there isn't any. You can make it home from the pictures or a pub but you'll hit trouble if you're out later than that.

Pubs Auckland has got a pretty good variety of places to go after the sun sets, many of them with music. Try the *Alexandra Tavern* in trendy Parnell or the nearby *Windsor Tavern* and the *Exchange*.

In the city the *London Underground Bar* of the *Civic Tavern* (corner of Queen and Wellesley Sts) serves food and has music (no cover charge) on weekends. Or try the *Shakespeare Tavern* at 61 Albert St with entertainment and locally brewed Falstaff beer. The pleasant *Alexandra Hotel* on the Federal St/Kingston St corner is another good place for a beer. On the corner of Wellesley and Hobson Sts in the city the *Albion* has a wide selection of bars.

There's more entertainment at *Abby's* on the corner of Albert St and Wellesley St East. Later you can retire to the nightclub in the basement. *Hotel De Brett's*, on the corner of Shortland St and High St in the city, is another hotel with entertainment in its bars. Its wine bar is a popular meeting place.

On the Ponsonby Rd/Jervois Rd corner in Ponsonby the *Ponsonby Hotel* has entertainment most nights of the week, even poetry readings on some nights. There's no cover charge.

Rock Music Next door to the Ponsonby is the *Gluepot*, a very popular rock venue with a cover charge which varies depending on whom is playing. The *Galaxy* is probably the other major rock venue in Auckland.

Other Nightclubs come and go with some rapidity. You could try *Club 21* on Queen St next to the Civic Theatre or the *Metropolis* downstairs in Abby's Hotel on the corner of Wellesley and Albert Sts.

For folk music try the *Poles Apart Folk Club* or the *Devonport Folk Music Club*. Some of the cruise boats do evening cruises with supper, music and dancing.

Getting There & Away

Air Auckland is the major international arrival point for flights to New Zealand. See the Auckland Information section for airline office locations and the Getting There chapter for flight details.

Air New Zealand connects Auckland with the other major centres in New Zealand. See the introductory Getting Around chapter for fare details. Ansett New Zealand also have a variety of flights in and out of Auckland and there are Mt Cook flights to Rotorua and other destinations in the South Island. A number of local operators like Eagle Air also have flights in and out of Auckland. See the Hauraki Gulf Islands section and the Northlands chapter for details of flights to those locations.

Road NZRRS have services to all the major North Island centres from Auckland. See the relevant sections for details. NZRRS buses operate from the railway station, phone 794-600 for details. Other companies with services to and from Auckland include:

Clarks Northliner (tel 796-056), Downtown Airline Terminal – services north to Whangarei and the Bay of Islands.

Mainline Coachways (tel 771-878), Downtown Airline Terminal – services south to Taupo, Rotorua and Tauranga/Mt Maunganui.

Mt Cook Landline (tel 395-395), 75 Queen St – services south through Hamilton and Taupo to Napier or Wellington. Departures are from the Downtown Airline Terminal.

Newmans (tel 399-738), 205 Hobson St – services to Whangarei in Northland and south through Hamilton to New Plymouth, Wanganui and Wellington.

Hitching If you're hitching north the best way to get out of the urban sprawl is to get a bus from the Downtown Bus Terminal to Waiwera (895) or to Hatfields Beach (894). Going south, take an NZRRS bus to Bombay Hills Cross Rd. These buses cost from $2 to $3.

Rail New Zealand rail services continue to contract and the Auckland-Wellington service is all there really is to consider from Auckland. It's become a bit faster of late principally because they're cut out more of the stops in between. The Auckland-Wellington fare is $68.

Getting Around

Airport Transport The Auckland Airport is a fair way out (21 km) from the centre. There's a bus service running half-hourly from the city from 5.35 am to 8.35 pm, from the airport starting at 7 am and last departure at 10 pm. From the airport the bus goes from the International Terminal to the Domestic Terminal, the Airport Travelodge and then into the city stopping at the Sheraton Hotel, the Hyatt Kingsgate and the Farthing Hotel opposite the Railway Station before finally terminating at the Downtown Airline Terminal. Going out it starts from the Sheraton, not from the terminal. Fare is $7 ($2 for children) or $12 return.

Between four people a taxi would work out at much the same price. To downtown Auckland a taxi costs about $26 during the 'green' period from 6 am to 10 pm on weekdays. From 10 pm to 6 am and all weekend is the red period and the fare then is about $31.

Between the terminals at the airports the bus costs $1.50 or a taxi will set you back about $4. There's a signposted footpath between the two terminals, the distance is about 900 metres, good practice for tramping the park trails!

The airport has a tourist information counter, a bank, a couple of rent-a-car desks and a dial-it-yourself hotel booking facility. There's a left luggage facility at the Downtown Airline Terminal.

Bus The Downtown Bus Terminal is on Commerce St, behind the CPO, but not all buses leave from here. Timetables for local bus routes are available from the bus terminal or from newsagents or you can phone Buz-a-Bus on 797-119 for information and schedules. It operates 7 am to 10.30 pm although on weekends you may have trouble getting an answer as there aren't enough people to answer the phone. There's a bus info kiosk during regular hours at the Downtown Bus Terminal.

Inner city fares are 30c, further distances cost 90c, then $1.70 and so on. Busabout passes are available for unlimited bus use from 9 am (anytime on weekends) for $5.60 (children $2.80). The passes can be bought on board the bus. Weekly passes are also available or there are family passes for $7.

There's an inner city shuttle bus (yellow with red destination band) which runs from the railway station along Customs St and up Queen St to Karangahape Rd, returning to the station via Mayoral Drive and Queen St. It costs 30c for any distance.

Taxis There are plenty of taxis in Auckland but, as elsewhere in New Zealand, they rarely cruise. You usually have to phone for them or find them on taxi ranks.

Ferries For harbour-ferry information phone 33-319 for the Devonport ferry, and 394-901 for the Birkenhead ferry. See also the Islands off Auckland section.

Rental Cars The major rental operators plus a host of smaller ones have offices in Auckland. Many of them have offices at Mangere, near the airport. They include:

Avis
22 Wakefield St (tel 795-545)
Auckland Airport (tel 275-7239)
Budget Rent-A-Car
73-83 Beach Rd, Auckland (tel 796-768)
Auckland Airport (tel 275-7097)
Dollar Rent-A-Car
183 Hobson St, Auckland (tel 395-658)
Hertz Rent-A-Car
154 Victoria St West (tel 390-989)
Auckland Airport (tel 275-9953)
Johnston's Rental Cars
corner Richard Pearse Drive & Brigade Rd,
Mangere (tel 275-9396)
Mutual Rental Cars
corner Cook & Nelson Sts, Auckland (tel
794-294)
Percy Rent-A-Car
219 Hobson St (tel 31-122 or 129)
Travellers International Motor Inn, Kirkbride
Rd, Mangere (tel 275-7674)
Southern Cross Rental Group
20 Moa St, Otahuhu (tel 276-3603)
Thrifty Car Rental
154 McKenzie Rd, Mangere (tel 276-7161)

The various campervan operators also
have Auckland offices. As with the car
rental operators many of them are at
Mangere. They include:

Adventure Vans
142 Robertson Rd, Mangere (tel 275-8994)
Blue Sky Motor Homes
41 Veronica St, New Lynn (tel 876-399)
Endeavour Motor Homes
72 Barry's Point Rd, Takapuna (tel 495-
860)
Horizon Motor Homes
154 Mackenzie Rd, Mangere (tel 275-
1159)
Maui Campas
100 New North Rd, Eden Terrace (tel 793-
277)
Mt Cook Line Motor Homes
Ascot Rd, Mangere (tel 275-5063)
Newmans Motor Homes
Richard Pearse Drive, Mangere (tel 275-
0709)

Bicycle Rental The Penny Farthing Cycle
Shop (tel 792-524) on the corner of
Symonds St and Khyber Pass Rd rents out
10-speed bicycles for $15 a day or $60 a
week plus a $30 deposit.

AROUND AUCKLAND
Walks around Auckland
The Auckland City Council has a series of
free guided walks available. Most walks
take about 1¼ hours. Contact the
Auckland Visitors Bureau for details.

For those footing it a coast-to-coast
walkway has been marked out between
the Waitemata Harbour on the east coast
and the Manukau Harbour on the west.
The walkway encompasses Albert Park,
the university, Auckland Domain (the
museum), Mt Eden and One Tree Hill, as
well as other points of interest. It keeps,
as much as possible, to reserves rather
than city streets. Total walking time for
the 13 km route, at an easy pace, is four
hours and it's near bus routes all the way.
An information pamphlet is available
from the Auckland Visitors Bureau.

New Zealand Walkway
Sections of the New Zealand Walkway
have been opened in the Auckland area,
the closest and most accessible being that
on Motutapu Island which is connected
by causeway to Rangitoto and has a
campsite at Home Bay. For more
information see the Lands & Survey
Department, Walkway Section, 14th
floor, State Insurance Building on the
corner of Rutland and Wakefield Sts (near
the Town Hall). They have a pamphlet on
the Auckland district walks.

Other New Zealand Walkway walks in
the area include Mt William (south of
Auckland near Bombay), Mt Auckland
(north of Auckland on SH 16 beyond
Helensville), Moir Hill (just south of
Warkworth on SH 1 north of Auckland) and
Dome Forest (just north of Warkworth).

Other Walks
There is more bush on the western fringe of
Auckland at the Waikakere Ranges where
there's a scenic drive, miles of bushwalks
and tracks (some not recommended for the
inexperienced) and wild, open beaches.
Whitcoulls on Queen St and the Auckland
Visitors Bureau have good maps. Apart

from tour buses on the scenic drive, bus services are almost non-existent so it is best to catch a bus to the fringing suburbs of Titirangi, Glen Eden, Henderson or Ranui, then walk or hitch.

Vineyards

New Zealand's wines have suddenly earned themselves an excellent worldwide reputation and there are numerous vineyards in the west Auckland area. There's a leaflet available which details the vineyards, their addresses, opening hours and shows their locations on a map. If you don't want to taste and drive or you don't have a car, vineyard tours are offered by AGM Productions (tel 398-670). Tours operate Monday to Saturday, from 10 am to 3 pm and include lunch.

A number of vineyards are within walking distance of Henderson, which you can reach by public transport.

Vineyards include:

Abel & Co Estate Wine
Pomana Rd, Kumeu (Monday to Saturday 10 am to 6 pm)
Babich Wines
Babich Rd, Henderson (Monday to Saturday 8 am to 5.45 pm)
Coopers Creek Vineyard
Main Rd, Huapai (Monday to Saturday 10.30 am to 6 pm)
Corbans Wines
426-448 Great North Rd, Henderson (Monday to Saturday 9 am to 6 pm)
Delegat's Vineyards
Hepburn Rd, Henderson (Monday to Friday 8.30 am to 5 pm, Saturday 10 am to 6 pm)
Lincoln Vineyards
130 Lincoln Rd, Henderson (Monday to Saturday 9 am to 6.30 pm)
Matua Valley Wines
Waikoukou Valley Rd, Waimauku (Monday to Friday 9 am to 5 pm, Saturday 9 am to 6 pm)
Nobilo Vintners
Station Rd, Huapai (Monday to Friday 9 am to 5 pm, Saturday 10 am to 6 pm)
Pleasant Valley Wines
322 Henderson Valley Rd, RD1 Henderson (Monday to Saturday 9 am to 6 pm)

San Marino Vineyards
Kumeu River Wines, Old North Rd & Highway 16, Kumeu (Monday to Saturday 9 am to 6 pm)
West Brook Winery
Panorama Vineyards, 34 Awaroa Rd, Henderson (Monday to Saturday 9 am to 6 pm)

Islands off Auckland

The Hauraki Gulf off Auckland is dotted with islands. Some are within minutes of the city and are popular for daytrips. Waiheke Island in particular is a favourite weekend escape and has become almost a dormitory suburb of the city. Waiheke also has some fine beaches and two hostels so it's a popular backpackers' destination. Great Barrier Island, on the other hand, is much more remote, much larger and much less suitable for a short visit. The islands are generally accessible by ferry services or light aircraft. There are a couple of 'getting there is half the fun' possibilities, like the Sea Bee Air amphibious flights and the elderly wooden auxiliary schooner *Te Aroha*.

Information

There are leaflets produced by the Lands & Survey Department on several of the islands. If you're planning to spend some time exploring the islands look for the Lands & Survey maps *Waiheke & Adjacent Islands* (NZMS 307) and *Great Barrier Island & Little Barrier Island* (NZMS 259).

RANGITOTO & MOTUTAPU ISLANDS

These two islands are joined by a causeway, both are part of the Hauraki Gulf Maritime Park and administered by the Department of Lands & Survey. Rangitoto is just 10 km from the city. It's a fascinating volcanic island – the last eruption was only 250 years ago. It's a good place to go for a picnic, there are lots of pleasant walks, a swimming pool,

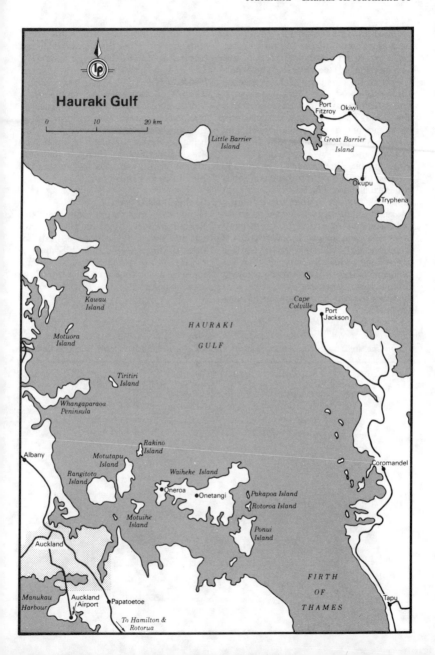

barbecues near the wharf and a great view from the summit of the 260-metre cone. Lava caves are another attraction, but you need good footwear as the whole island consists of lava with trees growing through it – no soil has developed as yet. If you're feeling lazy, go on a bus tour around the island. There's an information centre with maps of the various island walks and a shop which is open while cruise ships are at the island.

Motutapu, in contrast, is mainly covered in grassland and sheep and cattle are grazed there. The island was bought from the Maoris in 1842 for 10 empty casks, four double-barrelled shotguns, 50 blankets, five hats, five pieces of gown material, five shawls and five pairs of black trousers! There's an interesting three-hour roundtrip walk between the wharf at Islington Bay and the wharf at Home Bay. Islington Bay, the inlet between the two islands, was once known as 'Drunken Bay' as sailing ships would stop there to sober their crews who had overindulged in the bars of Auckland.

Places to Stay

There's a campsite at Home Bay, Motutapu Island. Toilets, water, garbage bins and barbecue sites are provided at this fairly rudimentary campsite but bring cooking equipment as open fires are not permitted. Camping fees are night and you can book by phoning the island's Senior Ranger on 727-674.

Getting There & Away

Rangitoto, Motutapu, Motuihe and Rakino are served by Blue Boats ferries but not every day. Phone 394-901 for details. Fullers Captain Cook Cruises go to Rangitoto twice daily. The fare includes a bus tour up to the top of the volcano cone.

'Finding shells on Takapuna' by Kristeen Lockett – Rangitoto Island from Takapuna Beach

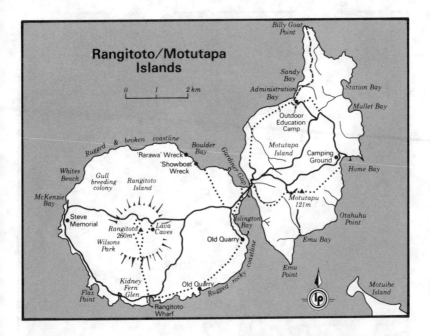

Rangitoto/Motutapa Islands

WAIHEKE

Waiheke is the most visited of the gulf islands and at 93 square km it's one of the largest. It's reputed to be sunnier and warmer than Auckland and there are plenty of beaches so it's a popular day trip from the city. There's also plenty of accommodation should you want to stay longer – everything from hotels and motels to two hostels.

The main settlement is Oneroa, at the western end of the island. From there it's fairly built up through Palm Beach to Onetangi in the middle. Beyond this the eastern end of the island is lightly inhabited although a rough road runs right round it. The island is very hilly so riding all the way around it on a bicycle is hard work.

Waiheke was originally discovered and settled by the Maoris. Legends relate that one of the pioneering canoes came to the island and traces of an old fortified pa can still be seen on the headland overlooking Putiki Bay. The Europeans arrived with missionary Samuel Marsden in the early 1800s and the island was soon stripped of its kauri forests. It's still a good place for bushwalking, however.

Information

The ferry operators have information on the island. *Gulf News* is a weekly newsmagazine of island events. *Waiheke Island – A Tour* is an interesting little booklet produced by the Waiheke Historical Society.

Waiheke is a local telephone call from Auckland but you have to dial 72 before the Waiheke number. There's a bank open Monday, Tuesday, Thursday and Friday in Oneroa.

Beaches

Popular beaches with good sand and good swimming include Oneroa Beach and the

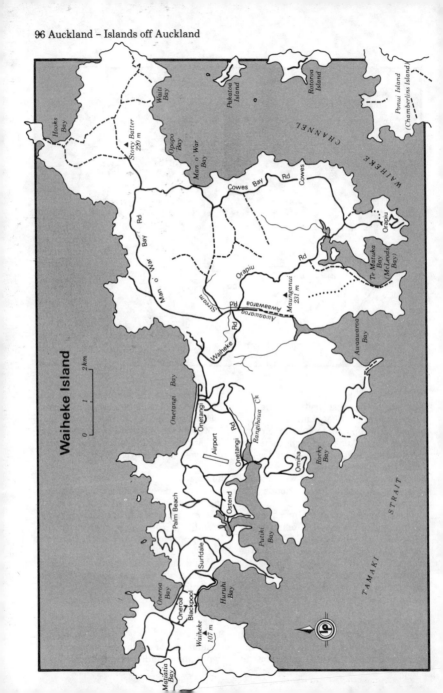

Waiheke Island

0 1 2 km

Top: Duke of Marlborough Hotel, Russell (TW)
Left: Signpost at lighthouse, Cape Reinga (MC)
Right: Large kauri tree in the Waipoua Forest, Northland (NZTP)

Top: Bay of Islands (MC)
Bottom: Stone Store, Kerikeri (TW)

adjacent Little Oneroa Beach, Palm Beach and the long stretch of sand at Onetangi Bay. There's snorkelling at Hekerua Bay and Enclosure. Waiheke enjoys more sunshine than Auckland and a number of the beaches have shady pohutukawa trees growing in the sand.

Historical Society Museum

There's a small historical museum at Ostend, midway between Oneroa and Onetangi. It's open 10 am to 1 pm on Saturday, 11 am to 2 pm on Sunday. The society is also planning to restore the old woolshed near Onetangi, one of the few remaining buildings built by the early settlers.

Stony Batter Walk

At the eastern end of the island the farmland derives its name from the boulder-strewn fields. There's an interesting walk leading to the old WW II gun emplacements with their connecting underground tunnels. The site is reached along the private road to the Man 'o War Station but vehicles are not permitted to go beyond the car park. From the gun emplacements you can continue walking north to Hooks Bay or south to Opopo Bay. From the entrance the walk to the WW II site takes 1½ hours return. From the site it's an additional 1½ hours return to either of the bays.

Activities

Fishing, horse riding, bushwalking, scuba diving and generally lazing around are all popular activities on Waiheke. Films are shown at the Surfdale Hall. There are a number of craftspeople on Waiheke and local craft shops show their work.

Tours

There's a three-hour tour of Waiheke at 9.30 am for $16.50 or a 3½ hour tour to Stony Batter at 1.30 pm for $22. Phone 7151 for details. You can also travel round Waiheke on the post office bus (refer to the Getting Around section).

Places to Stay

Hostels The two hostels on Waiheke are fiercely competitive. *Hekerua House* (tel 8371) is just beyond Oneroa at 11 Hekerua Rd. From the ferry terminal take the bus and get off when you get to Hekerua Rd, just up the hill from Oneroa. The hostel is pleasantly situated in one of the island's few patches of native bush. It has dorm beds at $11 or double rooms at $13 per person. In summer you get the seventh night free, in winter there are special lower weekly rates but whenever you come phone ahead from Auckland and make sure there's room. And bring your guitar! Bicycles are available for hire from the hostel.

The other hostel is the *Waiheke Island Youth Hostel* (tel 728-971) at Onetangi. To get there just take the bus from the ferry right to the end of the line. Nightly cost is $9 in this pleasantly situated hostel, up the hill overlooking the bay. The YHA offer two and three night packages including your return ferry fare and the return bus fare on the island.

Cabins & Guest Houses There's no campsite on the island but a couple of places have cabins. *Hide-Away Pacific* (tel 7897) at 4 Bay Rd, Palm Beach, has cabins for two at $30. The *Midway Motel & Cabins* (tel 8023) at 1 Whakarite Rd, Ostend has a variety of cabins from around $20 to $36. There are communal showers, toilets and kitchens.

Kiwi House (tel 8626), 23 Kiwi St, Blackpool offers bed & breakfast. *Hauraki House* (tel 7598), at 50 Hauraki Rd, Oneroa, is quite popular and has wonderful views.

Motels & Hotels The *Onetangi Hotel* (tel 8028) on the beachfront at Onetangi has rooms at $25/42 for singles/doubles. Also on the beachfront *Uncle McGinty's Lodge* (tel 8118) is rather more luxurious, the rooms all have attached bathrooms and cost $50/65.

The *Midway Motel*, see cabins above,

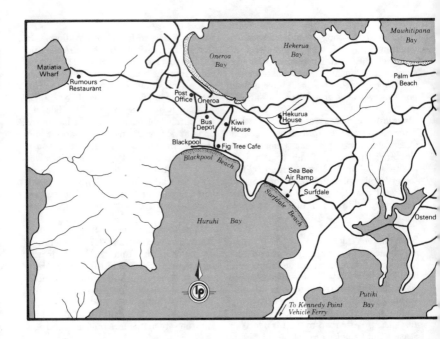

and the *Waiheke Hilton Holiday Chalets* (tel 7093) at 223 Oceanview Rd, Oneroa are both around $55/65. The new *Roanna-Maree Motel* (tel 7051) at Onetangi is more expensive.

Places to Eat

Oneroa There are all sorts of places to eat at Oneroa including a string of snacks bars and takeways. Try *Aoreno's Pizza*, *Poppy's*, the *Pickle Palace Deli*, the *Breeze Inn* or the *Schooner Cafe*. They're all along Ocean View Rd in the centre. Back close to the wharf at Matiatia Bay is the more expensive *Rumours Restaurant*.

The *Fig Tree Cafe* is near the waterfront on the corner of the Esplanade and Moa Avenue in Blackpool, between Surfdale and Oneroa. It's open for lunch every day and for dinner from Thursday through Sunday. There's a pleasant courtyard in this quiet and relaxed byo place. The food is good although a bit expensive – great

French bread rolls with salad and vegetables for $5.50, chicken and ham for $6.50, other lunch dishes from $4 to $8. At night main courses are $13 to $16.

Onetangi The *Onetangi Hotel* has good bistro meals and gives a 10% discount if you're staying at the YHA hostel. The hotel also has a pleasant beer garden and the more exclusive *Country Kitchen Restaurant* where you're advised that booking is essential. There's also a restaurant at *Uncle McGinty's Lodge* or you can get sandwiches and snacks in the somewhat scruffy Post Office Store.

Getting There & Away

Air You can fly to Waiheke right from Mechanics Bay in Auckland with Sea Bee Air (tel 774-404, 5 & 6). A trip on their amphibious aircraft is quite an experience and costs $30, or $50 return. It takes just 10 minutes to zip across the gulf to Surfdale on

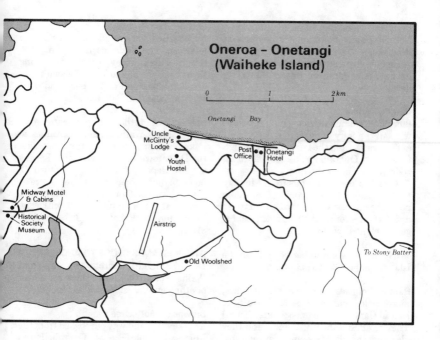

Oneroa – Onetangi
(Waiheke Island)

0   1   2 km

Onetangi Bay

Uncle
McGinty's
Lodge

Post
Office

Onetangi
Hotel

Youth
Hostel

Midway Motel
& Cabins

Historical
Society
Museum

Airstrip

To Stony Batter

● Old Woolshed

Waiheke but landing *in* Huruhi Bay and then taxiing up onto land is great fun.

The only trouble with this way of getting to Waiheke is that having arrived in Huruhi Bay you then have to wait for a bus to go by on its way to or from the ferry at Matiatia Bay, which is at the western end of the island. Alternatively, you could walk – it takes about half an hour, or plan ahead and arrange to be met.

You can also fly to Waiheke from Ardmore and Auckland with Waiheke Air Services (tel 298-7142). Fares from Auckland to Waiheke are \$40 one way or \$70 return (children \$35 and \$57 respectively). The Waiheke landing strip is between Ostend and Onetangi.

Boat *Quick Cat* is a high-speed, 500-seat catamaran service out to the island. It zips you out in about half an hour at a return cost of \$19 (children \$9.50). From Auckland the boat departs from opposite the Downtown Airport Terminal at 8 am, 10 am, 2 pm and 5.30 pm every day. Weekdays there is also a 6 am departure and on Fridays there's an additional 8.45 pm service. From Waiheke the departures are 8.45 am, 12.50 pm, 4.45 pm, 6.15 pm every day, 6.45 am weekdays and 10 pm Fridays. The late Friday service is made with a slower boat which takes about an hour. The slower boat is also used as a relief boat during peak periods or when the *Quick Cat* is out of operation. The ferries arrive and depart from Matiatia Bay at the western end of the island. Some of the services continue on from Waiheke to Pakatoa Island.

If you've got your own car the Subritsky Shipping Company (tel 534-5663) operates a ferry service twice a day during the week and once on Saturdays and Sundays. The cost depends on the size of the car plus there's a charge for each passenger additional to the driver. The ferry goes from Half Moon Bay on the mainland and from Kennedy Point on Putiki Bay on Waiheke.

There's also a service down the Tamaki Estuary from Panmure, phone 790-092 for details.

Getting Around

Bus There's a bus service which connects with all the ferry arrivals and departures and operates from the ferry wharf through Oneroa to Onetangi. The fare is $2.20 right to the end of the line.

There's a post office bus from Monday to Friday at 9.15 am from the Surfdale post office. It costs $6 just to Stony Batter or $10 for the round the island trip and it gets back at 12 noon.

Taxis There are a number of taxis on the island, phone 8038 to get one.

Rental Vehicles You can rent cars, motorcycles and bicycles from Waiheke Rental Cars (tel 8635 or 8386 after hours) They're at 13 Tahi Rd, Ostend and they also rent windsurfers and catamarans. Their office is right by the ferry wharf at Matiatia Bay.

Bicycles cost $15 a day, motorcycles are $33 plus $4 for a crash helmet and cars are $50 plus 44c a km. Petrol is included with motorcycle or car hire. Hekerua Lodge also has bicycles for hire. Remember, although it is compact, this island is very hilly and riding a bicycle around it is *hard* work.

PAKATOA ISLAND

Pakatoa Island is a small tourist resort 36 km out from Auckland and just beyond Waiheke. The resort has a restaurant, bar, coffee shop, swimming pool and various sporting facilities. There are great views of the gulf and across to the Coromandel Peninsula from the island's high point.

Places to Stay

Phone 796-780 or 734-084 in Auckland about accommodation at the island's resort.

Getting There & Away

Air Sea Bee Air's seaplane flies daily to Pakatoa. The flight costs $70, or $125 return. This is an even more interesting flight than the one to Waiheke as it takes you across the gulf and right over the island to Pakatoa.

Boat *Quick Cat*, the high speed catamaran which serves Waiheke, also continues to Pakatoa. Departures are from opposite the Downtown Airline Terminal. There's a daily departure at 10 am (return 12 noon), a daily except Friday departure at 2 pm (return 3.45 pm) and a Fridays only service at 7 pm (return 10.30 pm). The return fare to Pakatoa is $25 (children $12.50).

OTHER ISLANDS CLOSE TO AUCKLAND

Dotted around Rangitoto-Motutapu and Waiheke or further north there are a host of other smaller islands. They include:

Browns or Motukorea Island

This small island was purchased from the Maoris by John Logan Campbell and William Brown in 1840 and used as a pig farm. It's now part of the Hauraki Gulf Maritime Park. The old wharf collapsed long ago and along the west coast lie the rotting wrecks of five old ferries that ran aground and were abandoned.

Motuihe Island

Half way between Auckland and Waiheke this small two square km island with its fine beaches is a very popular daytrip from the city. At one time the island was used as a quarantine station and the cemetery at the north-west tip has graves of victims of the 1918 influenza epidemic. In WW I it was used as a prisoner of war camp and it was from there that the German captain Count Felix von Luckner made a daring, but ultimately unsuccessful, escape.

The peninsula pointing out north-west has fine sandy beaches on both sides so one side is always sheltered from the wind.

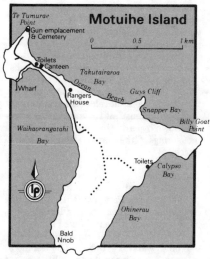

On a sunny weekend there may be over 500 boats anchored in the bay! There are some walking tracks on the island, it takes about three hours to walk all the way around.

Rotoroa Island
Another small island, just south of Pakatoa Island

Ponui Island
Also known as Chamberlins Island this larger island is just south of Rotoroa and has been farmed by the Chamberlin family ever since they purchased it from the Maoris in 1854. South again from Ponui is Pakihi or Sandspit Island and tiny Karamuramu Island.

Rakino Island
This small island is just to the north of Motutapu Island. Beyond Rakino there is a cluster of tiny islands collectively known as The Noises.

Tiritiri Matangi
Part of the Hauraki Gulf Maritime Park this island is further north, about half way

between the islands close to Auckland and Kawau Island. The island is an 'open sanctuary' where native wildlife is protected but visitors are permitted. Attempts are being made to re-vegetate the island with native species and re-establish native birds.

Motuora Island
Motuora Island is half way between Tiritiri Matangi and Kawau. There is a camp ground on the west coast of the island but there is no regular ferry service to Motuora. A camping permit must be obtained from the ranger on Kawau (tel Kawau Island 882), and camping costs $5 per site.

Getting There & Away
The Blue Boat Ferries (tel 394-901) service to Rangitoto also goes to Rakino and Motuihe.

KAWAU ISLAND
Kawau is fairly close to the North Island coast but well north of the other islands off Auckland. The ferry to Kawau departs from Sandspit, 45 km from Auckland. To get there, you turn off the main road north at Warkworth and travel a few km east to Sandspit.

On Kawau Sir George Grey's old home, Mansion House, which was used as a hotel for many years has now been restored to its original state and is open to the public. Sir George, an early governor of New Zealand, built Mansion House 150 years ago. There are many beautiful walks on Kawau, starting from Mansion House and leading to beaches, an old copper mine, a lookout, etc. You'll see numerous wallabies around here – they're not native to New Zealand so they're an unusual sight in this part of the world.

Places to Stay
You can camp at *Heavens Camping Ground* (tel 822) at Moores Bay, Bon Accord harbour for $9 per person. You have to book ahead to arrange boat pick

up from Bon Accord Harbour. Many good bushwalks lead from the site to various places on the island.

Getting There & Away

Air Although there are no scheduled services Sea Bee Air can arrange flights from Auckland to Kawau.

Boat Fullers operate the ferry service from Sandspit to the island. It operates four or five times daily and costs about $12 return. Fullers also have a daily tour to Kawau by bus from Auckland to Sandspit and then by launch to the island. You leave Auckland at 9 am and get back at 4.45 pm. The tour is a good idea as it's not always easy to connect with the ferry if you're taking public transport from Auckland. The old schooner *Te Aroha* also travels from Port Fitzroy, on Great Barrier Island, to Kawau for $35; and from Port Fitzroy to Kawau to Auckland for $60.

GREAT BARRIER ISLAND

The largest island in Hauraki Gulf is Great Barrier Island, 88 km from the mainland. Swimming, walking and generally lazing around are the popular activities on the island. Great Barrier has hot springs, historic kauri dams and a network of tramping tracks. There are three huts along along the trails in the State Forest and free camping grounds at Harataonga Bay, Medlands Beach and Awana Bay.

The island was originally sighted and named by Captain Cook. Later it became a whaling centre, a number of ships were built there and the island has also been the site for some spectacular shipwrecks including the *SS Wairarapa* in 1894 and the *Wiltshire* in 1922.

There's a cemetery at Katherine Bay where many of the victims of the *Wairarapa* wreck were buried.

Travelling out to the island on the *Te Aroha* is quite an experience.

Great Barrier Island is decidedly isolated. There are periodic complaints in the Auckland papers about how lousy the roads

are and how the government on the mainland forgets about the islanders' existence. The island doesn't even have a pub. Tryphena is the main town and arrival and departure port. Whangaparapara is an old timber town and the site of the island's whaling activities. The Great Barrier State Forest between Whangaparapara and Port Fitzroy is being developed for tramping although almost all the kauri trees were cut down by early this century. There are hot springs off the Claris-Whangaparapara track.

Information

The NZ Adventure Centre (tel 399-192 & 4) at Victoria Park Market, Auckland specialises in Great Barrier Island. The Forest Service office (tel Port Fitzroy 4K) in Port Fitzroy has information about the island's walking tracks. The island's manual telephone exchange only operates during business hours during the week and on Saturday mornings.

Places to Stay & Eat

There are no restaurants or takeaways on the island, you either have to fix your own food or eat at the place you stay. Guest house prices on the island are usually quoted inclusive of all meals.

Tryphena *Pohutukawa Lodge* (tel Tryphena 20) on Tryphena Harbour beachfront has camping facilities, a bunkroom for $13 ($12 for YHA members) plus a guest house with double and twin rooms at around $60. They do meals here at $8 for breakfast, $6 for lunch, $21 for dinner but you can also fix your own food and there's a shop at the lodge.

The *Mulberry Grove Motel* (tel Tryphena 16) has motel rooms at $55 a double and is right behind the Tryphena General Store which has a reasonable food selection.

The *Pigeons Guest House* (tel Tryphena 8A) is at Shoal Bay on the beachfront and including all meals costs $80 per person or there are two motel rooms at $60 a double.

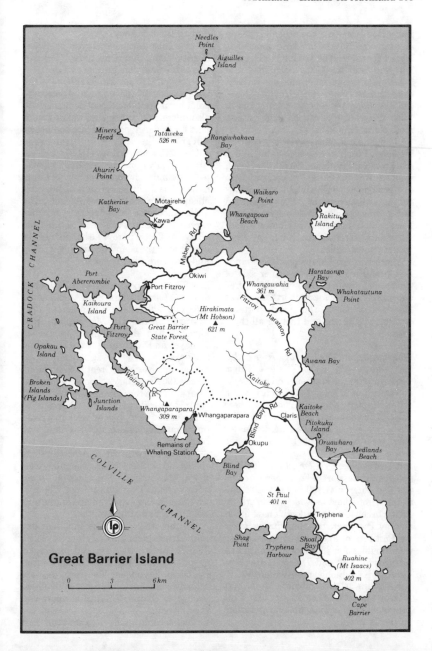

Great Barrier Island

0   3   6 km

Needles Point
Aiguilles Island

Miners Head
▲ *Tataweka 526 m*
Rangiwhakaea Bay

Ahuriri Point

Katherine Bay
Motairehe
Waikaro Point

C R A D O C K   C H A N N E L

Kawa
Whangapoua Beach

Rakitu Island

Mabey Rd

Okiwi

Port Abercrombie

Port Fitzroy

Harataonga Bay

Kaikoura Island
▲ *Whangawahia 361 m*
Whakatautuna Point

Port Fitzroy
Hirakimata (Mt Hobson) 621 m ▲

Fitzroy

Harataon

Rd

Opakau Island
Great Barrier State Forest

Awana Bay

Broken Islands (Pig Islands)
Wairahi

Junction Islands

Kaitoke Ck

▲ *Whangaparapara 309 m*
Whangaparapara

Kaitoke Beach

Blind Bay Rd

Claris

Pitokuku Island

Remains of Whaling Station

Okupu

Oruawharo Bay
Medlands Beach

C O L V I L L E
Blind Bay

▲ *St Paul 401 m*

C H A N N E L

Tryphena

Shag Point
Tryphena Harbour
Shoal Bay

▲ *Ruahine (Mt Isaacs) 402 m*

Cape Barrier

Shoal Bay is south of the other Tryphena accommodation and it's also somewhat more expensive. The setting is pleasant, however, and they have dinghies and fishing equipment for guests' use without extra charge. *Tipi & Bob's Holiday Home* (tel Tryphena 5A) and the nearby *Valley View Lodge* (tel Tryphena 6D) are two more central guest houses.

Medlands Beach Across the island, about five km from Tryphena, Medlands Beach is on the way to Claris. You can stay here at *Rangimarie*, a lovely old homestead-cum-guesthouse which has vegetarian food and reasonably priced accommodation. Nearby on Mason Rd is *Golden Goose Farmhouse* (tel Claris 6U), a more modern guest house.

There's a free campsite at Medlands Beach and another on the other side of Claris at Awana Bay. A third free campsite can be found north again at Harataonga Bay. You need portable cooking equipment and fuel for all these sites.

Whangaparapara *The Great Barrier Lodge* (tel Claris 4H) is at Water's Edge, Whangaparapara Harbour and has rooms at $70, cabins at $50 to $60. There is also a self-contained cabin and a cottage where you can fix your own meals. The town also has a free *Forest Service Hut*, useful for those walking across the island.

Port Fitzroy There's a *Forest Service Hut* and a campsite near the Forest Service office (tel Port Fitzroy 4K). They're both some distance from the store, which doesn't really matter because the store doesn't have much anyway. Port Fitzroy also has *Fitzroy House* (tel Port Fitzroy 2), which is a guest house with doubles for $85 and self-contained cottages for $70; and *The Jetty* (tel Port Fitzroy 1K), which is more expensive.

Kaikoura Island, offshore from Port Fitzroy, has the *Lost Resort* (tel Port Fitzroy 8) with cabins. You can get there on the *Te Aroha*.

Getting There & Away

Air Sea Bee Air have flights to Great Barrier Island four times a day. The trip only takes about half an hour and costs $75 one way or $135 return. Tryphena is the Great Barrier Island arrival and departure point but if there's sufficient demand it will also operate to Whangaparapara and/or Port Fitzroy. Adverse weather conditions can ground the Sea Bee Air flights.

Great Barrier Airlines (tel 275-9120 in Auckland) fly from Mangere and Ardmore to Claris and Okiwi on Great Barrier Island daily. This flight is less exciting but a bit cheaper than the Sea Bee Air one. The airline operates a connecting minibus service from Claris to Tryphena and from Okiwi to Port Fitzroy. Other flights are operated to the island by Air North Shore and Ardmore Air Charters.

Boat There are boat services to Tryphena on Great Barrier Island from Auckland for $35. Try Gulf Trans Shipping (tel 734-036) who operate the *MV Tasman* from Kings Wharf departing at 10 am on Fridays and returning at 11 am on Sundays.

You can also get to Great Barrier Island on the 1909 auxiliary schooner *Te Aroha*. She sails from the Captain Cook Wharf in central Auckland, every Tuesday in summer and every second week in winter, on a four-day cruise to the island and back.

You can sail with the *Te Aroha* direct to the island, without taking the full cruise, if you like. It leaves Auckland at 10 am and arrives at Tryphena at 5 pm. The one-way fare is $50, which includes morning tea, lunch and afternoon tea.

On the other hand the full, four-day round trip is great fun and costs only $250. The *Te Aroha*, its crew and passengers spend the first night on Great Barrier Island at Tryphena. The next day the schooner moves up the coast of Great Barrier to Okupu, Whangaparapara and Port Fitzroy.

The second night is spent at Port

Fitzroy, then the schooner heads over to Kawau Island, where again she spends the night before travelling back to Auckland. In winter the Kawau stop is skipped and she goes direct from Port Fitzroy to Auckland.

You can sleep on the deck or on bunks in the hold. There's lots of good food, booze, diving, snorkelling and fishing and if you like you can even help load and unload. The boat is also a supply vessel and a means of local transport. If the islanders don't have a wharf that allows the *Te Aroha* to dock close to shore, then they row out in dinghies to collect their goods.

All in all this is a great trip. Check with the NZ Adventure Centre (tel 399-192/4) for more details.

Getting Around

Roads on the island are rough and ready. It's about 40 km from Tryphena in the south, via Whangaparapara, to Port Fitzroy in the north, using the forestry walking tracks. The roads are bad enough that you may decide walking is a good idea! Alternatively you can take the *Te Aroha* on its weekly voyage along the coast.

There are a handful of taxis on the island but they aren't cheap. You can hire motorcycles from Bob Elvey (tel Tryphena 22K). They cost $38.50 for one day, $33 a day for two to four days, $30 a day for five or more. There is one solitary rental car on the island and Safari Tours (tel Tryphena 22M) has island tours, they'll take you one way as well.

Northland

The region known as Northland is like a finger pointing north from Auckland. Often referred to as the 'winterless north' its climate tends to be mild compared to the rest of New Zealand. It's a popular holiday resort area with beaches and water sport activities and close enough to the big city for weekend trips. Northland is also modern New Zealand's cradle – it was here that Europeans first made permanent contact with the Maoris, here the first squalid sealers' and whalers' settlements were formed and here the treaty of Waitangi was signed between the settlers and the Maoris. To this day there are a greater proportion of Maoris in the population than elsewhere in New Zealand.

Western Route

From Auckland there are two main routes through Northland to the Bay of Islands – the major attraction of the area. The simplest and fastest route is to head straight up through Whangarei on the east side of the peninsula. The west coast route is slower – the road is unsealed for a stretch – and longer, but it takes you through Dargaville, the Waipoua Forest and the Hokianga Harbour. You can get to Northland by going via Helensville or Warkworth to Wellsford, then on to Brynderwyn, 112 km north of Auckland, from where you take the east or west coast route.

AUCKLAND TO DARGAVILLE
Moir Hill Walkway
A few km before you reach Warkworth there is a waterfall, lookout and views of the Hauraki Gulf from the Moir Hill Walkway. The track is directly off the main road so the bus services can drop you there. The return trip takes three to four

hours and walking boots are only necessary in winter. Just north of the walkway is New Zealand's satellite tracking station.

Sandspit
East of Warkworth, a few km from the main road, is Sandspit, where a ferry service departs for Kawau Island. See the Kawau Island section in Islands off Auckland for more details.

Warkworth
Just north of Warkworth is a track to The Dome. It leaves from the main road and thus is easily accessible. There are some beautiful beaches between Warkworth and Whangarei, especially Pakiri, Mangawhai Heads and Waipu Cove. Access is not very easy for the traveller without wheels, but you can often hitch a ride with surfies.

Mangawhai Cliffs Walkway
The Mangawhai Cliffs Walkway leads from Managawhai Heads to Bream Tail (1½ to two hours one-way) giving extensive views both inland and of the Hauraki Gulf islands. The return trip can be made around the foreshore at low tide when the sea is not rough.

Brynderwyn Hills Walkway
Also in the same area is the Brynderwyn Hills Walkway (eastern section) starting from the Mangawhai-Waipu Cave road. It's an easy two-hour return climb which gives panoramic views of Northland and the Hauraki Gulf from the highest point. The road continues to Largs Beach, where it's possible to camp, before it rejoins the main highway at Waipu.

Kauris
As you travel through the Northland region you'll hear and see a lot about kauris. Kauris are gigantic native New Zealand trees, a competitor in size to the Californian redwood

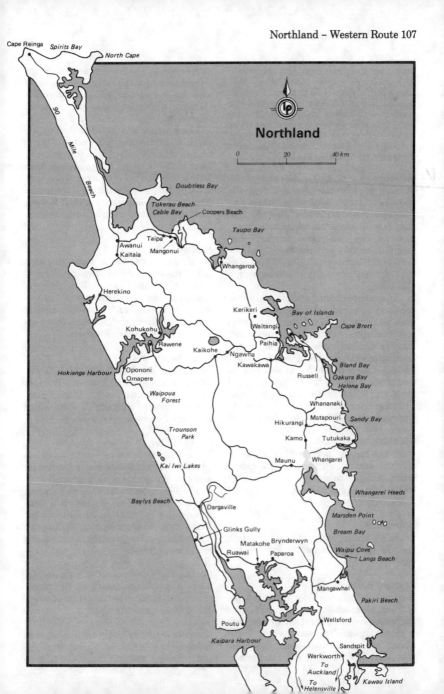

but entirely different in type. They only grow in the northern part of the North Island. They were once ruthlessly cut down for their excellent timber and Northland is covered with evidence of the kauri days. Kauri gum was found to be an important ingredient for making varnish and at one time there were many 'gumdiggers' who roamed the forests, poking in the ground for hard lumps of kauri gum.

Matakohe

Turning off at Brynderwyn for Dargaville you pass through Matakohe, where the Otamatea Kauri & Pioneer Museum has a strange and wonderful collection of kauri gum in the basement. It also has magnificent lifelike displays of various aspects of the life of the kauri bushmen and a very extensive photographic collection.

This is a superb museum and well worth the short detour off the road to see it. The museum shop has some excellent bowls and other items crafted from kauri wood. They're expensive but very well made. Look for the items made of 'swamp kauri', ancient kauris which lay in swamps for thousands of years, their gum-saturated wood still remaining in good condition. The museum is open daily from 9 am to 5 pm, admission $3 (children 50c).

DARGAVILLE

Once the busiest port in New Zealand, and the centre of the country's export trade, Dargaville's population is only 4800. It's about 185 km north of Auckland.

Information

There's a handy little information kiosk (tel 7056) on Normanby St in the centre.

Northern Wairoa Museum

Dargaville's eccentric little museum is not of the same standard as Matakohe but it's still worth visiting. Maori exhibits include a pre-European era war canoe, found buried in sand dunes, and there are also early settlers' items and kauri

gum samples. The feature of the museum is the maritime section. Hundreds of ships were built and worked on in Kaipara Harbour which was also notorious for shipwrecks.

The museum is situated at the top of a small hill in Harding Park on the outskirts of town about three km from the centre. In front of the museum are the masts from *Rainbow Warrior*, the Greenpeace boat sunk by French government terrorists in Auckland in 1985. The museum is open daily from 9 am to 4 pm and admission is $2 (children 50c).

Harding Park

Harding Park itself is an interesting area as it is the site of an old Maori pa. Tucked into the bottom of the hill is an early European cemetery. There are great views over Dargaville and the surrounding countryside from the park and there are picnic tables near the museum.

Ocean Beach

Only 15 minutes from Dargaville is Ocean Beach, site of many shipwrecks. It's said that the hulks of a French Man o' War, and an ancient Spanish or Portuguese ship can occasionally be seen.

Places to Stay

The tourist info centre on Normanby St has a leaflet on accommodation in Dargaville and can also arrange accommodation in local homes and on farms in the area. If you are interested in staying on a farm contact Ron Stocken (tel 38-576) who has cheap farm accommodation at Ruawai, 12 km south of Dargaville and a km south of Tokatoka Tavern.

Hostels The *Dargaville Youth Hostel* (tel 6342) is at 13 Portland St on the corner of Gordon St, close to the centre of town. A bed there costs $11.

Camping & Cabins Both are available at *Selwyn Park* (tel 8296), 1½ km from the post office. Camping costs about $6 a night per person ($2 extra with power) while a cabin costs $15 for one person, $25 for two.

Hotels & Motels There are several hotels in Dargaville or near it. The *Central* (tel 8034) 18-22 Victoria St, has B&B singles from $40; the *Northern Wairoa* (tel 8923) Hokianga Rd, costs from $25 to $30 a single; the *Commercial* (tel 8018), River Rd, Mangawhare, also ranges from $25 to $30 a single; and the *Aratapu* (tel 523), on the road to Te Kopuru, eight km from Dargaville, costs $40 including breakfast and dinner.

The *Kauri House Lodge* (tel 8082) on Bowen St is a more expensive place with rooms from $60/75, all with attached bathroom. The rooms in this old colonial homestead are all furnished with antiques and there's a swimming pool too.

The *Dargaville Motel* (tel 7734) at 217 Victoria St has rooms at $48/58.

Places to Eat

There are a number of takeaway places and cafes including the *Chicken Inn* on Kapia St across from the bus station or the *Bella Vista* on Victoria St. The old *Northern Wairoa Hotel* has recently modernised its restaurant and menu, which features standard pub food from $9 to $11. Or there's the fancier *Lorna Doone* restaurant on the corner of Victoria and Gladstone Sts.

Getting There & Away

NZRRS have bus services between Auckland and Dargaville up to three times daily. The trip takes about 3½ hours. Monday to Friday one of the services continues north through the Waipoua Forest to Opononi and Kaikohe to Paihia. Another NZRRS service from Auckland goes through Kaikohe en route to Kaitaia.

AROUND DARGAVILLE

Kaipara Lighthouse

A worthwhile trip from Dargaville, if you

can find a way to get there, is the 71-km run south-east to Kaipara Lighthouse, the last 6½ km is on foot along the foreshore. If you can't get there any other way check with the Dargaville information centre about the four-wheel drive Kauri Coaster Tours down the coast to the lighthouse, Kai-Iwi Lakes and through the kauri forest. They're expensive, but worth it. Built in 1884, the lighthouse has now been restored to its original condition.

Beaches

From Kaipara unbroken sand stretches 109 km north to Manganui Bluff. There is access at Bayly's Beach (14 km west of Dargaville), Glinks Gully, Mahuta Gorge and Omamari – the main road does not touch the beach. There the famous toheroa, a large shellfish, is found, however it's rigorously protected and can only be taken during an occasional open season. A French boat sank off Bayly's Beach in 1851, you can read about it at the Dargaville museum.

Kai-Iwi Lakes

Only 34 km north of Dargaville are three superb freshwater lakes called the Kai-Iwi Lakes (Taharoa Domain) and although they've been developed as a resort for swimming, trout fishing and so on, the area is still relatively unspoilt. The largest of the lakes, Taharoa, is fringed with pines and dotted with gleaming whitesand beaches.

A walking track leaves from the Kai-Iwi Lakes out to the coast, along the beach to Manganui Bluff where it climbs to the summit and drops down to the beach again. The track continues past the Waikara Beach campsite to the Kawerua campsite and on to Hokianga South Head near Omapere. Allow three days for this walk and make sure you organise to cross the Waipoua and Waimamaku Rivers at low tide. More details can be had from the ranger at Trounson Kauri Park, just north of Kaihu. There are some fine kauri stands in the park and you can take a half hour walk past a fallen kauri and the 'four sisters' – two trees each with two trunks.

Places to Stay

Bayly's Beach Motor Camp (tel 4453) is at Bayly's Beach, 13 km from Dargaville. Again there are camping facilities and cabins. You can also camp at the Kai-Iwi Lakes for $5 per adult and at Trounson Kauri Park. The latter is a stunning place to stay, ringed by superb kauris. It has showers, toilets and excellent cooking facilities and a camping site is $7.50.

WAIPOUA TO HOKIANGA
Waipou Kauri Forest

The road north enters the Waipoua Kauri Forest 50 km out of Dargaville. The Waipoua Forest Sanctuary, proclaimed in 1952 after much public pressure and antagonism at continued milling, is the largest remnant of the once extensive kauri forests of northern New Zealand. There is no milling of mature kauri trees now – except under extraordinary circumstances such as the carving of a Maori canoe. The kauri management programme which allowed for some thinning of adolescent trees to make room for others is under review. Milling in the Puketi State Forest was stopped some years back not only to protect the kauri but also because this area was the home of the rare native bird, the kokako.

The road through the forest passes by some huge and splendid kauris. Turn off to the forest lookout just after you enter the park. A little further north another turn-off leads to the park HQ where a hut used by the first ranger is now set up as an interesting small museum. Here you can pick up a brochure on the park which tells the full story of the trees. A fully grown kauri can reach 30 to 40 metres high and have a trunk four metres or more in diameter. They are slow growing, some kauris are over 1500 years old.

Several huge trees are easily reached from the road. Te Matua Ngahere, which means 'father of the forest', has a trunk over five metres in diameter. This massive tree is a short drive then a 10-minute walk from the main road. From the access road you can follow a walking track to the Yakas Tree and on to the Forest HQ. Do the walk in that direction as it's downhill.

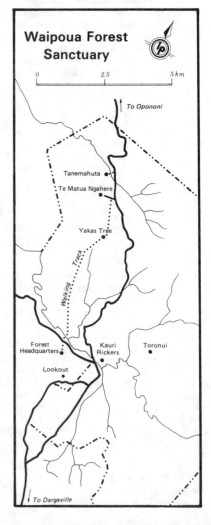

Waipoua Forest Sanctuary

Further up the road is Tanemahuta, 'lord of the forest', which stands much closer to the road and is estimated to be 1200 years old. At 52 metres it's much higher than Te Matua Ngahere but hasn't got the same impressive bulk – although its cubic volume is said to be even greater. The park contained an even larger tree called Toronui but it fell, apparently from old age, in the '70s.

Places to Stay Just across the bridge from the Kauri Rickers there's a picnic area where you can camp for free in the off season. The facilities are absolutely minimal – only a pit toilet and you have to get water from the river, but it is free.

Near the village of Waimamaku, just north of the Waipou Forest, is the *Solitaire Guest House* (tel Waimamaku 891). It's a pleasantly friendly place with accommodation in the beautifully restored old kauri house for $60 per person including breakfast and dinner. There are plenty of good walks from here.

Hokianga Harbour

Further north the road winds down to the Hokianga Harbour and the township of Omapere. The Hokianga is a popular area for city slickers wishing to escape to an alternative lifestyle, but it's still fairly unspoilt – much less commercial than the Bay of Islands – and a great place for travellers who want to take time out and drift for a while. From Omapere it is a 15-minute walk to the South Head where the coastal track from Manganui Bluff and the Kai-Iwi Lakes finishes. Here there is a swimming beach and views of the harbour entrance, the massive sand dunes of the North Head and the Tasman Sea. Boat trips across to the dunes are often organised from the House of Harmony hostel in Opononi.

OPONONI

Only 3½ km past Omapere the road passes through the tiny settlement of Opononi. The stone walls along Opononi's seafront were constructed from rock ballast used in timber ships which were sailed out from Sydney by convicts.

Back in 1955 a dolphin paid so many regular, friendly visits to the town that it became a national attraction. Opo, as the dolphin was dubbed, played with children and learned to perform numerous tricks with beach balls. Unfortunately, Opo was killed, some say accidentally, by illegal dynamite fishers. A sculpture of Opo marks the dolphin's grave outside Opononi's pub.

Beyond Opononi is Pakanae where the Waiotemarama Gorge road turns south for six km to Waiotemarama bush track. This track climbs to Hautura, 680 metres high. The highest point in Northland, 774 metres, is nearby but there is no regular track. Between Waima and Taheke is the old Waoju coach road, once the sole route to Dargaville and because of the rainfall only open during summer. The track at the end of the road leads to some old, hand-made culverts and excellent views of the valley. It takes about three hours there and back. If you continue to follow it, it winds south to Tutamoe and then west to Wekaweka Valley.

Places to Stay

Hostels The *Opononi Youth Hostel* (tel 792) is three km east of Opononi at Pakanae and costs $9 a night. It's a good hostel but a little far from the town. Right in the centre of town is the beautifully situated privately-run hostel, *Te Ranginarie – Harmony House*, which also costs $9 a night. It's more convenient than the YHA hostel but can be a little crowded and cramped.

Camping & Cabins The *Opononi Beach Motor Camp* (tel 791) costs $6 per adult to camp and there are also a handful of on-site vans at $18 to $25. You can also camp at the *Omapere Tourist Hotel* for $6, or $6.50 with power.

Hotels & Motels The *Opononi Hotel* (tel 858) has rooms, most of them without

attached bathrooms, at \$26/38 for singles/
doubles. Smack on the bay is the
Omapere Tourist Hotel & Motel (tel 737)
which has such a great setting it's almost
worth staying for that alone. Hotel rooms
are \$40 (\$48 to \$53 at the height of the
season), motel rooms \$53 (\$66 in season).
They also have boats to hire.

Places to Eat

On the main road in Opononi the *Blue
Dolphin Restaurant* has the usual grills
and the like for around \$8, plus burgers
and sandwiches. If you want a splurge try
the restaurant at the *Omapere Tourist
Hotel* where the food is good and the
setting is great for lunch too. You can eat
outside watching the boats and all the
activity in the bay.

ROUTES TO KAITAIA

From the Hokianga you can head north to
Kaitaia and the 90 Mile Beach or east to
the Bay of Islands. There are two routes
north to Kaitaia. The longer and busier
route goes via Kaikohe and is easier for
hitchhikers. The alternative route is 70 km
shorter and takes you on the Rawene-
Kohukohu ferry.

The ferry departs Rawene every hour
between 7.30 am and 5.30 pm and goes
from the Narrows on the Kohukohu side
at 7.45 and 8.30 am and then every hour
from 9 am to 6 pm. Starting time may be
an hour later and finishing time an hour
earlier in winter; the crossing takes 20
minutes. Fares are \$7 for cars, \$2 for
motorcycles, \$1 for people.

Rawene & Kohukohu

While you wait for the ferry at Rawene you
can visit historic Clendon House which is
open from 10 am to 4 pm daily. Admission
is \$2 (children \$1). Outside the Westpac
bank there's Te Hawera, an old Maori
dugout canoe. Rawene is quite a pleasant
little settlement, you might decide to stay
longer than just the wait for the ferry.

Kohukohu, on the other side of the river,
is a minor arty-crafty-trendy centre.

Places to Stay Rawene has a motor camp
(tel 720) in Manning St, which charges \$6
a night per adult for tent sites (\$1 more
with power) and has cabins for \$13 per
person. The *Masonic Hotel* (tel 822), just
a few steps up from the ferry landing, has
rooms from just \$20/35 a night.

Ngawha

Near Kaikohe is Ngawha which has a
series of hot springs of varying temperatures
called the Domain Pool – pick one to suit
your mood. It's very basic but it's a great
way to spend a bleak day and only about
three km off the main road.

Fairburn Glow-worms

Between Pamapuria and Rangithi, shortly
before Kaitaia, a turn-off leads east to
Fairburn. Sullivan's Glow-worm Grotto is
open in the evenings to 10 or 11 pm and
costs \$4 (children \$3).

KAITAIA

Kaitaia is a dull little town of no great
interest in itself. It's just a jumping off
point for trips up 90 Mile Beach to Cape
Reinga. Buses leave every morning on this
trip; see the section on 90 Mile Beach.

Information

There should be a new Information Office
on Commerce St.

Far North Regional Museum

To most people Kaitaia is merely a staging
point for the trip up the 90 Mile Beach to
Cape Reinga, but the Far North Regional
Museum houses an interesting collection
including a giant moa skeleton, various
bits and pieces from shipwrecks and the
Northwood Collection – hundreds of
photographs taken around 1900 by a
professional photographer. The 1759 de
Surville anchor is one of the museum's
prize pieces. It's open from 10 am to 5 pm
on weekdays, 1 to 5 pm on weekends and
admission is \$1.10 (children 25c). From
Christmas to the end of February there are
extended evening hours.

New Zealand Walkway

The Kaitaia section of the New Zealand Walkway, also known as the Kiwanis Bush Walk, makes a good day trip and has excellent views. Originally planned as a road, the track has a gentle gradient along its nine km, for which you should allow five hours. To get to it head south from Kaitaia on State Highway 1 for three km, then turn right into Larmer Rd and follow it to the end at the Kiwanis Club Bush Camp Hut where you can overnight if you've made prior arrangements.

The track finishes at Veza Rd, off Diggers Valley Rd, which can be an awkward place to get out of as there is no transport and it is quite a long way from the main road. Back the way you came is one option or you could try your luck hitching. Keen bushwalkers can get permission from the farmer on Diggers Valley Rd to cross the few km to Takahue Valley where the Mangamuka Gorge Walkway is a good full day's tramp to State Highway 1.

Places to Stay

Hostels The *Kaitaia Youth Hostel* (tel 1080) is very central at 160 Commerce St (the main drag). It sleeps 39 and since there are plenty of twin rooms and family rooms you've got a pretty good chance of getting a room to yourself. Nightly costs are $11.

Camping & Cabins *Dyer's Motor Camp* (tel 39) is at 69 South Rd, at the southern end of town, and has camp sites for $6 per person. There are also tourist flats at $40 for two and motel units at $38/50.

The *Pine Tree Lodge Motor Camp* is 18 km west on the coast at Ahipara while the *90 Mile Beach Holiday Park* is 18 km north on the Cape Reinga road.

Hotels & Motels Kaitaia has a number of hotels including the old *Kaitaia Hotel* (tel 406 & 446) on Commerce St. This venerable hotel has rooms at $36/48 with attached bathroom. There are also a surprising number of motels, presumably in part because the town is so popular as a 90 Mile Beach jumping-off point. See the Dyer's Camp note above or try one of the places along the road into town on the Bay of Islands side. The *North Highway Motel* (tel 1101) at 118 North Rd has rooms at $41/52. The *Motel Capri* (tel 202) at 3-5 North Rd is similarly priced.

Places to Eat

Kaitaia is not a great place for eating out but *Steve's Snapper Bar* at 123 Commerce St is pretty good. It's across the road and a

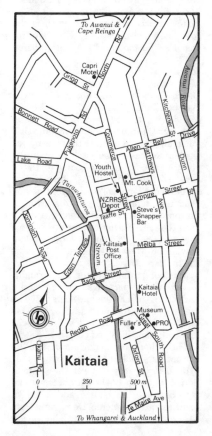

To Awanui & Cape Reinga

Capri Motel

Grigg St

North Rd

Bonnett Road

Puke noto Rd

Commerce

Kitchener St

Ananui River

Allen St

Bell St

Matthews St

Dunn Drive

Lake Road

Youth Hostel

Mt. Cook

Street

Taraui aturua

NZRRS Depot

Empire Ave

Street

Taaffe St

Steve's Snapper Bar

Dominion Road

Eden Terrace

Stream

Kaitaia Post Office

Melba Street

Bank Street

Kaitaia Hotel

Museum

Redan Road

Fuller's

PRO

South Road

Okahu Rd

Kaitaia

Oxford St

0   250   500 m

Te Maire Ave

To Whangarei & Auckland

little down from the YHA and although it's essentially a takeaway place you can eat your 'takeaways' there. Across the road there's the *Kurry Kai* which is definitely takeaway only. There are several other cafes.

Otherwise try the *Beachcomber* or the *Kaitaia Hotel* where the bar looks like it was time-warped from the '50s and the restaurant from an even earlier era. Main courses are around $11 to $14 but the service is so slow you'll probably give it away and look somewhere else before they even get a menu to you.

Getting There & Away

Air Air New Zealand have daily flights between Auckland and Kaitaia, the fare is $116.

Road NZRRS have services between Auckland and Kaitaia both directly via Whangarei or round the coast via the Bay of Islands. You can also go via Kaikohe and down the west side of the peninsula through the Waipoua Forest to Dargaville. The fare from Auckland is $47 and by the direct route it takes about 7½ hours.

Getting Around

Haines Haulage provides airport transport for $2 per person.

90 MILE BEACH

The tip of Northland – ending in Cape Reinga – is known as 90 mile beach. When they metricate it to 90 km beach the name will be a lot more accurate as it's a good bit short of 90 miles! Trips up the beach are very popular. The buses travel up the beach and down the road, or vice versa, depending on the tides.

The bus trips start from various other centres as well as Kaitaia including from the Bay of Islands. The major advantage in setting out from Kaitaia is that you're that much closer to Cape Reinga. Going from the Bay of Islands you've got a couple of hours extra travel at each end of the day to contend with so if you're going through

Kaitaia anyway you might as well head north from there. The bus from the Bay of Islands passes through Taipa, where Kupe is said to have made his first New Zealand landfall around 900 AD.

If you want to spend longer in the Cape Reinga-90 Mile Beach area than the one-day bus trip allows, a network of tracks has been opened up connecting the various beaches, and there are a couple of campsites with road access. The New Zealand Walkway continues down the 90 Mile Beach but you'll need to be well prepared as there are no huts and although it may not be as long as 90 miles it certainly seems like it to walk! The main attraction of the far north is the coastline which is scattered with beautiful beaches – far too many to mention here.

Tours

Mt Cook and Fullers both operate 90 Mile Beach Tours from Kaitaia and from the Bay of Islands. See the Bay of Islands section for details of tours from there. Although the tour operators proclaim that you really should go up to the cape by bus there's no reason you can't do it under your own steam. Even hitching up to the cape is not too difficult. Of course driving up the beach is not going to do your car any good and rent-a-car operators strongly disapprove – stick to the roads. A catch with the tours is that they're strictly one way and one day. You can't ride up and stay to camp or walk back without paying the full fare.

Mt Cook have two tours. The straight-forward one departs Kaitaia at 9.30 am and returns at 4.30 pm and costs $31. The longer Fun Bus tour leaves at 8.30 am, gets back at 5.30 pm, includes a barbecue lunch on the beach and costs $36.

The Fullers tour departs from Kaitaia at 9 am, gets back at 4.30 pm and costs $31 ($15.50 for children). Over the summer period they stop at a beach where you can get a barbecue lunch for an additional $8, or bring your own picnic. Departures from Mangonui, Coopers Beach, Cable Bay or

Taipa cost an additional $3. If you're not going on a barbecue lunch trip take food with you, the places where the buses stop are crowded and the food not that special.

Fullers also have a Seaspray trip which takes you along the beach, over a rocky headland and on through the old kauri gumfields in a six-wheel drive, 40-seat 'overgrown dune buggy'. This trip runs from Kaitaia around Ahipara and Reef Point at the southern end of 90 Mile Beach. The trip operates from 10 am to 2 pm and costs $27 (children $13.50). It operates daily most of the year but in June and July only on Tuesday, Thursday and Saturday.

Fullers (tel 724) and Mt Cook (tel 575) both have offices on Commerce St in Kaitaia.

Places to Stay

If you do plan to stay on the cape there are several campsites in the Cape Reinga area, one at *Spirits Bay* – this is a sacred area. There's a site at *Spirits Bay*, which has water and limited toilet facilities, and another at *Tapotupotu Bay*, which has toilets, showers and basic kitchen facilities. Spirits Bay is an area sacred to the Maoris as a place where the spirits depart from the dead by leaping off the cliffs and plunging into the sea. Both bays are infested with mosquitoes, so come prepared with coils and insect repellent.

There's another campsite at *Rarawa Beach*, three km north of Ngataki – water and toilet facilities only. No prior bookings can be made and fires are only allowed in the fireplaces provided. Pukenui, also known as Houhora, has the *Pukenui Motor Camp* (tel Houhora 803) with camping sites and on-site vans. There's also the *Pukenui Lodge Motel & Hostel* (tel Houhora 837) with hostel accommodation from $10. The campsite is opposite Wangener's Museum, claimed to be the largest privately owned museum in New Zealand.

DOUBTLESS BAY

From Kaitaia to the Bay of Islands it is 115 km via State Highway 10 through Mangonui. This route heads north a few km to Awanui, then down the east coast. In Doubtless Bay you pass the beach resorts of Taipa, Cable Bay and Cooper's Beach, arriving at Mangonui, an attractive but rather touristy place. On the wharf there is a saltwater aquarium. There is also a nice old hotel, a travel information centre and boats are available for hire. Tours up 90 Mile Beach also depart from Mangonui and this could be a better jumping-off point than Kaitaia since the town is rather more interesting.

Places to Stay

The *Old Oak* (tel 60-665) in Mangonui is an 1861 house with hostel accommodation from $10. It's a pleasant lodge with only two beds in most rooms. Mangonui also has a hotel, several motels and campsites.

WHANGAROA

The main road to the Bay of Islands passes close to Whangaroa, where in 1809 the ship *Boyd* was attacked and burnt by Maoris, who killed all the crew and passengers except a woman, two children and a young cabin boy. Whangaroa is six km off the main road and is a popular big game fishing centre. The outer harbour is surrounded by high, rugged cliffs and curious hills. The domed summit of St Pauls, above the town to the south, offers fine views.

Cruises, Fishing & Walks

Fishing trips and harbour cruises with Whangaroa Harbour Cruises on the *MV Friendship* (twice daily in summer, $20) are available. Much of the harbour is completely unspoilt since there is no road access to it. You can book boats through the Marlin Hotel or the Boyd Gallery. In the holiday season a special lunch cruise goes to the famous *Kingfish Lodge*, a licensed fishing lodge accessible only by boat.

On the north side of the harbour an old track from Totara North to Taupo Bay has been opened up – five hours return at a sedate pace.

Places to Stay

Hostels *Sunseeker Lodge* (tel Kaeo 183S) is a YHA associate hostel. It costs $11 per night and there are also some motel units at about $48 for a double. It's about a half km beyond the wharf. At Totara North the *Historic Gumstore Hostel* (tel 75-703) dates from 1890 and has hostel accommodation from $10. You can rent dinghies here.

Camping & Cabins The *Whangaroa Motor Camp* (tel Kaeo 36) costs $6 a night to camp and has cabins for $14 for one, $20 for two. The camp is about 2.5 km before the wharf.

Hotels & Motels There are several average-priced motels at around $50 for two, the small *Motel Whangaroa* is a bit cheaper. Right by the wharf the *Marlin Hotel* (tel Kaeo 131) has rooms at $28/40 for singles/doubles.

Places to Eat

You can get regular pub meals at $12.50 plus lunch and breakfast at the *Marlin*.

Bay of Islands

The Bay of Islands was the site of New Zealand's first permanent European settlement and today it has become one of the country's major tourist attractions. The two routes north through Kaitaia and Whangarei, together with the direct route east from the Hokianga, all meet at the Bay of Islands.

Orientation

The townships around the Bay of Islands are all on the mainland, there are no island resorts. To the north is Kerikeri –'so nice they named it twice', claim the tourist brochures. Paihia, the main centre on the bay, is virtually continuous with Waitangi. A little south again is Opua from where a car ferry shuttles across the Waikare Inlet to take you to Russell. You can also reach Russell from Paihia by road but it's a long and roundabout route.

PAIHIA & WAITANGI

The main town in the area, Paihia, was settled by Europeans as a mission station in 1823 when the first raupo hut was built for the Reverend Henry Williams. Paihia still has a pretty setting but the missionary zeal has been replaced with an equally fervent grab-the-tourists-and-show-em-a-good-time attitude and as a result positively reverberates with the sound of the cash registers. Nevertheless it's basically an accommodation, eating and tours centre and a good starting point to see the rest of the Bay of Islands.

Adjoining Paihia to the north is Waitangi, site of the historic signing of the 6 February 1840 treaty between the Maoris and the representatives of Queen Victoria's government. Since this is where modern New Zealand history commenced, Waitangi is a particularly interesting place to be on New Zealand Day, 6 February.

Information

Most of the information places are conveniently grouped together in the Maritime Building right by the wharf in Paihia. Here you'll find the helpful PR office together with the Mt Cook and Fullers counters so you can find out what's going on, organise accommodation and book cruises all in one go. The offices are generally open 7.30 am to 5 pm every day.

Cruises

The Bay of Islands is a very popular holiday area, so there's quite a bit to see and do although it's the bay itself which is the main attraction. Nearly 150 islands

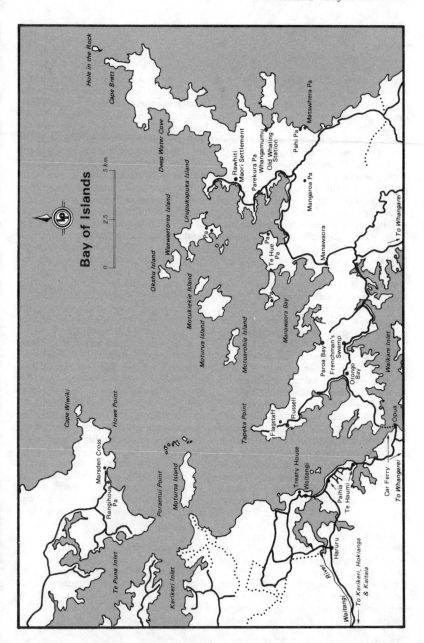

Bay of Islands

0   2.5   5 km

dot the waters of the bay – it's aptly named.

The best way to introduce yourself to the area is to spend the money and take a cruise. Fullers and Mt Cook both operate very popular regular cruises and they're supplemented by a host of other cruises from smaller operators including two of the hostels.

Best known of the cruises is Fullers' 'cream trip' which has had quite a history. Back in 1920 Captain Lane started a boat service around the bay, picking up dairy products from the many farms. As more roads were built and the small dairy farms closed the cruise became less and less of a working trip and more of a tourist one. The trip takes about five hours and passes a number of historical sites including Captain Cook's landing spot of 1789 and Otehei Bay where western writer Zane Grey went big game fishing. Other cruises follow a roughly similar pattern.

Weather permitting the cruises may go through the 'hole in the rock' off Cape Brett and stop at a deserted island bay for lunch. If you're not planning to bring your own lunch make sure you order it in advance. The cruises go past Te Hue where the French navigator Marion du Fresne was killed by Maoris in 1769.

The Fullers 'cream trip' takes from 10 am to 3.15 pm daily and costs $31 (children $15.50). At the same price they also have a 9 am to 12 noon Cape Brett trip and a similar trip from 12.30 to 4 pm. Mt Cook's Tiger Lily cruises cost $30 for the 9.30 am to 12.30 pm cruise and $35 for the 1 to 5 pm cruise. Lunch is included on the latter cruise, it's extra on the Fullers cruises.

Other options include a Fullers 'subsea' trip in a tourist submarine, this costs $15 plus $12 to get to the submarine in the first place. Mt Cook operate a night time disco cruise from 8.30 pm to 12 midnight for $20. Bring plenty of money for drinks and food as well. There are all sorts of smaller cruise operators, fishing trips, boat charter operators and so on in the Bay of Islands.

The hostels here generally fix up cheaper trips.

Walks, Boats & Other Activities

There are a variety of good short and long walks around the Bay of Islands and on the islands themselves. The park information centre in Russell has lots of walk information. You could start with the two-minute stroll to the top of the headland at the south end of Paihia or take the mangrove walk near the *Tui* or the coastal walk from Paihia to Opua.

There are small boats for hire at both ends of the Paihia beach. At the Waitangi end 12-foot catamarans cost $17 an hour, 14 footers are $22 an hour. Or you can hire powerboats for $30 an hour or $100 for four hours – plus fuel. Sportskis, those noisy motorcycle-on-water creations, cost $20 for 20 minutes. Or more mundanely you can paddle yourself around on an aquabike at $8 for half an hour. Half an hour on one of those things is about all the average human can stand. Smith's Camp also have small dinghies to hire.

At the more serious end of the boating scale there are a number of yacht charter operators on the bay. Of course you have to be able to prove you can handle a boat competently but assuming you can then Rainbow Yacht Charters (tel Paihia 27-821) and Freedom Yacht Charters (tel Russell 781) are the people to talk to. Yachts are available from around seven metres up

Moving from above the water to under it Paihia Dive Hire (tel 27-551) on Williams Rd has scuba gear to rent to qualified users. Full equipment and two tanks cost $50 a day. Or back on dry land you can hire horses to ride in the area.

Cape Reinga Trips

If you've read the 90 Mile Beach section and the info on the Cape Reinga trips you will know why it's easier to make the trip from Kaitaia rather than the Bay of Islands. If you do go from the Bay of Islands, the trips cost $42 (children $21), with Fullers.

Waitangi Treaty House

The Treaty House in Waitangi has special significance as the starting point for the European history of New Zealand. Built in 1832 as the home of British Resident, James Busby, eight years later it was the setting for the signing of the historic Treaty of Waitangi. It was here that many Maori chiefs accepted British 'sovereignty' and 'protection'. The house, with its beautiful sweep of lawn running down to the bay, is preserved as a memorial and museum. Admission is $3.50 (children free) and it's open from 9 am to 5 pm daily.

You can also see the Maori Whare Runanga (meeting house) completed in 1940 to mark the centenary of the treaty. The carvings represent the major Maori tribes. Down by the cove is a huge Maori war canoe (it could carry 150 people!) also built for the centenary. Beyond the Treaty House a road climbs Mt Bledisloe, from where there are commanding views of the area.

The Tui

Beached beside the bridge over the Waitangi River is the barque *Tui*, an old sailing ship, imaginatively fitted out as a museum of shipwrecks. Admission is $3 (children $1.50), open 9 am to 5.30 pm daily and extended hours during holiday periods. Recorded sea chants, creaking timbers and swaying lights add to the eerie mood as you look at the collection of bits and pieces diver Kelly Tarlton dragged up from wrecks around the coast.

A hundred metres from the *Tui*, in Te Kamara Avenue, is a mini-golf course.

Haruru Falls

A few km upstream from the *Tui* are the very attractive Haruru Falls which are also accessible via a walkway from Waitangi (2½ to three hours). The walkway has a unique boardwalk among the mangroves so you can explore them without getting your feet wet.

Places to Stay

The Public Relations Office will tell you what is available and make bookings. They're particularly good for bed & breakfast bookings which can be a worthwhile deal in Paihia, where accommodation is often quite expensive. *Abba Villa* (tel 28-066) on School Rd is one of the Paihia bed & breakfast places and has rooms at $35/55.

Hostels There is no YHA hostel in Paihia (it's out at Kerikeri) but there are a number of private hostels. The handiest and most popular of these is *Centabay Travellers' Hostel* (tel 27-466), on Selwyn Rd, just behind the shops and a short stroll from the Maritime Centre. It was a motel that's been converted to a hostel. There are four individual self-contained flats, each with two bunkrooms, a fully-equipped kitchen, and a lounge with TV. Cost per night is $12 and there are plans to add additional double or twin rooms. There are some old bicycles here, available free to guests. There's also a hostel boat which operates cruises at a cost of $27.50 per person.

Down at the Waitangi end of Paihia the *Mayfair Lodge* (tel 27-471) at 7 Puketona Rd costs $12. Again there are some twins and doubles at $26 and $25 respectively. Plus there are the usual kitchen and lounge facilities, a pool table and table tennis table, bicycles for hire and even a hot spa pool. The owner operates boat cruises on board the 43-foot *Mayfair*. A seven-hour trip including lunch will probably be about $40.

The new *Lodge Eleven* (tel 27-487) is on the corner of King and MacMurray Rds and a bed costs $12 a night. The bunkrooms sleep four to six and, as usual, there are kitchen and lounge facilities.

Camping & Cabins There are a number of campsites around Paihia and Waitangi, most of them are a few km back from the coast near the Haruru Falls. The *Panorama Motor Lodge & Caravan Park* (tel 27-525) faces the falls beside the river. There are camping facilities from $8 per person and also motel rooms.

Twin Pines Motor Camp (tel 27-322) on Puketona Rd at the falls has camping facilities from $7 per person plus cabins at $13 per person, on-site caravans at the same cost, tourist flats and also dormitory accommodation. Then there's the *Falls Caravan Park* (tel 27-816) also on Puketona Rd at the falls and *Puketona Park* at Puketona Junction. *Lily Pond Holiday Park* (tel 27-646) is three km from the falls (6½ km from Paihia) on Puketona Rd and has camping facilities at $8 per person plus cabins at $28 for two or on-site caravans at around $30 for two.

Smiths Holiday Camp (tel 27-678) is 2½ km south of Paihia towards Opua and right on the waterside. Camping here costs $8 per person, cabins are available from around $32, motel units from $55 to $75. It has its own beach and dinghies are available for hire.

Motels With about 40 motels to choose from you'd think the competition would keep prices down but they're as expensive as anywhere. Motels stand shoulder to shoulder along the waterfront but you'll be lucky to find anything as low as $50. Finding places asking over $100, on the other hand, is no trouble at all.

The motel units at *Smiths Holiday Camp* (see camping) used to be a bargain but now they're around the $60 mark as well and no longer so special. At other motels rates tend to vary with the room, the season, current demand and probably a few other secret factors as well. With so many to choose from the best advice is probably to ask the information centre, cruise the motel strip looking for a likely vacancy sign or simply take pot luck. On the plus side most of the Paihia motels offer pretty good standards and most have good kitchen facilities, which probably tells you something about the restaurants in Paihia! Some places where you might get a room for $50 to $60 include:

A1 Motel (or Aywon) (tel 27-684), Davis Crescent, nine units with kitchen facilities.

Aloha Motel (tel 27-540), Seaview Rd, 14 units with kitchen facilities, swimming pool.

Ala-Moana Motel (tel 27-745), Marsden Rd on the waterfront, eight units with kitchen facilities.

Ash Grove Motel (tel 27-934), Blackbridge Rd, Haruru Falls, seven rooms with kitchen facilities, swimming pool.

Hotels If you really want to spend up there's plenty of opportunity but the *THC Waitangi Hotel* (tel 27-411) with its fine setting, expensive but excellent restaurant, Zane Grey bar, heated pool and room prices from around $90 to $200 shouldn't be forgotten. Suites are much more!

Places to Eat
Paihia is not a great place for eating out, prices tend to be high, quality can be low.

Takeaways & Cheap Eats There are a number of takeaway places scattered around, particularly in the shopping centre across from the Maritime Centre and the post office. This centre includes a good bakery and *Waltons Carvery* while across Selwyn Rd there's *The Pantry*. The *Bon Appetit* cafe is open for lunch and from 6 to 8 pm from Monday to Friday. *Clinkers* (steaks and seafood) and *King Wah* (Chinese) share a pleasant outdoor eating area.

If you want to sit down and eat, the *Anchorage Grill* at the THC Waitangi Hotel is about the cheapest. It has the pub food standards, with chicken schnitzels, T-bones and the like at around $8 to $10. Trouble is it's distinctly second rate pub food accompanied by some of the limpest salads you'd never wish to see.

On Williams Rd the *Night Club Cafe* is behind the record and video store and has a variety of crepes served with salad for $7.50 to $9, plus a wide range of other snacks and desserts.

More Expensive & Much More Expensive There are quite a number of restaurants where the prices tend to be somewhat higher than the quality they have to offer. *Tides*, on William St, is one of the better places although main courses are often around the $20 mark. It's byo and the nearest place to bring it from is the bottle shop at the Waitangi Hotel. Other similarly pricey places include *La Scala* on Selwyn Rd and the *Bella Vista* (with its appalling flashing neon lights) on Marsden Rd. The *Courtyard Restaurant* in the Beach Haven Motel on Marsden Rd is said to be good.

Entertainment
Surprisingly Paihia has no pub at all – you have to go to the *Roadrunner*, in the middle of nowhere en route to Opua, or the *Waitangi Hotel*, which has a couple of cheap and plain public bars in a separate building. The Waitangi also has the expensive 'Zane Grey' bar in the hotel itself.

During the summer Fullers and Mt Cook have evening cruises with entertainment on their boats. Several times a week you can take a five-hour evening cruise on Fullers' *Supercat*.

Getting There & Away
Air Mt Cook Airlines flies to Kerikeri daily, but the closest that Air New Zealand can take you is Whangarei. The fun way to fly to the Bay of Islands, however, is with Sea Bee Air. Not only do you fly from Mechanics Bay, near the centre of Auckland, but you arrive right beside the Maritime Building in Paihia. The flight by amphibious aircraft costs $132.

Road NZRRS have regular buses from Auckland to the Bay of Islands. The trip takes about six hours and costs $34 to Paihia. They drop off (and collect for that matter) at the Opua ferry station, outside the Maritime Building in Paihia and at the Waitangi Hotel. To or from Kaitaia, jumping-off point for the 90 Mile Beach

Trip, takes around three hours at a fare of $18.

Clarks Northliner have an Auckland-Whangarei-Bay of Islands video bus service. It departs from the Downtown Airline Terminal in Auckland. There's a connecting service to Russell and also a direct Whangarei-Russell service four times a week.

Getting Around
A passenger ferry connects Paihia with Russell. It operates from Russell between 7 am and 6 pm (to 10 pm in summer); and from Paihia between 7.30 am and 6.30 pm. The fare is $3.50.

Or you can carry on a few km to Opua where the car ferry runs a continuous shuttle service during the day to Okiato Point, still some distance from Russell. This vehicle ferry operates from 6.30 am to 7 pm (9 pm in the summer, 10 pm on Fridays). The fare is $5.50 for car and driver, $1 for each additional passenger, $2 for a motorcycle and rider.

RUSSELL
A short ferry ride across the bay is Russell, originally a fortified Maori settlement which spread over the entire valley then known as Kororareka. Russell's early European history was turbulent. In 1830 it was the scene of the 'war of the girls' which occurred when two Maori girls from different tribes each thought they were the favourite of a whaling captain. This resulted in conflict between the tribes, which the Maori leader Titore, who was recognised as the chief of chiefs in the area, attempted to resolve by separating the two tribes and making the border at the base of the Tapeka Peninsula. A European settlement quickly sprang up in place of the abandoned Maori village.

In 1845 the government sent in soldiers and marines to garrison the town when the Maori leader, Hone Heke, threatened to chop down the flagstaff – symbol of Pakeha authority – for the fourth time. On 11 March 1845 the Maoris staged a

diversionary siege on Russell. It was a great tactical success with Chief Kawiti attacking from the south and another Maori war party attacking from Long Beach. While the troops rushed off to protect the township, Hone Heke felled the hated symbol of European authority on Maiki Hill for the final time. The Pakehas were forced to evacuate to ships lying at anchor off the settlement. The captain of *HMS Hazard* was wounded severely in the battle and the first lieutenant ordered the ships' cannons to be fired on the town, during the course of which most of the buildings were razed.

Russell today is a relaxed, peaceful and pretty little place. It's a marked contrast to the neon hustle of Paihia across the bay.

Information
The tourist information office is out at the end of the pier. There's a Fullers office at the land end of the pier. The excellent Bay of Island Park HQ information centre is next to the Captain Cook Museum and has displays about the area and lots of information on walks.

Captain Cook Memorial Museum
The Captain Cook Memorial Museum was built for the bi-centenary of his Bay of Islands visit in 1769. It houses the usual collection of early settlers' relics plus a fine 1:5 scale model of his barque *Endeavour* – a real working model. The museum is open 10 am to 4 pm weekdays and Sundays, admission is $1.50 (children 25c).

Pompallier House
Close by is Pompallier House, built for the French missionary Bishop Pompallier in 1841. It is one of the oldest houses in the country and has a small museum. Admission is $2.50 (children 50c) – open 10 am to 12.30 pm and 1.30 to 4.30 pm.

Other Attractions
You could carry on through the town and

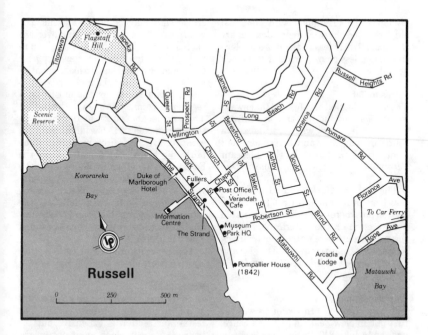

up the hill to look down on Russell from Maiki (Flagstaff) Hill – the fifth flagpole has stood for a lot longer than the first four. Mt Tikitikioure, behind the Orongo motor camp, also gives fine views and it's only a 15 minute climb to the top.

Christ Church in Russell is the oldest church in the country. Built in 1835, it is suitably scarred with musket and cannon ball holes.

Tours & Cruises
Russell Mini Tours cost $6 (children $3.50). The Fullers and Mt Cook cruises out of Paihia pick up passengers at Russell about 15 minutes after their Paihia departure. You can charter yachts out of Russell, just as from Paihia.

Places to Stay
Camping & Cabins The *Orongo Bay Motor Camp* (tel 37-704) is three km from Russell on the Opua car ferry road.

Nightly camping costs are $5.50 per person. They also have cabins from $25. The *Russell Holiday Park* (tel 37-826) on Longbeach Rd costs $6.50 per person for camping and has cabins from $32.

The *Jack 'n Jill Beach Camp* (tel 37-325) is 17.5 km east of Russell and has tent sites for $6 per person, an additional $2 for sites with power. There are also cabins from $26 plus motel flats from $50.

Close to the town *Arcadia Lodge* (tel 37-756) on Florence Avenue is a popular place with rooms from $30 to $50 for doubles. There's an extra charge to hire bedding.

Hotels & Motels Motels in Russell generally cost from $60 a night, particularly during the summer season when minimum rates often apply.

The fine old *Duke of Marlborough Hotel* (tel 37-829) on the waterfront would certainly be the place to stay if money was no object. This is a place with some real old-fashioned charm. Singles/doubles are $80/100, slightly less in the more modern (but much less characterful) motel block next door.

Places to Eat

There's a selection of cafes and takeaways in Russell including the waterfront *Strand* with sandwiches, snacks, a courtyard out back and a verandah out front. Back a block is the pleasant *Verandah Cafe* and the *Flower Day* cafe.

The *Duke of Marlborough* has typical pub food in its modern Reef Bar Bistro section plus more 'refined' dining in its old hotel section on the waterfront. Also on the waterfront there's the *Quarter Deck Restaurant* (main courses $13 to $14) and the expensive and licensed *Gables* (main courses up around $20).

Entertainment

The 'new' *Duke of Marlborough* was the first pub in New Zealand to get a licence, back on 14 July 1840. Its three predecessors all burnt down. There's a much more modern, and much less pleaseant, public bar a block behind it.

THE ISLANDS

Camping is permitted at *Urupukapuka Bay* on Urupukapuka Island but you must make your own transport arrangements and be completely self-sufficient. You need food, stove and fuel and a shovel for digging a toilet. Contact the Maritime Parks Board.

OPUA

As well as being the car ferry terminus, Opua is a busy, deep sea port from which primary produce – meat, wool and butter – is exported. The town was established as a coaling port in the 1870s when the railway line was constructed. Before the wharf was built, after WW I, the coal was transported out to ships on lighters (flat bottomed barges). Today, the occasional cruise ship may be seen alongside the wharf, as well as many local and overseas yachts during the summer. If you're trying to hitch a ride to far away places this could be a good spot to look. Yachties are often willing to take more crew.

The Opua Forest, for the most part a regenerating forest, is open to the public. There are lookouts up graded tracks from the access roads and a few large trees have escaped axe and fire, including some fairly big kauri. Get a leaflet from the Forest Service office in Waitangi or the Paihia Public Relations Office. A popular walk is Harrisons Bush Walk. Coming from Paihia you turn left at the intersection before the Opua Forest turn-off. Information on the walk can be found where it begins.

There's a historic steam train service which operates from Opua to Kawakawa.

Places to Eat

At Opua there's the *Ferryman's Restaurant & Bistro* by the car-ferry dock. The restaurant section is expensive but the bistro is a great place to sit out on the waterside and enjoy a light meal, sandwich or burger.

KERIKERI

Nestled into the north end of the bay, Kerikeri is an attractive town with a sleepy, laid-back atmosphere. The word Kerikeri means 'to dig' and it was right here, in 1820, that the first agricultural plough was introduced to New Zealand; and here that the Maoris grew large crops of kumaras (sweet potatoes) before the Pakeha arrived. Kerikeri was also the site of the first mission station to be opened in New Zealand. Early in November 1819 the Reverend John Butler arrived at the head of the Kerikeri inlet to set up the mission headquarters, now known as the Stone Store and completed in 1832.

Kerikeri is occasionally subject to flooding and in March 1981 it was inundated when the river burst its banks. It's the centre of a major fruit growing area

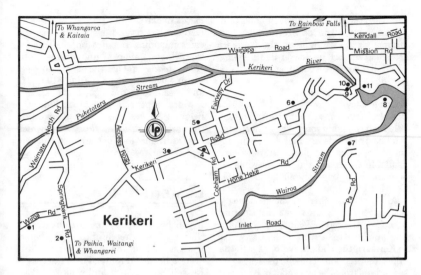

Kerikeri

1	Hideaway Lodge
2	The Orange Centre
3	Aranga Holiday Park
4	Post Office
5	Homestead Lodge & Restaurant
6	Youth Hostel
7	Pagoda Lodge Caravan Park
8	Kororipo Pa
9	Stone Store
10	Kemp House
11	Rewa's Maori Village

and many people come here to get fruit-picking work from late April through July. Kerikeri is a major centre for a wide variety of arts and crafts.

Kemp House
Near the Stone Store, Kemp House, a wooden building erected in 1822 by John Butler, is the oldest European structure in New Zealand. It's open from 10.30 am to 12.30 pm and 1.30 to 4.30 pm, admission is $2.50 (children 50c)

Stone Store & Museum
The Stone Store & Museum still operates as a general store selling refreshments and souvenirs. It has a museum upstairs – cost $1 (children 50c) – open from 9 am to 4.30 pm. Yachts moor in the inlet right in front of the Stone Store and there is a signposted historical walk starting up the hill behind the store.

Rewa's Maori Village
Just across the river from the Stone Store the Maori village is built on a site thought to have been occupied at one time by Chief Rewa. The various buildings there are an authentic reproduction of a pre-European Maori village with various habitations, kitchen buildings, storerooms and so on. Admission is 50c and there are fine views across the inlet.

Other Attractions
Fairy Pool, by a stream near the Youth Hostel, is a good spot to have a picnic. Only a couple of km or so from the Stone Store on Waipapa Rd is another good place for a picnic, the Rainbow Falls. Out on State Highway 10 you can see potters at work at 'The Potting Shed', or go on the Kerikeri Orchard Railway (more for the kids, maybe). At the Orange Centre you

can learn all about citrus fruits and tour the orchards in the 'orange-mobile'. The Orange Centre is right by the Kerikeri crossroad on SH 10. If you like messing about in boats hire a row boat and explore the inlet.

Places to Stay

Hostels The *Kerikeri Youth Hostel* (tel 79-391) is on the main road. The atmosphere is relaxed and it has a small shop, which is convenient for supplies. Bicycles are available for rent, and it's possible to organise boat trips through the hostel. Cost is $11 a night.

Alternatively there's the *Hideaway Lodge* (tel 79-773) on Wiroa Rd. Coming to or from the Bay of Islands on the main road you have to turn off the highway east to Kerikeri, the Hideaway Lodge is in the opposite direction. There's free transport twice daily from the bus depot in Kerikeri. Per person cost in a twin or double room is $10, there's a kitchen, laundry, swimming pool and also camping facilities. Many people stay here for the seasonal fruit picking.

Camping & Cabins There are several campsites at Kerikeri. The *Pagoda Lodge Caravan Park* (tel 78-617), is on Pa Rd at the inlet near the Stone Store, and nightly costs are $7 per person. They have free dinghies and canoes that you can use to explore the inlet.

Aranga Holiday Park (tel 79-326) is on Kerikeri Rd beside the Puketotara River only a few minutes walk from town. Camping costs $8 per person and there are also cabins from $32. It's a well equipped and beautifully situated site.

Motels Although most of the motels are similarly priced to elsewhere in the Bay of Islands there are a couple of cheaper alternatives. The *Citrus Motel* (tel 78-919) on Mission Rd has rooms from $40/50. The *Merriethought Motel* (tel 78-295) at 134 Kerikeri Rd is slightly more expensive.

Places to Eat

Kerikeri has several fast food places and cafes including *Goodies Cafe* with good sandwiches, snacks and cakes. The *Homestead Hotel* has the usual pub-meal menu with main courses from $10 to $14 and is said to be quite good.

More expensive places include the licensed *Spokes* and, out of Kerikeri on the Paihia road, *Jane's Restaurant* which has traditional food of the steak, chicken, seafood variety.

Eastern Route

If you head directly south from Russell there's a long stretch of dirt road before you get back on the main road, but it is quite a beautiful route. There's access to Russell State Forest and walkway along this route. You can camp at Papakauri Rd or Punaruku Rd or at Whangaruru North Head. It's also possible to walk out to Cape Brett lighthouse and stay there, but you must get permission and book accommodation with the ranger at the Park HQ in Russell.

The main road south to Whangarei leads out to State Highway 1 at Kawakawa, known to most people as the place where the railway line runs down the middle of the main street. Just south of Kawakawa, a km off the main road, are the Waiomio Caves which are open 9 am to 4 pm. Like Waitomo they have glowworms, but they're not as impressive. You can return from the caves via a hill walking track or through the cave.

WHANGAREI

Population 43,000

Back on the main road you soon reach Whangarei, the major town of Northland and a haven for yachties. Boats from all over the world are moored in Town Basin, an attractive area right on the edge of the town centre.

Information

The Information Office (tel 81-079) is in the glossy Forum North civic centre on Cafler Avenue. They have lots of information and the staff are helpful and friendly. There's a small information kiosk on the Auckland side of town. The AA has an office near the Mall.

Clock Museum

If you're interested in time and timepieces don't miss one of Whangarei's claims to fame, the Clapham Clock Museum in Central Park Rose Gardens. It has an awesome variety of clocks - big, small, musical, mechanical or just plain weird, and all ticking away furiously. The museum custodian will show you round and demonstrate various oddities. Check the great collection of Disney clocks. Hours are 10 am to 4 pm on weekdays, 10.15 am to 3 pm on weekends and holidays, admission $2, children 65c.

Whangarei Falls

The nearby Whangarei Falls are rated one of the most photogenic in New Zealand. Adjacent to the Ngunguru Rd, the falls may be reached by catching a Tikipunga bus and walking the last bit (but there's no bus on Sundays). There are three natural swimming pools in the river.

Other Attractions

There are two scenic reserves handy to the centre of town, situated on the hills on either side of the valley. Coronation Scenic Reserve, on the west, has a lookout, an old pa site, Maori pits and an old gold mine, as well as lots of bush - access from Kauika Rd. On the east side is the Parahaki Scenic Reserve. There is a road to the summit of Parahaki, turning off Riverside Drive (the road towards Onerahi and the airport). Three tracks lead down from the summit, two finishing at Mair Park and one at Dundas Rd.

There's an Art Gallery at Forum North and historic Reyburn House is also an art gallery. Ten minutes up from Dundas Rd

are some falls. Doing a round trip from the bottom is a good idea, but avoid going up Drummond Track as it is quite steep.

Other Whangarei attractions include the 1885 Clarke Homestead. Scuba diving is possible at Poor Knights.

Tours

You can take tours of Whangarei ($20 for a 3½ hour bus tour) or take bus or plane tours which connect with tours further north at the Bay of Islands or 90 Mile Beach.

Places to Stay

Hostels The *Whangarei Youth Hostel* (tel 488-954) is across the river at 52 Punga Grove Avenue. It has 20 beds and costs $11 per night.

Langstrath (tel Mangakahia 822) is a farm hostel about 35 km out of Whangarei towards Kaikohe. To get there from Whangarei take the road to Dargaville and at Maungatapere turn towards Kaikohe. Three km beyond Titoki turn into Fraser Rd and the farm is one km. Including all meals accommodation is about $28 but you must book ahead. You can get there on the daily (except Sundays) Newmans bus.

Camping & Cabins There are quite a few campsites with cabins in Whangarei or close to it. The *William Jones Camp* (tel 487-846), on Mair St (by Mair Park), 2.5 km from the centre, costs $5 per person to camp and has cabins from $9 per person. *Alpha Caravan Park* (tel 489-867), 34 Tarewa Rd is less than a km from the centre and has caravan sites from $12 for two people plus a variety of units from $33 for the cheaper ones to over $50 for the fancier self-contained units.

Otaika Caravan Park (tel 481-459) at 136 Otaika Rd is at the southern entrance to Whangarei. It has powered sites for $7 per person plus well-equipped tourist flats with TV, radio, in fact everything except bedding and towels, for $36/42 for singles/doubles.

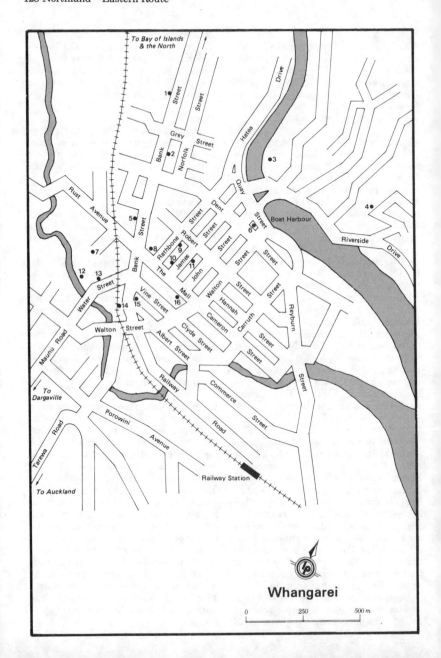

Whangarei

1	McDonald's
2	Pizza Hut
3	Swimming Pool
4	Youth Hostel
5	Plumes Restaurant
6	Reyburn House Art Gallery
7	Forum North Centre & Information Centre
8	Automobile Association
9	Post Office
10	Air New Zealand
11	Pizza Parlour
12	Clapham Clock Museum
13	Quo Vadis
14	City Bus & NZRRS Station
15	The Grand Establishment Hotel
16	Whangarei Hotel

Other sites include *Kamo Springs* (tel 51-208) at 55 Great North Rd, Kamo; *Tropicana Holiday Park* (tel 60-687) at Whangarei Heads Rd by the beach (10 km from Whangarei); and *Whangarei Falls Motor Camp* (tel 70-609) at the falls (five km from the centre). The falls camp also has a bunkroom which costs $10 a night and there's a swimming pool and all the usual camp facilities.

Hotels & Motels Whangarei has a surprisingly large number of hotels and motels. The *Grand Establishment* (tel 484-279) is right in the centre on the corner of Bank and Rose Sts. Rooms cost from around $32 to $50 for singles, $35 to $65 for doubles. The *Whangarei Hotel* (tel 483-379) on Cameron St has rooms from $37/50 for singles/doubles. Rooms with private facilities are more expensive.

Whangarei's motels generally cost from at least $50 for a single and $60 for a double. A couple of marginally cheaper ones to try are the *Kauri Lodge* (tel 483-526), 15 Lupton Avenue or the *Hibiscus Motel* (tel 488-312), 2 Deveron St.

Places to Eat

Fast Food & Snacks You can have a pleasant and economical lunch on a sunny day in Whangarei's Mall, there are even tables and chairs provided. The *Village Deli Lunchbar* or *Upper Crust*, both by the Rathbone St junction with the Mall, have good sandwiches.

Fast food fans can find a *McDonald's* and a *Pizza Hut*, both a km or so from the centre on the road north. Alternatives include the *Pizza Parlour* at 22 James St. Small pizzas are $4.50 to $8, big ones $10 to $16, medium ones in between.

Pub Food The *Forum Bistro* in the Forum North civic centre (see Information) does typical pub meals from 12 noon to 2 pm and 5 to 7 pm with main courses around $6 to $9. Also in the pub category there's the Carvery in the *Whangarei Hotel* on Cameron St. It does meals from Monday to Saturday from 12 noon to 2 pm and 5.30 to 8 pm. The Carvery is good value and they also have a family restaurant and bar where kids are especially catered for.

At 2 Bank St the *Grand Establishment* has the Ivory Room Restaurant which serves breakfast, lunch and dinner seven days a week. Sunday night it's a buffet-style smorgasbord. A couple of km north of the centre at Kamo there's a *Cobb & Co* restaurant at the Kamo Hotel, 567 Kamo Rd, with the same menu as all the other Cobb & Cos.

Restaurants *Quo Vadis*, at 24 Water St near the railway overbridge, has been going so long it's almost a piece of Whangarei history. It's open Wednesday to Monday and has a pretty standard menu from sausage and chips on up, main courses generally around $9.

Finally for a fancy night out Whangarei has several possibilities including *Plumes* at 63 Bank St and *Timothy's Myth* at 58 Vine St. Both are a bit pricey as is the *Forum Restaurant*, next to the Forum Bistro in that popular civic centre. The Forum is well thought of locally and has starters in the $6 to $10 bracket, main courses at $14 to $18. Avoid Whangarei on Sunday if you want to eat, nearly every place is closed that day!

Entertainment

The best music places are out of town. The *Tutukaka Hotel*, about 25 to 30 minutes north-east, really rocks on Friday and Saturday nights. The *Parua Bay Hotel*, south-east at Whangarei Heads, is also popular.

Closer in, there's entertainment at the *Onerahi Hotel* (buses go there) and the suburban *Tikipunga Tavern* on Derby Crescent.

The *Whangarei Hotel*, the *Settlers Motor Inn* and the *Kamo Hotel* also have music from time to time. Whangarei discos and nightclubs include *Oscar's Bar* on Vine St and the nearby *Pips*.

Getting There & Away

Air Air New Zealand has one or two flights daily between Auckland and Whangarei at a fare of $93. Air New Zealand can be found at Roseman & Warren Travel (tel 484-939) in the James St Arcade in Whangarei.

Road There are frequent NZRRS buses between Auckland and Whangarei, the trip takes 3½ hours and costs $24. It takes a further 2½ to 2¾ hours to Paihia in the Bay of Islands on the services that continue north. The fare is $12. Buses also continue to Kaitaia from Whangarei either via the Bay of Islands or via the direct road. The fare is $26.

Clarks Northliner have an Auckland-Whangarei-Bay of Islands service. At the Bay of Islands there are connections to Russell and four times a week there is also a direct Whangarei-Russell service. In Whangarei the bus operates from the Clarks Terminal (tel 483-206) at 3 Albert St. Newmans (tel 488-291) have an Auckland-Whangarei service as well.

Getting Around

Whangarei Bus Services provides transport between town and the airport, but only on weekdays. The adult fare is 80 cents.

AROUND WHANGAREI

Maunu

A few km west of Whangarei, on the Dargaville road, is Maunu. The main attraction is a settler's museum which is open Tuesday to Sunday from 10 am to 4 pm.

Whangarei Heads

There is magnificent scenery at Whangarei Heads, though it's hard to get to without a car. On the way is the Waikaraka Scenic Reserve on Mt Tiger, which has excellent views (turn off at Parua Bay). The coast is beautiful at Matapouri, Tutukaka and Ocean Beach.

There are great views from the top of the 419 metre high Mt Manaia, looking across the narrowest stretch of the heads to the oil refinery at Marsden Point. The trail to the top starts from the main road beneath the mountain (but it's easy to miss), and you climb up through forest. Close to the top there are cables to help you scale a steep rock. Two hours hard work will get you to the summit where there are incredible views of the sea, the mountains, the surrounding dairyland and, just as a contrast, the oil refinery.

Marsden Point

New Zealand's oil refinery is at Marsden Point, across the harbour from Whangarei Heads. If you're interested, there's an information centre you can visit to learn all about oil refining.

New Zealand Walkway

Continue past Maunu on the Dargaville road and 16 km south-west of Whangarei you reach the Maungatapere section of the NZ Walkway. A round trip takes 1½ hours through farmland and regenerated scrub with extensive views inland and out to sea. The track starts at the end of Pukeatau Rd, past which the infrequent bus on the Whangarei-Dargaville route goes. Hitching is probably easier.

Other Attractions

Heading south towards Brynderwyn and

Auckland the Otaika Valley Walkway is off to the right just beyond the town limits. After passing through Waipu from Whangarei it is nine km to Waipu Cove, a popular surfing beach. The main road turns inland from Waipu, climbing over the hills back to the Dargaville turn-off. Remember to look over your shoulder at the magnificent view of Whangarei Heads and the entire area. On the top of the hill is the entrance to Brynderwyn Hills Walkway (western section) and if you walk just a little way down the track you'll get great views – worth the time if you have it. This walkway eventually links up with the eastern section near Mangawhai Heads.

Whangarei

South of Auckland

Auckland to Hamilton

The trip to Hamilton by road from Auckland takes about two hours and there are a few points of interest along the way. If you're a steam train enthusiast and heading towards Hamilton on a Sunday or public holiday (except Christmas Day) then pause at the Glenbrook Vintage Railway where between 11 am and 4 pm you can take a 12-km steam train ride. Phone Patumahoe 669-361 on operating days only. From 26 December to 4 January the line operates every day. To get there follow the yellow signs after leaving the southern motorway at Drury, 31 km south of Auckland, and head for Waiuku. There is also a farm and deer park at Glenbrook.

Te Kauwhata, 67 km south of Auckland and just off the main road, is a good place for a bit of wine-tasting. From here the road follows New Zealand's longest river, the Waikato, all the way to Hamilton. After Huntly, a coal-mining town with a large power station, it enters Taupiri Gorge, a gap through the ranges. On your left, as you emerge from the gorge, is a Maori cemetery on the hillside.

If you're fit there is an excellent view from Taupiri Mountain and on the opposite side of the river the Hakarimata Track also gives good views. To walk the length of the track takes seven hours. Access to the north end is by crossing the river at Huntly, following the Ngaruawahia-Huntly West Rd to Parker Rd, off which the track leads. The south end meets the Ngaruawahia-Waingaro Rd just out of Ngaruawahia.

A shorter walk, and easier if you have no transport, is a three-hour return trek from Brownlee Avenue, Ngaruawahia to Hakarimata Trig (371 metres). The top part of this is fairly steep but the view is

rewarding. Tracks from each access point meet at the trig, or triangulation station, a point used as a basis for making maps. About 25 km east of Ngaruawahia, which is the main centre for the Waikato Maori people, are the popular Waingara Hot Springs. A few hundred metres off the main road, on River Rd, is Turangawaewae Marae.

Hamilton

Population 102,000
New Zealand's largest inland city and fifth largest overall, Hamilton is 129 km south of Auckland. The town is the centre of a rich farming area, the Waikato. The Waikato River was once Hamilton's only transport and communication link, but it was superseded by the railway 100 years ago and since then by roads. Frankton Junction is New Zealand's largest and busiest railway junction. Hamilton Station is on a branch line; the main line doesn't pass through the city centre.

History
White settlement of the region was initiated by the 4th Regiment of Waikato Militia, who were persuaded to enlist with promises of an acre (less than half a hectare) in town and another 50 acres in the country. The advance party led by Captain William Steele travelled up the Waikato River on a barge, drawn by a gunboat, and on 24 August 1864 went ashore at the deserted Maori village of Kirikirioa. The township built on that site was named after Captain John Hamilton, the popular commander of HMS *Esk*, who had been killed in battle at Gate Pa four months earlier on April 30.

Information
In the past few decades the city, which

looks new and glossy, has undergone spectacular population growth. The Waikato Visitor Information Centre is at 865 Victoria St, on the Auckland side of the centre. It's open from 9 am to 4.30 pm Monday to Friday, and 9 am to 12 noon on Saturday. The AA office is on Anglesea St.

You'll find most of the government offices you need in Victoria St. These include the Chief Post Office, the Department of Conservation, in the South British Building, and the agents for the Government Tourist Bureau.

Around the Town
Hamilton hasn't much to offer travellers; it's more a convenient overnight stop or a base for visiting the many attractions within day-tripping distance. Two relaxing spots right in Hamilton are Hamilton Lake and the various reserves along the Waikato River behind the main shopping centre.

The Waikato Museum combines the old Waikato Museum and the Waikato Art Gallery under one fancy new roof. The move to the new building on Grantham St near the river was made in 1987. Only a few doors away on Victoria St is the Hamilton Arts Centre Gallery with regular exhibitions by New Zealand artists.

Centennial Pool is in Minogue Park, Te Rapa and has indoor and outdoor pools, hydroslides and pleasant surroundings.

Hilldale Zoo Park
Hilldale Zoo Park is quite good, though really more fun for the kids. It has 40 different species of animals including deer, wallabies, opossums, pigs, pumas, jaguar, bison, camels, monkeys, llamas, raccoons and donkeys as well as reptiles, pheasants and various other kinds of birds. The zoo is eight km from the CPO, take Highway 23 westwards towards Raglan, turn right at Newcastle Rd and straight into Brymer Rd. Admission is $3 for adults, $1.50 for children, kids under

five free. Telephone 495-157 for additional information, open daily 9 am to 5 pm.

Temple View
People interested in comparative religious studies might want to take a trip to Temple View, eight km south-west of Hamilton, site of a Mormon Temple and college. The unworthy are not allowed inside but there is a visitor's centre, open from 9 am to 9 pm daily, where you can see pictures of the interior rooms; questions are answered and the reasons for building such a temple explained. There is a regular bus service from the city.

Farmworld
At Mystery Creek, 16 km south of Hamilton, there is the interesting Clydesdale Agricultural Museum or Farmworld. The museum's aim is to 'obtain, preserve and restore agricultural equipment and articles relating to New Zealand's pioneering and rural development and to breed, work and display the associated animals.' There are stage shows at 10.30 am and 2.30 pm and if you ever wanted to have a go at milking a cow this is your chance.

The museum is a km south-east of Hamilton Airport on Mystery Creek Rd. It's a little difficult to get to by public transport. Buses run by the airport turn-off but that still leaves you four km from Farmworld. It is open every day except Christmas, from 9 am to 5 pm, admission is $5 (children $2.50).

Cruises
River cruises on the Waikato River are a popular attraction from Hamilton. The cruises depart from Memorial Park, right across the river from the town centre. In season the *MV Spirit of Waikato* does 2¼ hour cruises twice daily for $12 (children $6) or there are one-hour Kingfisher cruises about five times daily for $6 (children $3).

Fanciest of the Waikato cruisers is the paddlewheel *MV Waipa Delta* which does

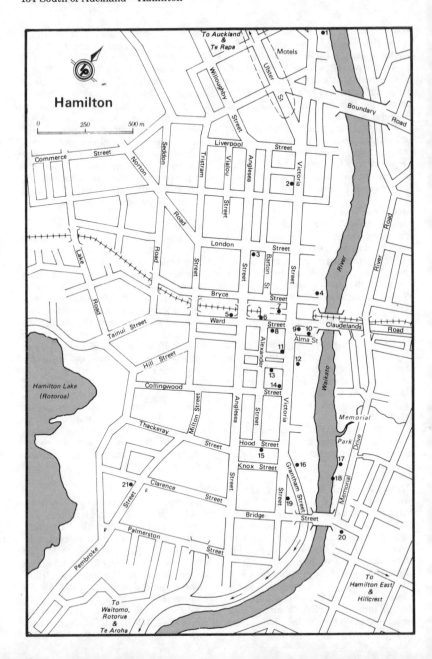

1	Youth Hostel
2	Waikato Visitors Information
3	Automobile Association
4	Governor's Tavern
5	NZRRS Travel Centre
6	French Bakery
7	Centreplace
8	Air New Zealand
9	McDonald's
10	Eldorado & No 8 Restaurants
11	Singapore Restaurant
12	CPO
13	Italian Pizza
14	Cobb & Co
15	Grand Central Guest House
16	Waikato Museum
17	SS Rangiriri
18	Cruiseboats
19	Riverview Private Hotel
20	Parklands Travel Hotel
21	YMCA & YWCA

morning cruises for $12 (children $6); lunchtime cruises (with lunch) from 12.30 to 2 pm for $27 (children $13.50); and dinner cruises (with dinner) from 7 to 10 pm for $55 (children $27.50).

Embedded in the riverbank walkway you can see the remains of the gunboat *SS Rangiriri* which played a part in the Maori Wars in 1864.

Places to Stay

Hostels The *Hamilton Youth Hostel* (tel 80-009) is at 1190 Victoria St, just north of the city centre on the river. Cost is $11 per night in the modern hostel and there are some family and twin rooms.

The *YWCA* (tel 82-218), takes both men and women casuals when they have room for $13.50 a night without meals, $17.60 including meals. There's a weekly rate of $88 but at weekends no meals are served – you can use the kitchenette then. It's on the corner of Pembroke and Clarence Sts, not far from the centre. The *YMCA* has no accommodation.

Camping & Cabins The *Municipal Camp* (tel 58-255) is on Ruakura Rd, Hamilton East and costs $8 a night for one or two

people on a tent site, $4.50 for each extra adult.

Camping at the *Hamilton East Tourist Court* (tel 66-220) in Cameron Rd, Hamilton East, costs $6.50 per person. They also have a variety of big and small cabins at a variety of prices ranging from $13 for one person and $29 for two. There are also self-contained flats (equipped apart from bedding) at $34 for two.

Guest Houses The wonderfully old fashioned *Grand Central* (tel 81-619) at 27 Hood St costs $30 per person for bed & breakfast. It is indeed quite central. Just round the corner and close to the new museum is the *Riverview* (tel 393-986) at 60 Victoria St with small and straightforward rooms at $23 per person including breakfast.

Just across the river at 24 Bridge St the *Parklands Travel Hotel* (tel 82-461) has bed & breakfast in its regular rooms at $30 per person. There are also motel-style rooms at $45/60 for singles/doubles.

Hotels Right in the centre on Victoria St the *Commercial Establishment* (tel 391-226) has rooms at $38 or with attached bathroom at $70.

Motels Hamilton has plenty of motels, particularly along Ulster St, the main road into the city from the Auckland side. In fact Hamilton has one of the biggest concentrations of motels in New Zealand. The Parklands Travel Hotel, mentioned under Guest Houses, is OK but some of the other moderately priced places include:

Abbotsford Court Motel (tel 390-661), 18 Abbotsford St, just off Ulster St, units have kitchen equipment, $55/64 for singles/doubles.
Bavaria Motel (tel 392-520), 203-207 Ulster St, from $46/58 for singles/doubles.
Classic Motel (tel 496-588), 451 Ulster St, swimming pool, from $44/58 for singles/doubles.
Motel Whitiora (tel 81-695), 157 Ulster St, swimming pool, from $48/57 for singles/doubles, some cheaper units.

Places to Eat

Snacks & Fast Food There are plenty of restaurants in Hamilton including a full complement of international fast-fooderies. At the Auckland end of Victoria St there's a *Pizza Hut* and a *Kentucky Fried*. Continue into town on that same road and you come to a large *McDonald's* right in the middle on the corner with Claudelands Rd. Continue out the other side and you'll find a much smaller *Wimpy Bar* – an example of the British attempt at the international burger market.

For a quick and cheap breakfast the modern new Centreplace shopping centre is a good place to go. On the mezzanine level there's the pleasant *Cafe Lonez* or try *Presto* for good sandwiches. Down below there's the takeaway only *Whole Food Cafe* (pies, samosas and the like) and a fruit shop. Just outside the centre at 68 Ward St there's a *French Bakery*. That selection should provide an economical breakfast or lunch but if you want more move over a block or two to the *Italian Pizza/Gelato Arlecchio* for pizza and gelati ice cream.

Pub Food Moving on to pub food there's a very popular *Cobb & Co* in the Commercial Establishment on the corner of Victoria and Collingwood Sts. It's open 7 am to 10 pm daily and has the usual Cobb & Co menu with main courses from around $8 to $12. Or there's the *Governor's Tavern* on Bryce St by the river. Other pub-food possibilities include the Jolly Roger at the *Chartwell Tavern* and the Bloody Steak out at the *Tavern Hillcrest* (see Entertainment).

Restaurants You can spend plenty of money in this category if you want but try the excellent *Eldorado* at 10 Alma St. They do good Mexican food with main courses at $10 to $16. They're also open for lunch when a $3 to $4 taco, enchilada or tostada with salad can make a pleasant lunch and an interesting escape from the usual New Zealand fare.

Right next door at number 8 you'll find the pleasant looking *No 8* which does Italian food with starters at $5, pastas at $11, main courses at $14. Right across Victoria St is the *Singapore Restaurant* on Garden Place. It's one of many Chinese restaurants in Hamilton but since the food features that spicy Malaysian flavour it's a good change from the usual Chinese dishes. *Uncle Sam's* on Ward St offers counter lunches from Tuesday to Friday, dinner from Tuesday to Saturday and a Sunday evening buffet. See Entertainment below as well.

Other possibilities include the *Left Bank Cafe* and *Friday's Restaurant & Bar* down Victoria St at the Hamilton Arts Centre Gallery. Or move right up market, break your fancy clothes out, grab the plastic money, phone 395-957 for a reservation and head for *Anderson's* at 104 London St. With main courses at $20-plus you'd better count on something up towards $100 for two by the time you've added a few drinks, starters, dessert and coffee.

Entertainment

Pubs The *Tavern Hillcrest*, corner of Clyde and York Sts, is one of the best music places in Hamilton – lots of uni students and live music most nights. Others to try include the *Eastside Tavern* and the *Chartwell Tavern*. The *Cobb & Co* in the Commercial Establishment on Victoria St has light entertainment from Wednesday through Sunday.

Nightclubs & Other As usual this category comes and goes but you can try *Shakes* at 30 Alexandra St or *Zaks* at Te Rapa. *Uncle Sam's* on Ward St just off Victoria St has a variety of weekend entertainment and a disco.

Cafe Lonez at Centreplace sometimes has entertainment. Try *Founders Theatre* for rock and other performances.

Getting There & Away

Air Air New Zealand have direct flights between Wellington and Hamilton

($142). Eagle Air have regular flights between Auckland and Hamilton with a fare of $76. They also fly between Hamilton and Gisborne, Napier, Nelson, New Plymouth, Palmerston North, Rotorua and Wanganui.

In Hamilton Air New Zealand's phone number is 399-800, Eagle Air is 389-500.

Road There are NZRRS, Mt Cook and Newmans buses through Hamilton. NZRRS (tel 81-979) are at Ward St where you will also find Newmans. Mt Cook operate from Dalgety Crown Travel at 630 Victoria St.

Services to and from Auckland are very frequent. The trip takes about 2½ hours at a fare of $17. Buses are also frequent to and from Rotorua and the trip takes just over two hours at a cost of $13. From Wellington there are about five buses daily, the 10-hour trip costs $57.

There are a number of local bus operators such as Buses Ltd and Hodgsons. There are regular services to Te Awamutu, Raglan, Te Aroha and Paeroa (for the Coromandel Peninsula). Any bus to Tauranga, Rotorua or Taupo passes by the Karapiro turn-off.

Hitching There's lots of traffic for hitching but getting out of Auckland can be a hassle as pedestrians are not allowed on the motorway – a law which is enforced. Hamilton itself can be a tricky place to hitch through with a pack. In Hamilton, State Highway 3 leads off towards Otorohanga, Waitomo and New Plymouth, while SH 1 continues towards Taupo and Wellington (take the road for Rotorua).

Rail There are daily passenger services between Hamilton and the main North Island centres from the railway station outside the city. The main rail line does not go via the branch station in the centre of town.

Getting Around
Airport Transport Weekdays and Sunday afternoons there is a bus from the City Mini Bus Terminal, opposite NZRRS, for Air New Zealand flights. Fare is $4 (children $2).

Local Transport Keep in mind that Hamilton's local bus service does not run on weekends. Mopeds (no motorcycle licence required) or motorcycles can be rented from Road & Sport (tel 394-445) at 56 Rostrevor St, Hamilton North.

AROUND HAMILTON
Raglan
The nearest beach is Raglan, 48 km west of Hamilton, a popular place in summer with both surf and sheltered beaches. Nine km south-west of Raglan, past the ocean beach, is the Bryant Memorial Scenic Reserve on Whaanga Rd. From here a track leads down to the beach. An easy bushwalk to the Bridal Veil Falls starts off the Kawhia road, 20 km south of Raglan.

Karapiro & Arapuni
Karapiro, one of a chain of hydro-electric power stations and dams on the Waikato River, is 28 km south-east of Hamilton, just off State Highway 1. You can arrange to see over the power house if you're interested. The road in passes over the dam, and the lake is popular for aquatic sports.

Further upstream is Arapuni, the first government-built hydro station on the river. It's 66 km from Hamilton via Highway 3 and Te Awamutu. (You then turn left at Kihikihi.) It is also accessible from Karapiro or Tirau on SH 1. The dam, built across the Arapuni Gorge, is worth seeing. Visitors are allowed access to most of the works.

Te Aroha
Te Aroha, 53 km north-east of Hamilton on Highway 26, is at the foot of the mountain (952 metres) of the same name. From the top you can see as far as Tongariro and Mt Egmont so it is well worth the climb. There are also hot mineral baths and other bushwalks.

If you want to spend longer there is a *Youth Hostel* (tel 48-739) at Te Aroha in Miro St. It's a pleasant small hostel (just 12 beds) and costs $9 a night.

Maungakawa Scenic Reserve

Turn off SH 1 at Cambridge, 20 km east of Hamilton, and you'll reach Maungakawa Scenic Reserve, a regenerating forest with some exotic timber species. There's a fairly easy short bushwalk here. From the east side of Mt Maungakawa a track suitable for experienced trampers ascends from Tapui Rd; it takes half a day there and back.

Other Attractions

Kawhia is another west coast port, with harbour and ocean beach, 98 km south-west of Hamilton via Temple View or 57 km west of Otorohanga. There is a driveable track over the dunes. At low tide you can find the Puia Hot Springs in the sands. The coast is reputed to be dangerous for swimming. A round trip can be made to include Bridal Veil Falls and Raglan. Between the Raglan and Kawhia roads is Pirongia Forest Park with its focal point Pirongia Mountain. For information on tramping contact the New Zealand Forest Service. Pirongia Mountain is 961 metres and is usually climbed from Corcoran Rd on the Hamilton side. The township of Pirongia is 32 km from Hamilton.

Te Awamutu

Mid-way between Hamilton and Otorohanga on SH 3, Te Awamutu is noted for its rose gardens. November through April is the time to see the roses at their best.

On the third Sunday of each month, from 10 am to 4 pm, the Waikato Railway Museum has the biggest static display of large steam locomotives in New Zealand. At other times railway enthusiasts can ring Te Awamutu 7950 or 4887 to enquire about the possibility of other opening times.

Otorohanga

Otorohanga is just under 60 km south of Hamilton and only a short distance before the Waitomo turn-off. Principally a dairying district, it is in the upper Waipa basin and the first township you come to at the northern end of The King Country, the stronghold of the Maori chiefs who held out against the whites longer than anywhere else in New Zealand. This area was forbidden to the Pakehas by Maori law until the 1880s.

Most people go through Otorohanga or stay overnight there on the way to the Waitomo Caves (see Waitomo) – 16 km away. It is the nearest town to the caves and a convenient base to visit them, Kawhia and Pirongia (see Around Hamilton).

History

The earliest Europeans to settle in Otorohanga were timber millers; the first of them arriving in 1890. From 1884, when the Pakehas were allowed into the district, until 1955 The King Country was 'dry'. This condition was apparently imposed by Maori chiefs when they agreed to the Europeans building the Main Trunk Railway Line through their country, opening it up even more to the outside world. Needless to say there are now numerous hotels everywhere, so you won't go thirsty.

Information

The Otorohanga Public Relations Office has lots of information on things to do and see, places to stay, etc. It's on Manipoto Rd, the main road through town, right by the town hall and is open seven days a week. They do the accommodation arrangements for YHA members but if there's no one there phone numbers to call are posted on the door.

Kiwi House

The Otorohanga Kiwi House is the town's

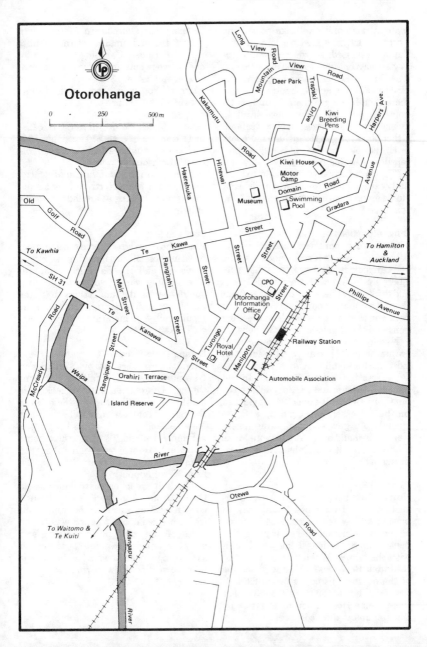

Otorohanga

0 · 250 500 m

main attraction, it's well sign-posted and worth a visit. In a kiwi house night and day are reversed, so you can watch the kiwis in daytime under artificial moonlight. The centre also has various other native birds on display including some keas who more than live up to their reputation for being inquisitive. The huge walk-in aviary here is the largest in New Zealand. Other birds you can see include morepork owls, various hawks and wekas plus reptiles including tuataras.

The centre is open from 10 am to 5 pm daily except June through August when it closes an hour earlier. Admission is $4.50 (children $1).

Other Attractions

There is a deer park near the kiwi centre. It's basically a high-fenced paddock where you can look at the deer from a distance. There's also an enclosure with peacocks and ducks, etc. There's no entry charge but there is a donation box. Between the deer park and the kiwi house are kiwi breeding pens and the Rhododendron Gardens.

Nearby there is an Olympic-sized swimming pool open daily in the summer. Cost is $1.50 (children 75c). Also in the same area is the Otorohanga Historical Society Museum (tel 7374 or 8462) in the old Court House. It's open Sunday, 2 to 4 pm but at other times call up and the friendly old guy who maintains it will wander over and open it up for you. Make a donation, it's a nice little local museum.

Places to Stay

Hostels Otorohanga has no youth hostel as such, but YHA members can stay in private houses registered as *Associated Home Hostels*. Each place has two to five beds available to hostellers, who live in with the family. When you arrive, go to the Public Relations Office and phone one of the numbers listed, or phone 8951. If that fails then try 8908, 8239 or 8375. For these Home Hostels you must arrive by 8.30 pm and nightly cost is $9.

Camping The *Otorohanga Motor Camp* (tel 8214) is on Domain Drive adjacent to the Kiwi House. Camping costs $10 for one or two people and there are some on-site caravans at $15 plus the camp charges. You may hear kiwis calling between 7 and 9 pm.

Hotels & Motels The *Royal Hotel* (tel 8129) in Te Kanawa St costs $30 for singles, $44 to $50 for doubles. Meals are available there at reasonable prices.

There's also the *Otorohanga Motel* (tel 8289), on the Main North Rd. For a room there you're looking at around $50 to $66 a night.

Places to Eat

Along the main street there are a number of eating possibilities including a Chinese takeaway and the *La Kiwi* restaurant where you're warned you won't get in if you're wearing 'denium'. I think that's the nuclear version of denim. You'll find the regular pub-food menu at the *Royal Hotel* on Te Kanawa St.

Getting There & Away

Otorohanga is serviced by NZRRS and Newmans buses. The railway line runs through Otorohanga but this looks like another station likely to get the chop in the general contraction of rail services in New Zealand.

From Auckland it's about three hours by bus at a fare of about $25. It's about $10 from Hamilton, $19 from Rotorua, $28 from New Plymouth.

The daily excursion bus to the Waitomo Caves from Auckland goes through Otorohanga at about 12.50 pm, from where it costs about $4 each way to the caves. A taxi could be competitive and more convenient for a group of people. You can arrange for it to wait for the hour it takes to visit the glow-worm cave.

Waitomo

The limestone caves at Waitomo are famous for their glow-worms which you see as you float through the caves in a boat. Waitomo is about 200 km south of Auckland, 75 km from Hamilton, 16 km from Otorohanga and 183 km north of New Plymouth. The Waitomo Caves are the feature attraction but the whole region is riddled with caves and strange limestone formations. There are also some good bushwalks so it's an interesting area to visit for a day or two.

In English Waitomo means water (wai) hole (tomo) – the river flows into a hole.

Rivers going underground, great springs emerging from the ground, independent hollows and basins instead of connecting valleys, deep potholes and vast caves, isolated tower-like hills .... these are some of the distinctive features of karst, the name given to the kinds of country that owe their special characteristics to the unusual degree of solubility of their component rocks in natural waters.

from *Karst* by J N Jennings (1971, Australian National University Press, Canberra)

Information

The Waitomo Caves are eight km off the main highway. There's an information centre (tel Te Kuiti 87-640) at the Caves Museum, a km or so before the caves themselves. There's lots of caving information available at the Tomo Group Hut – see the Hostel section under Places to Stay.

The Caves

There are three caves in Waitomo and you can visit them independently or get a combined ticket for all three. Tickets are sold at the Glow-worm Cave & Grotto, best known of the three, at the Caves Facility Building and at the Waitomo Hotel. Entry to just the glow-worm cave costs $9 (children $4.50). The other two cost $7 each or the combined ticket is $15.

Tours of the glow-worm cave leave at least every hour between 9 am and 4.30 pm, plus at 5.30 pm from November to February. There may be additional tours at the height of the summer season.

The caves are just caves with the usual assortment of stalactites and stalagmites until you board a boat and swing off onto the river. As your eyes grow accustomed to the dark you'll see a Milky Way of little lights surrounding you – these are the glow-worms. They are a type of beetle, the female and larvae of which have luminescent organs which produce a soft, greenish light. The larval grubs weave webs with threads hanging from them to catch unwary insects attracted by their 'lights'. The adult of the species, which resembles a large mosquito, is often caught and eaten by the larval glow-worm – its own offspring. Even if it avoids that fate, the adult insect does not live very long because it does not have a mouth; perhaps as a punishment for eating its own parents before its metamorphosis.

The other two caves are four km further up the road from the glow-worm cave but quite close to each other. Ruakuri Cave tours last 40 minutes and take place at 10 am, 1 and 3 pm most of the year; at 10 am, 12 noon, 2 and 4 pm in the Christmas through January peak period. The Ruakuri Caves also have a river, a hidden waterfall and more glow-worms. Aranui tours also last 40 minutes and take place at 11 am and 2 pm most of the year and 11 am, 1 and 3 pm during the peak period.

Cave Museum

If you want to find out more about caves visit the excellent Waitomo Caves Speleological Museum. You'll learn about how caves are formed, the fauna and flora that live in caves, the history of caves and cave exploration. Exhibits include a working cave model, extinct birds and animals, and a cave crawl for the adventurous. It's open daily, admission is $2.50 (children free) and the museum is open 8.30 am to 5 pm daily. You can get a combined ticket to the museum and the glow-worm cave for $10 (children $4.50). The museum has a 10-minute audio-visual presentation about caves.

Bushwalks
The information centre has leaflets on various walks in the area. There's a 45 minute return walk to Opapaka Pa, a short forest walk near the glow-worm cave and a variety of other short walks in the area.

Other Attractions
There are now several other tourist attractions on the road in from the main highway to the caves. The Ohaki Maori Village is a replica of a pre-European Maori pa and visitors can also see demonstrations and displays of Maori weaving. The village is open 10 am to 5 pm daily and admission is $3.50 (children $1).

Merrowvale Model Village is a miniature New Zealand village complete with farm, pine forest and railway line. It's open 9 am to 5 pm daily and admission is $3 (children $1.20). At Roselands Farm you can see sheep shearing, sheepdog handling or enjoy a barbecue but you are asked to make reservations in advance by phoning Te Kuiti 87-611.

Places to Stay
Hostels For the hostel go straight on by the centre and about a km past the caves to the Waitomo Caves – Tomo Group Hut. Accommodation here is hostel style and there's room for 30 people in bunks (lots more with a squeeze). Cost is $5 per person and the hut officer lives next door – phone Te Kuiti 87442 or write RD4, Te Kuiti. If you're walking up to the hostel from the centre grab (well buy) some goods at the store or you'll have a km-plus walk back from the hostel.

If you're lucky you may be invited on a caving trip by club members, to one of the many non-tourist caves in the area. It's not recommended that you go off caving alone in the area, unless you are an experienced caver. Caves can be dangerous, some have networks spanning several km and people have been lost underground.

Camping & Cabins The Waitomo Caves Camp & Caravan Park (tel Te Kuiti 87-639) charges $5 per adult, $2.50 per child. There are also cabins for two to four people in two-tier bunks. They cost $16 or $18 for two and $3.50 for each extra person. It's directly opposite the general store – you can book into the camp there. Ask about special rates for hitch-hikers.

Hotels & Motels The THC Waitomo Hotel (tel Te Kuiti 88-227 & 8) has rooms at $40/48 or $80/90 for singles/doubles. Most THC hotels are definitely at the top end of expensive but here the cheaper rooms are very reasonably priced. On the other hand if it's not expensive enough there are suites at over $200! It is very convenient for the caves and the restaurant is virtually the only place at Waitomo where you can sit down to eat.

Other accommodation is some distance from the caves. The Hangatiki Motel (tel Otorohanga 8882) is at the turn-off and rooms cost from $50 to $65 a night. Near the turn-off the Waitomo Country Lodge (tel Otorohanga 8109) costs $45/55 for singles/doubles. The Waitomo Colonial Motel (tel Otorohanga 8289) is eight km north from the turn-off, so it's 16 km from the caves. Rooms there are $50 to $65.

Places to Eat
The THC Waitomo Hotel has the only real restaurant at Waitomo but it's expensive and there's no cheaper pub-style food available. You can get snacks at the general store or, a few km back towards SH 3, at the model village. Supplies are available at the Waitomo general store but the choice is wider at nearby towns like Otorohanga so if you're planning to camp or stay at the hostel and prepare your own food it's worth bringing supplies with you.

Getting There & Away

The caves are several km off the main road. Getting a ride from the main road is not always easy although there's a bus which runs out to the main road (SH 3) passing by the Tomo Hut at about 8.40 am each morning. The same bus returns via Waitomo and may continue to Te Anga and some of the way towards Kawhia before heading off for Taharoa. Iron sands are being mined at Taharoa but it is not really worth the trip out.

There are NZRRS day trip services to the caves from Auckland and Rotorua. You only get an hour at the caves so it's a real rush trip. Fares from Auckland are about $24, from Rotorua about $20. There are also return excursion fares offered including admission to the cave. Since the Auckland and the Rotorua excursion buses arrive and depart from the caves at the same time if you are not planning to stay in Waitomo you can arrive from Auckland and leave an hour later for Rotorua. Or vice versa.

Other bus services that go along SH 3 will drop you off at the Hangatiki junction (Waitomo turn-off) from where it is eight km to the caves. Hitching along that stretch of road is usually pretty good.

Getting Around

If you don't have your own transport you can walk from the glow-worm caves to Aranui and Ruakuri, hitch or even take a taxi.

AROUND WAITOMO

Heading west from Waitomo the road follows a rewarding and scenic route. A sign, 26 km from Waitomo, marks a track (20 minutes one-way) to the Mangapohue Natural Bridge, a natural limestone formation. The impressive 36-metre-high Marakopa Falls are 32 km from Waitomo. You can view them from the road or walk to the foot of them.

To travel to Marakopa, which is situated on the west coast 48 km from Waitomo, you turn left at Te Anga.

The whole Te Anga-Marakopa area is also riddled with caves. The tar seal ends just out of Marakopa, but it is possible to continue, on a difficult but scenic road, for 60 km south until you meet the main Hamilton-New Plymouth road at Awakino. From Te Anga you can also get to Kawhia (see Hamilton section), 53 km away on a sealed country road.

South from Waitomo on the road to Wanganui at Ohura the District Museum has an interesting King Country exhibit.

New Plymouth

Population 46,000

New Plymouth is about midway between Auckland (373 km) and Wellington (357 km) on the west coast. From Waitomo it's 177 km on the main road, which has two scenic, but winding sections: the Awakino Gorge and Mt Messenger. Between these two parts of the road is a strip of exposed west coast beaches, broken every now and again by river estuaries.

History

Back in the 1820s the Taranaki Maoris took off to the Cook Strait region in droves to avoid a threatened attack by the Waikato tribes but it was not until 1832 that the Waikatos attacked and subdued the remaining Ngati-awa, except for Okuku Pa (New Plymouth) where the whalers had joined in the battle. So when the first European settlers arrived in the district in 1841 the coastlands of Taranaki were almost deserted. Initially it seemed there would be no opposition to land claims, so the New Zealand Company was able to buy extensive tracts from the Ngati-awa who had stayed.

When the others returned after years of exile and slavery they objected strongly to the sale of their land. Their claims were substantially upheld when Governor Fitzroy ruled that the New Zealand Company was only allowed to retain just

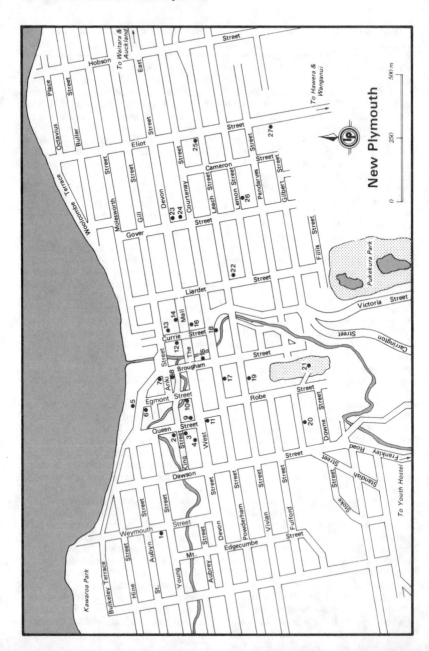

New Plymouth

1	Aotea Private Hotel
2	Newmans Coachlines
3	Govett Brewster Art Gallery
4	NZRRS Station
5	Tasman Hotel
6	City Council Bus Depot
7	Richmond Cottage
8	Library & Museum
9	White Hart Hotel
10	Black Olive Restaurant
11	Clocktower
12	Bellisimo Restaurant
13	CPO
14	Duke of Devon Tavern
15	L'Escargot Restaurant
16	Air New Zealand
17	Automobile Association
18	Egmont Steam Flour Mill
19	St Mary's Church
20	YWCA Hostel
21	Observatory
22	Information Office
23	Cobb & Co
24	The Steps Restaurant
25	McDonald's
26	Inverness Guest House
27	Central Motel

over 10 square km – around New Plymouth – of the 250 it had claimed. The Crown slowly acquired more land from the Maoris, but the Maoris became increasingly reluctant to sell and the European settlers increasingly greedy for the fertile land around Waitara.

The latter's determination finally forced the government to abandon its policy of negotiation and in 1860 war broke out. For 10 years the Maoris kept the military engaged in guerrilla warfare. During this time the settlers had moved in on Waitara and were in control there, but the Maoris came and went as they pleased throughout the rest of the province. The Taranaki chiefs had not signed the Treaty of Waitangi, nor did they recognise the sovereignty of the queen, and consequently were treated as rebels. By 1870 over 500 hectares of their land was confiscated and much of the remainder was acquired through extremely dubious transactions.

Today, the district of Taranaki is undergoing an economic boom, due to the discovery of natural gas and oil at Kapuni in 1959 and more recently at Maui off the coast of South Taranaki.

Information
Devon St (East and West) is the main street, the central section is a mall. The Public Relations Office (tel 86-086) in Liardet St is very helpful and has lots of printed information. It's open Monday to Friday from 8.30 am to 5 pm and they have a city map.

Around the Town
New Plymouth has numerous historic buildings, described in a leaflet available from the Public Relations Office. The 1853 Richmond Cottage on Brougham St is open Monday, Wednesday and Friday from 2 to 4 pm and on weekends from 1 to 4 pm, admission $1 (children 20c). Unlike most early cottages, which were timber, Richmond Cottage was built in stone.

On Vivian St, St Mary's Church dates from 1846 and its graveyard has numerous interesting gravestones of early settlers and of soldiers who died during the Taranaki Wars with local Maori tribes. Impressed by their bravery the British also buried several of the Maori chiefs here. Brooklands Park was once the land around an important early settler's home; the fireplace and chimney is all that remains of the house after the Maoris burnt it down.

On Brooklands Park Drive The Gables is an early hospital built in the late 1840s. In 1854 a notable Maori chief died here from wounds received in a tribal feud. The hospital consequently became tapu, which saved it during the Taranaki wars as its forbidden status prevented the Maoris from burning it down! On Devon Rd at the eastern end of town the Fitzroy Pole was erected by Maoris in 1844 to mark the point beyond which Governor Fitzroy had forbidden settlers to acquire land. The carving on the bottom of the pole depicts a sorrowful Pakeha topped by a cheerfully triumphant Maori.

Wandering around the city check the curious transparent clocktower on the corner of Devon St West and Queen St. It was erected in 1985 to replace the old post office tower which was demolished 16 years earlier. There is an observatory and planetarium on Marsland Hill off Robe St, open, depending on the weather, Tuesdays from 7.30 pm or during daylight saving at 8 pm. There's also a carillon here and fine views over the central city and St Mary's Church which is directly below.

Parks

New Plymouth is an attractive city renowned for its superb parks. A visit to Pukekura Park, just 10 minutes' walk from the city centre, is a must. There are numerous magnificent display houses which are open from 9 am to 12 noon and 1 to 4.30 pm during the week, 2 to 4.30 pm on Sundays, closed Saturdays.

Adjoining it is Brooklands Park, another beauty spot, and between the two, the Bowl of Brooklands, an outdoor soundshell in a beautiful bush and lake setting. In Tisch Avenue on the waterfront is Kawaroa Park, which has a pool, squash and tennis courts. The pool is only open in summer.

Power Station

At the western end of town is the New Plymouth Power Station, designed to run on oil or gas. The original intention was to burn coal, but the discovery of natural gas in Taranaki changed this. The station is dominated by its towering 200-metre high chimney. Conducted tours of the power station are made on Wednesday mornings at 10 am and Sunday afternoons at 2 pm. You can get to it on the port bus service on Wednesday but there is no bus on Sunday.

Above the power station is Paritutu, a steep hill with a magnificent view from the top. The name means 'rising precipice' and it's worth the tiring but quick scramble to the summit. Not only do you look down on the station but out over the town and the rocky islets rising just offshore.

Arts & Crafts Centre

Just below the Paritutu car park is the Rangimarie Arts & Craft Centre (tel 512-880) in Centennial Drive. It features a display of traditional Maori arts and crafts and you can watch the members working on their carving and weaving, etc. It's open from 10 am to 5 pm from 24 December to 10 January, and from 8 am to 4.30 pm the rest of the year.

Museums & Galleries

The Taranaki Museum (tel 89-583) on the corner of Brougham and King Sts, has a collection of Maori artefacts and an early colonists' exhibition. It's open Tuesday to Friday 10.30 am to 4.30 pm, weekends 1 to 5 pm.

The Govett-Brewster Art Gallery, a modern gallery in Queen St, is open weekdays 10.30 am to 5 pm, weekends 1 to 5 pm. It has a good reputation for its adventurous shows.

Beaches & Walks

For beaches head to Fitzroy and East End Beach at, you guessed it, the east end of town. Fitzroy is a surf beach. There's also good surf at Oakura, out of New Plymouth to the west. The information office has a leaflet on walks around New Plymouth including coastal walks and walks through local reserves and parks.

Tours & Flights

The local bus and tour company Neuman's (tel 84-622) at 23A Devon Mall have a variety of local sightseeing tours. They range from an $18 city tour to a day tour around Mt Egmont for $55. Pioneer Tours (tel 86-086) also have tours of the Taranaki area and they can be booked through the information office. Tui Safaris (tel Stratford 7652) in Stratford have a round Mt Egmont day tour.

Rafting and canoeing on the Waiwhakaiho and the Waitara Rivers is another local activity. Check with Waiawaka Rafting/Canoeing (tel 68-311) at Inglewood. Air New Plymouth (tel 70-500) offer flights around the area including a flight over the snow-capped summit of Mt Egmont – superb if the weather's clear.

Places to Stay

Hostels The *New Plymouth Youth Hostel* (tel 35-720) is at 12 Clawton St. It's fairly new, well-equipped and comfortable, but a bit of a walk (1.5 km) from the centre. Get there on a Frankleigh Park bus (Nos 4 or 10) which departs from Liardet St in the centre of town. There's room for 18 and nightly charges are $11.

The *YWCA* (tel 86-014) at 15 Bulteel St has accommodation for women and men when it's not full. It costs $6.50 a night or $35 a week. Cooking facilities and pots, plates, etc are available for use. The Y is cheap and central but phone to see if it has any vacancies first. There is no sign outside it either, so don't think you're at the wrong place when you arrive. The local YMCA has no hostel.

Camping & Cabins There are several camps within easy reach of the centre. The *Belt Rd Camp* (tel 80-228) at 2 Belt Rd is only 1½ km out – sites are $11 a night for two, a couple of dollars more with power.

In Fitzroy, about 3½ km from the centre, the *Fitzroy Camp* (tel 82-870) is beside the beach down Beach St and has camping sites at $11 for two and again a couple of dollars more with power. There are on-site caravans for $24 for two. The *Marantha Holiday Park* (tel 82-566) at 29 Princes St, Fitzroy, has camping sites for $6.50 per person. There are also cabins for about $32 and motel flats for $50 (both prices are per double).

Aaron Court Caravan Park (tel 34-012) is three km from the centre. Camping here is $10 for two, $3 more with power. Cabins are available for $28, tourist flats $48.

Guest Houses At the *Aotea Private Hotel* (tel 82-438), on the corner of Young and Weymouth Sts, singles/doubles are $25/35. Meals are also available – breakfast for $5 or dinner for $10.

Inverness Guest House (tel 80-404) at 48 Lemon St is $30/45 for room only, an additional $5 per person for breakfast. Both are only about five minutes' walk from town.

Hotels There are several hotels of the old school around central New Plymouth, with simple rooms without attached bathrooms. Try the *White Hart* (tel 75-442) on the corner of Queen and Devon Sts. Rooms here are $27.50/40 for singles/doubles. Others include the slightly more expensive *Royal* (tel 80-892) on Brougham St which also has more expensive rooms at $42/50 with private facilities. The newer *Tasman Hotel* (tel 86-129) on St Aubyn St is in the same price range. This modern-looking six-storey hotel looks like it should be pricier but it was actually built just before attached bathrooms became the norm and this oversight has forced them to price their rooms at a lower level.

On the corner of Devon and Gover Sts the *State Establishment* (tel 85-373) has rooms with attached bathroom from $55/60 and it has a Cobb & Co restaurant.

Motels New Plymouth has plenty of motels, starting around the $50 per night price range. Good value places include:

Aaron Court Motel (tel 34-012), 57 Junction Rd on the main south highway, three km from town. It's part of the Aaron Court Caravan Park and has a swimming pool.
Aloha Motel (tel 86-109), corner St Aubyn & Weymouth Sts, spa pool.
Central Motel (tel 86-444), 86 Eliot St, small but fairly convenient.
Oakura Beach Motel (tel Oakura 680), Wairau Rd, Oakura, 13 km out of town but a bit cheaper than the ones in town.
Timandra Unity Motel (tel 86-006), 31 Timandra St off Coronation Avenue, within walking distance of town.

Home Hosting New Plymouth has a home hosting scheme which provides local guides to show you the sights and a host panel who welcome you into their homes. Contact the Public Relations Office.

Places to Eat

Fast Food & Takeaways New Zealand is a small country and New Plymouth is a small town but the *McDonald's* on the corner of Leach and Eliot Sts is absolutely huge. This is a monster McDonald's. There's also a *Pizza Hut*, away from the centre on the corner of Sackville St and Clemow Rd in Fitzroy.

That apart there's not a great selection of quick snack places although *The Steps* at 37 Gover St is a pleasant place for a sandwich or snack. Health food is the specialty and it has a pleasant outdoor patio area. Up in Pukekura Park the *Park Kiosk* has good snacks.

Pub Food Once again there's a *Cobb & Co*, this one is in the State Establishment on the corner of Devon St East and Gover St. The usual Cobb & Co menu, the usual excellent hours of 7 am to 10 pm daily. Breakfast costs $3.75 (tea and toast), $6.50 (continental) or $7.50 (with eggs). Also on Devon St East, on the Liardet St/Gover St block, is the *Duke of Devon* with quite fancy bars, an extensive list of what patrons may not wear and pretty reasonable pub food at $9 to $12 from 6 to 9 pm.

Other places with pub food include the *Tasman Hotel* on St Aubyn St and the *Westown Motor Hotel* out on Maratahu St. Old-style hotels in the centre with restaurants include the *Royal Hotel* on Brougham St which was doing a special $3 breakfast and the old-fashioned *White Hart* on the corner of Devon St West and Queen St.

Restaurants *Black Olive*, on Egmont St near the Devon St West corner, has a curious menu half made up of absolutely straightforward pub-style dishes (schnitzel,

steak, ham steak, etc) and the other half of Indonesian dishes. Main courses are $11 to $14 and it's byo, as is *Bellissimo* upstairs at 38 Currie St near the Devon St East corner. Here the flavour is Italian with pasta dishes around $11, main courses at $14 to $16 and desserts at $4. It's a surprisingly large and locally popular restaurant. Their blackboard, at the top of the stairs, announces *Bonjorno* – which is obviously Italo-Australian for 'good journalist'.

There's a whole host of Chinese places including the *Tong*, at 39 Devon St West, which also does takeaways. *Gareth's*, at 182 Devon St West, is good but more pricey. And right up towards the New Plymouth stratosphere, price-wise, is *L'Escargot* at 37-39 Brougham St, which is *the* licensed place for a fancy night out.

Entertainment

Head to the *Westown Motor Hotel* in Maratahu St, where there's a band, lots of people and a moderate cover charge on weekends. It's fairly near the youth hostel. Just out of town, the *Bell Block Hotel* also has bands at weekends. Other central hotels with entertainment include the *Tasman* and the *White Hart*.

Getting There & Away

Air Air New Zealand has direct flights from Auckland for $113 and Wellington for $117. It's about an hour's flight in either direction. Air New Zealand (tel 87-674) is at 12-14 Devon St East.

Several small airlines also operate to and from New Plymouth. Eagle Air (tel 71-292) connect New Plymouth directly with Hamilton and Palmerston North with onward connections to Auckland, Rotorua, Nelson, Wanganui and other centres. Nationwide Aviation (tel 70-721) also fly between New Plymouth and Auckland.

Road The NZRRS depot (tel 87-729) is in Devon St West. The Newmans office is nearby at 32 Queen St (tel 75-482). Don't confuse the national Newmans who operate long distance services with the local Neuman's who do sightseeing tours.

Newmans connect New Plymouth with Auckland via Hamilton and with Wellington via Wanganui and Palmerston North with connections from Palmerston North to Napier. The Auckland and Wellington services go up to four times daily. NZRRS also operate on these routes but while their Wellington service is even more frequent they don't have so many buses on the Auckland-New Plymouth run. To or from Auckland or Wellington takes about 6½ to 7½ hours, to or from Wanganui about three hours. The fares are Auckland $49, Wanganui $19, Wellington $39.

Hitching Hitching is reasonable from the south (Wanganui and Wellington). From Auckland, you might have to wait a long time around Awakino Gorge. As ever, it's all a matter of luck.

Getting Around
Airport Transport Withatruck (tel 511-777 or 512-328 after hours) operate an airport bus service Sunday to Friday. The fare is $4 (children $1.50).

Local Transport There are local buses in New Plymouth but they don't run particularly often and not at all on Sundays. There is no public transport to the Egmont National Park.

Taranaki

MT EGMONT – TARANAKI
The coastal city of New Plymouth is backed by the cone of 2518 metre high Mt Egmont – a dormant volcano looking remarkably like Japan's Mt Fuji or the Philippines' Mayon. The mountain was supremely sacred to the Maoris, both as a burial site for chiefs and as a hideout in times of danger. According to legend,

Taranaki – Mt Egmont's Maori name – was once a part of the other group of volcanoes at Tongariro. He was forced to leave rather hurriedly when Tongariro caught him with Pihanga – Tongariro's lover. Pihanga is the volcano near Lake Taupo. So angry was Tongariro at this betrayal that he blew his top (as only volcanoes can when upset) and Taranaki took off for the coast. Heading south he gouged out the Wanganui River on the way and then strolled across to his current location where he's remained ever since.

Geologically, Mt Egmont is the youngest of a series of three large volcanoes on one fault line: the others being Kaitake and Pouakai. Egmont last erupted 350 years ago, but it is regarded as being dormant rather than extinct. An interesting feature of Egmont is the small subsidiary cone on the flank of the main cone and two km south of the main crater, called Fantham Peak (1962 metres). The top 1400 metres of Egmont is covered in lava flows and there are a few that descend to 800 metres.

The Maoris did not settle the area between Taranaki and Pihanga very heavily, perhaps because they feared the lovers might be reunited with dire consequences. Most of the Maori settlements in this district were clustered along the coast between Mokau and Patea, and concentrated around Urenui and Waitara in particular.

The mountain is a popular winter skiing centre and in the summer you can climb it in a day. The Taranaki Alpine Club, the Public Relations Office or the Lands & Survey Department can provide more information and will be able to put you in touch with a licensed guide. Egmont should not be climbed by the inexperienced without a guide. In good conditions, Egmont can be a reasonably easy mountain to climb, but it has precipitous bluffs, steep icy slopes, and is subject to very rapid weather changes. It has claimed over 30 lives. Don't be put off, but don't be deceived.

The Egmont National Park was created in 1900 and is the second oldest national park in New Zealand. There are quite a few points of access to the park but three roads lead almost right up to where the heavy bush ends. The closest to New Plymouth is Egmont Rd, turning off SH 3 and leading to North Egmont (24 km). Even a trip to the end of the road is worth it for the view, but there are numerous long and short tracks and bushwalks as well. The Visitors' Centre at North Egmont has lots of interesting displays on the park and the mountain, an audio visual and a cafe.

The other two roads lead from the east (to Stratford Mountain House) and south-east (to Dawson Falls). These also have many worthwhile tracks and bushwalks. From Stratford Mountain House the road continues to the Plateau and from here a 1½ km walk takes you to the main ski field on Egmont (not much by Ruapehu standards, the main skiing area of North Island).

There's a saying in Taranaki – Taranaki also refers to the region surrounding Egmont – that if you can see Egmont it's going to rain, and if you can't see Egmont it's already raining! There is some truth in this, but Egmont really is a spectacular sight on a clear day, even if it does try to cover itself in protective cloud. There's an on-going dispute at present about whether the mountain's official name should be Mt Egmont or if it should revert to its pre-Pakeha name of Taranaki.

Information
If you plan to tramp in Egmont National Park get a map from the Lands & Survey Department, Atkinson Building, Devon St West in New Plymouth. There is a National Park Interpretation Centre open daily at Dawson Falls, a Visitors' Centre at North Egmont also open daily, and a ranger station on the road to Stratford Mountain House. Around the mountain there are also Information Centres in Opunake, Stratford, Kaponga, Eltham and Hawera.

Wilderness Treks (tel Hawera 87-400) at Hawera organise guided bushwalks and mountain climbs including summit climbs on Mt Egmont.

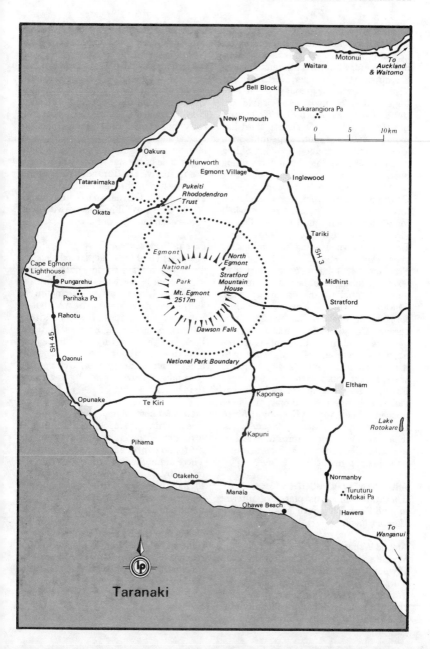

Taranaki

Places to Stay

At North Egmont the *Camphouse* (tel Egmont Village 710) provides accommodation for 32 at $7 (children $3) each. Enquiries to the Manager, North Egmont Visitors' Centre, Egmont Rd, RD 6, Inglewood – bookings are advisable. On the east side the *Mountain House* (tel Stratford 6100) at RD 21, Stratford has rooms at $60/70 or motel-type units with kitchen facilities at about $5 more. Skiing and climbing equipment and tramping boots may be hired here.

At Dawson Falls by the park Information Centre there is trampers accommodation for 38 in *Konini Lodge* (tel Stratford 5457) for $7 per person (children $3). There's also The Cottage which sleeps eight. Bring your own sleeping bag and eating gear. *Dawson Falls Tourist Lodge* (tel Stratford 5457) has accommodation at $60/85 including breakfast. A courtesy car will meet public transport in Stratford. The address is RD 29, Kaponga. Bookings for Konini Lodge and The Cottage also go through Dawson Falls Tourist Lodge.

There are also tramping huts scattered about the mountain. Most of them cost $7 a night, some are only $2. If you intend tramping get a map for these and consult a Park Ranger, as some tracks have been closed and other planned ones may have opened. The *North Egmont Chalet*, marked on many maps, no longer exists. There are also motor camps in Stratford and Eltham, handy to the east and southeast side of Egmont.

AROUND NEW PLYMOUTH

There are numerous places of interest around New Plymouth apart from Mt Egmont itself.

Around Waitara

Waitara is only 13 km from New Plymouth on the road towards Auckland. Turn off SH 3 at Brixton, just before Waitara, and seven km south is the site of the Pukarangiora Pa. It's beautifully sited on a high cliff by the Waitara River but historically this was a particularly bloody site. Just beyond Waitara on SH 3 east of New Plymouth is a conversion plant which converts natural gas to petrol.

Hurworth

On Carrington Rd, about eight km out of New Plymouth en route to Pukeiti, this early homestead dates from 1856. Its builder and first occupant, Harry Atkinson, later became premier of New Zealand four times. The house was the only one at this site to survive the Taranaki Wars and is today owned by the New Zealand Historic Places Trust. Further on towards Pukeiti is the Pouakai Wildlife Reserve with deer, donkeys and other animals.

Pukeiti Rhododendron Trust

Founded in 1951 the Pukeiti Rhododendron Trust is a private rhododendron garden surrounded by native bush, 29 km from town (just keep following Carrington Rd all the way from town). The road passes between the Pouakai and Kaitake Ranges, both part of Egmont National Park, but separated by the Trust. Peak flowering of rhododendrons generally takes place in September, October and November, though it's worth going up any time of year.

Around Mt Egmont

The mountain route follows SH 45 around to connect with SH 3 again at Hawera (186 km round trip) or short cuts can be taken. There are numerous attractions en route or nearby. Lucy's Gully, 23 km from New Plymouth on SH 45, is one of the few places where exotic trees are being maintained in a national park. A pleasant picnic area, it is also the start of a couple of tracks into the Kaitake Ranges. Turning right at Pungarehu on Cape Rd, one reaches Cape Egmont Lighthouse, an interesting sight, but not open to visitors.

Parihaka

Inland a km or two from Pungarehu is the

Maori village of Parihaka, formerly the stronghold of the Maori prophet and chief Te Whiti and once one of the largest native villages in New Zealand. Te Whiti led a passive resistance campaign against the ruthless land confiscation that was taking place with the expansion of white settlement. In the last military campaign in Taranaki, Te Whiti was defeated and jailed, and Parihaka was razed (1881). The heavily armed troops found themselves opposed only by dancing children. The spirit of Te Whiti still lives on and descendants and followers meet at Parihaka annually. Many other places in Taranaki are steeped in their Maori past.

Oaonui

Further around, Oaonui is the landfall of the gas pipeline from the Maui platform, and the site of the on-shore processing plant. The Information Centre at Oaonui houses scale models of the Maui Platform and of the on-shore processing plant. You can't visit the plant itself.

Kapuni

Just over 70 km from New Plymouth, off the main road to the south of Egmont, is Kapuni. Natural gas discovered at Kapuni was the first petroleum find of any size in New Zealand. It is now piped to Auckland and Wellington. The oil condensate is also piped out of Kapuni, first to New Plymouth from where it is shipped to New Zealand's oil refinery at Marsden Point.

Hawera

At Hawera SH 45 around the coast meets SH 3 which runs inland around the mountain. You could always visit the Kevin Wasley Elvis Presley Record Room on Argyle St! Phone 87-624 for details. Two km north of Hawera on the Turuturu road are the remains of the pre-European Turuturu Mokai Pa.

Eltham & the Lakes

Back on SH 3 you come to Eltham – well known for its cheeses – where 11 km down the Rawhitiroa Rd you will reach Lake Rotokare, the largest stretch of inland water in Taranaki. Here there is a 1½ to two-hour walk around the lake in native bush. Lake Rotorangi is also nearby and this artificial lake is popular for boating and fishing. Cruises are operated on the lake.

Stratford

North of Eltham is Stratford, named after Stratford-on-Avon in England and with all the streets named after Shakespearian characters. Stratford has a Pioneer Village.

Taumarunui

From Stratford, the Whangamomona-Tangarakau Gorge route heads off towards Taumarunui in central North Island. A good trip if you can put up with the road; the worst part is unsealed and it's hilly bush country.

Wanganui

Population 40,000

The coastal city of Wanganui is midway between Wellington and New Plymouth. Its tourist brochure proclaims it as 'The Friendly City' and the people really do seem very friendly and helpful. The city has a number of attractions and it's the jumping-off point for jet-boat and canoeing trips on the Wanganui River.

History

Kupe, the great Maori explorer and navigator, is believed to have travelled up the Wanganui River for about 20 km around 900 AD. The Maoris established themselves in the area soon after the great migration from Hawaiki (after 1350), and by the time the first white settlers moved in, around the late 1830s, there were

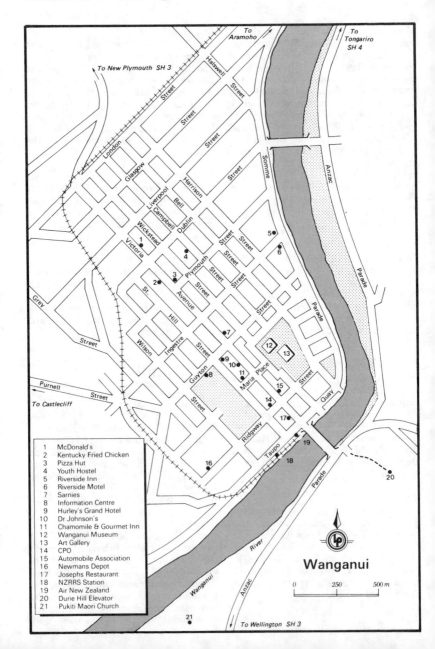

To Aramoho
To Tongariro SH 4
To New Plymouth SH 3
Halswell Street
London Street
Glasgow
Liverpool
Bell
Harrison Street
Somme Street
J Campbell
Dublin
Wickstead
Victoria
Grey Street
St. Hill
Wilson
Ingestre
Guyton Street
Plymouth Street
Avenue
Maria Place
Ridgway
Taupo
Quay
Parade
Anzac Parade
Purnell Street
To Castlecliff

1 McDonald's
2 Kentucky Fried Chicken
3 Pizza Hut
4 Youth Hostel
5 Riverside Inn
6 Riverside Motel
7 Sarnies
8 Information Centre
9 Hurley's Grand Hotel
10 Dr Johnson's
11 Chamomile & Gourmet Inn
12 Wanganui Museum
13 Art Gallery
14 CPO
15 Automobile Association
16 Newmans Depot
17 Josephs Restaurant
18 NZRRS Station
19 Air New Zealand
20 Durie Hill Elevator
21 Pukiti Maori Church

Wanganui River
Anzac Parade
To Wellington SH 3

Wanganui

0   250   500 m

numerous Maori settlements scattered up and down the river.

White settlement of Wanganui was hastened along when the New Zealand Company was unable to keep up with the supply and demand for land around Wellington. In 1840 many Wellington settlers moved to Wanganui and founded a permanent settlement there, the signing of the deed being conducted on the site now known as Moutoa Gardens.

The settlement was initially called Petre after one of the directors of the New Zealand Company, but his name wasn't destined to last on the maps for long. In 1854 it was changed to Wanganui, the name that Kupe had given the river, meaning large bay or stretch of water. When the Maoris understood that the gifts the Pakehas had presented them were in exchange for the permanent acquisition of their land seven years of bitter opposition followed. The whites brought in thousands of troops to occupy Queen's Park and the Rutland Stockade dominated the hill. Ultimately, the struggle was settled by arbitration and when the Maori wars were waged with the Taranaki tribes, the Wanganui Maoris actively assisted their Pakehas.

Information & Orientation
Victoria Avenue is the main shopping street, you'll find most points of interest along or close to this busy avenue. The Information Centre (tel 53-286) is on Guyton St between St Hill St and Wilson St. It's open Monday to Friday, 8.30 am to 5 pm and on weekends and public holidays from 9 am to 2 pm. The people here are very helpful and there's a great model of the country from Wanganui right up to the Tongariro Park. The CPO (tel 58-349) is on Ridgway St.

Wanganui Museum
The Wanganui Museum is the largest and one of the best regional museums in New Zealand, so if you've not had the chance to study Maori culture elsewhere stop here. Apart from the Maori collection, which includes a fine war canoe and some nasty looking *meres* – those elegant but lethal greenstone clubs, the museum also has a good wildlife collection, particularly the selection of moa skeletons. The giant moa is so tall its head disappears into a skylight! The museum is across from the Civic Centre on Wickstead St. It's open 9.30 am to 4.30 pm on weekdays, 1 to 5 pm on weekends and holidays, admission is $1.75 (children 60c).

Sarjeant Gallery
Above the museum is Wanganui's equally good art gallery. There is an extensive permanent exhibition and frequent special exhibits. The gallery is open Monday to Friday from 10.30 am to 4 pm, Saturday from 10.30 am to 12 noon and 1.30 to 4 pm, Sunday from 1.30 to 4 pm. Admission is free.

Other Buildings & Parks
Also in the Civic Centre area is the War Memorial Hall – comprising a concert chamber, convention hall and pioneer room. The good public library is up behind the gallery.

Wanganui has several parks right in the city centre including the pleasant little park in which the museum, gallery and library are situated. The complex is up a hill right beside the town centre and there are good views from the war memorial. If you cross the bridge at the end of Victoria Avenue (the main street) and turn left, there's a very pleasant riverside park.

Durie Hill
Take Victoria Avenue across the river from the town centre and immediately to the left you'll see the carved gateway entrance to the Durie Hill elevator. You follow a tunnel into the hillside then, for 35c, ride up through the hill to the summit 65 metres above. There are two viewpoints at the top, one on top of the lift machinery room, the other a 31-metre watchtower, built of fossilised shellrock. From here you'll get a fine view over the town and

clear to Mt Egmont, Ruapehu or the South Island if the weather is clear.

The elevator operates from Monday to Friday from 7.30 to 11 am and from 11.30 am to 7 pm. On Saturdays hours are 9 to 11.30 am, 12 noon to 5 pm and 5.30 to 8 pm. Sundays it operates from 10 am to 6 pm. In winter operating hours are shorter.

Putiki Church
If you turn right after the bridge and continue for a km or so you come to Putiki Church (St Pauls) – a plain enough little place from the outside but the interior is magnificent, completely covered in Maori carvings and Tukutuku wall panels.

Wairike Estate
If you're in Wanganui on a Sunday follow the Aramoho road four km past the Aramoho Park Camp to Upper Aramoho where you'll find the Waireka Estate on Papaiti Rd. John and Margaret-Anne Barnett, the young couple who own the house, have been restoring the property and its grounds. On Sundays they open the gates to visitors and conduct tours around the curious museum collection housed in what was once the 'gentlemen's smoking room'. Margaret-Anne's great-grandparents, who built the house in 1912, brought some of the items with them from England in 1876 and added others in New Zealand. John explains the various items, shows you how to handle a *mere* and caps the visit by firing the cannon on the lawn. The estate is open Sundays from 2 to 5 pm and entry is $3.50. It's open other days as well in summer, phone 25-729 to check. There are donkey cart rides for the kids and devonshire teas are served in the garden.

The Wanganui River
The Wanganui River, which exits to the sea at Wanganui, is the longest navigable and the second longest river in New Zealand. It starts off on Mt Tongariro and travels 315 km to its mouth in the Wanganui basin. The estuary is over 30 km long and it was this area that was known to the early Maoris as Wanganui or big inlet. The Visitors' Information Centre has information on jet-boat trips and canoeing.

Cruises The historic *MV Waireka* runs trips from the city wharf six km up-river to the Holly Lodge winery. They go at 10 am and 2 pm, cost $11 return and the round trip takes about 3½ hours. In summer there are cruises further up river to Hipango Park. Holly Lodge also operate the paddlewheeler *Otonui*. Holly Lodge Estate is interesting in itself being the only winery in New Zealand which can be visited by river. There's also an antique-replica porcelain doll factory here.

Jet Boat Trips Before the Wanganui calms down, it has a whole series of spectacular rapids – ideal for jet-boating. Jet-boats are a New Zealand invention, they have an inboard engine but no propeller. Instead water is drawn in and shot out the back, like a jet. Since there is no easily damaged prop they can run in extremely shallow water – shooting rapids going up-river as well as down is a jet-boat speciality.

There are several operators running jet boat tours. Holly Lodge Estate (tel 39-344) have a trip up-river as far as Hipango Park. Tours depart daily from Upper Aramoho at 10 am and 2 pm, take two hours and cost $30. Longer or shorter trips can be organised by arrangement.

Eric Hammond (tel 27-796) has trips which include the 45-minute bushwalk to the 'Bridge to Nowhere' for $80. Built in 1937 the bridge has hardly been used since. That trip takes 10 hours in all. Shorter trips include Drop Scene for $50 or local excursions from $12 to $25. They range from short half hour trips to Hipango Park up to a 2½ hour trip to Kawana Mill.

It's 77 km up river to Pipiriki from where you can make shorter trips but although this back road is scenic there is not much traffic and no regular public transport. Check with John Hammond (tel 54-635) about the mail bus service on weekdays. The section between Pipiriki and Drop Scene is the most exciting part of the river. There's a free campsite at Pipiriki. Arawhata Tours (tel Raetihi (0658) 54-575) or Pipiriki (0658) 54-674) have tours to Bridge to Nowhere and Drop Scene. Pipiriki Jet Boat Tours (tel Raetihi (0658) 54-733) have trips to Drop Scene for $17 or Bridge to Nowhere for $45. There are tours which combine a bus trip to Pipiriki with a jet boat trip from there.

A minimum of three to four people is usually required for the trips and on all-day jaunts you'll need to bring lunch. Parkas and leggings are provided but take warm clothing with you.

Canoeing Trips The Wanganui River is also a popular river for canoeing. Baldwin Canoe Adventures in Wanganui run six-day trips up the river and also rent out kayaks and two-person canoes by the hour or the day. Yeti Tours (tel Palmerston North (063) 70-202) also run six-day trips up the river. Two people, plus camping gear and food would cost about $750. They also have shorter two-day trips on the Rangitikei River.

If all this paddling sounds like too much effort there are five-day trips on the *MV Wakapai* for about $500. Check with Dalgety Crown Travel (tel 50-969) in Wanganui.

Places to Stay

Hostels Wanganui's inconveniently located seasonal hostel was replaced in early '87 by a much more central *Wanganui Youth Hostel* (tel 56-780) at 43 Campbell St. It's pleasantly run and has beds for 21 including several rooms for couples. Nightly costs are $11.

For women only there's a small *YWCA* (tel 57-480) at 232 Wickstead St – so small that you're unlikely to get in unless you book well ahead. The *Alwyn Motor Court*, see Camping & Cabins below, has bunkroom accommodation at $12 per person.

Camping & Cabins Most of Wanganui's camps and cabins are out at Castlecliff. There's no camping at the *Alwyn Motor Court* (tel 44-500) at 65 Karaka St but it has cabins, tourist flats and motel flats. The cabins start at $24 for two people, the tourist flats at $34 and the motel flats at $50. It's a pleasant place right on the beach. *Castlecliff Camp* (tel 45-699) charges $5 a night per person, a dollar more with power. Find it on the corner of Karaka and Rangiora Sts. There are also some on-site caravans. Both camps are adjacent to the beach, about eight km from town. Get there on a Castlecliff bus but not on a Sunday.

Aramoho Park Camp (tel 38-402) is 6½ km north of town on the city side bank of the Wanganui River. Aramoho buses run there but not on Saturday or Sunday. Camping here costs $14 for two, $16 with power. They also have cabins from $18 to $26, tourist flats from $30 to $40.

Closest to the city is the *Avro Caravan Court* (tel 58-462) at 36 Alma Rd. It's just 1½ km from the centre and has sites at $18 for two but unlike most motor camps there are no kitchen facilities. There are motel rooms here from around $55/65. *Gonville Caravan Park* (tel 42-012) is at 86 Bignell St, three km out. Sites cost from $12 for two and there are also on-site vans.

Hotels & Guest Houses There's been a spate of closures of the traditional old hotels but there are still some bed & breakfast places. The *Riverside Inn* (tel 32-529) at 2 Plymouth St is a restored colonial building with singles/doubles at $28/38 or with breakfast at $30/45. There are also some units which cost $40 or $45 with breakfast. And there are some budget cabins at $10 per person. Don't confuse it with the nearby *Riverside Motel* on Somme Parade.

Just round the corner at 24 Somme Parade by the river there's the *Cairnbrae Private Hotel* (tel 57-918) with rooms at $20 per person or $25 with breakfast.

Older hotels include the up market *Hurley's Grand Hotel* (tel 50-955) on Guyton St. All rooms have private facilities and cost from $65 a single or $75 to $90 for doubles. Cheaper hotels include the basic *Imperial* (tel 57-505) on Victoria Avenue or the *Station Hotel* (tel 57-363) on Taupo Quay across from the NZRRS station. Rooms at these hotels cost around $22 to $25 per person.

Motels There are plenty of motels in Wanganui including the *Alwyn Motor Court* and the more expensive *Avro Motel*, both covered in the Camping & Cabins section. Other cheaper motels include *Acacia Park Motel* (tel 39-093) at 140 Anzac Parade at $48 for singles, $52 to $60 for doubles. The *River City Motel* (tel 39-107) on Halswell St below St John's Hill has rooms from $50/60. At 181 Great North Rd (SH 3), *Motel Oasis* (tel 54-636) is similarly priced.

Places to Eat

Takeaways & Fast Food There's the usual collection of sandwich places along Victoria Avenue but Wanganui's slightly old-fashioned air is seen at its worst in these places. Most of them have terrible, limp, white-junk-bread excuses for a sandwich. They're the sort of places that give McDonald's a good name.

Places a bit better than this dubious standard include *Chamomile* and the *Gourmet Inn*, both in the Maria Mall, just off Victoria Avenue on Maria Place. *Erick's* at 178 Victoria Avenue is also pretty good. *Sarnies* on Victoria Avenue close to the Guyton St intersection has a wide range of individually wrapped sandwiches. Or try *Dr Johnson's Coffee House* in the 'Tudor Court', Victoria Avenue which has sandwiches and light refreshments.

Or give up on sandwiches and head for

McDonald's, it's further down at 314 Victoria Avenue. Before you come to it you'll pass the *Pizza Hut* and across the road from that is *Kentucky Fried Chicken*.

Pub Food & Restaurants Wanganui is a long way from the best place for eating out in New Zealand but hidden away in the innermost recesses of Hurley's Grand Hotel on the corner of Guyton and St Hill Sts is the *99 The Strand* bistro. It features the pub food standards at around $9 or $10. It's open for lunch and dinner from Monday to Saturday.

Joseph's at 13 Victoria Avenue has main courses at $15 to $17. It's open Tuesday to Saturday for dinner.

Getting There & Away

Air Air New Zealand's office (tel 54-089) is on the corner of Taupo Quay and Victoria Avenue. Air New Zealand has direct flights daily to Auckland ($131), Wellington ($95) and Whakatane ($119) and connections to other centres. Eagle Airways connects Wanganui directly with Hamilton and Palmerston North and also has connections to other towns including Nelson in the South Island.

Road The NZRRS depot (tel 54-439) is on Taupo Quay. Newmans (tel 55-566) is at 156 Ridgway St. Both companies have services that run from Auckland through New Plymouth to Wanganui and on to Palmerston North and Wellington. NZRRS have services from Taupo and Tongariro. By road Wanganui is two to three hours from New Plymouth, Tongariro or Wellington. Fares include Auckland $61, New Plymouth $19, Palmerston North $8.50 and Wellington $21.

The road down from Tongariro (SH 4) passes through the Paraparas, an area of interesting papa hills, with some beautiful views. Alternatively you can turn off at Raetihi, cross to Pipiriki and follow the Wanganui River to Wanganui. The Parapara route is much preferable if you're hitching and you want to actually get a ride! The SH 4 route also passes close by the impressive Raukawa Falls.

Rail The rail service has suffered the fate of most New Zealand rail services – it's been chopped!

Getting Around
A taxi to or from the airport is about $7. A suburban bus service is run by Greyhound Buses (tel 57-100) who are at 160 Ridgway St, by the Newmans depot. Buses run out to Aramoho and to Castlecliff. There are no buses on Sunday.

Palmerston North

Population 69,000
Although Palmerston North is a major crossroads, few people pause there. It's basically just somewhere you pass through. The city is on the banks of the Manawatu River and is the site of the Massey University.

Information & Orientation
The wide open expanse of The Square is very much the centre of Palmerston North, it's a long way around it on foot on a wet and windy night! There's a lookout on top of the Civic Centre building in The Square. It's open 10 am to 3 pm on weekdays. Broadway is the main street in the town.

There's an Information Centre (tel 85-003) in the Civic Centre on the south-west side of The Square. It's open Monday to Thursday from 8.30 am to 5 pm, Friday 8.30 am to 4.30 pm, Saturday from 9.30 am to 1 pm. The CPO is also on The Square. Bennetts Bookshop on Broadway is one of the better bookshops in New Zealand.

Manawatu Museum & Art Gallery
At 221-225 Church St, only a few steps from The Square, the museum specialises

in the history of the Manawatu region of which Palmerston North is the centre. It is open 2 to 4.30 pm on weekends and holidays, 10 am to 4 pm from Tuesday to Friday. Outside there are some old buildings including a schoolhouse and blacksmith's workshop.

Nearby on Main St West is the town's spacious and modern art gallery. It's open 1 to 5 pm on weekends, 10 am to 4.30 pm from Tuesday to Friday. At the south-east corner of The Square the Square Edge Community Arts Centre has exhibits, displays, workshops, shops and a pleasant little cafe.

Other Attractions
The Esplanade park includes gardens, bushwalks, a nature trail, an aviary, a conservatory, rose gardens and even a miniature railway. The Lido Swimming Centre is also there. New Zealand's famous rugby mania is glorified in the National Rugby Museum on the corner of Carroll and Grey Sts. It's open 1.30 to 4 pm daily and admission is $1 (children 20c).

Outside of the city you can visit the Tokomaru Steam Engine Museum with its display of working engines. It's 18 km south of Palmerston North and is open every day but phone Tokomaru 853 first and check opening hours. Himatangi Beach (29 km) and Foxton Beach (40 km) are popular beaches near Palmerston North. North of the town SH 2 to Hawke's Bay and Napier runs through the spectacular Manawatu Gorge.

Places to Stay
Hostels The *Palmerston North Youth Hostel* (tel 64-347) is at 10 Linton St but is only open during the summer. Nightly cost is $9.

Camping & Cabins The *Municipal Camp* (tel 80-349) at 133 Dittmer Drive, off Ruha St and Park Rd, has camping sites at $6 per person or $13 for a site with power. Tourist flats are $35 for two, cabins from

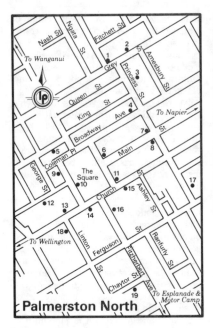

1   Rugby Museum
2   Grey's Inn
3   Newmans Bus Depot
4   Mid City Motel
5   Hard Rock Cafe
6   CPO
7   Air New Zealand
8   Empire Establishment (Cobb & Co)
9   Pizza Piazza
10 Public Relations Office
11 McDonald's
12 Manawatu Art Gallery
13 Manawatu Museum
14 Square Edge Art Centre
15 NZRRS & City Bus Depot
16 Majestic Hotel
17 Kentucky Fried Chicken
18 Youth Hostel
19 Chaytor House

Palmerston North

around $20 to $28 for two. The site is very pleasantly situated in the Esplanade Park area and right next to the Lido Swimming Centre. It's only about two km from The Square.

Guest Houses At 18 Chaytor St, *Chaytor House* (tel 86-878) has rooms at $33 to $38 for singles, $45 to $55 for doubles including breakfast. The more expensive rooms have attached bathrooms. *Grey's Inn* (tel 86-928) at 123 Grey St is around $30 to $35 for singles, $50 for doubles, again including breakfast.

Hotels The *Majestic* (tel 80-079) on Fitzherbert Avenue has rooms at $38 for singles, $45 to $55 for doubles. The *Masonic* (tel 83-480) on Main St West is a little more expensive.

Motels Palmerston North has a wide selection of motels. The *Consolidated*

Mid City Motel (tel 72-184) at 129 Broadway is very conveniently located, only a short walk from The Square. Singles/doubles are $55/65. Further along at 259 Broadway the *Broadway Motel* (tel 85-051) has rooms at $53/60.

The *Central Motel* (tel 72-133) at 26 Linton St is also reasonably central and has rooms at $45/54. *Bryn Teg Motel* (tel 79-978) at 877 Main St is similarly priced. At 451 Ferguson St the *City Court Motel* (tel 72-132) has a swimming pool. Rooms here are $50/60.

Places to Eat

Fast Food & Takeaways The *Pizza Piazza* on The Square does pretty good pizzas, small from $5, medium from $6.50, large from $9. In the Square Edge arts centre at the south-east corner of The Square *Sage* is a pleasant health food place for breakfast or lunch. It's open from 7.30 am for tea, coffee or light meals. Fridays it closes at 8.30 pm, other weekdays at 4.30 pm, on the weekends it only opens on Saturday mornings.

Truelife Takeaways, at 47 The Square, is a good sandwich place. There's a *McDonald's* on The Square and a *Kentucky Fried Chicken* on Princess St.

Top: Tudor Towers, Rotorua (TW)
Left: Mt Tarawera, Rotorua (TW)
Right: Geyser at Whakarewarewa Thermal Reserve, Rotorua (MC)

Top: New Plymouth Power Station (TW)
Left: Wairakei Geothermal Power Station (TW)
Right: Dairy, Tauranga, Bay of Plenty (MC)

Pub Food & Restaurants There are a number of pub-food places in the centre, including the *Britannia Restaurant* in the *Majestic Hotel*, on Fitzherbert St just below The Square. It's open for lunch and for dinner until 10 pm every day of the week. The *Brasserie* in the same hotel is good for breakfast or lunch. There's a *Cobb & Co* in the Empire Establishment on the corner of Princess and Main Sts. It has the usual Cobb & Co menu and the usual seven days a week opening hours.

The *Hard Rock Cafe* on Cuba St behind The Square is no relation to its famous international namesakes but it is open late from Wednesday to Saturday.

Entertainment
Apart from pubs you could try *Champers* or *Zeds* nightclubs on Cuba St near The Square.

Getting There & Away
Air Air New Zealand (tel 64-737) are on the corner of Princess and Main Sts. There are direct flights to Auckland ($141) and Wellington ($92) and connections to other centres. Eagle Air have direct flights to Hamilton ($123), Napier ($86), Nelson ($116), and Wanganui ($52).

Road NZRRS (tel 81-169) are right by The Square on Church St East. Newmans (tel 77-079) are on Princess St. Allans buses to Masterton also operate from the Newmans station. It takes about three hours to get from Palmerston North to Wellington ($18) or to Napier ($24), and 1½ hours to Wanganui ($8.50). Most direct Auckland-Wellington services actually by-pass Palmerston North.

Getting Around
A taxi to or from the airport costs about $6. The City Bus Depot shares the same facilities with NZRRS beside The Square on Church St. There's a flat fare system anywhere in town and the buses operate all weekend.

Rotorua

Population 51,000
Rotorua stands 280 metres above sea level on the shores of the lake of the same name. It's 109 km south-east of Hamilton, 368 km west of Gisborne, and 84 km north of Taupo. Rotorua is probably the most touristed area of the North Island if not of New Zealand. Despite a strong smell of rotten eggs Rotorua's got a lot going for it, including:

1 The most energetic thermal activity in the country – bubbling mud pools, gurgling hot springs, gushing geysers, evil smells. It's sometimes nicknamed 'Sulphur City' and some say it's sitting on a time bomb.

2 A large Maori population with the most interesting cultural activities to be seen in New Zealand.

3 The world's best trout fishing and some interesting trout springs and wildlife parks.

Despite all these attractions and the consequent hordes of tourists it's not too much of a rip-off place. The blaze of signs outside the motels may be an assault on the senses but the assault on the wallet is not as devastating as you might think.

New Zealand's main belt of volcanic activity stretches in a line from White Island, north of the Bay of Plenty, down to the Tongariro National Park. At one time it must have continued even further as Mt Egmont is a dormant volcano and Wellington Harbour is the flooded crater of a long extinct volcano. Rotorua is the most active area, all around the city steam drifts up from behind bushes, out of road drains and around rocks.

Where Has All the Steam Gone?
The geysers, hot springs, bubbling mud pools and so on at Rotorua have performed faithfully as long as the Maori and Pakeha can remember but recently the geysers have erupted less

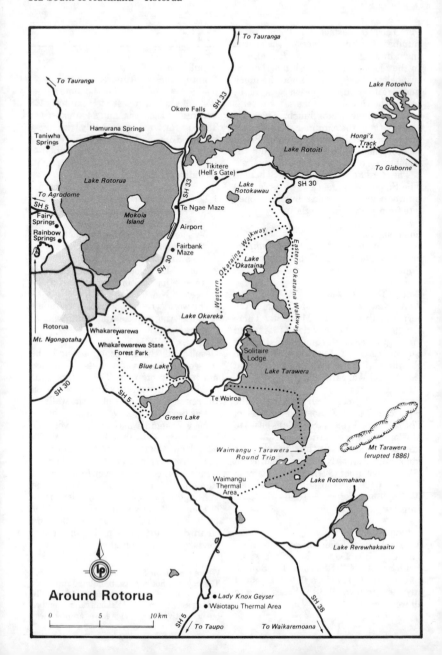

Around Rotorua

0   5   10 km

frequently, the hot water hasn't been so hot and some of the thermal attractions have simply dried up. There's considerable argument over the cause but undeniably a century ago there were not rows of hotels and motels all cashing in on the free hot water. Less obviously all that thermal activity is also widely tapped for industrial use, for heating and for power.

This is all fine but Rotorua is built around tourism and if the geysers dry up so may the tourists. This fear has prompted all sorts of new rules about tapping Rotorua's steam potential. In particular the city government wants to cap all bores within a km of the Whakarewarewa reserve since this is the major Rotorua thermal attraction. A lot of residents blame the whole thing on the huge Wairakei thermal power station near Taupo.

History

The district of Rotorua was probably first settled during the middle of the 14th century by descendants of the navigators who arrived at the central Bay of Plenty in the *Arawa* canoe from Hawaiki. Originally, they were of the Ohomairangi tribe, but soon after they reached Maketu, they changed their tribal name to Te Arawa to commemorate the vessel that brought them so far in safety. Much of the inland forest was explored by the Maori Ihenga in the late 1300s and it was he who discovered and named the lakes of Rotorua and many other geographical features of the area.

In the next few hundred years various sub-tribes spread into the area and as they grew in numbers, they split into more sub-tribes and began to fight over territory. In 1823 the Arawa lands were invaded by the Ngapuhi chief, Hongi Hika, of Northland. Although their primitive stone weapons were no match for the newly acquired muskets of the Ngapuhi, the Arawa managed to rout the Northlanders and force them to withdraw.

The first white person to visit Rotorua was a Dane, Philip Tapsell, who set up a trading station on the coast at Maketu and gave the Maoris guns in exchange for flax, which he exported to Sydney where it was used for rope. In 1831 Thomas Chapman, a missionary, visited Rotorua, returning to settle permanently in 1838; a date signifying the beginning of European occupation.

During the 1850s wars between the Arawa and the Waikato tribes erupted. In 1867 the Waikato tribes attacked in retaliation for the part the Arawa had played in preventing the east coast reinforcements getting through for the Maori King movement. In the course of these wars the Arawa threw in their lot with the government and thus gained the backing of government troops.

With the wars virtually over in the early 1870s European settlement around Rotorua took off with a rush, particularly as the army and government personnel involved in the struggle had broadcast the scenic wonders of the place. People came to take the waters in the hope of cures for all sorts of diseases, and so Rotorua's tourist industry was founded. A road was cleared during 1883-84 to make access easier from Auckland and in 1894 the Auckland-Rotorua railway was completed.

Information & Orientation

The main shopping area is down Tutanekai St, the central part of which is a parking area and pedestrian mall. Fenton St starts in the Government Gardens by the lake and runs all the way down to the Whakarewarewa (just say Whaka) thermal area three km away. It's lined with motels for most of its length.

Tourist Information The NZTP (tel 85-179) is at 67 Fenton St. It's open 8.30 am to 5 pm every day of the week. Other local tourist information is available at the Rotorua Tourist Information Centre (tel 82-256) at the corner of Sala and Tryon Sts in Whakarewarewa. Incidentally, this is one place where the national tourist organisation (the NZTP) is much better than the local one.

The Automobile Association (tel 83-069), is on the corner of Hinemoa and Hinemaru Sts. The excellent *Gateway to*

Geyserland map, widely available in Rotorua, has a good map of the city on one side and of the surrounding area on the other.

Whakarewarewa

Whakarewarewa is Rotorua's largest and best known thermal resort and it's also a major Maori cultural area. If you can't get your tongue around Whakarewarewa it's known simply as Whaka. This is where you'll see the bubbling mud pools, gurgling hot springs and mineral pools, and gushing geysers.

The most spectacular geyser is Pohutu (Maori for 'big splash' or 'explosion'). It is also the most unpredictable, erupting anywhere from two to nine times a day. Pohutu spurts hot water about 20 metres in the air but sometimes shoots up over 30 metres in brief 'shots'. Each display lasts about 20 minutes, although one is reputed to have lasted 14 hours! You get an advance warning because the Prince of Wales' Feathers geyser always starts off shortly before Pohutu.

Other Whaka attractions are the replica Maori village and, on weekdays, the Maori craftspeople working in the carving centre. There are lots of Maori concerts around Rotorua but the daily one at Whaka is rated one of the best.

Whaka is straight down Fenton St from the town centre – three km distance. There's a bus roughly once an hour but at weekends the service is so infrequent you may have to walk. The reserve is open daily from 8.30 am to 5 pm. Admission is $5.50 (children $2.20). The Maori concert costs $6 (children $2.20) or you can do both for $10.50 ($4).

Performing to Schedule

How do the on-time geysers manage to perform so neatly to schedule? Simple – you block them up with some rags so the pressure builds up and you shove a couple of kg of soap powder in to decrease the surface viscosity. And off they go.

Museum & Art Gallery

The small city museum and art gallery are housed in Tudor Towers, an 'olde English' Tudor-style building in the city park, Government Gardens. The museum displays interesting Maori artefacts and there's a fascinating model explaining the Tarawera eruption of 1886. Have a look at this before you do the Waimangu-Tarawera round trip covered below. The museum and art gallery are open 10 am to 4.30 pm weekdays, 1 to 4.30 pm on weekends, admission is free. In the gardens are typical English things like croquet lawns and rose gardens – not to mention untypical steaming pools!

Rotorua also has the Te Amorangi Museum with Maori artefacts plus agricultural machinery. It's at Holdens Bay and open on Sunday afternoons. The Rotorua Settlers Museum in Kuirau Park has items relating to early Pakeha settlement of the area.

Ohinemutu

Ohinemutu is a Maori village by the lakeside with a finely carved meeting house and the historic Maori Church of St Faiths. In the church a Maori-cloaked Christ is etched on a window so he appears to be walking on the waters of Lake Rotorua!

Lake Rotorua

Lake Rotorua is the largest of 12 lakes in the Rotorua district. It was formed by volcanic activity in the area. There are various cruises on the lake – they depart from the jetty at the end of Tutanekai St. There are cruises every day to Mokoia Island on the *Ngaroto* from $20 (children free) for a two hour excursion. Or you can take the *Lakeland Queen* paddleboat for cruises, some with lunch and dinner included. You can also hire boats, charter yachts or simply pedal yourself around on the lake.

Trout Springs

There are several trout springs around Rotorua – the springs run down to Lake Rotorua and the trout, lured by thoughts of free feeds waiting for them from the tourists, swim up the streams to the springs. They are not trapped there; if you watch you may see a trout leaping the little falls to return to the lake or come up to the springs. Try to latch on to a bus tour group or alternatively ask one of the people there to explain things – after half an hour you'll be able to tell a rainbow trout from a brown trout, a male from a female or a young one from an old one.

Rainbow & Fairy Springs are by far the best known of the trout springs. There are a number of pools, one with an underwater viewer, an aviary and a nocturnal kiwi house. The first time I was there a male kiwi was being 'introduced' to a female kiwi and getting a damn good kicking for his troubles! Say hi to Ray Puntner, the knowledgeable 'keeper of the trout'. At the springs you'll also find eels, wallabies, deer, birds, doves and sheep. The springs

are four km around the lake from the city centre and they are open 8 am to 5 pm daily. Admission is $6 (children $2).

Across from the springs is Rainbow Farm, another farm show with sheep shearing, sheep dogs and a chance to try your hand at milking a cow. There are shows three times daily and entry is $5 (children $2).

Although the Rainbow Springs are the best known and most conveniently located there are several others around the lake. Paradise Valley Springs (admission $6, children $2.50) are close to Rotorua on the Ngongotaha Valley Rd. Further round the lake on the north-west side are the Taniwha Springs (admission $5, children $2.50). There's also a fortified Maori pa site near the springs. Finally Hamurana Park is at the northern end of the lake and admission there is $3.50 (children $1.75)

Waimangu-Tarawera Round Trip

There are all sorts of tours and trips around Rotorua but this day-trip is not to be missed. From Rotorua the tour takes you to the Waimangu Tea Rooms, where you can start the day off right with a Devonshire tea before you have to walk a km or two.

The walk, an easy downhill stroll, first passes by the Waimangu Cauldron – a pale-blue lake steaming quietly at 53°C. In this valley the Waimangu Geyser used to perform actively enough to be rated the 'largest geyser in the world'. Between 1900 and 1904, when it became extinct, it would occasionally spout jets to nearly 500 metres! The walk continues down to Rotomahana ('warm lake') where a launch meets and carries you across the lake by the site of the Pink and White Terraces. These were one of the wonders of Rotorua but in 1886 nearby Mt Tarawera disastrously erupted. The Maori village of Te Wairoa was obliterated, the Terraces destroyed, 153 people were killed and Lake Rotomahana was formed.

After you leave the launch it's a short, half km walk across to Lake Tarawera

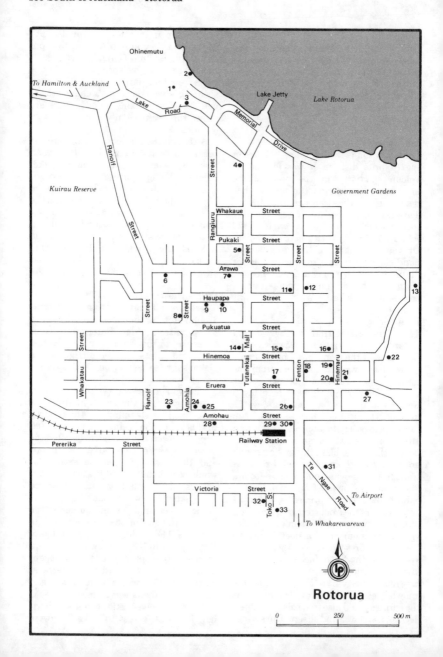

Rotorua

0   250   500 m

1	Ohinemutu Meeting House
2	St Faiths Church
3	Lake Tavern
4	Pizza Hut
5	Gazebo Restaurant
6	Ranui Guest House
7	Palace Tavern
8	Zanelli's Restaurant
9	Ivanhoe Lodge
10	Floyd's Cafe
11	NZTP Office
12	Municipal Council Chamber
13	Tudor Towers, Museum & Art Gallery
14	CPO
15	Grand Establishment, Cobb & Co
16	Automobile Association
17	Mt Cook
18	Chez Bleu
19	Eaton Hall
20	Youth Hostel
21	Hyatt Kingsgate
22	Polynesian Pools
23	Kentucky Fried Chicken
24	H&H & Mainline Terminal
25	Spa Tourist Hotel
26	Fentons
27	Travelodge
28	NZRRS Travel Centre
29	Air New Zealand
30	McDonald's
31	YWCA
32	Tresco Guest House
33	Morihana Guest House

where another launch takes you across to Te Wairoa now known – rather crassly – as the Buried Village: a sort of Maori Pompeii. At a waterfall nearby, your bus will collect you for the drive back to Rotorua. En route it stops at the Blue and Green Lakes (usually the difference in colour is striking) and Redwood Grove where Californian Redwoods have been planted and, like the Californian rainbow trout, have done better then they ever did at home.

The tour is operated by H&H (now part of Mt Cook), departs daily at 9.30 am, returns at 5 pm and will set you back $45 (children $22.50). It's byo lunch as well, but you'll probably reckon the tour is well worthwhile anyway.

Hell's Gate

Hell's Gate, another highly active thermal area, is 16 km from Rotorua on the road to Lake Rotoiti. It's open 9 am to 5 pm daily, admission is $5 (children $3), and (as by now you'll feel is pretty usual) the mud bubbles, the water boils, the geysers spout.

Agrodome

An unusual Rotorua attraction is the Agrodome. Going to see a bunch of sheep seems a rather strange thing to do in New Zealand, but for $6.50 (children $3.25) you get a really interesting show at 9.15 am, 10.30 am and 2.30 pm daily. There's sheep shearing, sheep dogs displaying their expertise and by the time you're through you may even be able to tell the difference between some of the 19 breeds on show. The Agrodome is seven km north of Rotorua.

Mazes

The New Zealand maze craze has spread to Rotorua and there are a couple of mazes near the airport. The Te Ngae Park is a three-dimensional maze similar to the original Wanaka maze in the South Island. It's three km beyond the airport, open every day and admission is $3 (children $1.50). The Fairbanks Maze is opposite the airport and is a hedge maze. There's an orchard here as well, both are open daily and admission is $2 (children $1).

Other Attractions – in town

The Rotorua Experience is on Te Ngae Rd near the centre. It's a multi-screen audio-visual and costs $5.50 (children $2.20). Or you could try Little Village, an 'olde worlde' village replica across from the Rotorua International Hotel. There's an orchid garden ($5.50) and a herb garden ($4) or you can ride the chairlift at Skyline Skyrides and whistle down on the luge – a sort of sled without snow. One ride is $3, less per ride for multiple trips.

Last but not least, exhausted by all the

heavy sightseeing, you can relax in Polynesian Pools on Hinemoa St. The public hot thermal pools cost $4.40 (children $2.20) and $5.50 per person for the private ones.

Other Attractions – out of town

If you don't go on the Waimangu day trip it is possible to visit the attractions individually. Entry to the Waimangu Thermal Valley costs $6 (children $2) or for the valley and the lake it's $10.50 (children $5.50). At the other end of the Waimangu day trip there's the buried village of Te Wairoa where entry is $4.40 (children $1.65). You can also go on the boat across Lake Tarawera which goes to meet the Waimangu round trip. The round trip across the lake, with time to walk across to Lake Rotomahana, costs $7.50 (children $3.75).

Further out beyond Waimangu at Waiotapu is the Lady Knox Geyser. It performs (with a little prompting) at 10.15 am daily. The Champagne Pool and the Bridal Veil Falls are other Waiotapu attractions. Entry is $4.50 (children $1.75) to the park and $5 (children $2) for the geyser as well which is one km beyond the thermal area.

You can also go on four-wheel drive expeditions on Mt Tarawera or go whitewater rafting down the Rangitaiki River. Rafting trips cost $60 from the river or $70 including transport from Rotorua, and include equipment and a barbecue at the end.

Trips & Tours

The NZTP can advise you about the many tours in and around Rotorua and further afield. NZRRS have tours from $19 to $40 (children $9.50 to $20). They include city tours, tours to the thermal attractions, tours to Te Wairoa (the buried village), a visit to the Agrodome and so on. H&H also have tours including the excellent Waimangu-Tarawera day trip covered earlier.

Tours further afield include Waitomo

Cave day trips for $37 including the cave entrance fees.

Flights

All Rotorua's attractions can be seen from the air and some, like the Tarawera volcano, are best observed from above. Flightseeing trips depart either from the airport or by floatplane from the lake and are priced from about $35 and up.

Volcanic 'Wunderflites' from Rotorua Airport are particularly popular. They will fly you up and over the awesome chasm of Mt Tarawera on a half hour flight for $60. For an additional fee you can land beside the volcano and wander over to look over the edge. They also have longer flights over the lakes, out to White Island or even down to Mt Ruapehu and Mt Ngaruahoe in the Tongariro Park. You can spend up to $400 for the complete volcano tour.

My Rotorua flightseeing favourite is White Island Airways who operate an all-biplane fleet of Tiger Moths and Dragon Rapides. In their Tiger Moths they'll fly you over the city for $55, over Mt Tarawera for $99 or, if your stomach is strong, will take you up for some aerobatics for $88. You're out in the open air in a Tiger Moth but in your flight suit, leather helmet and goggles you'll feel as warm as the Red Baron. The larger Dragon Rapide is a real museum piece and in this a Mt Tarawera trip costs $55 or you can take trips further afield, including to White Island, for $121 to $165.

Other operators include the Helicopter Line (tel 476-086) who operate from the City Helipad on Te Ngae Rd near the centre or Floatplane Airservices (tel 84-069) by the lake.

Parks & Walks

Whakarewarewa State Forest Park is just on the edge of town. This is an exotic (non-native) forest, planted earlier this century as an experiment to find the most suitable species to replace New Zealand's rapidly dwindling and slow-growing natives.

The Forestry Information & Visitor Centre is open 9 am to 5 pm from October to May, and 11 am to 4 pm from June to September. It has displays on the history and management of New Zealand forests and forest industries. Check in here if you want to go walking. There are many walks, including routes to the Blue and Green Lakes. A 1½ hour tour of the Waipa State Sawmill is available free of charge at 10.30 am on Mondays, Tuesdays and Thursdays, except between 20 December and 20 January. Other local mills also have tours: enquire at the NZTP.

Other walks in the Rotorua area include the 22½ km Western Okataina Walkway, from Lake Okaraka to Ruato, this time in native bush. There's public transport past the Ruato end only; the whole walk takes about six hours, and you need boots or stout shoes. There is now an Eastern Okataina Walkway as well. It goes along the eastern shoreline of Lake Okataina to Lake Tarawera - eight km long, about a 2½ hour walk. At present you have to walk out the same way you walked in and access to the mountain is difficult - see map. There are also shorter walks around Okataina.

You can tramp up Mt Tarawera (1111 metres) but take some water: it's a scarce resource up there. Be selective about which streams you drink from anywhere here; being a thermal zone, much of the water isn't pure. Mt Tarawera is actually on private property so before you go you must obtain permission from the Te Arawa Maori Trust Board on Pukuatua St, or check at the NZTP office. It's not a hard walk (about 2½ to three hours each way) and no technical expertise is required. Solitaire Adventure Walks (tel 28-208) offer guided walks to the summit.

Fishing

And, of course, there's trout fishing. You can hire guides or go it alone, but remember you need a licence and there are various regulations about how you may catch them. The guided fishing trips aren't cheap but they all but guarantee that you'll catch a fish.

Places to Stay

With all the Rotorua region's tourist attractions, it's not surprising that it is well endowed with places to stay. Hot mineral pools are a Rotorua bonus in almost any establishment, no matter how humble.

Hostels The *Rotorua Youth Hostel* (tel 476-810) is on the corner of Eruera and Hinemaru Sts, close to the centre. Formerly known as the *Colonial Inn*, there are twin and family rooms available and the nightly charge is $13. You can hire bicycles from the hostel.

Ivanhoe Lodge (tel 86-985) is also very central at 54 Haupapa St. This popular though somewhat crowded hostel has a variety of accommodation ranging from bunkrooms to heated cabins to rooms which come complete with bedding. In the bunkrooms a bed is $11. In the cabins per person costs are $15 in the singles, $12 or $13 in the twins and doubles. In the rooms it's $17 for singles, $15 or $16 for twins or doubles. There's a good communal kitchen with eating and cooking utensils provided, and a shop where you can buy small quantities of food. It also has a comfortable lounge and hot pool (swimming gear unnecessary) and the people who run it are very helpful. Ivanhoe also has bicycles for hire.

Thermal Lodge (tel 70-931) is at 60 Tarewa Rd, a km or two from the centre. This brand new hostel has single, double and larger rooms. Per person costs are $20 in singles, $13 in doubles or larger rooms. If you've not got bedding you can hire linen packs for $3.50 single or $4 double. There are also tent and campervan sites for $6. There's a spacious and modern kitchen, dining area and TV lounge, laundry facilities and plenty of showers. Bicycles can be hired and there's a courtesy bus which meets the most popular bus services into Rotorua.

The *YWCA* (tel 85-445) on Te Ngae Rd doesn't usually have any casual accommodation available. If it does it will probably be women only, but it's a place to try in emergencies.

Camping & Cabins Rotorua has a very good selection of campsites, although some are 'caravan only' places. Almost all have cabins.

On Whittaker Rd (turn left towards the lake just before you get into town, coming from Auckland or Hamilton), *Cosy Cottage* (tel 83-793) has camping sites (only a limited number for tents) at $13 for two. Cabins cost from $25 for two, tourist flats from $40 for two. The tourist flats have toilets, showers, heating and self-contained kitchens.

Lakeside Motor Camp (tel 81-693) is also on Whittaker Rd, beside the lake and only two km from the town centre. Sites here also cost $13 for two and again there are cabins ($26 for two) and tourist flats ($33 to $40 for two).

The large *Rotorua Thermal Motor Camp* (tel 88-385) on the south end of the Old Taupo road near the golf course, has both camping sites and cabins and there's a swimming pool. Sites are $8 per adult. There are a variety of cabins from around $25 to $34 for two.

If you don't mind staying a little further out there are many more camps and cabins in the area. *Holdens Bay Holiday Park* (tel 59-925) is about half a km from the lake and 6.5 km out on the Tauranga-Whakatane Highway. Camping is $7.50 per person and there are a bunch of cabins and tourist flats. The cabins range from $20 a night for the most basic ones to $35 for the fancier ones with kitchens. In peak season the base charge will be about $10 higher. The tourist flats cost from $44.

Blue Lake Camp (tel 28-120) is 11 km out and has camping at $6 per person and cabins from $18 and up or tourist flats from about $30. Again there are minimum charges at peak seasons. You can hire canoes and a ski boat on the Blue Lake

here, as well as going horse trekking. At *Fisherman's Lodge* (tel 28-318) near the Buried Village, camping is $7 per person and there are on-site caravans, cabins and tourist flats. They have fishing charters and you can hire boats.

There are a couple of places to camp at Ngongotaha, eight km out of Rotorua on the western shore of the lake; and plenty more places nearer to and further from the city. All in all there's no shortage of camping sites here:

Beachcomber Lakeside Family Resort (tel 56-330), camping from $6 per person, one night surcharge, also tourist flats.
Moana Auto Park (tel 56-240), Lee Rd, Hannahs Bay, off Tauranga-Whakatane Highway 7.5 km out, camping from $7.50 per person, also tourist flats.
Ngongotaha Caravan Park (tel 74-289), 24 Beaumonts Rd, Ngongotaha, eight km out, camping from $7 per person, also on-site caravans, cabins and tourist flats.
Waiteti Stream Holiday Park (tel 74-749), 14 Okana Crescent, Ngongotaha, beside Waiteti Stream, camping from $7 per person, also on-site caravans, cabins and tourist flats.
Willow Haven Holiday Park (tel 74-092), 31 Beaumont Rd, Ngongotaha, on lake side, camping from $6.50 per person, also cabins.

Guest Houses There are a number of guest houses and bed & breakfast places around Rotorua. The *Spa Tourist Hotel* (tel 83-486) is a straightforward little place at 69 Amohau St, right across from the Travel Centre where NZRRS buses arrive and depart. Singles are $28, twins and doubles $37 to $40. All rooms have washbasins with hot and cold water. Although this is a rather busy and noisy street during the daytime, Rotorua is a quiet place at night.

There are a couple of places on Toko St, off Victoria St which is just across the railway line from McDonald's. At number 3 there's *Tresco Guest House* (tel 89-611) with singles/doubles for $33/44 including breakfast. There are sinks in the rooms and it's a neat, tidy and comfortable place. Ditto for the *Morihana Guest*

House (tel 88-511) a bit further down at 20 Toko St. Rooms here are $27/38. Although it's reasonably central, Toko St is a quiet street and well away from the tourist hustle of central Rotorua.

Traquair Lodge (tel 86-149) at 126 Ranolf St is not quite as central as the places above. It's a homely though slightly scruffy and dog-eared sort of place but a major attraction here is breakfast time. 'The best breakfast we had in the North Island,' reported one well fed visitor. If you like to start the day with bacon and eggs and the other essentials of a truly British morning feast then this is the place. Singles/doubles, including breakfast, are $24/39.

Other guest houses include *Eaton Hall* (tel 70-366) at 39 Hinemaru St, centrally located across from the Hyatt Kingsgate. Or there's *Ranui* (tel 83-691) at 114 Arawa St, also near the centre.

Hotels Right in the centre on the corner of Hinemoa and Fenton Sts the *Grand Establishment* (tel 82-089) has rooms at $70/80. Rooms have tea and coffee making equipment and there's a laundry and sauna.

Rotorua has some big hotels, to cater for those big tour groups. There's a *Quality Inn*, *Rotorua Travelodge*, *Sheraton Rotorua*, *THC Rotorua*, *Geyserland Resort*, *Voyager Resort* and even the *Hyatt Kingsgate*. At these establishments even singles can cost from $100 a night. Still, that's nothing on the *Solitaire Lodge* (tel 28-208 at Lake Tarawera where singles/doubles including all meals run from around $450/650 a night!

Motels There are also plenty of motels in Rotorua and the competition has kept some prices down. Several campsites also have motel-style rooms in addition to their cabins and tourist flats. Just a few of the cheaper places to try include:

Aloha Motel (tel 87-149), 105 Amohau St, rooms from $50/60.

Amber Lodge (tel 80-595), 48 Hinemaru St, rooms from $50/60.
Aywon Motel (tel 477-659), 18 Trigg Avenue, rooms from $45-52 single, $54-65 double.
Bel Aire Motel (tel 86-076), 257 Fenton St, rooms from $45/52.
Colonial Motel (tel 84-490), 22 Ranolf St, rooms from $46-52 single, $58-64 double.
Eason Court Motel (tel 82-093), 13 Eason St, rooms from $44/50.
Eruera Motel (tel 88-355), corner Eruera & Hinemaru Sts, rooms from $44/55.
Havana Motel (tel 88-134), 12 Whakaue St, rooms from $44/58.
Manhattan Motel (tel 85-483), 130 Hinemoa St, rooms from $44-50 single, $55-60 double.
Monterey Motel (tel 81-044), 50 Whakaue St, rooms from $46-50 single, $56-66 double.
Punga Court (tel 80-552), 19 Union St, rooms from $45/56.
Racecourse Motel (tel 81-131), 258 Fenton St, rooms from $38/45.
Waiteti Stream Holiday Park (tel 74-749), 14 Okono Crescent, Ngongotaha, rooms from $45/50.

Places to Eat

Takeaways & Fast Food There are plenty of sandwich places and assorted fast food joints around Rotorua. Try, for example, the *Bakery Boutique* or the *Tudor Cottage Bakery*, both up towards the lake end of Tutanekai. In between them is the *Coffee Bean* where you can sit down and enjoy your sandwiches. This is a good place for breakfast too. Other good sandwich places include *Taste Tease*, opposite Air New Zealand on Amohau St.

The American big three are all represented in Rotorua. There's a large *McDonald's* on the corner of Fenton and Amohau Sts. *Kentucky Fried* is further down Amohau while *Pizza Hut* is right up the lake end of Tutanekai St. And there's even a poor little *Wimpy* as well, it's at the other end of Tutanekai, near Amohau St. *Chez Bleu* is another non-chain imitation of the chain hamburger places, it's on Fenton St between Hinemoa and Eruera.

Pizza Forno at 44 Hinemoa St is open seven days but, apart from Friday and

Saturday, it closes by 8 pm. Pizzas range from around $4 for small ones to $8 for large ones. Two doors away, *Chez Maison* does good sandwiches. Also on Hinemoa St pizza fans can try *Al Capone Pizzas*.

Pub Food Yes there's a *Cobb & Co* as well. It's in the Grand Establishment on Hinemoa St between Tutanekai and Fenton Sts and has the usual good-value Cobb & Co menu. It's open the usual 7.30 am to 10 pm hours, the usual seven days a week.

Other pub food alternatives include the bistro in *Fentons*, right across from McDonald's at the Amohau/Fenton Sts junction. Or there's the *Palace Tavern* on Arawa St and the *Lake Tavern* on Lake Rd near the lake in Ohinemutu. These latter two are pretty basic, rough-edged grog houses although the bistro areas are peaceful enough.

Restaurants Plenty of these in Rotorua, particularly up at the lake end of Tutanekai St where the Pukaki St-Whakaue St block is real restaurant territory.

At 46 Haupapa St, just a few doors from the Ivanhoe Lodge, *Floyd's Cafe* is a pleasant, modern-looking, comfortable little byo with dishes like moussaka or various pastas at around $7 to $9 or main courses at $10 to $13. On Amohia St near the junction with Pukuatua St, *Zanelli's* is somewhat similar in mood but here the food is strictly Italian, the colour scheme decidedly red, white and green. Pasta dishes are around $6 to $7 as starters, $10 as main courses, other main courses are around $13, and there are great gelatis.

In that popular restaurant quarter on Tutanekai St *Gazebo* is a very popular little byo at lunch or dinner time. Main courses here are $15 to $16 and the menu is very straightforward. Nearby is *Lewishams* where the menu is Eastern European – or Austrian-Hungarian as they say. At 259 Tutanekai St *Karl's Dining Room* is a place for straightforward food – if you miss

the Sunday roast then come here for moderately priced and good food.

Entertainment

Maori Concerts & Hangis Maori culture is a major attraction in Rotorua, the unofficial Maori capital, and although it's decidedly commercialised it's a worthwhile investment to get out and enjoy it. There are two big activities – concerts and hangi feasts – and in many cases the two are combined. Some places simply put on the concerts, others combine them with a hangi although you can sometimes watch the concert without the feast to go with it.

The 12.30 pm Maori concert at Whakarewarewa is rated one of the best around. Cost is $6 (children $2.20) or you can combine it with entry to the thermal reserve. Another popular concert is the one at the Municipal Concert Chamber at the Haupapa St and Fenton St junction across from the information office. The concert is on from 7 to 8 pm daily, tickets go on sale at 6.30 pm and cost $6 (children $2.50). The third concert-only performance is at the Ohinemutu Meeting House at 8 pm. This is the longest running of the various concerts put on in Rotorua each night – once upon a time it was the only one – but it doesn't seem to be up to the best standards these days.

The combined concerts and hangis are generally at the big hotels. Although you can sometimes just go to the concert, if they're full it's possible they'll only let people in for the concert if they've paid for the hangi as well. An exception is the Sheraton where you can do either the hangi or the concert separately. The concert at the Rotorua International Hotel has for some years had an excellent reputation. Another place for hangis and concerts is Tudor Towers, at the museum and art gallery building in the Government Gardens. You should book ahead at any of these places. Prices for concerts and hangis are:

Geyserland Hotel – concert $6, concert and hangi $26 (tel 82-039)

Hyatt Kingsgate – concert $10, concert and hangi $30 (tel 87-139)

Rotorua International Hotel – concert $8.25, concert and hangi $27.50 (tel 81-189)

Sheraton – concert $15, hangi $15, concert and hangi $30 (tel 87-139)

Travelodge – concert $5.50, concert and hangi $27.50 (tel 81-174)

Tudor Towers – concert and hangi $24 (tel 477-238)

The concerts are put on by local people and they seem to get as much a kick out of them as you will. Chances are by the time the evening is over you'll have been dragged up on stage, experienced a Maori *hongi* – nose-to-nose contact (as you touch say 'aaaah'), joined hands for a group sing-in, and thought about freaking out your next-door neighbour with a haka when you get home. *Hakas* are war dances which are intended to demonstrate how tough you are. The high point of the haka is to stick the tongue out as far as it will go, demonstrating derision and aggression. Other features of a Maori concert are poi dances, action songs and hand games.

Poi dances are performed by women only and consist of whirling round the *poi* (flax-fibre balls that are swung and twirled on lengths of string). Action songs are a recent addition to the Maori activities – story-songs illustrated by fluid hand and arm movements. There are also hand games – a reaction-sharpening pastime. The best game is where the two players make rapid gestures and try to catch their opponent making the same one!

A *hangi* is a Maori earth oven – a large pit is dug and a fire is lit to heat stones placed in the pit. Then food in baskets, covered with wet cloths, is buried with earth and steamed to perfection. The traditional Maori food (smoked eels, kumara – sweet potatoes, marinated fish and mussels) is supplemented with dishes to the Pakeha taste (wild pork, lamb,

venison stew) and dessert to follow. A full (and filling) evening.

Pub Entertainment Rotorua has the usual pub music – but not every night. Rock regulars include the rough and ready *Palace Tavern* on Arawa St and the *Lake Tavern* on Lake Rd near the hospital.

There's also the smaller and more intimate *Cobb & Co* in the Grand Establishment on Hinemoa St. They have a jazz band and reasonably priced beer. Or try *Fentons* on the corner of Amohau and Fenton Sts.

Other Disco and nightclub-style activity can be found at *Tudor Towers* later in the evening and at *Club Keets* opposite the CPO.

Getting There & Away

Air Air New Zealand's offices (tel 87-159) are at 38-42 Amohau St. They have direct flights to Tauranga ($73) and Wellington ($141) and onward connections to other centres.

Mt Cook Airlines (tel 477-451) is at 33 Eruera St and has direct flights to Auckland, Christchurch and Mt Cook and onward connections to Queenstown and other centres. Ansett New Zealand (tel 70-599) is at 113 Fenton St and has similar services. Fares include Auckland $111, Christchurch $192, Mt Cook $329 and Queenstown $410.

Eagle Airways (tel 389-500) has direct flights to Hamilton ($59) connecting with their services to other centres including Gisborne, Napier, Nelson, New Plymouth, Palmerston North and Wanganui.

Road Rotorua is a little less than two hours from Hamilton by road and around 1½ hours from Taupo. Waikaremoana (see Tramping section) is about 4½ hours drive, some of it on a fairly difficult unsealed road.

Trains (but there are no passenger trains) and NZRRS buses come into the Travel Centre (tel 81-039) on Amohau St and this is also where you leave for the NZRRS area tours. Mainline Coachways (tel 82-786) can be found at 77 Amohau St, just across from the Travel Centre. This is where the H&H tours depart from. Or at least did, since H&H has been taken over by Mt Cook it's possible there may be some amalgamation of their operations.

By NZRRS, bus fares from Rotorua include Auckland $28, Hamilton $13, Gisborne $41, Napier $37, Taupo $16, Tauranga $13, Wellington $54. Rotorua is about five hours to or from Auckland. Two days a week you can get to Waikaremoana for $23. The service continues on to Wairoa.

Between Auckland and Rotorua, Mainline's service is cheaper and faster though less frequent than NZRRS. It costs $23 but one of their Auckland departures is at 1.30 am (yes!) delivering newspapers. Note that the bus does not go via Hamilton, but via Morrinsville and Matamata.

Hitching Hitching to Rotorua is generally not bad except for Highway 38 from Waikaremoana – once past Murupara heading out that way, count on about four cars per hour going past depending on the time – although more people will stop than on the major roads. The hitching problem out of Rotorua is often just the sheer number of backpackers leaving town! You may have to simply join the queue and wait.

Getting Around

Airport Transport The airport is about 10 km out, on the north-east side of the lake. There is a minibus service operated by Aroha Tours for $5, phone 88-703 for details.

Local Transport Suburban bus services operate from the NZRRS Travel Centre on Amohau St but apart from a limited Saturday service they mainly operate Monday to Friday. There is nothing at all on Sundays. Route 3 runs to Whakarewarewa,

route 2 round the lakeside to Rainbow Springs.

There's also a Shuttle Bus service which connects the main tourist sites. It runs from Whakarewarewa to the NZTP office, Rainbow Springs, the Skyline chairlift and the Agrodome. Fares from the NZTP are Whakarewarewa $1.50, Rainbow Springs $2, Agrodome via Rainbow Springs $3.75. Timetables are available from the NZTP on Fenton St.

Bicycle & Motorcycle Hire Rotorua is fairly spread out, public transport is not that good so a bicycle is a nice thing to have. All the hostels seem to have bikes for hire. Ivanhoe has bikes at $5.50 an hour or $11 a day for guests, rather more for outsiders. At Thermal Lodge 10-speeders are $8 a half day, $15 a day. They also have mountain bikes.

Rotorua Motorcycles (tel 89-385) at 65 Amohau St rent small capacity Yamaha motorcycles, ideal for exploring the Rotorua area.

Taupo

Taupo, 85 km south of Rotorua, is the world's trout fishing capital. If you thought those trout in the Rotorua springs looked large and tasty they're nothing to the monsters here. All New Zealand's rainbow trout are descended from one batch of eggs brought from California nearly a century ago. The lakes here are everything a trout could dream of and they grow to a prodigious size. Lake Taupo is in the geographic centre of the North Island.

The largest lake in New Zealand, it is 606 square km in area and 357 metres above sea level. The depression Lake Taupo occupies is thought to have been formed by a gigantic volcanic explosion and subsequent subsidence. Pumice from Lake Taupo is found as far away as Napier and Gisborne and forms a layer, from a cm to some metres thick, over a vast area of central North Island.

History

Back in the mists of time a Maori chief named Tamatea-arikinu visited the area and, noticing that the ground felt hollow and that his footsteps seemed to reverberate, called the place Tapuaeharuru – 'resounding footsteps'. Taupo, as it became known, was first occupied by Europeans as a military outpost during the Maori wars. Colonel J M Roberts built a redoubt in 1869 and a garrison of mounted police remained there until the defeat of Te Kuti.

In the 1870s the government bought the land from the Maoris who asked that it be named Bowen in honour of Governor Sir G F Bowen who visited the lake in 1872. While this was agreed to, it was never carried out. Taupo has grown slowly and sedately from a lakeside village of 750-odd in 1945, to a resort town with a permanent population of 13,500. The town itself is on the lakeshore where the main road from the north first meets the lake.

Information

The Taupo Information Centre (tel 89-002 & 3) is on the main street (PO Box 142). Taupo has a brand new post office on the corner of Horomatangi and Ruapehu Sts. It's painted in amazingly un-post-office-like pastel shades of pink and blue.

Orakei Korako

Between the main roads from Hamilton and from Rotorua to Taupo is one of the finest thermal areas of New Zealand – Orakei Korako. Access is what stops people going there, but it's worth the trip if you can make it. It's 23 km off the Rotorua-Taupo highway and 15 km off the Hamilton-Taupo highway, or 37 km from Taupo itself. During the peak of the summer you can visit it on a NZRRS bus tour from Rotorua. Otherwise you can probably manage to hitch in. Admission is $6 (children $2.50), which includes the

jet-boat ride across Lake Ohakuri, formed by an electricity department hydro-electric dam.

After the destruction of the Pink and White Terraces by the Tarawera eruption, Orakei Korako was possibly the best thermal area left in New Zealand, and one of the finest in the world. Now three-quarters of it lies beneath the waters of Lake Ohakuri but the quarter that remains is still worth seeing.

A well laid out walking track takes you around the large, colourful silica terraces for which Orakei Korako is famous, as well as geysers and Aladdin's Cave – a magnificent natural cave with a pool of jade green water. The pool is said to have been used by Maori women as a mirror during hairdressing ceremonies; the name Orakei Korako means 'the place of adorning'.

Aratiatia

Heading in from Rotorua after the Orakei Korako turn-off there are a whole series of attractions along the Waikato River, at 436 km the longest river in New Zealand. The Waikato has its beginning to the east of Ruapehu, flows into Taupo at its southern end (here it's also known as the Tongariro River), leaves Taupo in the township and flows through the heart of northern North Island, before finally reaching the west coast at Waikato Heads just short of Auckland.

The first attraction is Aratiatia; two km off the main road on your left just before Wairakei are the Aratiatia Rapids. Unfortunately, the government, in its wisdom, went and plonked another power house and dam down here, shutting off the water from the rapids. To keep the tourists happy, they open the control gates at 10 am and 2.30 pm daily. That's the time to be there to see the water flow through.

Wairakei Thermal Valley

Just past the Aratiatia turn-off, SH 5 from Rotorua meets SH 1 from Hamilton and Auckland, and then you're in Wairakei, eight km from Taupo. If you are not too distracted by all the steam from the Geothermal Power Project, you'll see a 1½ km road on your right leading to the Wairakei Thermal Valley, where there are yet more mud-pools.

This is the remains of what was once known as Geyser Valley. Unfortunately, one of the most famous geysers is now extinct. According to the Maoris the Karapiti was a spectacular jet of steam which erupted with undiminished force for almost 500 years before the Europeans came to Wairakei. Now the neighbouring geothermal power project has sucked off the steam, and all you will see is a simulated geyser with cold water piped to the mouth of an extinct geyser. Entry is $3 (children 75c).

Wairakei Geothermal Power Project

New Zealand was the second country in the world to produce power from natural steam. If you dive into all that steam you will find yourself at the Wairakei Geothermal Power Project which generates about 150,000 kilowatts, providing about 5% of New Zealand's total electrical power. Although it is claimed the power will last 'indefinitely' in actual fact it has been decreasing at a rate of 2 to 3% per year.

There's a Geothermal Information Centre close to the road where you can make an educational stop between 9 am and 12 noon, or 1 and 4.30 pm daily. Information on the borefield and power-house is available and conducted tours of the powerhouse can be arranged. You can drive up the road through the project and from a lookout see the long stretches of pipe, wreathed in steam.

Huka Falls & Huka Village

Just after Wairakei a road on your left leads to the spectacular Huka Falls. A footbridge crosses the Waikato River above the falls, which plunge through a narrow cleft in the rock, dropping about 24 metres in all.

On the same spur road 2½ km before Taupo is Huka Village, a replica of an early New Zealand pioneer village. It's open daily from 9 am to 5 pm, admission is $2.50 (children free).

Craters of the Moon

Craters of the Moon is an interesting and non-exploited thermal area where admission is free! It's signposted on your left about five km north of Taupo towards Wairakei. It's not too well publicised or the commercial thermal area operators would complain. The area is well fenced for safety purposes, but not overdone as commercially exploited thermal areas can be. Be careful when you leave your car as things have been stolen from cars here.

Walks

You can walk all the way from Taupo to Aratiatia. From the centre of town turn up Spa Rd by Woolworths. Turn left at County Avenue and continue through Spa Thermal Park at the end of the street, past the skateboard bowl, and over the hill, following the rough roadway to the left until you hit the track.

The track follows the river to Huka Falls crossing a hot stream and riverside marshes en route (about one hour, or say two hours from the centre of Taupo to Huka). From Huka Falls you can cross the footbridge along the seven-km Taupo Walkway to Aratiatia (two to three hours). There are good views of the river, Huka Falls, and the power station across the river. It's easy walking.

If you're going to Craters of the Moon as well you can make it a round trip, using the walkway one direction between Taupo and Aratiatia, and the road the other. You would need all day, and should time it so you're at Aratiatia at 2.30 pm when the control gates are open and at Wairakei when the Info Centre is open.

Another walk worth mentioning is Mt Tauhara, with magnificent views from the top. Just south of the city centre, still in

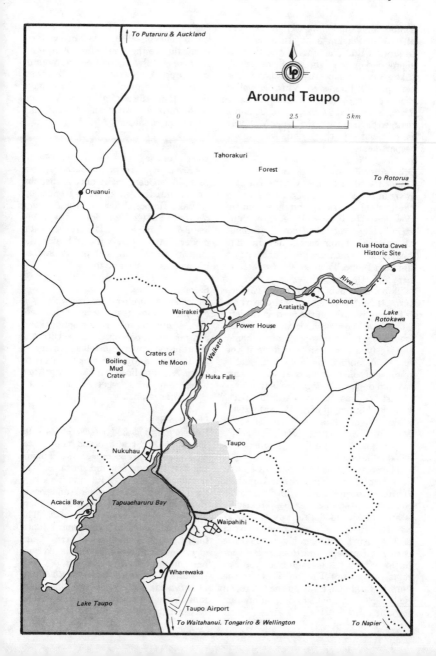

Around Taupo

Taupo, the Taupo-Napier Highway turns off. About six km along turn left into Mountain Rd. The start of the track is signposted on the right-hand side. It will take about two hours to get to the top at a slow pace. If interested in further walks, pick up a copy of the leaflet *Walks & Tramps in the Taupo Area*. A more detailed description of the Taupo Walkway is put out by the Lands & Survey Department.

Other Attractions

Under the SH 1 bridge over the Waikato River in Taupo are control gates regulating the level of Lake Taupo and the amount of flow down the Waikato River through its string of hydro-electric power stations. Just up the hill from here is the turn-off to Acacia Bay, a pleasant peaceful beach 7.5 km from Taupo. There's a short walk from here to Little Acacia Bay.

Two km north of Taupo is the Kinlock turn-off, Poihipi Rd. A km or so down here is Restpoint Park, off the road on the left. They have two glass hives where you can watch the bees at work. There's honey tasting (you can even buy some if you like!), an animal park for kids and a number of souvenir shops. It's open 9 am to 5 pm daily and admission is free.

Just off Spa Rd is a wildlife park, Cherry Island, right in the Waikato River. A km along Spa Rd turn left into Motutahae St, then right into Waikato St – open 9 am to 5 pm daily, admission is $5.50 (children $1.65).

The small Taupo Regional Museum & Arts Centre is behind the information centre. It's open 10 am to 3 pm, Monday to Saturday and admission is free. Trainsville is an extensive model railway display at 35A Heu Heu St. It's open 10 am to 5 pm daily. There's a mini-golf course on the corner of Ruapehu and Roberts Sts (not far back from the lakeshore) or you can relax in De Brett Thermal Pools up the Napier-Taupo Highway on the left (open daily 7.30 am to 9.45 pm, admission $2.50).

Flights

If you're feeling affluent you can go for a scenic flight either by the floatplane from the lake front by Taupo Boat Harbour or with Taupo Air Services (tel 85-325) from Taupo Aerodrome. They both have similar flights for similar prices. At 11 am on Sundays you can arrange to go gliding from Centennial Park Airfield.

Lake Cruises

You can cruise the lake on the *Waikare II*, the *Ernest Kemp* or on the *Barbary*, a 60-year-old wooden yacht once owned by Errol Flynn. Don't ask me how it ended up on Lake Taupo! Cruises on the *Barbary* cost from $15 (children $8) and typically last 2½ to three hours. The cruises visit a modern Maori rock carving beside the lake, it's reached through private land so it's not easy to visit on foot.

Fishing

There are a number of places where you can hire fishing gear in town. There are also a number of fishing guides and charter boat operators. Check with the information centre. Hostellers staying at the Rainbow Lodge can book fishing trips there. A fishing licence is $5 a day or $14 a week. You can also get licences by the month or season.

Places to Stay

Hostels *Rainbow Lodge* (tel 85-754) at 99 Titiraupenga St is a brand new hostel which has quickly become known as one of the best in New Zealand. In fact it's so popular that it's often full and it's a very good idea to phone ahead and book. Bunkroom accommodation is $11 or there are twin rooms available for $27. The hostel has the usual lounge and kitchen facilities. All manner of trips and activities in the area can be arranged from here, often at a useful discount.

Taupo also has a summer *Youth Hostel* at Nui-a Tia College, Spa Rd, open from mid-December to the end of January for $9 per night.

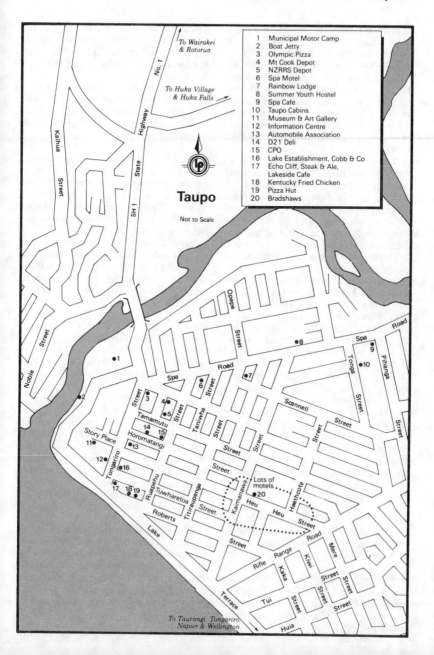

To Wairakei & Rotorua

To Huka Village & Huka Falls

Taupo

Not to Scale

1 Municipal Motor Camp
2 Boat Jetty
3 Olympic Pizza
4 Mt Cook Depot
5 NZRRS Depot
6 Spa Motel
7 Rainbow Lodge
8 Summer Youth Hostel
9 Spa Cafe
10 Taupo Cabins
11 Museum & Art Gallery
12 Information Centre
13 Automobile Association
14 D21 Deli
15 CPO
16 Lake Establishment, Cobb & Co
17 Echo Cliff, Steak & Ale, Lakeside Cafe
18 Kentucky Fried Chicken
19 Pizza Hut
20 Bradshaws

To Tauranga, Tongariro, Napier & Wellington

Camping & Cabins There are lots of camp sites in Taupo including, in the middle of town by the river, the *Municipal Camp* (tel 86-600). Located on Redoubt St, camping costs $10 a night for two people. There are also cabins at $15 for two. Hopefully this is once again a well run site, after a period when it was somewhat rundown. You can camp for free beside the river about 1½ km south of the Huka Falls towards Taupo.

Taupo Cabins (tel 84-346) at 50 Tonga Street, 1.5 km from the CPO, has a whole variety of cabins. They cost from $22 a night for the cheapies to over $40 a night for the fanciest ones with kitchen and shower. *Auto Park* (tel 84-272) is on Rangatira St 1.5 km from the centre. Here there's camping at $10 for two, a couple of dollars more with power, plus cabins and tourist flats.

Out of town *Acacia Bay Lodge* (tel 86-830) at 868 Acacia Bay Rd has just a few tent sites at $12 for two, $16 for caravan sites. There are also cabins from $33 a night and up. They all have kitchens but the cheaper ones don't have their own shower or toilet. *Acacia Holiday Park* (tel 85-159) is also on Acacia Bay Rd. Camping here costs $7 per person and again there are on-site caravans, cabins and tourist flats.

Other sites around Taupo include the *Wairakei Thermal Valley Motor Camp* at Wairakei, the *Windsor Lodge Caravan Park* at Waitahanui 12 km south and the *Rotongaio Lakeside Motor Camp* by the lake 15 km south. Also at Waitahanui the *Waitahanui Lodge* (tel 87-183) has units at $37 for two.

Guest Houses *Bradshaws* (tel 88-288) at 130 Heu Heu St has rooms including breakfast at $25 to $33 single, $44 to $55 for twins or doubles.

Hotels The *Spa Hotel* (tel 84-120) on Spa Rd has rooms at $30/50 including breakfast. It's a little far out from the centre and see the description under

entertainment. Right in the centre, the *Lake Establishment* (tel 86-165) is on the corner of Tongariro and Tuwharetoa Sts. Rooms are $38 to $50 for singles, from $55 for doubles.

If money is no object there's one of New Zealand's most expensive hotels just outside of Taupo. At the *Haka Lodge* (tel 85-791) at Huka Falls singles are over $400 a night!

Motels Taupo is packed with motels and, as in Rotorua, the competition tends to keep prices down although many of them have minimum rates during holiday periods. The *Spa Road Motel* (tel 89-292) is very close to the centre at 69 Spa Rd and has rooms at $45/55.

Dunrovin (tel 87-384) at 140 Heu Heu St, the *Continental Motel* (tel 85-836) at 9 Scannell St and the *Golf Course* (tel 89-415) on Tauhara Rd are all similarly priced. There are a lot of motels along Heu Heu St.

Places to Eat

Fast Food & Takeaways Taupo has the usual collection of sandwich places and take-away bars. Down by the lakefront there's a *Pizza Hut* and a *Kentucky Fried Chicken* side by side.

On Horomatangi St there's the *D21 Deli* with lots of sandwiches and snacks. Or try the *Olympic Pizza House* on the corner of Tongariro St and Spa Rd. Up Spa Rd past the Rainbow Lodge and the summer hostel on the corner of Pihanga St, the *Spa Cafe* is a good place for fish & chips and the *Spa Bakery* in the same small shopping centre has good sandwiches and baked goods.

Pub Food & Restaurants There is a *Cobb & Co* in the Lake Establishment, Tuwharetoa St, open every day 7.30 am to 10 pm with the usual menu and reasonable prices. The *Spa Hotel* has a menu that features dishes like fish & chips, pie & chips, sausage & chips or steak & chips, all at about $7 to $8.

The *Steak & Ale Bar* at 17 Tongariro St is open for dinner from Tuesday to Sunday. No messing about at this place, it's big hunks of meat served up straightforward and simple at around $16 for main courses. The food is well prepared though, so no complaints about the food. The absurdly uncomfortable tables and chairs are something else. There are some other expensive restaurants like *Brookes* at 22 Tuwharetoa St or *Echo Cliff* (with good views over the lake) right at the lake end of Tongariro St. There's even a French restaurant – *La Vielle France*, upstairs at 133 Tongariro St.

Entertainment

Trumps in the Lake Establishment on Tongariro St often has a band on Thursday, Friday and Saturday nights. There's also often entertainment at the *Spa Hotel*, some distance down Spa Rd from the centre. Actually the Spa Hotel is entertainment all by itself. The cavernous public bar is definitely a fishin', huntin', shootin' man's hangout. There are trophy heads mounted around the wall and the toilets are labelled 'stags' and 'hinds'. Nobody seems to buy beer less than a litre jug at a time but you feel unsteady on your feet even without any beer on board since the carpet seems to be underlaid with about five cm of foam rubber. Must make for softer landings when you fall over.

Getting There & Away

Air You can get to Taupo from Auckland ($112), Wanganui ($99) or Wellington ($131) with Air New Zealand. Contact James Travel (tel 87-065) on Horomatangi St.

Road Only an hour or so south of Rotorua, Taupo is about half way between Auckland and Wellington. It costs $16 from Rotorua to Taupo by NZRRS bus. From Napier it's $21 by Mt Cook and takes about 2½ hours. From Auckland the fare is about $31 for the 4½ to five hour trip. Mt Cook, Mainline and NZRRS all operate on this route. Mt Cook and NZRRS have their stations side by side on Ruapehu St. Mainline are handled by Mt Cook.

Getting Around

The airport is six km south and a taxi costs about $12. Bicycles can be hired from Roy's Cycles in Ruapehu St at $5 per day or from the Rainbow Lodge.

Tongariro

Tongariro was New Zealand's first National Park – established in 1887. It was given to the country by a far-sighted Maori chief who realised that this was the only way to preserve an area of such spiritual significance in its entirety. With its collection of mighty (and still active) volcanoes, Tongariro is one of the most interesting and spectacular parks in New Zealand. In the summer it's got excellent walks and tramps and in the winter it's an important skiing area.

There are two main ski fields – the Whakapapa Skifield up above the Chateau (the THC hotel) and the newer Turoa Skifield above Ohakune. See the Skiing section for more details. Clustered around the fine old Chateau are cabins and a 'skotel'. There are also huts scattered along the walking trails.

The Park Headquarters near the Chateau will supply you with lots of info on the park and the shorter walks. Mt Ruapehu is the highest of the volcanoes at 2796 metres and still active – it's also the site for all the ski runs! The upper slopes were showered with hot mud and water in the most recent activity in 1969 and 1975. The long, multi-peaked summit of Ruapehu shelters Crater Lake which you can climb up to if you're well prepared. The route follows the Whakapapa Glacier for part of the way. Don't go too close to Crater Lake – it's surrounded by dangerous precipices.

In 1945-47 the level of the lake rose

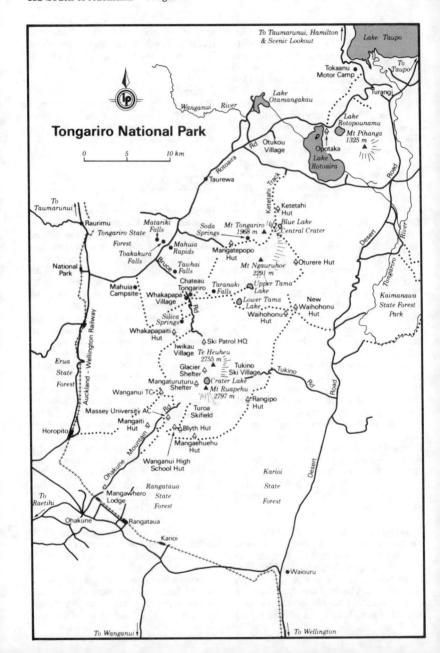

dramatically due to eruptions blocking off the overflow. On Christmas Eve 1953 the overflow burst and the flood that resulted led to one of New Zealand's worst disasters. The torrent swept away a railway bridge moments before a crowded express train arrived and in the resulting crash 153 people lost their lives.

Mt Ngauruhoe is much younger than the other volcanoes in the park – it's estimated to have formed in the last 2500 years and the slopes to the 2291-metre summit are still perfectly symmetrical. It can also be climbed by the experienced or with a guide although in winter it is definitely suitable only for experienced mountaineers. It's a very steep but rewarding climb. Mt Tongariro, at 1968 metres is much older and regarded as being dormant but has a number of coloured lakes dotting its uneven summit as well as hot springs gushing out of its side at Ketetahi. The Tama Lakes are crater lakes formed between Ngauruhoe and Ruapehu.

Information

For information on Tongariro National Park, walks, tramps, etc, see the Park Headquarters (tel Ruapehu 729), Whakapapa. It's behind the Chateau and across from the campsite and is open 8 am to 5 pm daily. There are also ranger stations at Ohakune (tel 58-578) and Turangi (tel 8520).

The Lands & Survey Department excellent *Tongariro National Park* map is well worth purchasing before you go.

Walks

The park has a number of really interesting walks including a long one described in the Tramping section. There are brochures on the various walks available from the park ranger stations and during the summer months there are regular guided walks at very low cost. You can go on a walk to the Crater Lakes or climb to the summits of Mt Ngauruhoe and Mt Tongariro for just a couple of dollars. Walks from the Park HQ include:

Taranaki Falls A 2½-hour walk to the Wairere Stream and along to the spectacular sheer drop of the Taranaki Falls. Excellent pamphlets describing this and the other short walks can be obtained from the Park HQ.

Silica Springs Another 2½-hour trip to springs where the rocks are coloured by silica and other minerals carried in the water.

Whakapapanui Track Starting from the same point as the Silica Springs track it takes two hours to follow this track alongside the Whakapapanui Stream downstream more-or-less parallel to the road.

Whakapapanui Gorge A full-day trip, needing boots. Follow the road above the Chateau up to the footbridge across the Whakapapanui Stream. Don't cross the bridge, but go to your left and follow the stream, rock-hopping up until you eventually enter the gorge itself with a sheer precipice at its head.

Ridge Track A 40-minute walk above the Park HQ.

Whakapapaiti Valley A full-day round-trip walk from the Park HQ or Scoria Flat, about four km above Park HQ on the Bruce road.

Tama Lakes To climb to these crater lakes takes two to three hours each way beyond Taranaki Falls.

Walks starting from other parts of the National Park include:

Mangatepopo Valley From the end of the access road this 1½-hour walk (each way) leads to the valley between Tongariro and Ngauruhoe.

Tawhai Falls A 10-minute walk off the entrance road four km below the Park HQ.

Waitongo Falls Two hours return from the Ohakune access road.

Mangawhero Forest A 2½-hour walk through one of the few remaining original forests near Ohakune.

Ketetahi Springs The track starts about 30 km from the Chateau, on the north side of Tongariro. It takes about 2½-hours to walk to the springs and you can bathe in the stream there.

Mt Tongariro Traverse It takes six to eight hours to walk right across the mountain in what has been described as the finest one-day walk in New Zealand. Come prepared for changeable mountain weather and you have to make transport arrangements at both ends.

Rotopounamu A beautiful, secluded lake, 20 minutes' walk from the Te Ponanga Saddle road in a separate part of the Tongariro National Park between Mt Tongariro and Lake Taupo, which includes Pihanga. See the chapter on New Plymouth for the legend about Tongariro, Taranaki and Pihanga. You can walk around the lake in 1½-hours – no camping though.

Other Attractions

North of the main part of the park on the shores of Lake Rotoaria are some interesting excavations of a pre-European Maori village site. West of here is Te Porere Redoubt Historical Reserve, the site of the last pitched battle in the Maori wars in 1869. Very different from the ancient Maori pa, Te Porere was typical of the type of fortification that followed the use of firearms. The earthworks have been restored. It's a 22-km drive from the Chateau, and then another 15 minutes from the road.

To the east of Mt Ruapehu is an area known as the Rangipo Desert. It's not a desert in the true sense of the word, but was so named because of its desert-like appearance caused by its cold, exposed, windswept situation.

Places to Stay

The choice at Tongariro is whether you stay in the National Park at Whakapapa, where there is an expensive hotel, a pretty expensive motel and a campsite, or whether you stay outside the park in one of the surrounding towns. See the following sections on National Park, Ohakune and Turangi for accommodation details about places outside the park.

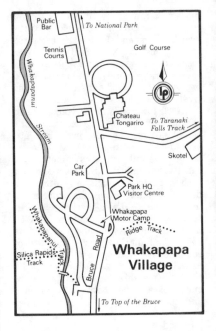

Places to Stay

Camping & Cabins The popular *Whakapapa Camp* (tel Mt Ruapehu 897) is up the road from the Chateau, across from the Park Visitor's Centre. If you're tenting (not recommended in winter!), it's $6 per adult, $3 per child. Caravan sites cost $7 per adult and $3.50 per child plus a standing fee of $3 most of the time, $5 during the 1 June to 30 October peak season and $16 (oh wow) on holidays and long weekends.

The camp also has pleasant cabins which cost $8 for adults, $6 for children but with a minimum charge of $27. And it has a lodge with bunks for 20 at $9 per person. Don't count on the bunkroom, sometimes it's filled up with school groups.

Around the park there are eight huts – access by foot only – scattered around the park. Contact the ranger stations about the tramping huts which cost $7 a night (children \$3) – maximum stay two nights at busy periods.

Hotel & Motel The hotel is called the *Chateau* (tel Mt Ruapehu 809) and apart from the Hermitage at Mt Cook, it is the best known hotel in New Zealand. Like the Hermitage it's run by the THC. It was originally built in 1929 and is still in like-new condition, and priced accordingly. Rooms costs about \$100 to \$120 in the off-season (1 October to 15 July). In season you're looking at about \$130 to \$200. The Chateau is not for economising.

Round behind the Chateau is the *Skotel* (tel Mt Ruapehu 719) which has gone through a recent renovation and expansion. Accommodation here includes plain no-facility rooms at around \$35, rooms with bathroom at \$60, deluxe rooms (you get a video and other luxuries) are about \$75. Those are the low-season summer rates for one person. In the winter, skiing, high season the rates jump about 50%. Add on \$5 per person for additional people in summer. In winter add on \$10 to \$12 per person. The Skotel also has chalets with kitchens and other goodies from about \$90 for two. There's a communal kitchen for the regular Skotel accommodation, as well as a spa pool, gym, games room, restaurant and bar.

Places to Eat

There's a reasonable selection of food in the camp store if you're preparing your own – as usual it's more expensive than down the road. It's 16 km down the road to National Park, the nearest crossroads town. Milk and bread are sold at the store and the Chateau cafeteria, but can be difficult to get sometimes. The camp has kitchen facilities, of course, but so does the Skotel.

The camp store also does pies and light snacks. You can also get pies, sandwiches and the like in the public bar across from the Chateau. Otherwise the *Skotel* has a bistro-bar with the pub regulars – main courses from around \$11 to \$14, desserts

for \$4, breakfast is \$7.50. And you can eat at the *Chateau* where breakfast costs from \$10 or at dinner main courses are around \$21 to \$25.

During the ski season there is a takeaway food van or if you're skiing there is food available up at the Top of the Bruce where the lifts and tows start.

Getting There & Away

Road State Highway 1 (at this point it's called the Desert Road) passes down the east side of the park. It was once a nightmare, but now it's a good sealed road, though sometimes temporarily blocked by snow in winter. State Highway 4 passes down the west side, Provincial Highway 47 crosses the top and 49 the bottom; so encircling it by roads. The main road up into the park is Provincial Highway 48 which leads to Whakapapa Village, where the Park HQ and the Chateau are, and on up the mountain is the Bruce road to the 'Top of the Bruce' at Iwikau Village. The Ohakune Mountain Rd leads up to the Turoa Skifield from Ohakune in the south-west.

In the winter ski season there are buses right to Whakapapa village but at other times of year the closest you can get by public transport is the small settlement of National Park, 15 km away. You can take a taxi from National Park to Whakapapa but at around \$24 it isn't cheap. See the National Park section below for bus details.

Whichever direction you come, hitching to Whakapapa is never that easy because traffic is usually so light. If you're coming south from Turangi use the shorter saddle road – the locals no longer use the SH 1 to SH 47 route.

Getting Around

The bus-truck service from Whakapapa up to the ski-runs at the Top of the Bruce cost \$4 one-way or \$7 return.

NATIONAL PARK

The small settlement of National Park is at

the junction of SH 4 and SH 47, 15 km from Whakapapa village. It's of no real interest, just a dormitory for Tongariro. The Auckland-Wellington railway line runs through National Park but this is another place where the trains no longer stop.

Places to Stay

Camping & Cabins The *Discovery Caravan Park* (tel National Park 744) is on SH 47 about mid-way between Whakapapa and National Park. Which means it's effectively in the middle of nowhere! Camping charges are $8 a night per person and there are also cabins with charges that vary from around $30 for two in the low (summer) season. Sometimes in the deepest troughs of the off-season they have special prices on the cabins which are even lower.

Six km south of National Park is *Erua Ski Lodge* (tel 87-144 or 84-216 for bookings), which can accommodate up to 200 people in bunks at $17 a night during the ski season. Occupants must supply their own bedding and blankets and the kitchen, dining room, showers and recreation area are communal. It's half-price out of season. There are also some on-site caravans. The management also organises summer camps which include windsurfing, horse riding, sailing and climbing.

Six km north is the *Slalom Ski Lodge* (tel National Park 856) with rooms at $55 in the off-season or beds in the bunkroom at $12 to $17.

Chalets & Motels The *Discovery Best Western Motel* (tel National Park 744) is at the same site as the Discovery campsite (see above), about half way between Whakapapa and National Park. Rates vary with the season but a double costs from about $65 off-season, over $100 in season.

Various sizes of chalet are available at *Buttercup Alpine Resort* (tel National Park 702) which is actually at National Park. Costs including breakfast and dinner are $55 per person (children $33). Various activities are also organised from here

including rafting trips on the lower Tongariro ($50 for a full day trip) or volcano hikes ($25 including lunch and transport to the trailhead).

There are several other motels in National Park including the *Highland Motel* (tel National Park 860) and the *Mountain Heights Motel* (tel National Park 833) both with rooms at around $48/60 but much more at the peak of the ski season. The *National Park Hotel* (tel National Park 805) has rooms at $32/42 and a bunkroom at $18.

Getting There & Away

From mid-87 trains no longer stop at National Park so there's only buses now. NZRRS services use the railway station as a depot – or at least they used to, that may change now that trains no longer stop there. Some of the Auckland-Wellington NZRRS bus services stop at National Park. Auckland-National Park is about five hours and costs $41; Wellington-National Park is about six hours and costs $37. To Ohakune it's $7 or to Hamilton $27. There's a taxi service to Whakapapa which costs $24.

OHAKUNE

In contrast to National Park, Ohakune is quite a pleasant little town with lots of motels and even more restaurants. It's very much a skiing town, a lot of effort goes into catering for those snow-season big-spenders.

Orientation & Information

The centre with the CPO and information office is at the southern end of town on SH 49. The Information Centre has lots of brochures and an excellent 3D model of Tongariro Park – great for tracing where you're going to walk. Up at the north end of town by the railway line there's a sort of second centre with a number of restaurants along Thames St. Just north of the line is the Ohakune Ranger Station with info on walking in the park and a book to sign before you set off.

Things to See

Ohakune is mainly a base for skiing or walking trips but while you're in town check the 'big carrot' on the Waiouru road and the weather stone on Thames St. Kids will like the old tank in the children's play park by the information centre. Helicopter flightseeing trips are available from Ohakune. Phone 58-888 for details.

Places to Stay

Hostel The *Ohakune Youth Hostel* (tel 58-724) is on Clyde St, near the CPO and Information Centre. It's a good hostel with lots of rooms and accommodation for 28 in total at $11. During the ski season it is very heavily booked so at that time you have to plan ahead.

Camping & Cabins The *Ohakune Borough Camp* (tel 58-561) is on Moore St and has camping sites at $6 per person. There are also powered sites, slightly more expensive in winter.

Hotels & Motels Costs are usually higher during the ski season at Ohakune's motels. The *Hobbit Motel Lodge* (tel 58-248) is on the corner of Goldfinch and Wye Sts. Singles/doubles are $50/60 in the summer low season. There are also bunkrooms where a bed costs $11 if you provide your own bedding.

At 2 Moore St the *Ohakune Mountain View Motel* (tel 58-675) has rooms at around $42 to $50. Or there's the *Ohakune Hotel* (tel 58-268) on Clyde St with singles at $30, doubles at $40 to $50.

Places to Eat

Friar Tuck in the centre off Goldfinch St does sandwiches and snacks. *Parklands* behind the YHA is good for cheaper sit-down meals. Or beside the YHA on Clyde St there's the *Lovin' Spoonful Restaurant* and the *Cafe de Kerb* takeaways. The Ohakune Hotel has the *Griddlestone Restaurant* while also on Clyde St you'll find the *Cafe Stua* and the Swiss *Grischuna Restaurant*.

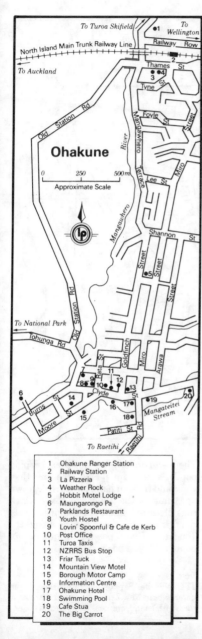

Ohakune

0   250   500 m

Approximate Scale

1   Ohakune Ranger Station
2   Railway Station
3   La Pizzeria
4   Weather Rock
5   Hobbit Motel Lodge
6   Maungarongo Pa
7   Parklands Restaurant
8   Youth Hostel
9   Lovin' Spoonful & Cafe de Kerb
10 Post Office
11 Turoa Taxis
12 NZRRS Bus Stop
13 Friar Tuck
14 Mountain View Motel
15 Borough Motor Camp
16 Information Centre
17 Ohakune Hotel
18 Swimming Pool
19 Cafe Stua
20 The Big Carrot

Up by the railway station there are a number of restaurants along Thames St including *La Pizzeria* which does pretty good pizzas.

Getting There & Away
Some of the NZRRS services on the Auckland-Wellington route go through Ohakune. The railway line does too but this is another place where the train may not be stopping.

Getting Around
There's transport up to the skifields during the winter with Ruapehu Outback Adventures (tel 58-799) and their snowbus. Check with Turoa Taxis on Clyde St (tel 58-573) about transport to or from trail heads if you're heading off tramping. They charge $28 for a taxi to the Lake Surprise track, $18 to the Blyth track.

WAIOURU
At the junction of SH 1 (south from Turangi) and SH 49 (east from Ohakune) is Waiouru where the Army Memorial Museum makes an interesting stop. It's open 9 am to 4.30 pm daily and entry is $5 (children $2.50).

TURANGI
At the north end of the park, beside Lake Taupo, Turangi is a new town, developed for the construction of the hydro-power station here. It's a good access point for the tracks at the north end of the park.

Information
There's an excellent new information centre just off SH 1 by the town centre. They have a model of the hydro-power project and are open 9 am to 5 pm daily. If you're planning to walk into the park from the north fill in the walker's intentions book at the ranger station first.

Trout Hatchery
Four km south of Turangi on SH 1 are the Tongariro Trout Hatcheries. They're open 9 am to 4 pm daily and entry is free.

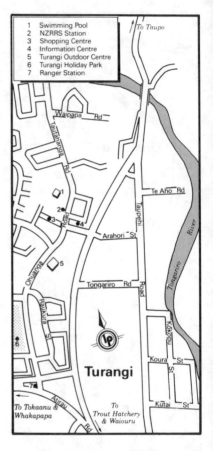

1 Swimming Pool
2 NZRRS Station
3 Shopping Centre
4 Information Centre
5 Turangi Outdoor Centre
6 Turangi Holiday Park
7 Ranger Station

There's an underwater view area, keeping ponds, a pleasant picnic area and then you could try your hand on the real, grown up, thing in the Tongariro River which runs close by. There's a fine little walk right from the town centre along the Tongariro River passing a number of popular fishing pools.

Trout
The Wildlife Service operates three trout hatcheries in New Zealand – one in Wanaka in the South Island, one near Rotorua and the one

in Turangi. The Wanaka hatchery is mainly for salmon while the two North Island hatcheries are almost exclusively for rainbow trout. There are other private hatcheries, some of which obtain their eggs from the Wildlife Service operations.

The first brown trout eggs arrived in New Zealand from Tasmania in 1867. They had originally come to Australia from England. Rainbow trout eggs first arrived from California in 1883. Hatcheries were established at that time to rear the first young fish and although many fish are hatched naturally there is still a need for artificial hatcheries. This is because New Zealand's lakes and rivers may be ideal for trout but some of them have insufficient good spawning grounds. Plus there's a hell of a lot of fishing going on!

In the wild fully grown trout migrate each winter to suitable spawning beds. This usually means gravel beds in the upper reaches of rivers and streams. Here a female fish makes a shallow depression and deposits eggs which are quickly fertilised by an attendant male fish. The female fish then sweeps gravel over the eggs. Over two or three days this process is repeated to create a *redd* with several pockets of eggs. All through this process the fish do not feed and a female fish may lose one third of its body weight by the time it returns to the lake. Male fish are in even worse shape because they arrive at the spawning grounds before the females and leave afterwards.

Less than 1% of the eggs survive to become mature fish. The eggs may be damaged or destroyed by movement of the gravel and even when hatched they may be eaten by other fish, birds or rats. Even other trout will happily make a meal of them.

Because there were only a few shipment of eggs originally, from which all today's trout are descended, New Zealand's rainbow trout are considered to be a very pure strain. The hatchery eggs are collected by capturing fish during their spawning run. Eggs are gently squeezed from a female fish and milt from males added and stirred together in a container. Incubator trays containing about 10,000 eggs are placed in racks and washed over by a continuous flow of water.

After 15 days the embryo fish eyes start to appear and by the 18th day the embryo, previously very sensitive and frail, have become quite hardy. They'd better be because on that day the eggs are poured from a metre height into a wire basket. Any weak eggs are killed off by this rough treatment, ensuring that only healthy fish are hatched out. The survivors are now placed 5000 to a basket and about 10 days later the fish hatch out, wriggle through the mesh and drop to the bottom of the trough. They stay there for about 20 days, living off the yolk sac.

When they have totally absorbed their yolk sac they are known as fry and although they can be released at this stage they are normally kept until they are 10 to 15 cm long. At this time they are nine to 12 months old and are known as fingerlings. They are moved outside when they are about four cm long and reared in ponds. Fingerlings are transported to the place where they will be released in what looks rather like a small petrol tanker, and simply pumped out the back down a large diameter pipe!

Tokaanu

About five km out of Turangi on the road round the western side of Lake Taupo towards Taumarunui is this pleasant little pioneer settlement with an interesting thermal area. There's a posted walk around the bubbling mud pools and also hot pools and a sauna. The walk is free, the public pool costs $2, private ones $3.

Other Attractions

Turangi is a popular base for fishing, walking and rafting. River Rats Rafting (tel 7492) will take you on a 12 km whitewater rafting trip down the Tongariro River for $59 per person. They operate at 1.30 pm midweek, 8.30 am and 1.30 pm on weekends. Turangi Scenic Flights (tel 7870) operate flights over the volcanoes of Tongariro National Park or over Lake Taupo.

On the slopes of Pihanga and near to Turangi it's a pleasant 1½ hour walk around Lake Rotopounamu with its prolific birdlife.

Places to Stay

Camping & Cabins Right in the centre the *Tongariro Outdoor Centre* (tel 7492) on Ohuanga Rd used to be the single men's hostel during the construction of the power station. They have a number of 12-room lodges each with a TV room, kitchen and dining area. Rooms are $20 single or $32 for twins or doubles or they have a backpacker's special of a bed in a triple room for $12. They also have tent sites for $4 per person.

There are a number of campsites in Turangi including *Turangi Holiday Park* (tel 8754) on Ohuanga Rd, off SH 41. Sites are $6 per person, slightly more with power. They also have cabins at $15 single or $27 double and some on-site caravans. This was also at one time quarters for the hydro-power construction workers, which accounts for the large number of cabins.

There are several other campsites out of Turangi on the road around the Taupo lakeside to Taupo. They are the *Motuoapa Domain Camp* (tel 5333), eight km out at Motuoapa, the *Tauranga-Taupo Lodge & Caravan Park* (tel 8385), 11 km out at Tauranga, and the *Motutere Bay Caravan Park* (tel 8963), 17 km out at Motutere Bay.

Hotels, Motels & Lodges There are plenty of motels and fishing lodges in Turangi. This is a very popular area for trout fishing and like the campsites some of them are round the lakeshore towards Taupo. There's some interesting accommodation in nearby Tokaanu including the expensive *THC Tokaanu* (tel 8873) with rooms at around $100 a night and a thermal swimming pool. Or there's the *Oasis Motel* (tel 8569) with rooms around $40/45 for singles/doubles.

Places to Eat

There are a scattering of takeaways and fast food places like *Golden Crust*, *Coffee Time* or *Tiki's Burger Bar* in the modern little shopping centre. Or try *El Burcio*, a solidly Italian reminder of the many Italian construction workers at the time the power station was built.

Getting There & Away

NZRRS buses stop right beside the shopping centre in Turangi. Auckland-Wellington buses which run down the east side of Lake Taupo from Taupo all go through Turangi. Fares include Taupo $8, Auckland $38 and Wellington $35. Mt Cook buses also go through Turangi and use the NZRRS depot.

Getting Around

Alpine Scenic Tours (tel 8392 at all hours) offer tours of the area but also provide transport for skiers and trampers. They'll take you to the start of the Ketetahi Trail for $10 ($6.50 per person for larger groups) or to the Mangatepopo Trail for $25 ($12.50). Access to these northern trails used to be a real problem so this is an excellent service.

Coromandel Peninsula

To the north-east of the Hauraki Plains is the Coromandel Peninsula, a rugged, densely forested region with very little flat land and rivers that force their way through gorges and then pour down steep cliffs to the sea. The Coromandel State Forest Park stretches almost the entire length of the peninsula. It's an intensely scenic spot, isolated and well worth going to before it becomes spoilt by tourism. There are a number of small towns scattered up and down both sides of the peninsula along the coast.

The Coromandel Peninsula is not the place to go if you're looking for entertainment, but if you're in the mood for lying around on beaches, fishing, lazing and walking it's superb.

History

The European history of the peninsula is steeped in goldmining, kauri-timber milling and gumdigging. The first gold discovered in New Zealand was at Coromandel in 1852 by Charles Ring, but the rush was short-lived once the miners found it was not alluvial gold, but had to

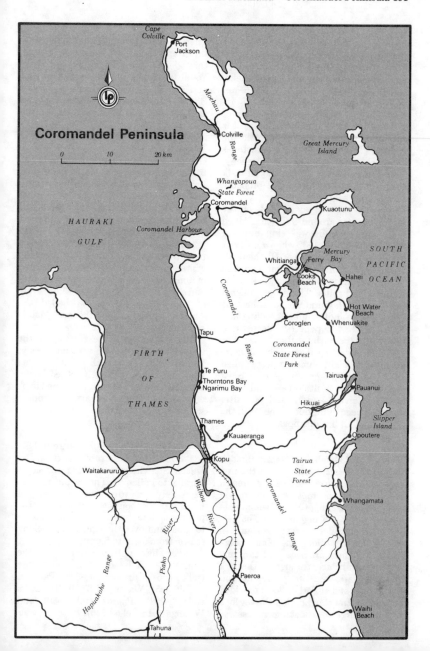

be wrested from the ground by pick and shovel. More gold was discovered around Thames in mid-1867 and over the next few years other fields were proclaimed at Coromandel, Kuaotunu and Karangahake. In 1892 the Martha mine at Waihi began production and by the time of its shutdown in 1952 around $60 million of gold had been won. Interest in minerals is still strong today as apart from gold the area is rich in semi-precious gemstones like quartz, amethyst, jasper, chalcedony, agate and carnelian. In fact if you walk along Te Mata beach you will probably stumble over some agate.

Kauri logging was big business on the Coromandel for around 100 years. Allied to the timber trade was ship building which took off after 1832 when a mill was established at Mercury Bay. By the 1880s Kauaeranga, Coroglen (Gumtown) and Tairua were the main suppliers of kauri to the Auckland mills. Things got tougher once the kauri around the coast became scarce due to indiscriminate felling and the loggers had to penetrate deeper and deeper into the bush for the timber. The problems of getting it out became more and more difficult. Some logs were pulled out by bullock teams; on the west coast tramways were built; others had to be hauled to rivers and floated out after dams had been built, but by the 1930s the logging had all but disappeared.

Walks

There are over 30 walks and tramps through Coromandel Forest Park covering the area from the Maratoto Forest near Paeroa to Cape Colville; the most popular region being the Kauaeranga Valley which cuts into the Colville Range behind Thames. The main entrance is from the southern edge of Thames along the Kauaeranga Valley Rd. There are overnight camping huts in several places throughout the park including Waikawau, Stony, Fletcher and Fantail Bays and at Port Jackson provided by the Department of Lands & Survey for a nominal charge – no bookings necessary.

Places to Stay

There are camp grounds administered by the Department of Lands & Survey throughout Coromandel Forest Park. You'll find them on the west coast and northern tip of the peninsula at Fantail Bay, Port Jackson and Fletcher Bay and at Stony Bay and Waikawau Bay on the east coast.

THAMES

Coming from Auckland, Thames is the first town you arrive at on the peninsula. Pakeha settlement of Thames was fairly late in the day but it began in the usual way as a mission station. The Maoris had settled the region much earlier and lived on high land near Thames until the 1820s, returning about 10 years later to occupy a new pa site on the Thames flat. After the whites moved in in 1833 Thames consisted of a mission station, two or three pa sites and a few traders. During the Maori Wars of the 1860s, gun boats shelled the Thames pa and in 1864 the local Maoris surrendered.

Today Thames is the gateway to the Coromandel Peninsula, a rather sleepy, laid-back little port with a small fishing fleet and lots of privately-owned boats. The main drag, Pollen St, is claimed to be one of the longest straight shopping streets in New Zealand.

Information

The Thames Information Centre (tel 87-284) is right in the centre of Porritt Park on Queen St, which runs along the coast parallel to Pollen St. The people here are extremely friendly and a mine of information about the whole of the peninsula. It is open every day from 10 am to 4 pm and over the Christmas holiday season from 9 am to 5 pm.

Other information centres on the peninsula can be found at Whitianga (tel 65-555), Tairua (tel 48-503), Pauanui (tel 48-395), Waihi (tel 8386), Te Aroha (tel 48-052), Paeroa (tel 8636) and Whangamata (tel 58-340).

Top: Brian Boru Hotel, Thames (TW)
Bottom: South of Coromandel, Coromandel Peninsula (TW)

Top: Wellington (TW)
Bottom: Chateau Tongariro at dusk (NZTP)

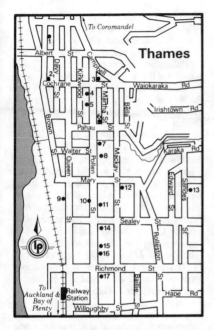

Thames

To Coromandel

To Auckland & Bay of Plenty

1 Sunkist Lodge
2 Mineralogical Museum
3 Historical Museum
4 NZRRS Depot
5 Pizza Cabin
6 Junction Hotel
7 Golden Dragon Restaurant
8 Majestic Restaurant (fish & chips)
9 Information Centre
10 Post Office
11 Boulangerie Cafe & Restaurant
12 Salutation Hotel
13 Brookby Motel
14 Imperial Hotel
15 Chevron Diner
16 Automobile Association
17 Brian Boru Hotel

Various leaflets and pamphlets on walks through the Coromandel Forest Park – giving map references, general description and approximate walking times – can be obtained from the Forest Service office in Pollen St or the Forest Park HQ which is about 15 km out of Thames on Kauaeranga Valley Rd. The Forest Park office is open weekdays and in season on weekends too. The Sunkist Lodge also has lots of walking information.

Gold Mining History

You can see some of Thames' old gold mining history at the eastern end of Cochrane St. The Hauraki Prospectors' Association has set up a stamper battery and there's a mine close by which you can look over on request.

Around the end of the 1800s Thames was actually the biggest town in New Zealand with over 100 hotels. There are still a number of fine old hotels like the Brian Boru on Pollen St, they're a solid reminder of the town's goldrush prosperity. The information office has a $3.50 map showing where all the old hotels once were. The popular Sunkist Lodge is just one of the venerable hotel buildings, now converted to other uses.

Museums

On the corner of Brown and Cochrane Sts you'll find the Mineralogical Museum which has the most comprehensive collection of New Zealand rocks, mineral and fossils in the country. Open Monday to Saturday from 2 to 4 pm and on public holidays from 10 am to noon, reopening 2 to 4 pm. Ask someone here and they may be able to put you in touch with one of the local prospectors so you can go fossicking yourself. Next door is the Thames School of Mines which is in the process of being restored by the Historic Places Trust.

The local Historical Museum is on the corner of Cochrane and Pollen Sts and is open Monday to Saturday from 10 am to 4 pm, Sunday from 1 to 4 pm.

Lookouts

If you've got wheels there's a nice drive to Kauaeranga Valley through bush country. Or you can walk or drive up to Monument Hill – a WW I peace memorial – at the northern intersection of Pollen St and State Highway 25 for a good view of the township and right across the Hauraki Plains. If you look north you can see the Hauraki Gulf.

Another good vantage point is Totara Pa Hill, which is a lookout over the Waihou Valley and the Hauraki Plains. There were several Maori inter-tribal battles fought in this area and if you look carefully you will see the remains of various fortifications and deep trenches.

Totara

At Totara, south of Thames on the main highway, there's a winery, Totara Vineyards, which has won awards for its wines. You can stop off for a tasting.

Places to Stay

Hostels *Sunkist Lodge* (tel 88-808) at 506 Brown St is a pleasantly relaxed hostel with beds at $11. There are some smaller rooms including singles at $15, and some twins or doubles (particularly the 'honeymoon suite') at $26. The upstairs verandah is a fine place to laze on a sunny afternoon. The fine old building was the Lady Bowen Hotel from 1868 to 1952 and it's reputed to have a resident ghost. The manager organises tours of the peninsula for $25.

Camping & Cabins *Dickson Park Motor Camp* (tel 87-308) is three km north of Thames, pleasantly situated beside a stream. Camping costs $6 per person, a bit more with power. There is bunkroom accommodation at $9; cabins starting at $22; and fancier cabins from $33 or $44 with bathroom. It's a quiet site with a swimming pool. There are a number of other campsites up the coast north from Thames, see the North to Coromandel section that follows.

Hotels There are still enough hotels remaining from the goldrush days to give Thames a good representation in this category. Top of the heap is the *Brian Boru* (tel 86-523) on Pollen St with rooms

at $25/40 or with attached bathrooms at $40/60. In the off season they'll probably quote you budget rates if you ask.

The *Imperial Hotel* (tel 86-200) is also on Pollen St and has rooms at $30/45 or a handful of doubles with attached bathroom for $55. Others are the *Junction Hotel* (tel 86-008) on Pollen and Pahau Sts or the cheaper *Warwick Arms* (tel 86-183) on Pollen St and the cheapest of all *Salutation* (tel 86-488) at 400 Mary St.

Motels There are plenty of motels in Thames and north along the coast towards Coromandel. None of them are price bargains, count on at least $50 for a single, $60 for a double. You could try the *Brookby Motel* (tel 86-663) at 102 Redwood Lane and the *Crescent Motel* (tel 86-506) on the corner of Jellicoe Crescent and Fenton St. The *Coastal Motor Lodge*, three km north of Thames on the main road, is more expensive but it's particularly attractive and pleasantly situated.

Places to Eat

There are a number of places to eat along Pollen St including the licensed *Pizza Cabin*, which has various pizzas for between $7 and $9 for a medium and $13 to $16 for a large. It also has Bluff oysters – not to be missed if you haven't tried them – and the usual steak, ham steak and fish dishes.

The *Hotel Imperial*, also on Pollen St, has the cheaper *Pan & Handle* restaurant and the more expensive *Regency Room*. The Pan & Handle is open for lunch and dinner, from 6 to 8.30 pm, and has main courses from $9.

Pollen St takeaways and snack bars include the *Chevron Diner* at 442 which has takeaways, burgers, sandwiches and an eat there menu. Opposite the post office is *The Boulangere* at 523, an OK coffee bar which provides meals on Wednesdays, Thursdays and Fridays only.

Getting There & Away

Road There are regular bus services between Auckland, Thames, Coromandel,

Whitianga, the Hauraki Plains, Paeroa, Waihi and Hamilton, but the easiest way to get around the peninsula is by car. The NZRRS services run Auckland-Thames-Coromandel and Auckland-Thames-Whitianga but do not connect Coromandel and Whitianga.

Hitching is OK between Thames and Coromandel but difficult beyond there. Be prepared for long waits if you're heading up to Colville or across to Whitianga. Down the east coast traffic is sparse except at holiday periods, so hitching can be slow going.

NORTH TO COROMANDEL

North from Thames, State Highway 25 snakes along the coast for 32 km past lots of pretty little bays and beaches on one side and bush on the other. Along the way you pass through Whakatete, Ngarimu Bay, Te Puru, Tapu and various other small settlements. Keep your eyes open for the square kauri as you whizz through Tapu, it's right by the side of the road. Six km inland from Tapu are the Rapaura Watergardens which are open 10 am to 4 pm daily from 1 October through April 30. Admission is $3.50 (children $1).

Places to Stay

There are a number of campsites and motels along the coast from Thames to Coromandel. *Boomerang Motor Camp* (tel Te Puru 879) is 11 km north of Thames and has camping facilities and cabins. Another couple of km brings you to the *Waiomu Bay Holiday Park* (tel Te Puru 777) with camping, on-site caravans, cabins, tourist flats and motel units. Further north towards Coromandel at Tapu there's the *Tapu Motor Camp* (tel Tapu 837) and also the *Birdwood Cabins* (tel Tapu 804).

Motels along the coast include *Puru Park* (tel Puru 686), 11 km north at Puru on the Thames-Coromandel road. At Tapu the *Te Mata Lodge* (tel Tapu 74-834) has hostel-style accommodation for $11. It's handy to the beach and there are

also rivers where you can swim nearby. To get there go 1½ km past Tapu on the coast road, turn right over the concrete bridge into Temata Creek Rd and follow the road to the end. There's a sign on the gate.

COROMANDEL

When you get to Wilsons Bay the road leaves the coast and cuts through hills and valleys until you arrive at the next major town Coromandel, named after *HMS Coromandel* which visited the harbour in 1820 to pick up a load of kauri spars for the navy. It's a soporific little township which, like Rip Van Winkle, seems to have been asleep for the past 100 years or so.

Around Town

The Coromandel Mining Museum is open 10 am to 12 noon and 2 to 4 pm and admission is $1. In winter, if it's closed, call 58-825. If you're interested in crafts, Coromandel is a centre for potting and weaving. Go into the Coromandel Craft Gallery on Wharf Rd and, if you want to see more of any particular potter's or weaver's work, check whether you can go to their home – most of the local potters welcome visitors.

Beyond Coromandel

At Coromandel either cut across to Whitianga, Mercury Bay on the other side of the coast – the road runs through forest and is not sealed so it's slow-going, but stunningly beautiful – or continue to Colville and Port Jackson. If you head for Colville drop by the Coromandel Fruit Winery and try their apple, apricot and apple, boysenberry, feijoa or kiwifruit wine – they sound rather more exotic than they are but they're good fun to try. The winery's on Colville Rd at Papa Aroha.

Places to Stay

There are several motor camps in and around Coromandel, including the *Long Bay* and *Tuck's Bay* camps where camping costs just $1.50 a night at Tuck's Bay or $4.50 a night at Long Bay

Coromandel Motel & Camp (tel 58-830) has camping facilities at $7.50 per person (a bit more with power), cabins from $22 single, $32 double and also motel units. The *Coromandel Hotel* (tel 58-760) is on the main street and has rooms at $25 per person. Most other motels in Coromandel start at around $50.

Other campsite possibilities include *Oamaru Bay* (tel 58-735) which is seven km north and has camping facilities ($6 per person), cabins (from $30 for two) and tourist flats (from $37). Or there's *Papa Aroha Motor Camp* (tel 58-818) at Papa Aroha, 12 km north, and the *Angler's Lodge & Motor Park* (tel 58-584) at Amodeo Bay, 18 km north.

Places to Eat

Try the *Bakehouse* on Wharf Rd or the bistro bar at the *Coromandel Hotel*. You can't buy stores or food beyond Colville so stock up here, there's an excellent market every Saturday in Main St from 9 am to 3 pm. Buy some fish from the local fishing fraternity and cook it yourself.

WHITIANGA

Whitianga is a big game fishing base for tuna, marlin, mako, thresher sharks and kingfish. Take the passenger ferry (no cars) from The Narrows to Ferry Landing, site of the original township. The stone wharf here was built in 1837 by Gordon Browne, who had a trading post, warehouse and boatbuilding business. Stone for the wharf came from Whitianga Rock, a pa site of which Captain Cook said 'the best engineers in Europe could not have chosen a better site for a small band of men to defend against a greater number'.

Information

There's an Information Centre (tel 65-555) on the main street right in the middle of town. Buffalo Beach takes its name from *HMS Buffalo*, wrecked there in 1840. There are a number of charter boat and yacht operators in Whitianga including the ketch *Hibiscus*, phone 64-180 for details.

Mercury Bay District Museum

This extensive little museum has some interesting stuff on game fishing and Zane Grey. It's open Wednesday and Saturday from 1 to 3 pm and on Sunday from 10 am to 12 noon. Admission is $1 (children 30c).

Places to Stay

Hostels Opening in late '87 the *Coromandel Travellers Hostel* (tel 65-380) at 46 Buffalo Beach Rd is a converted motel. Nightly costs are $10 to $13. There are five rooms, each with five beds, and catamarans and canoes are available to rent.

Camping & Cabins The *Buffalo Beach Tourist Park* (tel 65-854), adjacent to Buffalo Beach and the wharf, has camping facilities at $7.50 per person, a couple of dollars more with power. There are also on-site caravans and cabins. Other campsites at roughly similar prices include the *Waters Edge Lodge* (tel 65-760) at 44 Albert St and the *Mercury Bay Motor Camp* (tel 65-579), also on Albert St.

Whitianga has a lot more camps like the *Whitianga Holiday Park* (tel 65-896) at the northern end of Buffalo Beach or the *Aladdin Motor Camp* (tel 65-834) on Bongard Rd.

Sites at the *Hot Water Beach Camp* (tel Whenuakite 735) cost $8 per person, more with power. It's about 40 km from Whitianga by the road, shorter via the passenger ferry.

Hotels & Guest Houses The *Whitianga Hotel* (tel 65-818) on Blacksmith Lane has rooms at $25 to $38 for singles, $37 to $50 for doubles or twins. At 21 the Esplanade, opposite Buffalo Beach, *Esplanada 21* (tel 86-523) is a tourist hotel with bed & breakfast at $30 a night. They offer special rates to YHA members.

On Racecourse Rd the *Good Life Guest House* (tel 65-461) is on a six hectare 'self sufficiency farm' where they produce most of the food they provide. Bed & breakfast is $30 per person, dinner is also available, rates are lower in the off-season.

Motels Not only does Whitianga have a lot of campsites it has a lot of motels too. Most are in the $50 and up bracket but some of the cheaper ones include *Baileys' Motel* (tel 65-500) at 66 Buffalo Beach Rd on the beachfront, the *Seabreeze Motel* (tel 65-570 at number 71, the *Seafari Motel* (tel 65-263) at 7 Mill Rd, the *Waters Edge Lodge* (see the campsite section above) or the *Bay View Motel* (tel 65-527) at 7 Mercury St.

Places to Eat
There's a choice of several takeaways, pizzas at *Napoli's Pizza*, good pub food at the *Whitianga Hotel* or, right across from the information centre, there's *Snapper Jacks*.

Getting There & Away
The NZRRS bus services from Auckland run through Thames to Whitianga. There are also services from Waihi to Opoutere but there is not a continuing service up the coast between Opoutere and Whitianga.

SOUTH FROM WHITIANGA
The coast is wild and there are spectacular beaches all the way from Mercury Bay to Waihi, including Hahei, Hot Water Beach where thermal waters heat the sea, Tairua, Pauanui, Opoutere and Whangamata. Easterly is a fascinating crafts shop in Tairua.

At Waihi, once a booming goldmining town, there's a good museum with superb models and displays of Martha Mine. Railway buffs have acquired eight km of track between here and Waikino and are planning to run trains between the two townships.

Places to Stay
The rambling old *Opoutere Youth Hostel* (tel 59-072) is a fine place to get right away from it all although it can be difficult to get to by public transport. Nightly cost is $9. There are campsites and motels at various places down the east coast.

Bay of Plenty

Cook sailed into this bay aboard the *Endeavour* in October 1769 and named it the Bay of Plenty, because of the numbers of thriving settlements of friendly Maoris he encountered (and the amount of duty-free supplies they gave him). It was in sharp contrast to the 'welcome' he received from the natives of Poverty Bay several weeks earlier!

The Bay of Plenty forms a rough triangle, with Rotorua, Katikati and Opotiki at its apexes. The area is not as popular for tourists as the far more commercial Bay of Islands, but in summer it hums along rather nicely. The climate is consistently mild all year which might explain why beach fanatics don't find it a particularly attractive holiday proposition.

The region is rapidly becoming the horticultural centre of New Zealand, with its main exports being kiwifruit and timber by-products – logs, wood-chips, paper, etc. There is a growing mineral water industry, with springs popping up everywhere. Naturally there are several hot mineral spas around.

TAURANGA
Population 59,000
The principal city of the Bay of Plenty, and the largest export port in New Zealand, Tauranga, like the rest of the towns in the region, is thriving economically at present. The rapidly growing town celebrated its 21st year as a city in 1983.

Tauranga is the Maori name for 'resting place for canoes', and most appropriate it is, because apart from the 530 cargo vessels that dock there annually, this was where some of the first Maoris to arrive in New Zealand landed.

Information
There's an Information Centre on The Strand by Coronation Pier. It's open weekdays from 9 am to 5 pm.

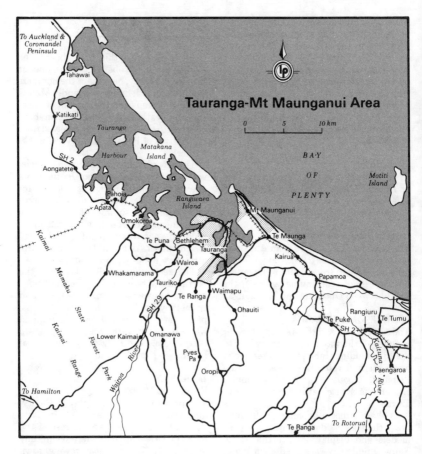

Tauranga-Mt Maunganui Area

Historic Village

The Historic Village (tel 81-302) on 17th Avenue features restored period buildings, vintage vehicles, farming equipment, an 1877 steam locomotive and even an old tugboat. There's also a Maori culture section and relics from the goldmining era. It's open every day from 10 am to 4 pm and entry is $4 (children $2).

Other Attractions

At the top end of The Strand, near the centre of the town, Te Awanui is a fine replica Maori canoe, on display in an open-sided building. Continue uphill beyond the canoe and you come to Monmouth Redoubt, the site for heroic scenes and displays of British stiff upper lip in an 1840 squabble with the Maoris.

On Mission St is the Elms Mission House, completed in 1847 by a pioneer missionary to the Bay of Plenty. The grounds are open daily except Sunday and there are guided tours at 2 pm. Fernland Natural Mineral Pools has hot pools both public and private. It's located

1	Monmouth Redoubt
2	Maori Canoe
3	Strand Motel
4	Tauranga Hotel
5	Information Office
6	NZRRS Station
7	Automobile Association
8	St Amand Hotel
9	Mid-City Tavern
10	Post Office
11	Youth Hostel
12	Bread of France
13	East Coaster
14	Le Cafe
15	Air New Zealand
16	The Salad Bowl
17	6th Avenue Tourist Court

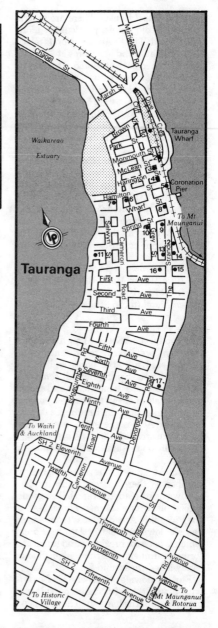

two km down Cambridge Rd off Waihi Rd and is open 10 am to 10 pm daily.

There are various charter and fishing trips operated from Tauranga. See the following Around Tauranga section for details about Mayor Island, offshore from Tauranga.

Places to Stay

Hostels The *Tauranga Youth Hostel* (tel 85-064) is on Glasgow St, off the end of Elizabeth St, very close to the centre. It's a modern hostel with nightly costs of $11.

Camping & Cabins *Mayfair Caravan Park* (tel 83-323) is off 15th Avenue on Mayfair St beside the harbour. Tent facilities are limited, power sites are $7 per person and there are also some cabins. *Silver Birch Motor Park* (tel 84-603) is at 101 Turret Rd, the extension of 15th Avenue, by the Hairini Bridge to Maungatapu. Sites here are $8 and there are cabins from $30 for two, tourist flats and motel flats.

The small *6th Avenue Tourist Court* (tel 85-709) is very close to the centre on 6th Avenue right beside the water. Sites are $14 for two and there are also cabins at $24 to $34.

Omokoroa Tourist Park (tel 480-857) and *Plummer's Point Caravan Park* are both 20 km out of Tauranga at Omokoroa.

Hotels & Guest Houses There are several traditional old hotels, particularly along The Strand. The *St Amand Hotel* (tel 88-127) on The Strand has rooms at $35/50 or with attached bath at $40/55. Also on The Strand at the corner with Harrington St the *Tauranga Hotel* (tel 88-059) has rooms at $30 to $35 single, $40 to $45 double.

Fitzgeralds (tel 62-860) at 46 Sutherland Rd has rooms at $25/38. It's about a five-minute drive from the centre.

Motels Right up at the Robins Park end of The Strand at number 27 the *Strand Motel* (tel 85-807) is an older motel, pretty plain and straightforward but very conveniently located. Rooms are $48/63. The *Sixth Avenue Motel* (tel 85-709) is on Sixth Avenue at the waterfront, at the Sixth Avenue campsite. Doubles here are $58.

Other reasonably priced motels include the *Blue Water Motel* (tel 85-420) at 59 Turret Rd and the budget priced *Shoal Haven Motel* (tel 86-910) at 67 Turret Rd.

Places to Eat
Fast Food & Takeaways Along Devonport Rd there are lots of restaurants in all categories. Up at the north end on the corner with the Spring St mall *Fenwick's Delicatessen* does sandwiches and snacks and has tables out in the mall so you can sit and enjoy them in Tauranga's famous sunshine. Across the street and hidden back in an arcade is the *Top Tastes Cafe*, a fancy cafe open 8 am to 4 pm, Monday to Friday.

Midway down Devonport Rd at number 58 there's *Bread of France* for sandwiches, bread, rolls and baked goods; a good place for a takeaway breakfast. In the Piccadilly Arcade across the road you can sit down and eat at *Potters Eatery* which is open for breakfast and lunch and for early dinners on Friday night. Fancy sandwiches are around $5.

Further down at number 82 is *Le Cafe* with a sundeck with chairs outside and great views of the harbour. They're open 7

am to 3 pm Monday to Friday and 5.30 to 7.30 pm on Friday. Round the corner at 32 Elizabeth St the *Salad Bowl* is another good place for vegetarians with a variety of good value salads.

Pub Food At the popular *Mid City Tavern* on the corner of Devonport Rd and the Spring St mall the *Boulevard Brasserie* is a big, bright and pastel-trendy place open for lunch and for dinner from 6 to 9 pm. Starters are $5 to $6, main courses $11 to $12, desserts $3.50 to $4.

Going away from the centre along The Strand there are standard pub meals for $10 to $16 in the *Cook's Cove Restaurant* in the *Hotel St Amand*. It's open Monday to Saturday for lunch and dinner, Sunday for dinner only. Out at Greerton there's a *Cobb & Co* in the *Greerton Motor Inn*.

Restaurants Across the road from the Mid City Tavern is the *Pink Pig* which is cheap, straightforward and nicely situated overlooking the waterfront. Main courses here cost from around $7.

Further down Devonport Rd is the upstairs *East Coaster*, a spacious and popular place specialising in Tex-Mex food and burgers. There's an obvious low-key effort to imitate the successful Armadillo places in Wellington and Auckland. Still the food's not bad, vegetarians are catered for and main courses are $9 to $14.

Other more expensive restaurants even include a *Chez Panisse* on Devonport Rd, no relation to the real Chez Panisse in Berkeley, California. Or right up at the north end of The Strand there's the expensive but quite good *La Salle*.

Entertainment
There's a band at the popular and crowded *Mid City Tavern* and entertainment Tuesday to Saturday at *Candyo's Nightclub* at 132 Devonport Rd.

Getting There & Away
Air The Air New Zealand office (tel 80-083)

is on the corner of Devonport Rd and Elizabeth St. There are regular flights to Auckland ($93), Gisborne ($103), Rotorua ($74) and Wellington ($149) with connections on to other centres.

Road The Bay of Plenty is south-east of Auckland, about 200 km away by the shortest route – SH 2 – which takes about three hours by car. From Rotorua, it is a mere 55 minutes along SH 33 and from Hamilton, it is a two-hour drive down SH 1, turning onto SH 29 at Tirau.

NZRRS have bus services between Tauranga and Auckland ($27), Rotorua ($13) and Taupo ($27). Their station (tel 82-839) is on the corner of Hamilton and Durham Sts, close to the centre. Mainline also operate Mt Maunganui-Tauranga-Auckland and are slightly cheaper than NZRRS – their Tauranga office is at Bay Travel (tel 85-105) at 40 Grey St. Auckland to Tauranga takes about 4½ hours.

Getting Around
Airport Transport Airport Coach Services operate a bus to the airport for each departure and arrival. The airport is actually over near Mt Maunganui and the fare is $4 (children $2).

Local Transport Although Mt Maunganui is right across the inlet from Tauranga it's a fair way by road. There's also a ferry that shuttles across, departing from Coronation Pier on The Strand eight times daily. The fare is $2.75 (children $1.35).

MT MAUNGANUI
The town of Mt Maunganui stands at the foot of the 232-metre-high hill of the same name. It's just across the inlet from Tauranga and its fine beaches make it a popular holiday resort for kiwis.

Information
Like Tauranga, Mt Maunganui is built on a narrow peninsula. There's a small information centre at 275 Maunganui Rd. In winter it's open weekdays 10 am to 1 pm,

in summer it's open 10 am to 3 pm and on Saturdays from 10 am to 12 noon.

Things to Do
There are hot saltwater pools at the foot of the mount. Moturiki Island, which is actually joined to the peninsula, has a long water slide and various other activities. It's been dubbed 'Leisure Island'. You can also hire a sailboard or catamaran, hang glide off the mount or even catch a scenic flight from the airport. Check with Airsports (tel 56-419) at the airport about flying in a microlight – a sort of powered hang-glider.

Places to Stay
Camping & Cabins Mt Maunganui is a popular summer resort so there are plenty of campsites. Right under the mount the *Mt Maunganui Domain Motor Camp* (tel 54-471) has sites at $12 for two people plus a handful of on-site caravans.

The *Omanu Beach Holiday Park* (tel 55-968) at 70 Ocean Beach Rd is also conveniently central and has sites at $9 per person and a variety of cabins, cottages and tourist flats. There are minimum charges at peak periods.

There are several other sites including *Ocean Pines Motor Camp* (tel 54-265) on Maranui St which has camping at $7.50 per person and also tourist flats. On The Mall, which runs along the waterfront on the Tauranga side of the peninsula, *Elizabeth Gardens Holiday Park* (tel 55-787) has caravan or campervan sites plus cabins from $25 to $30 for two and tourist flats from $38. They also have bunkroom accommodation from $12.

Hotels & Motels The *Oceanside Hotel* (tel 53-149) is pleasantly sited right below the mount on the corner of Marine Parade and Adams Avenue. Rooms here are $25 to $44 for singles, $44 to $50 for doubles or twins. The more expensive rooms have showers.

The *Anchor Inn* (tel 53-135) is also fairly central on the corner of Maunganui Rd and Rata St. Rooms here are $24 for

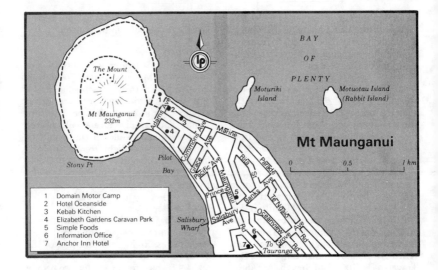

1 Domain Motor Camp
2 Hotel Oceanside
3 Kebab Kitchen
4 Elizabeth Gardens Caravan Park
5 Simple Foods
6 Information Office
7 Anchor Inn Hotel

singles, $38 for doubles. The doubles have attached bathrooms.

The motels at Mt Maunganui are not so numerous as in Tauranga and there are no price standouts.

Places to Eat

The *Anchor Inn* does pub food. On Maunganui St right in the centre of town *Simple Foods* has sandwiches and takeaways. Or try *Kebab Kitchen* on Marine Parade close to the mount.

Getting There & Away

Air The Tauranga airport is actually at Mt Maunganui.

Road The Mainline buses run Auckland-Tauranga-Mt Maunganui, with NZRRS you have to take another local bus or the ferry on from Tauranga. The Mainline office (tel 56-821) is on Tawa St.

Getting Around

See the Tauranga section earlier on for the details about the ferry service across the inlet.

AROUND TAURANGA
Mayor Island

Offshore from Tauranga, Mayor Island is an extinct volcano with numerous walking tracks through the now overgrown crater valley and an interesting walk around the island.

Places to Stay & Eat You need a permit from the Department of Maori Affairs in Tauranga to land on the island or to camp there. Camping costs $2 per person or there are cabins at $20 to $22 per night. The Tauranga Game Fishing Club (find them on Coronation Pier) have the *Mayor Island Lodge* with 'VIP' cabins at $28 per person and more spartan cabins at $14.

The canteen at the Mayor Island Lodge has some food items for sale but you should bring most supplies with you. The campsite has a fireplace and barbecue facilities but you need all your own utensils.

Getting There Cruises to the island operate from Coronation Pier in Tauranga and go out via Mt Maunganui. They last from 7 am to 7 pm and the cost is $23 (children $12).

Mayor is well out to sea and the trip takes about three hours in each direction. There's a $3 'landing fee' charged to each visitor to Mayor, it's included in the cruise costs.

Views

From Minden Lookout, about 10 km from Tauranga and four km off the SH 2 route to Auckland, there's a superb view back over the Bay of Plenty.

Historic Sites

There's a Maori pa site at Town Point, near the township of Maketu, to the north-east of Te Puke (pronounced Pookay), where you can see some ancient carvings. In Bledisloe Park, three km from Maketu, is the gun pit – still intact – from where, on 22 April 1864, Lieutenant-Colonel Thomas McDonnell and 12 Europeans shot 600 hostile Maoris.

Katikati

Off SH 2 near Katikati the Katikati Bird Gardens are a bird sanctuary and botanic gardens. The gardens are open daily. *Jacaranda Cottage* (tel 490-616) has bed & breakfast, full board or just the 'bare necessities'. It's a couple of km up Thompson's Track which is five and a bit km south of Katikati.

Kiwifruit Orchards & Wineries

The Bay of Plenty is kiwifruit country and there are several places you can learn a little more about this important, for New Zealand, fruit. Kiwifruit Country (look for the 'big kiwifruit') is six km from Te Puke or 36 km from Tauranga, right beside the main Rotorua-Tauranga road. There you can take a kiwi-kart ride through the kiwifruit orchards and see how they're grown and packed then sample some kiwifruit or kiwifruit wine. Kiwifruit Country is open 10 am to 4 pm daily and entry is $5.50 (children $3.30)

Prestons Kiwifruit Winery on Belk Rd off Highway 29 is another place where you can sample this uniquely New Zealand wine! Their hours are 10 am to 4.30 pm, Monday to Saturday. Another kiwifruit winery is Durham Light in Glen Lyon Place off Oropi Rd in Greerton, right in Tauranga. They're open 10 am to 5 pm, Monday to Saturday. Guided tours through the winery are made at 10 am and 2 pm.

Longridge Park, on SH 33 12 km south of Te Puke, is another kiwifruit farm with tours, walks and other activities. It's open 9 am to 5 pm daily and entry is $5 (children $3). May is the time to see kiwifruit picking and packing.

Kiwifruit

New Zealand's most famous fruit, and a major export crop, is also known as the Chinese gooseberry. The name kiwifruit was dreamed up in the 1950s. Imported from the Yangtze Valley in China the first kiwifruit climbers were grown as ornamental garden vines and it was only 50 years ago that attempts were made to grow it commercially. Growth of the industry was very slow at first and it was not until the last 20 years that it finally assumed the economic importance it has today. In part this is because the fruit, although fragile, keeps very well and properly packed and refrigerated it is ideal for exporting.

The kiwifruit is a fuzzy, brown, oval-shaped fruit about the size of a small lemon. The skin peels off to reveal its unique green flesh, high in vitamins and fibre. The area around Te Puke in the Bay of Plenty is a major centre for growing kiwifruit. New Zealand produces about two thirds of all the kiwifruit grown in the world. Over 100,000 tons are now exported each year and the total is still growing rapidly. May to July is the picking season and thousands of people flock to the area for harvesting work.

Walks

McLaren Falls in the Wairoa River Valley, 11 km from Tauranga on Highway 29, are worth a visit. Good bushwalking, rock pools and of course, the falls. It's picturesque, but not exactly awe-inspiring. There's more bushwalking in the Mamaku State Forest down SH 5 between Hamilton and Rotorua. There are spectacular views from Kaimai Summit and Wairere Falls.

Gisborne

Population 32,000

Gisborne is New Zealand's most easterly city and the closest to the International Date Line. Therefore dawn in Gisborne marks the new day for most of the world. It's 368 km east of Rotorua and 220 km north of Napier. It was here that Captain Cook made his first landfall in New Zealand on 9 October 1769. He was distinctly unimpressed by what he saw and named it 'Poverty Bay' because, as he wrote in his log ' . . . it did not afford a single article which we wanted, except a little firewood'.

Around Gisborne there are fertile alluvial plains which support intensive farming of subtropical fruits, maize and market-garden produce and also vineyards. In fact, maize, citrus, maize, grapes, maize and more maize is just about all the eye can see. If such a sight doesn't have a great deal of appeal for you, remember that seasonal work is available if you're there at the right time – sweet corn is picked from around the second week in January, peas at the beginning of February. The city itself is situated right on the coast at the confluence of three rivers, the Turanganui, Waimata and Taruheru. Often described as the city of bridges, it is also noted for its fine parks and recreational facilities.

History

European settlement of the region was very slow; much of the country was left unexplored until late in the 19th century. It was not until 1830 when whaling became increasingly popular that the missionaries began to move into the area. Two of them, Father Baty and Reverend William Colenso, were the first Europeans to tramp into the heart of Urewera and see Lake Waikaremoana.

Gradually more Pakehas arrived but there was no organised settlement. Several factors were against it, the main one being that the Maoris were opposed to the

idea. When the Treaty of Waitangi was signed in 1840 many chiefs from the East Coast did not acknowledge the treaty, let alone sign it. Another was that the first governor of New Zealand to visit the region, Gore Browne, was not given much of a welcome and warned against unauthorised European settlement in the region. More important, during the 1860s numerous Maori wars broke out which further curbed white settlement, but by 1866 the government had crushed the rebels and transported most of the survivors to the remote Chatham Islands. This paved the way for an influx of Europeans who brought with them their flocks of sheep.

Even today, however, much of the pasture land is leased from the Maoris and a large part of it is under their direct control. Unfortunately, the pioneer farmers were so anxious to make a buck they ripped out far too much forest cover with disastrous results. Massive erosion occurred as the steeply sloping land was unable to hold the soil after heavy rains.

Information

The Public Relations Office (tel 86-139) is at 209 Grey St. Look for the fine Canadian totem pole beside it. They have a good walking tours leaflet on Gisborne and they can probably supply some information on seasonal work. The office is open 9 am to 5 pm Monday to Friday, 10 am to 1 pm on Saturday. The AA is on the corner of Disraeli St and Palmerston Rd.

There's a Maori Arts & Crafts Centre at 31/33 Gladstone St. Gisborne also has a canoe and tramping club and there's a laundromat at the corner of Gladstone Rd and Carnarvon St.

Statues & Views

There's a statue of 'Young Nick', Cook's cabin-boy, in a playground named after him in Churchill Park on the beachfront. He was the first member of Cook's crew to sight New Zealand. Across the river on the foreshore at the foot of Kaiti Hill is a monument to Captain Cook. Also at the foot of the hill is the Poho-o-Rawiri Maori meeting house. From the hill top you get a wide-angle view of the area but the finest view of Gisborne is probably from Gaddum's Hill. To get there head out to the suburb of Kaiti on Wainui Rd (Highway 35 to East Cape), turn left at De Latour Rd and follow it up the hill. It's a short walk from here to the trig station; nine km return from Gisborne.

Maritime Museum

One wild night in 1912 the 12,000 ton ship *Star of Canada*, out of Belfast, Northern Ireland and only three years old, was blown ashore on the reef at Gisborne, quite close to where Captain Cook made his landing. Although the ship was only three years old all attempts to refloat it failed and eventually whatever equipment could be salvaged was removed, including the ship's bridge and captain's cabin, which the salvager removed and brought ashore to win a bet that it couldn't be done. At the waterside he sold the 26-ton bridge for £104 and it was eventually installed on the corner of Childers Rd and Cobden St and sat there for 15 years until in 1927 the second owner's daughter got married and needed a home. Additional rooms were added and the *Star of Canada* became the best known home in Gisborne.

When the owner died in 1983 she left her unique home to the city of Gisborne and it was moved to its present site, restored and turned into a fascinating little museum. There are displays on Maori canoes, early whaling and shipping and Captain Cook's Gisborne visit but the most interesting items relate, of course, to the *Star of Canada*. The Maritime Museum is on the riverside, right behind the Art Gallery & Museum and you pay the admission fee of $3 (children $1) in there. The Maritime Museum is open 10 am to 4 pm on weekdays, 2 to 4.30 pm on weekends and public holidays.

Museum & Art Gallery

That Gisborne and the surrounding district are strongly Maori is clearly exhibited at the small Gisborne Museum & Arts Centre at 18 Stout St. The gallery has exhibitions of local, national and international art which change regularly and the museum has numerous displays relating to the East Coast Maori and colonial history, as well as geology and natural history exhibits. Outside there are more exhibits – a sled house, stable and Wylie Cottage with a varied and well-labelled collection of household items.

The museum is open Tuesday to Friday 10 am to 4 pm, weekends and public holidays 2 to 4.30 pm – admission is $2 (children 50c). When you've had your fill of culture you can relax in the Top Deck Cafe in the museum, it's open Monday to Friday from 10 am to 4 pm.

Other Attractions

At the A&P Showgrounds, Makaraka, is a Transport & Technology Museum in the early stages of development. It's open Sundays from 9 am to 12 noon. At Matawhero, a few km south along the State Highway, is an historic Presbyterian Church. It was built in 1865-66, originally as a school-room, but has also been a church, meeting place and hospital. It was the only building in the immediate vicinity to survive the Poverty Bay Massacre by Te Kooti and his band in 1868, and is one of a handful still standing from this period.

You can swim right in the city at Waikanae Beach. There's good fishing and surfing the whole way along the coast. If you happen to be in Gisborne around the peak of the summer holidays, a reserves programme including walks and talks is held. Transport to walks is by private car but sharing is encouraged so you should get a ride without any trouble if you haven't got your own wheels.

Tours around the Gisborne area are operated by Cosmac Tours (tel 84-139) and cost $15 to $20.

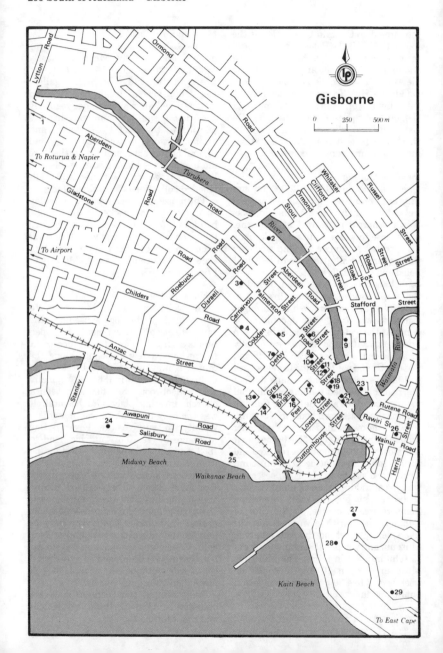

1	To Showgrounds & Camp
2	Botanical Gardens
3	Automobile Association
4	Aloha Travel Lodge
5	Royal Hotel
6	Dominion Bus Station
7	Meng Yee Restaurant
8	CPO
9	Museum, Art Gallery & Star of Canada
10	Air New Zealand
11	McDonald's
12	Robert Harris Coffee
13	Information Centre
14	Pizza Hut
15	Kentucky Fried Chicken
16	NZRRS Station
17	Lyric Cafe & Channels Guest House
18	Scrumples
19	Regent Cafe
20	Masonic Hotel
21	Bread & Roses Restaurant
22	Albion Hotel & Maori Crafts Centre
23	Arnhem Restaurant
24	Churchill Park Camp
25	Waikanae Beach Camp
26	Green Gables Travel Hotel
27	Kaiti Hill Lookout
28	Cook Memorial
29	Poho-O-Rawiri Meeting House

Places to Stay

Hostels The *Gisborne Youth Hostel* (tel 83-269) is at 32 Harris St, just 1½ km from the town centre across the river. Nightly charges are $11 and it has accommodation for 38 people. Advance bookings are essential from Christmas to the end of January.

Camping & Cabins Very close to the centre the *Waikanae Beach Municipal Camp* (tel 75-634) is on Grey St at Waikanae Beach. Sites cost $9 per person, a couple of dollars more with power. They also have cabins ranging from very simple ones at around $16 for two and tourist flats from $35.

The *Churchill Park Municipal Camp* (tel 74-555) is at Salisbury Rd, a km from the centre and near the beach. Sites here

are about the same price and again there are tourist flats. The *Showgrounds Motor Camp* (tel 74-101) is cheaper to camp but it's not so conveniently central, out at Makaraka. The cabins here are cheap at $12 to $16 but they're pretty spartan. This camp is closed, of course, at showtime.

Guest Houses Guest houses include the *Green Gables* (tel 75-6191) at 31 Rawiri St, Kaiti across the river from the centre. Nightly cost is $25 per person including breakfast. The neat and clean *Aloha Travel Lodge* (tel 79-032) at 335 Childers Rd has rooms including continental breakfast at $30/42 on the 1st floor, $40/61 on the ground floor.

The *Channels Private Hotel* (tel 75-037) is on the corner of Gladstone Rd and Peel St in the centre. Rooms here are $20 to $30 for singles, $35 to $45 for doubles. Although it's more central it's not as good a place as Green Gables or Aloha.

Hotels There are a number of hotels around the centre of town including the fine old *Masonic* (tel 84-099) on the corner of Lowe St and Gladstone Rd. Singles are $30 to $38, doubles $35 to $45, more expensive rooms have attached bathrooms.

Others include the *Royal* (tel 89-184) and the *Albion Club* (tel 79-639), both on Gladstone Rd.

Motels Most Gisborne motels start from around $60 double. Marginally cheaper ones include the *Travellers' Inn Motel* (tel 83-322) at 721 Gladstone Rd and the *Highway Motel* (tel 84-059) at 60 Main Rd.

Places to Eat

Snacks & Fast Food There's the usual selection of sandwich places, particularly along Gladstone Rd or try Peel St, up towards McDonald's, where there are two excellent up-market sandwich places. *Scrumples* has sandwiches, rolls, drinks and is a relaxed and pleasant place to eat them. Across the road in the centre leading through to McDonald's is the

Robert Harris Coffee Shop with an equally good selection of sandwiches. Here you can eat inside or out in the open air in the mall.

Apart from the *McDonald's*, main entrance on Bright St, there's also a *Pizza Hut* and a *Kentucky Fried Chicken* on Grey St down by the information centre. As usual there are a number of Chinese takeaways – try *Meng Yee* on Derby St.

Light Meals & Pub Food At 124 Gladstone Rd the *Lyric Cafe* is a fine, old fashioned fish restaurant with a variety of fish & chips at around $8.50 to $10.50. Across the road the *Regent* offers pretty similar fare at pretty similar prices.

The *Masonic Hotel*, on the corner of Gladstone Rd and Lowe St, has the usual pub-food menu, as does *Cooks Gallery Restaurant* in the *Royal Hotel* which is on Gladstone Rd between Cobden and Derby Sts.

Away from the centre, and for something completely different, the *Roadhouse* on Solander St near the Churchill Park Camp has takeaways and bargain priced food in its sit down area. It's open reasonably long hours as well.

Restaurants Restaurants include *Bread & Roses* on the corner of Lowe St and Reads Quay with interesting main courses in the $15 to $18 range. *Arnhem*, wonderfully situated beside the river, is very expensive.

Entertainment
The *Sandown Park* on Childers Rd and the *Gisborne Hotel* on Huxley Rd have live music most weekends of the year. At the *Albion Hotel River Bar* on Gladstone Rd the lineup's mostly good old rock & roll – lots of it. There are door charges at these venues. Gisborne's only nightclub, the *Silver Lair*, offers both disco music and live stuff. During the holiday period local bands, musicians and poets perform in the parks.

Getting There & Away
Air The Air New Zealand office (tel 84-075) is at 37 Bright St. They have direct flights to Auckland ($132), Napier ($92), Tauranga ($103) and Wellington ($145). Eagle Air (tel 81-608) also fly to Gisborne with direct connections to Hamilton ($110), Napier ($81) and Palmerston North ($125).

Road The NZRRS depot in Gisborne is on the corner of Bright St and Childers Rd. You can approach Gisborne from four directions.

From Napier in the south it's a pleasant 216 km, three hour trip on a road which runs close to, but rarely right on, the coast. Unusually NZRRS has no bus services along this route, it's operated via Wairoa by Dominion Coachlines (tel 89-083) whose Gisborne office is at 247 Palmerston Rd.

Coming from Rotorua, Auckland and other points north the most direct route is via Opotiki along the Waioeka Gorge. It takes about 3½ hours to drive between Rotorua and Gisborne, a 287 km trip by this route. There are bus services from Auckland and Rotorua via Opotiki to Gisborne. From Rotorua it's five hours at a fare of $41, all the way from Auckland it's 10½ to 12 hours at a fare of $66.

An alternative but much longer route runs from Opotiki around the coast of East Cape. There is no direct bus connection but services around the cape from Opotiki and Gisborne overlap and you can make the trip by bus in two days. See the following East Cape section for details. Opotiki to Gisborne is 345 km and it takes about eight hours by car, if you're pushing it.

The third route from Rotorua to Gisborne runs through the Urewera National Park, passing by Lake Waikaremoana and joining the Napier route at Wairoa, 99 km from Gisborne. It's about three hours by car between Gisborne and Waikaremoana but there is no direct bus. To travel this way by public transport you have to take the twice weekly NZRRS between Rotorua

Art Deco Architecture, Napier (TW)

and Wairoa where you can catch the Napier-Wairoa-Gisborne Dominion Coachlines service. It's difficult to make handy connections on this route. Travelling from Gisborne towards Rotorua you would have to travel to Wairoa one day and overnight there in order to catch the morning departure from Wairoa. In the other direction, heading to Gisborne, you can continue straight through Wairoa. If you do get stuck in Wairoa the *Borough Camp* is a pleasant place, right on the river with sites and cabins.

Hitching Hitching is OK from the south, not too bad through Waioeka Gorge to Opotiki (but it's best to leave early). To hitch a ride out head along Gladstone Rd to Makaraka a few km away where you turn left for Wairoa and Napier, right for Opotiki and Rotorua. Hopefully you may get a ride before you walk as far as Makaraka but most of Gladstone Rd is a built-up area.

Hitching from Wairoa to Waikaremoana is hard going. Gisborne is actually just off Highway 36 around East Cape so if you're hitching around East Cape head out along the Wainui road.

Rail There's a daily rail service Wellington-Napier-Gisborne. From Wellington takes about 10½ hours at a fare of $49. From Napier takes about six hours at a fare of $20. The railway station is about a half km from the town centre, beyond the Information Office.

Getting Around
A taxi to Gisborne airport costs about $6. You can hire scooters from Corrin Motorcycle Service at 441 Gladstone Rd for $20 a half day or $40 a day.

OPOTIKI
Historically, Opotiki was the centre of Hauhauism, a doctrine advocating the extermination of the white race. In 1865 the Reverend Karl Volkner was murdered in his church, St Stephen the Martyr, which culminated in the church being transformed into a fortress by government troops.

Today, Opotiki is a prosperous dairying and sheepfarming district. There are good surfing beaches nearby at Ohiwa and Waiotahi. An alternative route from Opotiki crosses over the Motu Hills through beautiful bush scenery but the road is unsealed and there's not much traffic, so it's no good for hitching.

Travelling directly from Rotorua to Gisborne you turn inland at Opotiki and travel up along the spectacular Waioeka Gorge. There are some fine walks, both day and longer, in the Waioeka Gorge Scenic Reserve. The Forest Services office in Opotiki has information. The gorge gets progressively steeper and narrower as you travel inland, before the route crosses typically green, rolling hills, dotted with sheep, on the descent to Gisborne.

Places to Stay
Patiti Lodge (tel 792) at 112 Ford St has rooms at $28/45. Opotiki has three hotels, all on Church St – the *Opotiki* (tel 56-078), the *Masonic* (tel 56-115) and the *Royal* (tel 56-364). There are also a couple of motels and several campsites with cabins.

EAST CAPE
The east coast is still one of the most isolated and least known regions of the North Island. The small communities that are scattered along the foreshore are predominantly Maori. Geographically, the area has few natural harbours and until the road network was completed goods had to be loaded off the beaches onto waiting barges. The coast is now circled by 480 km of highway, which took decades to build and is now open all-year round. The drive is worth it if only for the magnificent views of this wild coast.

It's 344 km from Opotiki to Gisborne along an interesting and scenic road via SH 35. The area is rich in history and has many beaches. Along the first stretch from Opotiki there are often fine views across to smoking White Island. It's worth

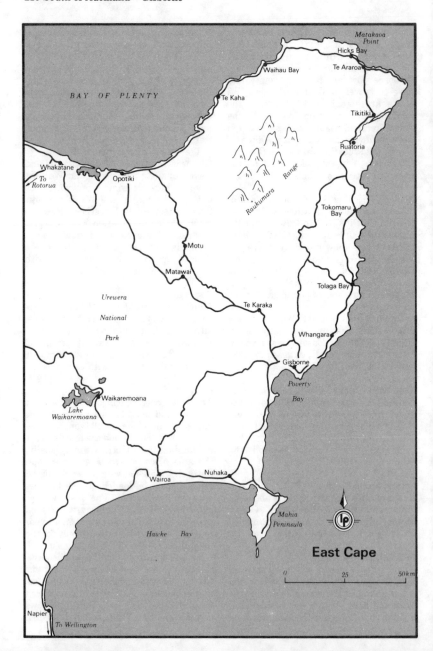

BAY OF PLENTY

Matakaoa Point

Hicks Bay

Te Araroa

Waihau Bay

Te Kaha

Tikitiki

Ruatoria

Whakatane

To Rotorua

Opotiki

Raukumara Range

Tokomaru Bay

Motu

Matawai

Urewera National Park

Te Karaka

Tolaga Bay

Whangara

Gisborne

Poverty Bay

Lake Waikaremoana

Waikaremoana

Wairoa

Nuhaka

Mahia Peninsula

Hawke Bay

East Cape

0   25   50km

Napier

To Wellington

stopping at Tikitiki to see the wonderful Maori carvings inside the little church. You can hire canoes and dinghies at Tolaga Bay. Inland the Raukumara Range offers tramping (including the highest mountain, Hikurangi, at 1754 metres), hunting and whitewater rafting on the Motu.

Places to Stay

On the way around East Cape there are various motor camps or you can camp on most beaches for nothing if you've got your own equipment. If you're travelling by bus the *Te Araroa Holiday Camp* (tel 873), midway between Te Araroa and Hicks Bay, is a convenient place to stay right on the beach. Camping costs $6.50 per person and there are also cabins and tourist flats.

Alternatives in Te Araroa are the *Kwakawa Hotel* (tel 809) where singles cost $35 to $38, doubles $45 to $54. Hicks Bay has the *Hicks Bay Motor Lodge* (tel 880) with a variety of units from around $48.

Getting There & Away

There is no bus service that goes right around East Cape, but there are regular NZRRS buses from Opotiki as far as Te Araroa and from Gisborne as far as Hicks Bay, thus the services overlap by only 12 km. So the trip can be made by bus, but it takes a minimum of two days (who wants to go faster?) and a bit more organisation.

It's about 4½ hours from Gisborne to Hicks Bay, another 3½ hours from Hicks Bay to Opotiki. There are buses four to six times weekly. Buses run more frequently between Gisborne and Ruatoria. Hitching is possible around East Cape in peak summer but at other times there is very little traffic.

UREWERA NATIONAL PARK

The Lake Waikaremoana turn-off is 97 km from Gisborne at Wairoa on the road towards Napier. This is a marvellous area of bush and lakes, with lots of day tramps or longer walks and much birdlife.

Places to Stay

There is a camp, cabins and motel 48 km from the turn-off. Or at Galatea on Lake Aniwhenua the *Urewera Lodge* (tel Galatea 556) has bunkroom accommodation at $15, a bit less in the off-season. They also have a variety of boats to hire. It's on the shores of Lake Aniwhenua, just off Whakatane-Murupara road.

Getting There & Away

NZRRS buses run from Rotorua to Wairoa, on the Gisborne-Napier road. See the Gisborne and Rotorua sections for more details. Most of the way between Frasertown and Murupara through the park, about 150 km, is unsealed, very winding and therefore very time consuming.

GISBORNE TO NAPIER

Heading south towards Napier the Dominion bus service follows the shorter coastal route on Highway 2. The road passes close to the Wharerata Forest Reserve – the Wharerata Walkway is a popular 10 km walking track. The Morere Hot Springs are 56 km from Gisborne and there are various pools and bushwalks at this spot which is open for 11 months of the year from 9 am to 6 pm and until 7 pm through January – last tickets sold one hour before closing time. A bit further on you reach Nuhaka and the turn-off to Mahia where there are good beaches and fishing, with camping, cabins and a motel.

Along the inland route to Wairoa and Napier (Highway 36) there are also several things to see and do. If you climb up Gentle Annie Hill you will get good views over the Poverty Bay area. Doneraille Park (53 km from Gisborne), a native bush reserve, is a popular picnic spot which is good for swimming when the water is clear. There's fine trout fishing at Tiniroto Lakes, 61 km from Gisborne, and about 10 km further the Te Reinga Falls are worth the few hundred metres detour off the main road.

Napier

Population 53,000
In 1931 Napier was rather dramatically changed when a disastrous earthquake measuring 7.9 on the Richter scale virtually destroyed the city. In Napier and nearby Hastings over 250 people died, but in partial compensation the waterlocked city suddenly found itself 40 square km larger. The quake heaved that amount of water-covered land above sea level! In places the land level rose by over two metres. The Napier airport is built on that previously submerged area.

Information
Napier's extremely helpful and well informed Information Centre (tel 57-182) is on Marine Parade close to the town centre. It's open Monday to Friday, 8.30 am to 5 pm, weekends 9 am to 5 pm.

Finding your way around Napier is slightly complicated by a lack of street name signs (pretty normal for NZ) but also by a lack of building numbers which is extreme even by NZ standards. People must simply know where places are, there

are so few numbers on buildings that they don't even bother to list them in phone directories or other sources.

Art Deco
The earthquake and fire of 1931 had a very interesting side effect. Most of the older brick buildings collapsed with the quake, survivors were mainly new buildings of reinforced concrete. Two frantic years of reconstruction rebuilt Napier in the years from 1931 to 1933. The end result is that much of the city architecture of Napier dates from the narrow period from the late '20s through early '30s – the peak years for art deco. In fact the British Museum has stated that:

Napier represents the most complete and significant group of Art Deco buildings in the world, and is comparable with Bath as an example of a planned townscape in a cohesive style.

Napier has an Art Deco Group which promotes and protects the city's unique architectural heritage and if you're in town on a Sunday you can take a guided 'art deco walk' starting from the museum at 2 pm for $3. If your Napier visit doesn't coincide with a Sunday you can guide yourself with a walk leaflet available from the information centre or the museum. The museum also has a book on Napier's art deco architecture and some excellent post cards and posters. Many of the finest buildings are very well preserved and looked after.

As you walk around town look for art deco motifs on the buildings such as zig-zags, lightning flashes, geometric shapes and rising suns. The soft pastel colours are another art deco giveaway. There are some excellent art deco buildings along Emerson St, check the Dijon Restaurant buildings or the Bank of New Zealand on the corner with Hastings St. On Dalton St the Central Hotel is a superb example of the style both externally and inside the foyer and stairs. Round the corner on Dickens St look for the extravagant

Spanish-style building which used to be the 'Gaiety de Luxe Cinema'.

On Tennyson St see the Desco Centre facing Clive Square. It used to be the Napier Fire Station and the doors are now glassed in. The Tennyson St-Hastings St intersection has more fine buildings particularly the block of Hastings St from Tennyson to Browning St. Look at Alsops storefront in particular, the window exhibit is terrific. On Marine Parade, the Soundshell is art deco as is the paving of the plaza which used to be a skating rink. From here you can admire the art deco clocktower (neon lit at night!) of the T&G building and the Masonic Hotel. Finally read the moving poem inside the colonnade beside the plaza.

Marine Parade

Rubble from the destroyed buildings was used to form a new Marine Parade that runs along the seashore. Many of Napier's attractions are found along here and there are also parks, a scented garden for the blind, an assortment of amusements, and

Pania of the Reef, a sort of Maori equivalent of Copenhagen's little mermaid and a symbol of the town. Napier's stony beach is most uninspiring.

Marineland & Aquarium

On Marine Parade, Marineland of New Zealand has the usual collection of performing seals and dolphins and is open daily 9.30 am to 4.30 pm, admission $4.50 (children $1.75). Also on the parade the Hawke's Bay Aquarium is claimed to be the largest in Australasia. The aquarium has a wide variety of fish, sharks, turtles and other displays including New Zealand's unique tuatara lizards. It's open daily from 9 am to 9 pm in summer, 9 am to 5 pm in winter, entry is $4.50 (children $1.75).

Lilliput & Planetarium

Lilliput is a miniature village and model railway together with a display of toy cars over the years. It's open Monday to Friday from 10 am to 4.30 pm, Saturday and Sunday from 2 to 5 pm. Adjoining it is the planetarium.

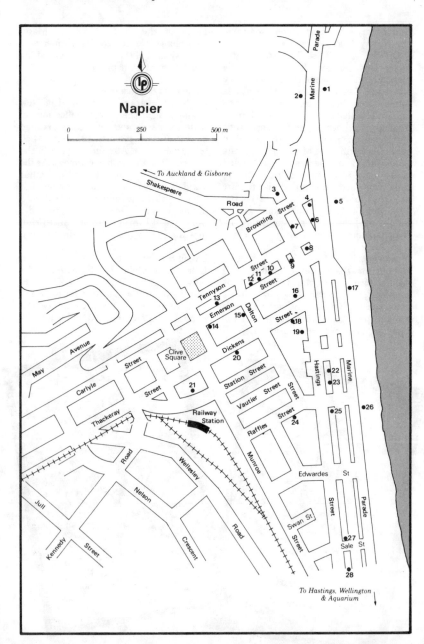

1	Nocturnal Animals Centre
2	Spa Private Hotel
3	NZRRS Buses
4	Art Gallery & Museum
5	Pania of the Reef
6	Lilliput
7	Old Bank Guest House
8	Masonic Hotel
9	Criterion Hotel
10	Dijon Restaurant
11	Lanterna Restaurant
12	National Cafe
13	Food for Thought
14	Juices & Ices
15	Cheers & Hotel Central
16	CPO
17	Information Centre
18	Golden Crown Restaurant
19	Air New Zealand
20	Automobile Association
21	Newmans Depot
22	Waterfront Lodge
23	Pinehaven Guest House
24	Drago's Restaurant
25	Youth Hostel
26	Marineland of New Zealand
27	Pizza Hut
28	Indonesian Restaurant

Hawke's Bay Art Gallery & Museum

Next down from the planetarium is the excellent small art gallery and museum. The museum has displays of Maori artefacts, European antiques, art deco items and they show a 20 minute audio-visual of the '31 earthquake. The gallery and museum are open Tuesday to Friday from 10 am to 4.30 pm, Saturday and Sunday from 2 to 5 pm. Entry is $2, children are free.

Nocturnal Wildlife Centre

If somehow you've missed seeing kiwis at nocturnal centres all over New Zealand you have another chance here. The centre actually has other animals as well as kiwis and feeding time is 2.30 pm. It's open 10 am to 4 pm daily in the summer peak period, on winter weekends the hours are 11 am to 3 pm. Entry is $2.50 (children $1).

Other Attractions

There's a swimming pool on Marine Parade which costs just 55c. The Onekawa Pool Complex is larger and fancier with hydro-slides and other attractions. Napier also has miniature golf, skating rinks, a waxworks and numerous other activities along Marine Parade. The Hawkes Bay Museum of Technology on Clive Square is open Saturday 9 am to 12 noon, Sunday 1 to 4 pm and admission is $2.50 (children 50c). A tour of the Leopard Brewery on Monday, Wednesday or Friday is followed by a glass of the amber fluid. Or you could visit Classic Decor sheepskins to see how sheepskins are processed. There are tours every weekday at 11 am and 2 pm.

Fishing trips and pleasure cruises from Napier are also popular and there are night cruises if there is sufficient demand.

Places to Stay

Hostels The *Napier Youth Hostel* (tel 57-039) is at 47 Marine Parade and costs $11 a night. Close to the beach and right across the road from Marineland, it's more luxurious than most hostels because it is a converted guest house. The dormitories are therefore smaller, while the kitchen, dining room and recreation area are all separate which make it more spacious.

The *Glenview Farm Hostel* (tel 266-235, 232) is a peaceful and pleasant independent farm hostel 31 km north on the road to Wairoa and Gisborne. It's a hill country sheep station where horse riding and walking are popular activities. Nightly costs are from $8.

Camping & Cabins Napier has a number of campsites but none of them conveniently located if you don't have transport. Closest to the centre is *Kennedy Park* (tel 439-126) at Marewa, 2.5 km from the CPO. Sites cost $7 per person, slightly more with power. There are also some basic huts ($22 for two), cabins ($30 for two) and tourist flats ($50 for two).

At Taradale (6.5 km out) there's the

Taradale Holiday Park (tel Taradale 442-732) at 470 Gloucester St. Sites here are similarly priced and there are also on-site caravans and a variety of cabins. The *Westshore Holiday Camp* (tel 59-456) is on Main Rd near Westshore Beach, four km from town. There are cabins and tourist flats as well as camping facilities.

Other sites include the *Clive Motor Camp* (tel 700-609) near Clive, the *Esk River Holiday Park* (tel 266-805) which is 17.5 km out at Eskdale and *Burden's Motor Camp* (tel Hastings 750-170) which is 19 km from Napier, towards Cape Kidnappers. Burden's Camp is the starting point for the tractor-trailer trip to the gannet sanctuary. Also near here is the *Clifton Reserve Camp* (tel Hastings 750-263) at Clifton.

Guest Houses Since it is a summer resort of the old fashioned school Napier has some good old bed & breakfast places, particularly along Marine Parade beside the beach.

Places to try include *Pinehaven Private Hotel* (tel 55-575) at 42 which is probably the best of the bunch. Rooms here are $33/50 for singles/doubles including breakfast. The front rooms have fine views of the seafront.

Or there's the cheaper *Waterfront Lodge* (tel 53-429) at 36 which costs $22/33 bed only, $30/46 with breakfast. Further along, near the kiwi house, the *Spa Private Hotel* (tel 58-119) at 10 Marine Parade costs $33/60 for bed & breakfast, dinner is also available.

Back from Marine Parade at 31 Hastings St the *Old Bank Guest House* (tel 59-691) costs $25/43 with continental breakfast but it isn't as good as the seafront guest houses.

Hotels Cheaper hotels include the *Provincial* (tel 56-934) on Clive Square at $25/42 or the *Shakespeare Inn* (tel 57-639) on Shakespeare Rd at $30 to $40. The *Victoria Hotel* (tel 53-149) at 76 Marine Parade has singles at $30 to $40, doubles at $40 to $60.

The fine old *Masonic Establishment* (tel 58-689) is on the corner of Marine Parade and Tennyson St so it's very central. There are a few cheaper singles but the rooms with attached bathroom are $70/77. Although it's a comfortable and nicely situated place it's rather sombre and some parts are a bit scruffy.

Motels There are plenty of motels, particularly around Westshore, but most are around $60 or more for a double. Some distance out, two km north of the airport, but lower priced is the *Airport Boomerang Motel* (tel 266-828) on Main Rd at Bay View, where rooms are $40/50 for singles/doubles. The *City Close Motel* (tel 53-568) at 16-18 Munroe St is conveniently located and has rooms from $46 single, $58 to $65 double.

Places to Eat

Fast Food & Takeaways There are plenty of sandwich places along Emerson St and the sandwiches here are often pretty good. Places to try include *Food for Thought* at 204 Emerson St with healthy looking sandwiches and snacks. Other Emerson St possibilities in the light meal bracket include the *National Cafe* for fish & chips and other snacks or *Hatters* at 247-249 for burgers. You can sit down at both these places. Across from Hatters is *Antonio's Pizzas* while a few steps further up Emerson St at Clive Square *Juices & Ices* has homemade ice cream, milkshakes and fruit smoothies.

Just off Emerson St on Dalton St is *Cheers*, a very up-market sandwich place – licensed and combined with a cocktail bar. The sandwiches may cost $4 to $5 but they're really excellent, in fact they're a meal in themselves. Cheers has another interesting variation on those ubiquitous NZ dress standards. Here it's denim shirts which get the thumbs down.

Of course there are plenty of Chinese restaurants and takeaways in Napier. Try the *Golden Crown* on Dickens St which does both. And yes, there is a *Pizza Hut* in Napier, on Marine Parade, but McDonald's hasn't made it here yet.

Pub Food & Restaurants There's a *Cobb & Co* in the fine old Masonic Establishment looking out on to Marine Parade. It's open the usual seven days a week, 7.30 am to 10 pm. The *Victoria Hotel* at 76 Marine Parade also has a restaurant with the pub-food regulars.

Further out at 90 Marine Parade the *Restaurant Indonesia* makes a pleasant break from the sometimes bland NZ fare. Main courses are around $12 to $14 and they also do a variety of rijstaffels, that Dutch-Indonesian-smorgasbord blend.

On Emerson St on the 1st floor *Lanterna* has a standard Italian menu with main courses around $15, pastas at around $7 as starters, $11 as main courses. It's open Tuesday to Saturday. Over at 14 Raffles St *Drago's Restaurant* is a long-standing upper bracket restaurant with their normal menu at around $16 for a main course. On Monday, Tuesday and Wednesday they also have a fixed-price Mexican menu. These three places are all byo.

Finally, and back on Emerson St at number 80, *Dijon's* is the only one of this restaurant bunch which is licensed and is said by many to be the best place in town for a real night out. Not only is the food stylish so is the art deco building itself and the internal fittings to go with it. Main courses average around $18.

Entertainment
Popular rock pubs include the *Cabana* on Shakespeare Rd and the *Onekawa*. *Cheers*, see Places to Eat above, also has a pleasant wine bar.

Getting There & Away
Air Air New Zealand (tel 53-288) is on the corner of Hastings and Station Sts. There are direct flights to Auckland ($132) and Wellington ($118). Eagle Air (tel 389-500) has flights to Gisborne ($81), Hamilton ($110) and Palmerston North ($78) with onward connections.

Road NZRRS buses (tel 54-849) operate from the railway station, not from the downtown depot. They have a service down to Wanganui ($31) and New Plymouth ($49) or to Auckland ($51) via Taupo ($21) and Hamilton ($38).

Mt Cook (tel 51-063) has an office at 20 Station St. They operate an Auckland-Taupo-Napier-Hastings service. Newmans's (tel 52-009) is on Dickens St and they have a service to Palmerston North with connections south to Wellington and north through Wanganui and New Plymouth to Hamilton and Auckland.

Dominion Coachlines have regular connections between Gisborne and Napier with services on to Wellington. The service goes through Wairoa, from where you can get an NZRRS bus to Rotorua via Waikaremoana twice a week. The Dominion office (tel 83-231) is in Hastings, in Napier they go from the Mt Cook office.

It's 220 km north to Gisborne, a three hour drive. Taupo is 148 km north-west on Highway 5.

Hitching Hitching is OK around here. If you're heading north catch a long distance bus and get off at Westshore, walk, or try thumbing closer in. Heading south stick to Highway 2. The alternative route, Highway 50, is much harder going with very little traffic. You can get an NZRRS bus to Hastings.

Rail The Railway Station is, oddly enough, on Station Rd. The train between Napier and Wellington costs $36. The service continues on to Gisborne at a fare of $20.

Getting Around
Airport Transport A taxi to the airport costs about $10.

Local Transport NZRRS operate the suburban bus services and there are regular buses between Napier and Hastings via Clive and Taradale plus other local services. Or at least there are on weekdays, Saturdays the services drop dramatically and on Sundays there's nothing at all. They stop on Dickens St near the Dalton St intersection.

Bicycle Rental You can hire bicycles from Cycle World, 104 Carlyle St.

AROUND NAPIER
Gannets & Cape Kidnappers

Between October and March one of Napier's unique sights is the Cape Kidnappers gannet sanctuary. These large, ungainly birds usually make their nests on remote and inaccessible islands but here they nest on the mainland and are curiously unworried by human spectators. The gannets usually turn up in late July after the last heavy storm of the month. Supposedly, the storm casts driftwood and other handy nest-building material high up the beach so very little effort has to be expended collecting it! In October and November eggs are laid which take about six weeks to hatch. By March the gannets have started to migrate and by April only the odd straggler will be left.

You can get to Cape Kidnappers (so named because Maoris tried to kidnap an obviously tasty-looking Tahitian servant boy from Cook's expedition here) by several methods. From Burden's Motor Camp at Te Awanga, 21 km from Napier, you can ride on a tractor-pulled trailer along the beach for $8 (students under 18 $5, children under 12 $4). It departs about two hours before low tide at the cape – the information centre has tide information or you can phone 750-400 or 750-334 for details. Alternatively you can walk along the beach from Clifton, just along from Te Awanga. The eight-km walk takes 1½ to two hours and you must leave no earlier than three hours after high tide and start back no later than 1½ hours after low tide. It's another eight km back and there are no refreshment stops so come prepared!

You can also get to Cape Kidnappers with Gannet Safaris from Summerlee Station beyond Te Awanga. The 18-km trip departs at 1.30 pm and takes about an hour each way with an hour at the sanctuary. A minimum of six people are required for the trip and the cost is $30 (children $15). This trip only operates from October through April.

Free permits and tide reports are obtainable at Clifton. There is a rest hut with refreshments available at the colony. This is also a place to see (or, even better, to avoid) New Zealand's only poisonous spider, the katipo. The natural habitat of this spider is in the driftwood above the high tide mark, so leave it alone!

The Department of Lands & Survey, who administer the reserve, have a handy leaflet on getting there and the gannets' habits. They also have copies of booklets titled *The Cape Kidnapper Gannet Reserve* and *The Geology & Fossils of the Cape Kidnappers Area*. Whichever route you take to the gannets there is no public transport to Te Awanga or Clifton from Napier, but you should be able to hitch.

Wineries

The Hawke's Bay area is one of New Zealand's premier wine producing regions and there are a number of vineyards you can visit and taste the wines. They include Brookfields Vineyards at Meeane, Mission Vineyards at Napier, Glenvale Vineyards in the Esk Valley, Vidal Wine and Ngatarawa Wines in Hastings, Te Mata Estate and Lombardi Wines in Havelock North and Cooks/McWilliams Wines in Taradale. Mission Vineyards is the oldest in the country and their tour at 3 pm on weekdays is excellent. The Napier information centre has a booklet on the wineries and their opening hours. They are all closed on Sundays. A fine way of getting round the wineries is on a bicycle (see above about cycle rentals) since most of them are within easy cycling distance and it's all flat land.

Hastings

Population 55,000
Neighbouring Hastings tends to get forgotten beside Napier but it also has

some interesting examples of art deco architecture and as well as the wineries listed above Hastings is also noted for its many fruit growers. The craft studios and honey houses in Havelock North, just a few km from Hastings, are worth a visit. *Rush-Munro's Ice Cream Garden* in Hastings is a local institution, it's been there since WW II, and has 'truly incredible ice cream'!

Sheep are one of the overwhelming influences on the New Zealand scenery; they're seen everywhere, from the country's rolling green meadows to its craggy southern hillsides. They've become a cliché of New Zealand, just like the Sydney Opera House shouts Australia or the Manhattan skyline America. Show somebody a green field with sheep dotted over it and a mountain in the background and they'll say 'New Zealand'.

The sheer number of sheep is astonishing. Of course it varies over the year, as there are lots more at lambing time in the early spring, but 60 million is a good figure to work on. That means there are 20 sheep for every man, woman and child in the country; or the reverse of the sheep:person ratio in Japan, where there are 20 humans for every sheep!

The first sheep to set hoof on New Zealand soil were the two survivors of six sheep taken on Captain Cook's second voyage. Although they happened to be a ram and a ewe, today's 60 million sheep did not descend from this ovine Adam and Eve, as both sheep died before Cook had even sailed away. So, it wasn't until the 1830s that sheep really arrived, migrating with the early settlers, missionaries and whalers; and in the decade that followed, many more of them were brought in from Australia.

Sheep began to appear in more and more places around New Zealand. Soon flocks of over 1000 sheep were not unusual and by 1855 the sheep population had exploded to three quarters of a million. By 1861 there were 2.8 million, then 4.9 million in 1864, 8.4 million in 1867 and 13 million in 1880. Even back then, visitors to New Zealand were commenting that sheep were the overriding topic of conversation. During this period the sheep and their owners came mainly from Australia and as the flocks at the time were run purely for their wool, the majority of the sheep imported were merinos, which are prized for their fleece.

As time went by, however, the merino's shortcomings became obvious; they may have had good wool, but for meat they were not so ideal. Furthermore they were not prolific breeders and the lambs were weak and grew slowly.

Crossbreeding with Lincoln and English Leicester sheep produced a sturdier, faster growing breed and by the 1890s almost all the sheep in the North Island were crossbred. In the South Island a different pattern of interbreeding was followed which eventually produced the unique New Zealand Corriedale sheep.

The change from running merinos was also hastened by the rapid spread of planting pastureland based on European grasses and clovers. While the merinos had coped well with the sparse native herbs and grasses, they were not so enthusiastic about the new exotic varieties.

Sheep farming went through another major change when freezer ships began to operate in the late 19th century. The first cargo of frozen mutton and lamb from New Zealand arrived in London in 1882 and despite inevitable problems (Victorian refrigeration equipment was not always 100% reliable), meat production soon began to gain importance. Today sheep are still one of the mainstays of the New Zealand economy, with meat and wool production both of great importance.

Sheep even play their part in the tourist trade with sheep shows a popular attraction in many centres; even though the sheep simply do what sheep do best, which is stand around looking bewildered and sheepish. The 'show' is actually provided by the sheep dogs who run around looking energetic and clever, having a great deal of fun making sheep run backwards, forwards and even round and round in circles. The Kiwi shearers also perform, demonstrating how quickly a short back and sides can be given if you're in a real hurry.

You meet New Zealand sheep in many other everyday situations as well. There are few visitors who don't, at some point, find themselves trying to get through a surging sea of sheep on some country road. A favourite sheep view during my last visit was on a late afternoon light aircraft flight between Te Anau and Queenstown. The green field below was dotted with countless sheep, looking for all the world like grains of rice spilt across a billiard table.

Wellington

Population 321,000

Wellington, as the capital of New Zealand, takes part in friendly rivalry with larger Auckland, but it's quieter and not so speedy. The town is hemmed in around its magnificent harbour, the buildings marching picturesquely up the steep hills. It's a pleasant and lively city with plenty to see and do – so long as the wind isn't blowing. Many travellers pass through Wellington as apart from its importance as the capital it's also a major travel crossroads between the North and South Islands.

History

Traditionally, the Maoris maintain that Kupe was the first person to discover Wellington harbour. The original Maori name for the place was Te Whanga-Nui-a-Tara, Tara being the son of a Maori chief named Whatonga who had settled on the Hawke's Bay coast. Whatonga sent Tara and his half-brother off to explore the southern part of the North Island but it was over a year before they returned. When they did, their reports of the land were so favourable that Whatonga and his followers moved to the harbour, founding the Ngati-tara.

The first white settlers arrived on 22 January 1840 in the New Zealand Company's ship *Aurora*, not long after Colonel William Wakefield had arrived to buy land from the Maoris. The idea was to build two cities: one a commercial centre by the harbour, the other further north was to be the agricultural hub. The settlers were to be allotted two blocks, a town section of an acre (less than half a hectare) and a back country block worth $2 an acre. But the Maoris denied they had sold the land at Port Nicholson – or Poneke as they called it – the result of hasty and illegal buying by the New Zealand Company and the start of land rights struggles which were to plague the country for the next 30 years and still affect it today.

Wellington began as a settlement with very little flat land. Originally the waterfront was along Lambton Quay, but reclamation of parts of the harbour began in 1852 and has continued ever since. In 1855 an earthquake razed part of the Hutt Rd and the area around Te Aro flat to the Basin Reserve, which initiated the first major reclamation. The city is built around a fine harbour formed by the flooding of a long extinct, and very large, volcano crater. The city runs up the hills on one side of the harbour, and so cramped is it for space that many Wellington workers live in two urban corridors leading northwards between the steep, rugged hills – one is the Hutt Valley and the other follows State Highway 1 northwards through Tawa and Porirua.

In 1865 the seat of government was moved from Auckland to Wellington and since then it has gradually become the business centre of the country – most major organisations operating in NZ have their head office here – and also the centre of the diplomatic corps.

Information & Orientation

Lambton Quay, the main business street, wriggles along, almost parallel to the seafront. Many of the older buildings in Wellington have been demolished in the past few years and modern concrete boxes have sprung up in their place. Thorndon is the area immediately north of the centre where you'll find a number of the major embassies and also the youth hostel. Mt Victoria is the area immediately south where you'll find a number of other hostels and cheap places to stay.

Tourist Offices The Public Relations Office (tel 735-063), is on the corner of Mercer

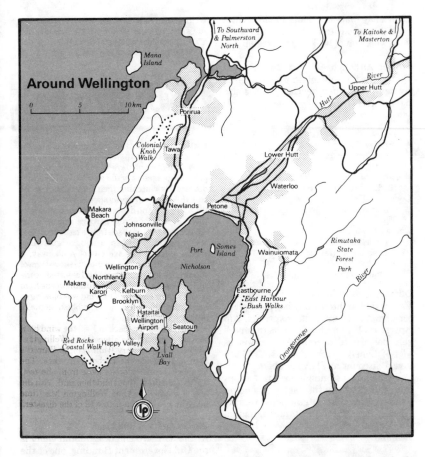

Around Wellington

0   5   10 km

To Southward
& Palmerston
North

To Kaitoke &
Masterton

Mana
Island

River

Upper Hutt

Porirua

Colonial
Knob
Walk

Tawa

Hutt

Lower Hutt

Waterloo

Makara
Beach

Newlands

Petone

Johnsonville

Ngaio

Port

Somes
Island

Wainuiomata

Rimutaka
State
Forest
Park

Nicholson

River

Wellington

Northland

Makara

Karori

Kelburn

Brooklyn

Eastbourne
East Harbour
Bush Walks

Hataitai

Wellington
Airport

Seatoun

Orongorongo

Red Rocks
Coastal Walk

Happy Valley

Lyall
Bay

and Victoria Sts. It's open 9 am to 5 pm every day. The NZTP is also on Mercer St but it's basically a travel agent rather than an information centre. It's open 8.30 am to 5 pm Monday to Thursday, 8.30 am to 8 pm on Friday, and 9.30 am to 12.30 pm on Saturday. The AA (tel 851-7450) is at 342-352 Lambton Quay.

Post Office The Wellington CPO suddenly disappeared in 1987 and nobody, including the post office, was quite certain where it got to. Whatever happened to it you can

now pick up poste restante mail at the post office in the Post Office Headquarters building on Waterloo Quay near the railway station.

Bookshops Wellington has some fine bookshops including Unity Books on the corner of Willis St and Manners Mall, Ahradsen's in the BNZ underground shopping centre or the usual Whitcoulls and London Bookshop branches. The Government Bookshop, with lots of Lands & Survey maps, is on Cuba Mall. Tala at 60

Courtenay Place is a South Pacific centre with Polynesian arts and crafts and also a good selection of books on the region.

Airlines Although Air New Zealand and Qantas are the only international airlines flying into Wellington other airlines also have offices there:

Air New Zealand
129-141 Vivian St (tel 859-922)
Ansett New Zealand
corner Featherston St & Lambton Quay (tel 711-044)
British Airways
199 Lambton Quay (tel 727-327)
Continental Airlines
corner Brandon & Featherston Sts (tel 736-665)
Qantas Airways
National Bank Building, corner Featherston & Panama Sts (tel 738-378)
UTA
Dalmuir House, The Terrace (tel 722-460)

Other Living Simply in the Phoenix Centre on Lambton Quay is a good place for camping equipment, maps, etc. Alp Sports at 125 Lambton Quay has a superb selection of outdoor equipment, as well as lots of Lonely Planet guidebooks. They give a discount to YHA members.

Wellington has numerous craft shops and galleries. On the last weekend in January there's an international touring car race through the streets of Wellington, the biggest car race of the year in New Zealand.

Windy Wellington

□ Yesterday's northerlies brought Wellington's strongest wind gust of the year, a Kelburn Weather Office spokesman said today.

The 76 knot (139km/h) gust shaded the year's previous best, recorded on February 4, by 13km/h, the spokesman said.

The strongest gust today, recorded just after midnight, was 113km/h.

Wellington really can get windy. When the sun's shining it can be a very attractive city but it's not called the windy city for nothing – one of the local rock stations even calls itself:

Particularly as winter starts to arrive you've got a fair chance of experiencing some gale-force days. The sort of days when strong men get pinned up against walls and little old ladies, desperately clutching their umbrellas, can be seen floating by at skyscraper height. Seriously the flying grit and dust can be uncomfortable to the eyes and the flying garbage can be a real mess. I was walking back from a restaurant late one windy night when a sudden gust blew several bags of garbage out of a doorway, a passing car hit one and a veritable snowstorm of soft drink cans, pizza boxes and assorted debris rushed down the street like tumbleweeds from an old western movie. The wind was blowing so hard that this blizzard of rubbish actually overtook the offending car!

One blustery day back in 1968 the wind blew so hard it pushed the almost-new Wellington-Christchurch car ferry *Wahine* on to Barrett's Reef just outside the harbour entrance. The disabled ship later broke loose from the reef, drifted into the harbour and then sank with the loss of many lives. The Wellington Maritime museum has a dramatic model of the disaster.

Old Government Building

At the northern end of Lambton Quay is the Old Government Building, one of the largest all-wooden buildings in the world – there's a wooden temple in Japan which beats it for 'the biggest' honours. Wood was widely used in the construction of buildings in Wellington's early days – there are some fine old wooden houses still to be seen.

Parliament Building

Across from the Old Government Building is the very modern new parliament building known as the Beehive – because that is just what it looks like. You can arrange to tour the Parliament Buildings by phoning 749-199.

Parliament Building, the 'Beehive'

Old St Paul's

One block away from Parliament in Mulgrave St, Thorndon (a couple of minutes' walk from the Railway Station) is Old St Paul's. It was built in 1863-64 but take a look inside as the interior is a good example of Gothic design in timber. Old St Paul's is open Monday to Saturday from 10 am to 4.30 pm, Sundays 1 to 4.30 pm – free admission but donations gratefully accepted.

Cable Car

From a narrow alley off Lambton Quay a cable car runs up to Kelburn overlooking the city – a ride to the top costs 60c (children 30c) on weekdays, 90c on weekends and holidays. It operates from 7 am to 10 pm at about 10-minute intervals on weekdays, 10.30 am to 6 pm on weekends and holidays. The cable car service began in 1902, carried nearly half a million passengers in its first year and by 1912 was transporting a million passengers a year. In the late '70s the track was reconstructed and the two cable cars were replaced with new ones. From the top you can stroll back down through the Botanic Gardens and by the University.

Maritime Museum

On Queen's Wharf and Jervois Quay is Wellington's interesting little Maritime Museum – open 9 am to 4 pm weekdays and 1 to 4.30 pm on Saturdays, admission free. It has many relics of shipping associated with the city and a fine three-dimensional model of the harbour. The collection of ship models includes a great one of the *Wahine* in the process of sinking.

National Museum

The National Museum (just look for the carillon on Buckle St) has a good Maori and Pacific Islands collection. There's an interesting leaflet describing the Maori exhibits. Amongst the most interesting items is a full-size moa, very realistically feathered with help from emus and kiwis. The marine-life models are also very well done and there's a good Pacific cultures section. Admission is free and it is open 10 am to 4.45 pm daily. Get there on a 1 or 3 bus to the Basin Reserve or an 11 to Buckle St.

The museum has an excellent cafe and a shop which is good for NZ souvenirs. In the same building is the National Art Gallery and New Zealand Academy of Fine Arts.

Zoo

Wellington Zoo, open daily 8.30 am to 5 pm, admission $4 (children $1.70), has a nocturnal kiwi house and a wide variety of native fauna and other wildlife. The kiwis are on view from 10 am to 4 pm daily but the best viewing time for them is 10 am to

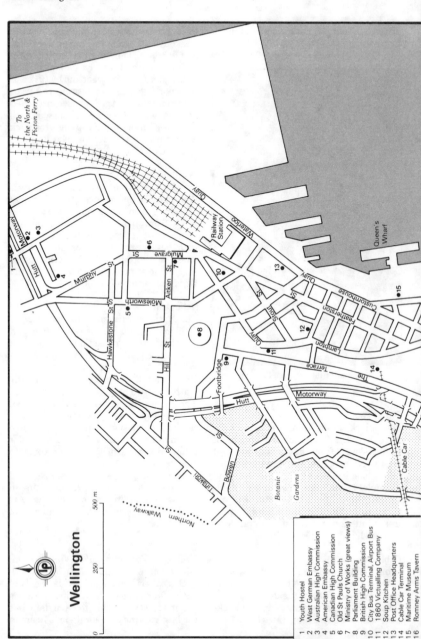

Wellington

1   Youth Hostel
2   West German Embassy
3   Australian High Commission
4   American Embassy
5   Canadian High Commission
6   Old St Pauls Church
7   Ministry of Works (great views)
8   Parliament Building
9   British High Commission
10 City Bus Terminal, Airport Bus
11 1860 Victualling Company
12 Soup Kitchen
13 Post Office Headquarters
14 Cable Car Terminal
15 Maritime Museum
16 Romney Arms Tavern

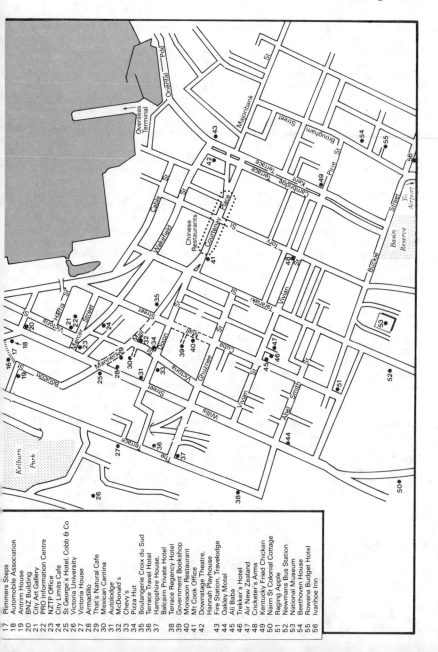

17 Plimmers Steps
18 Automobile Association
19 Antrim House
20 BNZ Building
21 City Art Gallery
22 PRO Information Centre
23 NZTP Office
24 City Limits Cafe
25 St George's Hotel, Cobb & Co
26 Victoria University
27 Victoria House
28 Armadillo
29 That's Natural Cafe
30 Mexican Cantina
31 Autolodge
32 McDonald's
33 Chevy's
34 Pizza Hut
35 Boulangerie Croix du Sud
36 Terrace Travel Hotel
37 Hampshire House,
   Balcairn Private Hotel
38 Terrace Regency Hotel
39 Government Bookshop
40 Monsoon Restaurant
41 Mt Cook Office
42 Downstage Theatre,
   Hannah Playhouse
43 Fire Station, Travelodge
44 Oakley Motel
45 Ali Baba
46 Trekker's Hotel
47 Air New Zealand
48 Cricketer's Arms
49 Kentucky Fried Chicken
50 Nairn St Colonial Cottage
51 Raging Apple
52 Newmans Bus Station
53 National Museum
54 Beethoven House
55 Rowena Budget Hotel
56 Ivanhoe Inn

12 noon. The zoo is four km from the city centre – you can get there on a No 11 bus marked Newtown Park Zoo, which leaves from the Railway Station at intervals of about 15 minutes on weekdays, 20 minutes on Saturday and 30 minutes on Sunday.

Walks

There are numerous walkways in the Wellington area, check at the PRO for a full range of city walks brochures. A new Southern Walkway has been opened which covers some 11 km and departs the city via Mt Victoria, Newtown, Melrose to Island Bay. You don't have to walk the whole 11 km as you can catch a bus at several points along the way.

There are several good walks around the harbour shore or outside the harbour – try the Red Rocks Coastal walk beyond the airport on the west side or the East Harbour Bush Walk above the harbour on the east side. The Colonial Knob walk near Tawa is also good. Longer walks can be found in the Rimutaka State Forest Park on the east side of the harbour.

Other Attractions

For a great view of the city look for the Ministry of Works Building (the Vogel Building) on the corner of Mulgrave and Aitken Sts on the way down to the station from the Youth Hostel. Take the lift to the 14th floor and walk up to the viewing area. Shame they don't clean the windows more often. Another great city view is from the top of Mt Victoria. A number 20 bus will take you there in 20 minutes, it starts from the railway station.

The fortress-like US Embassy building, also near the Youth Hostel, occupies the grounds where author Katherine Mansfield's family home once stood. There's a memorial to her in the park across the road.

The Colonial Cottage Museum at 68 Nairn St is open Wednesday to Friday from 10 am to 4 pm, Saturdays and Sundays from 1 to 4.30 pm. Antrim House, a restored house in Boulcott St, is now the restaurant Plimmers. It's open to visitors (as opposed to diners) from 12 noon to 3 pm on Fridays. The adventurous City Art Gallery is in Victoria St, close to the PRO and the NZTP. The Golden Bay Planetarium is on Harris St and has sessions on weekday afternoons. They cost $3 (children $2). The Carter Observatory in the Botanic Gardens is open from 7.30 to 9.30 pm on Tuesdays from March to October.

Tours

Wellington City Transport's 2½ hour afternoon bus tour is a good city intro. It costs $17 (children $8.50), the bus departs from outside the PR office daily at 10 am and 2 pm and after a circuit of the inner city it follows the Marine Drive out to Mt Victoria with fine views over the city and the airport. Beware of higher priced private operators who try to hook people intending to take the city transport tour!

Various other tours are also operated by companies which include Elite Tours (tel 727-281) and Wally Hammond (tel 720-869. They have a variety of local city tours and trips further afield. You can even make day trips across Cook Strait to Picton although most people find crossing that often stormy strait in one direction is quite enough!

Places to Stay

Wellington's location, crowded in against the bay by the surrounding hills, means that building land is limited and this has an effect on the accommodation picture. There are no campsites close to Wellington,

the number of motels is very limited and even the guest houses, of which there are plenty, are comparatively expensive. Backpackers, at least, are fairly well catered for as there is a fair choice of hostels.

Hostels The *Wellington Youth Hostel* (tel 736-271) is at 40 Tinakori Rd, just across the motorway beyond the American Embassy, uphill from the railway station. It's conveniently situated only 10 minutes' walk from either the ferry terminal or the railway station. Nightly costs are $13. It's a very popular hostel and it's so often full up that there's a permanent overflow hostel available. The overflow hostel was in the process of being redeveloped and upgraded in 1987.

There's another YHA *Youth Hostel* (tel 267-251) 52 km north of Wellington at Kaitoke at the top of the Hutt Valley. You'll find it in Marchant Rd and it sleeps 20. Nightly costs are $9. The hostel is located in attractive hill country close to bushwalking tracks and horse riding. Get there on a NZRRS Wellington to

Masterton bus (100-metre walk), or it's an eight-km walk from Maymorn Station on the Wairarupu line, or a 12-km walk from the Upper Hutt suburban train station.

Wellington has several private hostels, about the same distance south of the centre as the youth hostel is north. *Beethoven House* (tel 842-226) at 89 Brougham St, Mt Victoria, is probably the best known hostel in New Zealand and it's a must for anyone into eccentric places. For a start you have to like Beethoven's music – there's rarely a moment when one or other of his works is not being played. And if you're a smoker, you'll have to give it up – at least temporarily – as there's no smoking allowed anywhere on the property and a great number of signs warning you of the evils of tobacco. Allen (don't mention my name) Goh, the hostel's manager, accounts for a large measure of the eccentric atmosphere. He's been talking about leaving and it certainly won't be the same place if he does but meanwhile you'll keep running into people all over NZ wearing

Happy Hostellers, Beethoven House

Beethoven House T-shirts. All birthdays, including Beethoven's, the house's, yours and Christmas, are celebrated.

The hostel is open 24 hours a day, nightly costs are from $12 although if you arrive *very* late you'll be charged more on night one. After the first night the cost drops by $1. A light breakfast of cereal, toast and marmalade and tea or coffee is included; everybody breakfasts together. It's hardly the tidiest hostel on earth – in fact a long way from it. To get there from the Railway Station end of town catch a No 2 or 5 bus to Pirie St, or a 1 or 3 to the Kentucky Fried Chicken on Kent Terrace. From the Courtenay Place end of town it's only a five-minute walk. If you're arriving in Wellington by air get off the bus by the fire station/Travelodge at the bottom of Kent Terrace. There's no prominent sign outside, just a small 'BH'. Note that Beethoven House inspires love or hate and as many people positively hate it as love it!

Close to Beethoven House are two places which are part hostel, part guest house. At 115 Brougham St the *Rowena Budget Hotel* (tel 857-872) is up above the street with fine views down over the city. It's a well kept place and you can't miss its amazing colour scheme. There are no less than 60 rooms, three lounges, coin-in-the-meter kitchens, barbecue facilities, and costs of $12 dorm, $16.50 single, $35 double. Breakfast is available for $3 continental or $5 for a cooked breakfast.

Just round the corner at 52 Ellice St is *Ivanhoe Inn* (tel 842-264), 52 Ellice St. It's a little tired looking but there are rooms with handbasins at $16.50/22 as well as bunkroom accommodation from $12. There's the usual kitchen, lounge, laundry facilities.

Victoria House (tel 843-357), a university hostel at 282 The Terrace, has accommodation available during university vacations (mid-November to late February, mid-May and late August to early September) but it's not cheap. Including three meals the daily cost is $45.

Camping & Cabins If you're looking for a campsite or cabins you'll find Wellington a tough place – there is no flat ground. The best you'll do is out at Lower Hutt in the *Hutt Park Motor Camp* (tel 685-913), 14.5 km from the Wellington CPO. Sites cost from $10 for two or from $15 with power. They warn that the site is not suitable for tent camping over the winter months. Cabins and tourist flats are also available starting from around $15 single for the plainer cabins. To get there without your own transport take a bus to Gracefield – they go at least hourly, every 20 minutes during rush hour. Then walk half a km. Or take a train to Woburn (faster at rush hour) and follow the signs for two km.

Guest Houses Wellington has a limited number of conveniently situated motels but it has plenty of guest houses. A number of them are found along The Terrace where there are numerous attractive old wooden houses, many of them with great views over the city. The steep streets, the architecture of these old homes and the colours they're painted are all very reminiscent of similar areas in San Francisco. The *Cedar Tourist Lodge* (tel 720-868) is at 234 The Terrace. Continuing along the street you come to the Victoria University accommodation centre, see the Hostels section for details.

The *Ambassador Travel Lodge* (tel 845-697) at 287 The Terrace has rooms, including breakfast, at $45/70 without attached bathroom or with bathroom at $60/80 plus some motel-style rooms at $60/70. At 291 The Terrace the *Terrace Travel Hotel* (tel 848-702) is a homely old building but well kept and costs $33/44, room only.

On the corner of The Terrace and Ghuznee St is *Hampshire House* (tel 843-051) with rooms in the $50 to $60 bracket. Right next door at 151 Ghuznee St is the *Balcairn Private Hotel* (tel 842-274) with rooms at $30/40. Several other guest houses/private hotels are along The Terrace.

Other guest houses include *Richmond House* (tel 858-529) at 116 Brougham St. Under Hostels above see the Rowena Budget Hotel and Ivanhoe Inn both in the same area. They have bunkroom accommodation but also private single and double rooms. Ivanhoe is cheap and pretty basic, Rowena is larger and a bit fancier. Another alternative is the *Clinton Private Hotel* (tel 859-515) in the southern part of the central area at 35 Thompson St. Bed and breakfast is around $40 and there are also a few motel flats from $60.

At 10 Orchard St, up behind the youth hostel, *4 Orchard House* (tel 738-063) has three rooms on the top two storeys of a turn-of-the-century home. There are fine views over the city and rooms in this more exclusive family run guest house cost $40 to $55 single or $50 to $65 double but you must phone ahead to make reservations.

At 182 Tinakori Rd the *Tinakori Lodge* (tel 733-478) is the historic home of an early prime minister. Room cost from $40 single, from $55 double or twin.

Hotels *Trekkers Hotel* (tel 852-153) is on Dunlop Terrace, off Vivian St by Cuba St and right across from the Air New Zealand office. It's a recycled old hotel and although the changes are mainly in the reception and restaurant area it's been quite attractively done. There are rooms with and without attached bathrooms. The cheaper rooms are $45/62, with attached bathroom they're $65/90. There are also some more expensive motel-style rooms.

There are some cheaper old hotels and also plenty that head up towards the sky pricewise. Cheaper ones which are also centrally located include the *Cambridge Establishment* (tel 858-829) on Cambridge Terrace with rooms at around $38 to $45 for singles, $45 to $60 for doubles. This is one of the nation-wide Establishment chain although in Wellington the Cobb & Co restaurant is not also located there. *Flanagan's Hotel* (tel 850-216) on Kent Terrace is similarly priced.

The *Autolodge* (tel 851-304) is very

central at the corner of Willis and Dixon Sts and has 72 rooms from around $100 a night. It's a business hotel with slightly cheaper rates on weekends. Also very central is *St George's Hotel* (tel 739-139) on the corner of Willis and Boulcott Sts where the Cobb & Co Restaurant is located. Singles/doubles are $105/120 and again there are cheaper rates on weekends.

Much more expensive hotels include the *James Cook Hotel* (tel 725-865) on The Terrace, *Plimmers Towers Hotel* (tel 730-785) on the corner of Boulcott St and Gilmer Terrace, the *Terrace Regency Hotel* (tel 858-829) at 345 The Terrace, the *Wellington Parkroyal* (tel 859-949) at 360 Oriental Parade and the *Wellington Travelodge* (tel 857-799) at 40-44 Oriental Parade. In these a double will probably be in the $150 to $200 range.

Wellington has some apartment hotels, a cross between an apartment and a hotel. Some of the fine old wooden houses along The Terrace are being converted into apartments for longer term stays – contact *City Life Apartments* (tel 723-413) but you're looking at up to $200 a night. Or on the corner of Brougham and Ellice Sts, south of the centre, *Melksham Towers* (tel 851-569) has apartment-style rooms at $85 to $100.

Motels There are no motel bargains in Wellington. *Oakley Motel* (tel 846-173) at 331 Willis St is an old wooden building but the rooms are all self contained and cost $65/75. *Aroha Motel* (tel 726-206) at 222 The Terrace is another old wooden building but with self-contained rooms from $90. The *Wellington Luxury Motel* (tel 726-825) at 14 Hobson St has rooms from around $60. Otherwise you'll probably have to go out to the suburbs to find motels.

Places to Eat
Wellington probably has the widest variety of international cuisines to be found in New Zealand and there are plenty of restaurants to choose from.

Courtenay Place and Willis St in particular are packed with restaurants.

Fast Food The American fast food giants are well represented in Wellington. There's a *Kentucky Fried Chicken* on Kent Terrace near to the Brougham St/Ellice St accommodation places. In the centre there's a *Pizza Hut* on the corner of Dixon and Willis Sts. Only a block away on the corner of Manners Mall and Willis St there's one of the city's several *McDonald's*. Another one is on Courtenay Place near the Cambridge Terrace junction.

Takeaways & Lunchtime Wellington's a great place for a sandwich or snack at lunchtime. You'll find lots of choice along Courtenay St and Manners Mall, up Plimmers Steps and along Lambton Quay, or along Cuba St and Cuba Mall.

Try the basement level under the BNZ (Bank of New Zealand) building at the Willis St/Lambton Quay junction. This is the Wellington equivalent of the underground shopping centres of Montreal but while the French-Canadians go subterranean to escape the cold, the Wellingtonians do it to escape the wind. There's a bunch of places here selling sandwiches, tacos, pizzas, soup and other light meals.

Starting from the northern (parliament and railway station) end of town and moving south good sandwich places include *Stripes* in the Phoenix Centre on Lambton Quay. Or next door in the James Cook Arcade there's *Stickybun*. Climb Plimmers Steps off Lambton Quay and you'll come to *Cafe Mamba* with a great selection of appetising sandwiches. On the other side of the steps is *Cafe Cuisine*, a more expensive sit-down place which is open for breakfast too, hours are Monday to Friday, 7 am to 3 pm.

Along Cuba St at 157 there's *Food for Thought* with good wholefood sandwiches and snacks. Or at 101 Manners St close to the Cuba St junction there's a *Boulangerie Croix du Sud* French bakery with lots of good sandwiches and baked goods.

At 203 Cuba St *Ali Baba* is a great place for a doner kebab with salad and bread for around $2.50. It's essentially a takeaway but there's an alcove at the back where you can sit, on Turkish carpets of course. It's open Monday to Saturday from 9 am to 8.30 pm, to 10 pm on Friday.

An important port like Wellington naturally has plenty of fish & chip specialists. Try *Dominion Fisheries* at 128 Courtenay Place for excellent takeaways. Or at 12 Bond St the *Fisherman's Plate* will dish you up a fine fish & chip meal on a paper plate for $6.50 to $7.50. Another simple meal alternative is the big bowls of soup and crusty bread served up at *Soup Kitchen* at 32 Waring Taylor St, just off Lambton Quay. It's open 7.30 am to 3 pm Monday to Thursday, 7.30 am to 7.30 pm on Friday. On Wakefield St near the Information Centre and NZTP office *City Limits* is a pleasant and relaxing cafe for a coffee or light meal.

If you're staying at Ivanhoe or Beethoven House and need a quick meal there's a string of places providing pizzas, burgers and other takeaways nearby. They're all at the Ellice St/Kent Terrace junction. Finally if you're up at the *Dominion Museum* there's a coffee bar with excellent and economically priced sandwiches and snacks.

Wholefood Apart from some of the sandwich places there are also several excellent wholefood restaurants where vegetarians are well catered for. Try the very pleasant *That's Natural* at 88 Manners Mall. It's upstairs and has lunchtime snacks and sandwiches plus main meals at around $10 to $12. Or right up the end of Cuba St at 301 there's *Raging Apple*, also upstairs, with a similarly healthy wholefood menu. It's open Tuesday to Saturday until fairly late and on Fridays and Saturdays there's a live performance from 9 pm.

Pub Food Yes there's a *Cobb & Co*, it's in the St George's Hotel on Willis St right across from the Manners Mall McDonald's.

It's open the usual 7.30 am to 10 pm hours and serves the usual reliable Cobb & Co pub menu.

Other places with straightforward pub food include *Chloes* in the *1860 Victualling Company* at 152-172 Lambton Quay. They have a good choice of steaks, schnitzels, ham steaks and so on for around $9 to $11. It's open Monday to Saturday for lunch and dinner. Or move along Lambton Quay to the *Romney Arms* on Plimmer's Steps. The ambience, the food and the prices are very similar here.

On Plimmer's Steps in *Plimmer's Tavern* there's the fairly smooth and slick *Nickers Bar* with main courses around $12 or $13. The *Cricketers Arms*, on the corner of Tory and Vivian Sts, has pub food in the *Sticky Wicket* with main courses in the $10 to $11 range. *Flanagan's* on Kent Terrace also has pub food.

Restaurants - Chinese Wellington is positively weighed down with Chinese restaurants. They nearly outnumber everything else put together, in fact they probably outnumber all the rest of the Chinese restaurants in NZ put together. There are so many along Courtenay Place it's almost a Chinatown. The menus feature all the Cantonese regulars with main courses generally in the $5 to $8 bracket. Because of the great number of Chinese restaurants here there's a popular belief that the prices are lower and the quality higher than in NZ in general. My (admittedly limited) experience has been that Wellington's Chinese restaurants are very unexciting - the usual dollop of dull vegetables topped by the usual gluggy sauce. Why, when Cantonese food can be so terrific, is it almost always so dull?

Amongst the many, you might try the *Horn Kung* on Courtenay Place but Wellington's Chinese eating place all seem pretty similar.

Guidebook Award
When we publish the next edition of this guidebook we'll give 10 LP guidebooks (your choice) to the writer of the most dazzling, glowing and *verifiable* description of a Chinese restaurant in Wellington. *Verifiable* because I, or another LP researcher, has to try the restaurant and agree with your description or you lose no matter how dazzling or glowing you were. PS – our next edition is due in 1990. PPS – it doesn't even have to be good, if you describe in glowing terms how terrible a Wellingtonian Chinese restaurant was and we try it and agree it truly was bloody awful you'll still win.

Restaurants - Other The *Mexican Cantina*, at 19 Edward St just near the Manners Mall McDonald's, is great value. They have all the usual Mexican dishes – enchiladas, tacos, etc – at around $2.60 to $4.50 and some choice for vegetarians. Get there early though as last orders are taken around 9 pm and it can be crowded since it's very popular. Main meals are from around $10.

Nearby, at 95 Dixon St, *Chevy's* is a colourful pseudo-US restaurant with fancy burgers from $9 to $12 and plenty of other US-style fast meals including (for $9.50) a Ronald Reagan omelette. Made to Nancy's own recipe of course. It's licensed and wine costs $2.50 a glass, beers from $3.

In the same area, more or less behind the Mexican Cantina, is another Wellington institution – *Armadillo* at 129 Willis St. It proved so popular that it's been exported (in a much larger but equally crowded version) to Auckland where the menu is identical. The food here is Texan. Or 'cowboy'. Which means ribs, southern chicken, burgers, etc. It's not cheap at $15 for main courses, $5 for desserts. But you get plenty of food and the place, complete with its John Wayne decor is lots of fun. 'At one point the patrons started batting around a beach ball,' reported one visitor. 'When the firecrackers started flying we left.'

There are all manner of 'ethnic' cuisines around Wellington including Burmese food at *Monsoon*, 124 Cuba Mall. Burmese cuisine is nothing to get too excited about – just straightforward curries – but the only other place in the whole world I've seen a Burmese restaurant (apart from in Burma of course) is San Francisco so this is a rare opportunity. A complete soup, main course curry, rice and tea meal is \$17.50. They're open Monday to Saturday and also have Singapore-Chinese food.

More familiar territory is covered by a number of Italian restaurants including *La Spaghettata* at 15 Edward St, right next to the Mexican Cantina. The pasta is good and the setting pleasant. Or try *Mangiare* at 35 Dixon St, it's a long-standing favourite for pasta.

Wellington has a number of Indian restaurants including the licensed *Bengal Tiger* at 33 Willis St. Tandoori food is a speciality here but we're getting into the expensive night out category by this time. Of course if you really want an expensive night out there's plenty of opportunity for that in Wellington.

Entertainment

Pubs There are lots of pubs with music in the evenings and many good places just for a drink. In the centre, the *1860 Victualling Company* (see Pub Food) is upstairs at the parliament end of Lambton Quay. There are two popular bars here for a drink and they also have entertainment. It's a big, slightly plastic place done up in mock 'days of sail' decor.

Just off Lambton Quay beside the cable car entrance is the *Marble Bar*, a pleasantly relaxed after-the-office bar. Further along Lambton Quay is the *Romney Arms Tavern* on levels one and two of the Williams Centre on Plimmers Steps. Again it's a fairly new place, good for a drink or with evening entertainment. Further up Plimmers Steps is *Plimmers Tavern*.

If you're staying at the YHA hostel the *Thorndon Tavern* on Molesworth St is about halfway downhill towards the railway station. There's evening entertainment there too. There are also plenty of pubs south of the centre including the *Cricketer's Arms* on the corner of Vivian and Tory Sts. This is the rock venue for Wellington.

Other places with music include the *Western Park* at 285 Tinakori Rd, Thorndon and *Quinn's Post* at Ferguson Drive.

Other *Stardust* is a disco on the 1st floor at the corner of Dixon and Cuba Sts. Night-clubs include *Exchequer* on Plimmers Steps and *Spats* on the corner of Victoria and Harris Sts.

The popular *Downstage Theatre* presents plays in the Hannah Playhouse on the corner of Cambridge Terrace and Courtenay Place. The *Wellington Film Society* shows films either at the Regent, the University or the National Museum Theatre. Friday and Saturday nights there are live performances at *Raging Apple*, a wholefood restaurant at 301 Cuba St.

Vivian St around Cuba St is Wellington's very low key red light district with the odd extremely seedy strip joint or massage parlour. Plus, late at night, kiwi ladies-of-the-night leaning acutely into the wind.

Getting There & Away

Air Due to the lack of level land around the city Wellington Airport is very cramped and until recently this limited the international flights which could use the airport – it was simply too small for 747s. Now that Qantas and Air New Zealand both operate 767s there are regular flights to and from Australia.

Air New Zealand's travel centre (tel 859-922) is at 129-141 Vivian St. To get to the south island you have to take the ferry or fly so there are many flights in and out of Wellington. Direct connections include Auckland ($162), Blenheim ($78), Christchurch ($126), Dunedin ($186), Gisborne ($145), Hamilton ($143), Invercargill ($220), Napier ($118), Nelson ($92), New Plymouth ($117) and Rotorua ($141).

There are a number of small carriers hopping across the Cook Strait to towns at the north end of the south island. They can make an interesting alternative to the ferry but note that the strait can be just as bumpy up above as it so often is at sea level. Skyferry/Outdoor Aviation (tel 888-380) has flights to Picton for $39 and other connections to places on the South Island close to the straits. This isn't that much more than the ferry fare but you do have to get to and from the airports at both ends. On the South Island the airport is eight or nine km out of Picton and the shuttle bus into town costs $2.75 (children $1).

You can also fly Air Nelson to Nelson for $45, Motueka Air hops across the strait to Motueka, Kiwi Air flies to Blenheim.

Road Wellington is an equally important junction for bus travel, all the services meet here whether you're coming south from Auckland and the central North Island attractions like Rotorua, Taupo and Tongariro; east from New Plymouth and Wanganui; or west from Napier and Gisborne. It takes about 12 hours to or from Auckland, seven hours to Taupo, eight hours to Rotorua, seven hours to New Plymouth, 5½ hours or longer to Napier.

NZRRS buses operate from the railway station (tel 725-399). Fares include Auckland $70, Hamilton $57, Napier $40, New Plymouth $39, Palmerston North $18, Rotorua $53, Taupo $41 and Wanganui $21.

Newmans have two routes into Wellington – one from Napier, the other from Wanganui, New Plymouth, Hamilton and Auckland. The Newmans station (tel 851-149) is at 260 Taranaki St near the National Museum but their buses also pick up from the city bus terminal beside the railway station.

Mt Cook have a service from Auckland via Taupo to Wellington, with a Taupo-Napier connection. Their office (tel 844-136) is at 83-87 Courtenay Place.

Hitching It's not easy to hitch out of Wellington because that long stretch out of the city through Lower Hutt is built up all the way. It's probably best to catch a train at least as far as Porirua, or possibly to Paekakariki – it's an awkward road to hitch on wherever you are.

Rail Wellington Railway Station is a travellers' centre and meeting place; it would be a bad day not to come across at least one backpacker here. When it's open there's a friendly and helpful Information Office. You can only leave gear in the left luggage area if you hold a rail ticket (ie a train, Picton ferry, or NZRRS bus ticket). It's a free service open 7 am to 8 pm daily. You can walk from the station to the ferry terminal in 20 minutes but there's also a bus for each ferry departure.

New Zealand's railway services continue to contract but you can still travel by rail from Wellington to Auckland ($68) and Napier ($36).

Ferry The Cook Strait ferry service shuttles back and forth between Wellington and Picton. There are usually four services daily and the crossing takes about three hours. Fares are $18 bargain fare, $25 regular fare and $30 summer fare. Children travel at half fare. Bargain means off season, summer means mid-December to early February, regular is bits in between. Day return fares are only about 25% more than a one-way and there are a variety of short excursion fares, family fares, group fares and so on. Cars or motor homes cost from around $60 to $120, bicycles $12, motorcycles $18 to $30.

At peak periods you must book well ahead, the ferries can be booked solid at certain popular holiday times. There are connecting buses to and from the ferry and in Wellington there's a bus to the ferry from platform 9 at the railway station. It departs 35 minutes before the ferry departure.

If you're planning to hitch out of Picton note that the cars are driving off the ferry almost as soon as the ferry docks. Foot passengers are likely to find every vehicle has gone by the time their feet hit terra firma! Try to hitch a ride while you're still at sea. Also keep your baggage with you or remove all valuables. Travellers have discovered their packs have been gone through and cameras or other items of value removed during the crossing.

Getting Around

Airport Transport Guthrey's run a regular airport shuttle service to Wellington Airport for $3.50 with its city terminus in Bunny St, adjacent to the railway station. It comes into the centre along Oriental Parade and turns up Courtenay Place. For the Brougham Place hostels get off at the start of Courtenay Place (fire station/ Travelodge), for Trekkers Hotel get off at Cuba St, for the Youth Hostel go to the end of the line. Services operate regularly even on weekends, phone 872-018 for details. A taxi will cost $8 or $9. There are left luggage lockers at the airport.

Local Transport Wellington City Council (tel 856-579) runs most of the local central city bus services. Most local services and the airport bus start from beside the railway station. Bus fares start at 60c and step up to $1.90. A five-ride Downtowner ticket costs $1.80 or you can get a

Daytripper ticket which covers an adult and two children for $4.50. There's a useful Bus Route Guide leaflet with a map showing the routes and information on which bus you use to get to the various attractions.

New Zealand Railways run the country's only electrified suburban train operation in Wellington, with quite good services along the two northern corridors.

Bicycle Rental Bicycle Village at 39 Ghuznee St rents bikes for $4 an hour, $12 a day or $50 a week.

AROUND WELLINGTON
Tramway Museum

The Tramway Museum is 45 km north of Wellington in Queen Elizabeth Park, just past Paekakariki, where there are picnic and swimming spots. It's open weekends and holidays only from 11 am to 5 pm. You can have a ride for a small charge and there are static displays as well. The Engine Shed, a steam locomotive museum, is also at Paekakariki. It's open Saturday from 9 am to 5 pm.

An alternative way to get there is over the scenic Paekakariki Hill road. North of Paekakariki is a string of good, sandy beaches.

Southward Car Museum

Also out of town the Southward Car Museum at Paraparaumu has nearly 100 cars on exhibit. They include the three oldest cars in New Zealand including the 1895 Benz which is the oldest of the lot. Admission is $2.50 and it's open 10 am to 5 pm daily but getting there isn't too easy by public transport. Other attractions out of Wellington include the Gear Homestead at Porirua and Taylor Stace Historic Cottage at Pauatahanui.

Masterton

In the sheep raising Wairarapa area, Masterton has no notable attractions although it's a reasonable size town and on the Wellington-Palmerston North railway line. Queen Elizabeth Park in Masterton has a fine miniature railway where trains are run on weekends.

Just north of Masterton in the Tararua Forest Park at Mt Bruce there's the Mt Bruce Wildlife Centre, run by the New Zealand Wildlife Service. This native bird reserve has aviaries with examples of various rare or endangered species including the takahe and the black stilt.

The centre is open 9.30 am to 4 pm daily. There are several interesting places between Masterton and Napier. Mikimiki, 15 km north, has a pioneer museum.

Places to Stay Masterton has hotels, motels, campsites and the pleasant *Okiokinga Guest House* (tel 82-970) at 88 Cole St.

SOUTH
ISLAND

Marlborough & Nelson

Marlborough Sounds

For travellers coming across from Wellington the convoluted waterways of the
Marlborough Sounds are the first sight of
the South Island. Many visitors strike out
further afield immediately but there is
much of interest in this area including, of
course, the inlets and bays of the sounds.

History

The first European to come across the
Marlborough district was Abel Tasman,
who spent five days there sheltering under
the east coast of D'Urville Island in 1642.
It was to be over 100 years before the next
white man, James Cook, turned up in
January 1770, remaining there for 23 days.
Between 1770 and 1777 Cook made four
visits in all to the sound he named Queen
Charlotte. Near the entrance of Ship Cove
there's a monument which commemorates
the explorer's visits. Because Cook spent
so much time there he was able to make
detailed reports of the area which made it
the best known haven in the southern
hemisphere. In 1827, the French navigator
Dumont D'Urville discovered the narrow
strait, French Pass, and his officers gave
his name to the island just to the north.

In the same year a whaling station was
set up at Te Awaiti in Tory Channel,
which brought about the first permanent
European settlement in the district.
There was much activity in the next few
decades until the arrival, in June 1840, of
HMS Herald with Governor Hobson's
envoy, Major Bunbury, on the hunt for
Maori signatures to the Treaty of
Waitangi. On 17 June Bunbury proclaimed
the Queen's sovereignty over the South
Island at Horahora Kakahu Island.
Towards the end of that year a Wesleyan
mission was set up at Ngakuta Bay in the
north-west corner of the port.

In spite of this, the Marlborough area
was not the site of an organised company
settlement, more an overflow of the
Nelson colony. Around 1840, the oppor-
tunistic and unscrupulous New Zealand
Company attempted settlement of part of
the Wairua Plain after buying the alleged
rights from the widow of a trader, John
Blenkinsopp. He claimed to have bought
the land from the Maoris for one 16-pound
gun, and obtained a dubious deed signed
by illiterate Maori chiefs. The gun is now
on display in Blenheim.

By 1843 the pressure for land from the
Nelson settlers was so great that it led to
conflict with the Maoris who denied all
knowledge that any part of Wairau was
sold. Two Maori chiefs, Te Rauparaha
and Te Rangihaeata, arrived from Kapiti
to resist survey operations. The whites
sent out a hurriedly co-opted armed party
led by Arthur Wakefield and Police
Magistrate Thompson to arrest the chiefs.
The party was met peacefully by the
Maoris at Tuamarina, but a brief
skirmish precipitated by the Europeans
ensued during which Te Rangihaeata's
wife was shot. The whites were forced to
surrender and Rangihaeata, mad with
rage, demanded vengeance. Twenty-two
of the party, including Wakefield and
Thompson, were tomahawked or shot; the
rest escaped through the scrub and over
the hills.

In March 1847 Wairau was finally bought
and added to the Nelson territory. It was not
long before the place was deluged by people
from Nelson and elsewhere. However,
when the Wairau settlers realised that
revenue from land sales in their area was
being used to develop the Nelson district
they petitioned for the separation and
independence of the area. The appeal was
successful and the colonial government
called the new province Marlborough and
approved one of the two settlements,

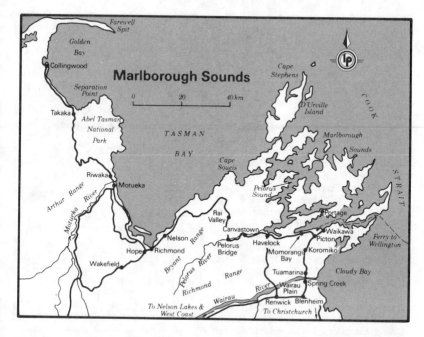

Waitohi – now Picton – as the capital. At the same time, the other settlement known as The Beaver was renamed Blenheim. After a period of intense rivalry between the two towns, including legal action, the capital was transferred – peacefully – to Blenheim in 1865.

THE SOUNDS

The convoluted waters of the Marlborough Sounds have many bays, islands, coves and waterways, formed by the sea invading its deep valleys – an ideal holiday area. Parts of the Sounds are now included in the Marlborough Sounds Maritime Park. The park is not a continuous entity of land, but a large number of separate reserves intermingled with private land. The best way to get around the Sounds is by boat, but the road system has been extended. Permits are required for hunting or camping and there's lots of good swimming, tramping

and fishing. Information on the park is available from the Chief Ranger at 26 Canterbury St, Picton.

Marlborough Sounds Adventure Company (tel Picton 42-301) organises sea-kayaking trips and bushwalks on the sounds. The kayaking trips range from daytrips for $75, to two and three-day expeditions for $175 to $250, or even longer trips. They will also hire out kayaks to experienced people for solo trips. Walks include the two-day Nydia walk ($175), the six-day Queen Charlotte trek from Anakiwa to Ship Cove ($350) and various other longer and shorter walks.

Places to Stay

There are various places to stay on the sounds, some of them accessible only by boat or floatplane. Prices are usually fairly reasonable. They include the well known *Portage Hotel* (tel Lochmara 34-309) on Kenepuru Sound. Rooms here cost from about $75 a night and there is also bunkroom accommodation. The hotel has all sorts of sporting facilities and it can be reached by road from Picton or Havelock.

Also on Kenepuru Sound the *Raetihi Lodge* (tel Lochmara 34-300) costs $70 a night including all meals and the *Hopewell Guest House* (tel 34-341) has self-contained cottages from around $40. The *Bulwer Guest House* (tel Rai 26-285) is on Waihinau Bay on Pelorus Sound and has guest house accommodation with meals, or units and flats. *Castaways Resort* (tel Picton Sounds 39-141) on Te Pangu Bay on Tory Channel and the *Tira-Ora Lodge* (tel Lochmara 34-253) on Northwest Bay on Pelorus Sound both can only be reached by boat or floatplane.

There are cabins at *Gem Resort* (tel Picton Sounds 39-245) at the Bay of Many Coves. Cabins for two cost $38 to $50. The *Blueseas Motel* (tel Lochmara 34-235) at Elie Bay can be reached by road or water and has tourist flats for just $20. The *Te Rawa Boatel* (tel Lochmara 34-285) is also low priced with rooms at $25 to $30. *Punga Cove Chalets* (tel Lochmara 34-361) on Endeavour Inlet on Charlotte Sound and the *Te Mahia Motel* (tel Lochmara 34-089) both cost $50 to $60. The Te Mahia Motel also has a small campsite for caravans and campervans.

Getting Around

See the following sections on Picton and Havelock for information about cruises, mail boat runs and floatplane flights on the sounds.

PICTON

The ferry from the North Island comes into Picton, a pretty little port at the head of Queen Charlotte Sound. Picton is a small borough with a population of about 3300, a hive of activity when the ferry is in and during the peak of summer, but rather slow and sleepy any other time.

Information

For detailed info on Picton there's an

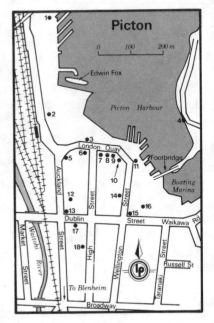

1	Cook Strait Ferry Terminal
2	Information Centre
3	Museum
4	'Echo' Marlborough Cruising Club
5	New Zealand Experience
6	Terminus Hotel
7	Dairy & Tea Rooms
8	Hotel Federal
9	Seaspray Cafe
10	Oxley's Hotel
11	Post Office
12	Bellevue Guest House
13	Top of the South Bakery
14	5th Bank Restaurant
15	Picton Hotel
16	Whalers Inn
17	Youth Hostel
18	Sunwick Private Hotel

Information Centre in the car park between the ferry wharf and the town itself. It's open Monday to Friday from 9.30 am to 4 pm and on Saturdays and Sundays from 10 am to 3 pm. They have

Top: Picton Harbour (TW)
Bottom: Mutton Cove, Abel Tasman National Park (VB)

information on yacht charters and on walking in the Sounds area as well as some interesting exhibits.

The Post Office is on the corner of Wellington St and London Quay. Picton has a convenience that you will not come across often in New Zealand – a laundromat. So if you've got a pile of dirty clothes in your backpack take them along to Picton Villa, Wellington St. The Creek Pottery on Wellington St has interesting pottery and other local crafts. The Marlin Motel, 33 Devon St is the AA agent (tel 784)

Museum

The excellent little Picton Museum is on the foreshore, right below London Quay. There are a number of interesting whaling exhibits including a harpoon gun and numerous other unusual items such as an old Dursley Pederson bicycle of around 1890. The museum is open 10 am to 4 pm daily and the admission price is $1 (children 50c).

The Edwin Fox

Between the museum and the ferry wharf is the battered, but still floating, hull of the old East Indiaman *Edwin Fox*. Built of teak in the Bengal region of India she was launched in 1853 and in her long and varied career she carried convicts to Perth, troops to the Crimean War and immigrants to New Zealand. Later she was one of the earliest vessels to operate as a cold store with the most up-to-date freezing machinery in its time. It arrived in Picton in 1897 and for some years was used as a coal hulk.

Edwin Fox Restoration Society

Picton   New Zealand

Boarding Pass N° 2059

In 1986 she was refloated and a comprehensive survey has been completed in order to draw up plans for her total restoration. It's hoped that this work will commence in 1987 but it will take over 10 years to complete. It's planned that the ship will remain open throughout the restoration process so that you can see the work actually underway. The metal-sheathed hull is open to visitors from 8.30 am to 5.30 pm every day and admission is $2 (children $1).

The Echo

On the other side of Shakespeare Bay, across the inlet from the town centre on the footbridge, is the scow *Echo* which is now used as the clubrooms of the Marlborough Cruising Club. Built on the Wairau River in 1905, the *Echo* used to trade between Blenheim and Wellington, shipping around 14,000 tons of freight a year, and was only retired in 1965 after the railway ferries were introduced.

Around Picton

The New Zealand Experience is a multi-screen show plus assorted amusements on the corner of London Quay – $6 or $3.50 for children.

Out of Picton is Port Underwood, the scene of great whaling activity in the 19th century. The narrow winding road from Waikawa to Rarangi has magnificent views of the North Island silhouetted against the horizon.

Only six km south of Picton, near Koromiko, is another of the ubiquitous deer parks – complete with picnic area and children's playground – that are scattered around both islands. Tuamarina, 13 km further on, is historically interesting as the site where the Wairau Massacre occurred. The tree near where the skirmish started still stands on the riverbank. In the cemetery, just above the road, is a white monument designed by Felix Wakefield, the youngest brother of Arthur Wakefield, who was killed in the affray.

Walks

There are many scenic bushwalks around Picton as well as longer tramps. An easy track of about a km runs along the eastern side of the harbour to Bob's Bay where there's a barbecue area. Queen Charlotte Drive, the 35-km road between Picton and Havelock, has nice scenery but hostile sandflies.

Tours

The main access around Queen Charlotte Sound is by water, which means there are innumerable cruises and fishing trips available as well as tours on land. Marlborough Scenic Tours (tel 36-262) and Bramley's Mini Bus Service (tel 37-866) are two local tour operators; winery visits are a speciality.

Out on the water there are Round the Bay cruises including a stop to feed the tame fish at Double Cove. The trips take about two hours and cost $22 (children $11). Day trips to the Portage Hotel on Kenepuru Sound are another possibility, they cost $25 (children $12.50). Mail boat cruises on the *MV Rawene* go on Monday, Tuesday, Thursday and Friday, departing at 8.30 am from the Picton Wharf.

Or you can get up above it all on floatplane flights. Float Air Picton (tel 36-433) is between the *Edwin Fox* and the ferry terminal.

Places to Stay

Hostels Wedgwood House is an associate *Youth Hostel* on Dublin St close to the centre of town. Nightly costs are $9.

Camping & Cabins The *Blue Anchor Holiday Park* (tel 37-212) is on Waikawa Bay Rd, only half a km from the centre, and has sites at $17. There are also a variety of different cabins from around $20 to $35 a night plus tourist flats.

Alexander's Motor Park (tel 36-378) is a km out on Canterbury St and has sites at $6 per person plus cabins and on-site vans. *Parklands Marina Holiday Village* (tel 36-343) is on Beach Rd at Waikawa Bay,

three km out. Other sites include *Waikawa Bay Caravan Park* (tel 37-434) and *Momorangi Bay Motor Camp* (tel 37-865) which is 13 km out. The Momorangi Bay site also has dinghies for hire.

Guest Houses Picton has a number of guest houses and private hotels including *Marineland* (tel 36-429) at 26-28 Waikawa Rd which claims to have a 'shark-free swimming pool'. Rooms are $30/52 with breakfast or there are four self-contained motel units which cost $52 without breakfast.

Others include the *Bellevue Guest House* (tel 36-598) at 34 Auckland St with rooms at $28/38, add $5 for breakfast. *Admiral's Lodge* (tel 36-590) at 22 Waikawa Rd and *Sunwick Private Hotel* (tel 36-268) at 75 High St are others.

Hotels The *Federal Hotel* (tel 36-077) on the waterfront has rooms including breakfast at $26/32.

Motels Picton has plenty of motels and the *Bell Bird Motel* (tel 36-912) at 96 Waikawa Rd is particularly good value at around $40 for a double. It's an older motel, a km or so out from the centre and there's a $1 surcharge for one night stays.

The *Sunnyvale Motel* (tel 36-800), five km out at Waikawa Bay, is also good value. The *Tourist Court Motel* (tel 36-331) at 45 High St has rooms from around $52 for two and is a simple and straightforward place right in the centre.

Other There are various guest houses, motels, 'boatels' and cabins dotted around the Sounds, some accessible by road and boat, but many with the main access being by boat. Most are on the Picton telephone exchange if you want to phone them.

Places to Eat

Most food would be better than the junk you get on the ferry, but early in the morning or late at night you're unlikely to find much on offer. In any case Picton doesn't offer many real taste treats although there are plenty of takeaways and fast food places around the centre. Try the *Villa Cafe* on Wellington St, 'A Good Place to Eat' their sign announces. Or there's the *Sandwich Maker* on High St, the *Dairy & Tea Rooms* at the London Quay/High St corner and the *Carousel* takeaway next door. On the Auckland St/Dublin St corner the *Top of the South* is a combination bakery and Chinese takeaway.

There are three pubs along London Quay and all three – the *Terminus Hotel*, the *Federal Hotel* and the *Oxley Hotel* – have pub food. In the Oxley there's bistro food in the $5.50 to $10 bracket, the Federal has bar lunches for just $5.50 to $6, while the Terminus also has its fancier George James Restaurant which is open for breakfast, lunch or dinner every day of the week.

The *5th Bank* on Wellington St is an expensive restaurant with main courses at $16 to $20. A block over at 33 High St the *Ship Cove* is heavily nautical in feel, also somewhat expensive and licensed. The byo *Tides Inn* is at the same arcade and is slightly cheaper.

Getting There & Away

Air Skyferry/Outdoor Aviation (tel 37-888) have a regular service across the straits to and from Wellington. The short flight costs $36 and operates about a half dozen times a day. The Picton airstrip is at Koromiko, eight or nine km out of town, and a shuttle bus connects to the flights for $2.75 (children $1).

Road Delta Coachlines has a daily service between Picton and Blenheim and on to Greymouth. They also have a weekday service from Blenheim to Nelson, Deluxe Motor Service run a bus from Picton to Blenheim ($5) to connect with this bus. Delta operate from the ferry terminal.

All and sundry seem to have services from Picton south to Christchurch. Mt Cook/H&H (tel 36-175) at 2 Wellington St

continue all the way to Dunedin and Invercargill. Newmans (tel 36-687) at the ferry terminal have services around the north coast to Nelson, Motueka and Takaka; south-west through Nelson to Westport and Greymouth; and south through Christchurch to Dunedin. Their fares include Nelson $23 and Christchurch $43. It takes about three hours from Picton to Nelson, five to six hours from Picton to Christchurch. NZRRS also get into the act with a Nelson-Christchurch bus service.

Hitching Hitching out on Highway 1 is possible if you've got patience. It can take a few hours to get a ride or at other times you may not get one at all. Most traffic is on the road just after a ferry arrives – there is not much between sailings. The trouble with being on the road just after the ferry docks is that every other hitch-hiker is there as well so it doesn't necessarily make for easier hitching at that time. See the Ferry section for further details.

On average it will take a day to reach Christchurch or Nelson. Queen Charlotte Drive between Picton and Havelock is the shortest way to Nelson but has little traffic so it's easier to hitch via Blenheim on the Spring Creek bypass (follow Blenheim road 22 km to Spring Creek, where you turn right).

Rental Cars Avis, Hertz, Southern Cross, Thrifty, Budget, Newmans and National all have rent-a-car offices at the ferry terminal.

Rail The rail service between Christchurch and Picton operates daily in either direction and takes about six hours. The fare is $38.

Ferry The Cook Strait ferry service shuttles back and forth between Wellington and Picton. There are usually four services daily and the crossing takes about three hours. Fares are $18 bargain fare, $25 regular fare and $30 summer fare.

Children travel at half fare. Bargain means off season, summer means mid-December to early February, regular is the times in between. Day return fares are only about 25% more than a one-way and there are a variety of short excursion fares, family fares, group fares and so on. Cars or motorhomes cost from around $60 to $120, bicycles $12, motorcycles $18 to $30.

At peak periods you must book well ahead, the ferries can be booked solid at certain popular holiday times. If you're planning to hitch out of Picton note that the cars are driving off the ferry almost as soon as the ferry docks. Foot passengers are likely to find every vehicle has gone by the time their feet hit terra firma! Try to hitch a ride while you're still at sea. Also keep your baggage with you or remove all valuables. Travellers have discovered their packs have been gone through and cameras or other items of value removed during the crossing.

The ferry terminal in Picton has few facilities, but it does have long padded seats, so if there aren't too many people around you can grab some sleep while you wait. But beware, the terminal is sometimes locked between sailings and Picton can be a cold place to hang around, waiting for the late ferry in winter.

Getting Around
Bicycles can be hired from the Renta Centre (tel 36-324) at 53 High St.

BLENHEIM
Population 23,000
The largest town in the area, Blenheim is 29 km south of Picton, on the Wairau Plains, a contrasting landscape to the Sounds. Situated at the junction of the Taylor and Opawa Rivers, Blenheim is particularly well laid out, but more by accident than design as the early surveyors confined their development to the high ground to avoid the swamp in the centre. The swamp has been reclaimed and is now Seymour Square with attractive lawns and gardens.

Near the square are relics of Blenheim's violent early history, including the old cannon known as Blenkinsopp's gun which is on the corner of High and Seymour Sts. Originally part of the equipment of the whaling ship *Caroline* which Blenkinsopp captained, this was supposedly the cannon for which Te Rauparaha was persuaded to sign over the Wairau Plains and a contributing cause of the massacre.

Te Rauparaha was a distinctly unsavoury character and indirectly was a major reason for the British government taking control of New Zealand. He cultivated the captains and crews of visiting whaling ships (they nicknamed him the 'old sarpint') and with muskets and other weapons he acquired, set out on wholesale and horrific slaughter of other South Island tribes. In his most gruesome raid he was aided by a white trader who transported his warriors and decoyed the opposing chiefs on board where they were set upon by Te Rauparaha's men. The ensuing slaughter virtually wiped out the tribe. When news of this event, and the captain's part in it, reached Sydney the British government finally decided to bring some law and order to New Zealand and to their unruly citizens operating there.

At least, that is the reputation that has been ascribed to Te Rauparaha. This reputation of wickedness has been questioned in a biography entitled *Te Rauparaha: A New Perspective*.

Information
There's an Information Centre on the corner of Queen and Arthur Sts. It's open 9 am to 5 pm from Monday to Friday. A three hour Wine Trail tour of local wineries costs $20 (children $10).

Places to Stay
Camping & Cabins At the north end of town on SH 1 at 78 Grove Rd the *A1 Motor Camp* (tel 83-667) has sites at $6 per person and also cabins from $20, tourist flats from $34.

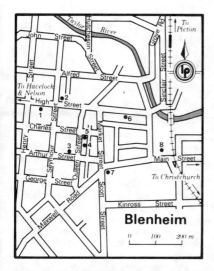

Blenheim

0   100   200 m

1   Cobb & Co
2   Blenkinsopp's Cannon
3   Information Centre
4   Air New Zealand
5   Ginger & Pickles Cafe
6   City Hotel
7   Post Office
8   Pizza Hut

The *Blenheim Auto Court* (tel 87-419) at 27 Budge St is a km from the centre off the main Picton highway. Sites for two cost from $10, more with power. They also have cabins and tourist flats.

Campsites further out from the centre include *Spring Creek Holiday Park* (tel 893) which is six km out towards Picton and about a half km off SH 1. *Sun Valley Caravan Park* (tel 28-196) is 11 km out. Both these parks have cabins as well as sites.

Guest Houses & Hotels There are a couple of guest houses to choose from. The *Maple Guest House* (tel 87-375) at 144 High St offers bed & breakfast for $18 per person. On Main St the more expensive *Koanui Guest House* (tel 87-487) has bed & breakfast at $28 per person.

Hotels include the *City* (tel 85-029) right in the centre at 25 High St. Rooms here all have attached bathrooms and cost $40/50 for singles/doubles. The *Criterion Hotel* (tel 83-299) on Market St is more expensive with rooms at $50/60.

Motels Reasonably priced motels include the *Raymar Motor Inn* (tel 85-104) at 164 High St which has doubles at $50. The *Alpine Motel* (tel 81-604) at 148 Middle Renwick Rd is similarly priced. At most other motels doubles cost from about $60.

Places to Eat
There are plenty of takeaways and cafes around the centre but this is another Kiwi town where they produce the sort of sandwiches and snacks that give McDonald's a good name. No McDonald's hasn't got to Blenheim (yet) but there is a *Kentucky Fried Chicken* establishment on the Picton edge of town and a *Pizza Hut* in Main St near the centre.

There's also a *Cobb & Co* at the Grosvenor Establishment at 91 High St on Seymour Square. It's open daily from 7.30 am to 10 pm. Cheaper bar meals are also available at lunchtime there. The *Criterion* at the Market St/Alfred St corner also does pub food. An exception to the generally low standards in Blenheim is *Ginger & Pickles Cafe* at 13 Charles St but fancy open sandwiches here will cost you about $9 and in any case it's only open for lunch.

Getting There & Away
Air Air New Zealand (tel 85-299) are at 29 Queen St. They have direct flights to Wellington ($78) with connections on to other cities from there. The Picton airstrip at Koromiko is about half way between Blenheim and Picton and you can fly from there to Wellington with Skyferry for just $36. Kiwi Air also have regular flights between Blenheim and Wellington for $48.

Road See the Picton section for details on bus services. Deluxe Motor Services (tel 85-467) have regular services between Blenheim and Picton ($5). Delta Coachlines (tel 81-408) are at 53 Grove Rd and operate Picton-Blenheim-Nelson and Picton-Blenheim-Greymouth.

Newmans (tel 85-189) are also on Grove Rd and operate Picton-Blenheim-Christchurch-Dunedin and Picton-Blenheim-Nelson with connections on from Nelson to Motueka-Takaka and to Westport-Greymouth.

Mt Cook/H&H (tel 81-408) operate from the Delta office on Grove Rd and have a service Picton-Blenheim-Christchurch-Dunedin-Invercargill.

NZRRS also have services south from Picton through Blenheim to Christchurch.

Rail The daily Picton-Christchurch railway service operates through Blenheim.

Getting Around
A taxi to Blenheim airport costs about $9.

HAVELOCK
Founded around 1860 and named after Sir Henry Havelock of Indian Mutiny fame, this attractive little town is situated at the confluence of the Pelorus and Kaituma Rivers. Havelock is 43 km from Blenheim and 73 km from Nelson and the only place where a main road touches the Pelorus Sound. Historically it was the hub of the timber trade, both for milling and export, and later on the service centre for gold mining activities in the area. Today it's a thriving small-boat harbour and a pleasant place to drop off the planet for a couple of days.

There's not much to do around town but if you stroll up the hill to the top of Hughes St before dusk you'll get a good view of the town and the Sounds, followed by a good sunset – if you're lucky – and the flicker of glow-worms when it gets dark. There's a tiny museum in Havelock and also many good walks in the area. The walk to Nydia

Bay is particularly popular and the youth hostel can supply information on this and other walks.

Mail Boat Trips
Glenmore Cruises takes passengers along on the mail run boat, stopping at isolated homesteads to deliver post and supplies. Tea and coffee are available free on board and fishing enthusiasts can try their hand with the bait and handlines which are supplied. If you want to camp or tramp anywhere along the way you can get dropped off and collected again on a specified day. You're on your own so take what you need. Fresh water is available in some places; check with locals whether you need to take any. To get an idea of how convoluted the Sounds are, Pelorus Sound is 42 km long, but has 379 km of shoreline.

The trips operate Monday to Saturday departing at 9.30 am and returning at 5.30 or 6.30 pm. The round trip fare is $35 (children $17.50) and there's a discount to YHA members. On Wednesdays and Saturdays you can have lunch, at extra cost, during the stopover at Beatrix Bay Homestead. On Sundays during the summer season there's a shorter day cruise which costs $30 (children $15).

For information and bookings check with the Glenmore Cruises office (tel 42-276) right in the middle of town. If they should be shut then try the tea room across the road. Newmans buses stop outside Glenmore Cruises. Various other cruises and fishing trips are also operated from Havelock with costs of $18 to $25.

Places to Stay
Hostels The excellent *Havelock Youth Hostel* (tel 42-104) is on the corner of Lawrence St and the main road through the town. Nightly cost is $11 and much information is available about walks and other local activities.

Camping & Cabins The *Havelock Motor Camp* (tel 42-339) on Neil St is low-priced with sites from around $10 or a couple of dollars extra with power.

Motels Havelock has a couple of small motels, both on the main road through town. The *Anchor Motel* (tel 42-019) has rooms at $55, the *Havelock Garden Motel* (tel 42-387) is a bit cheaper with rooms from around $40 to $50.

Places to Eat
There's the *Tea Rooms* on the main road for snacks and light meals or you can get counter meals at the *Pelorus Tavern* and dine overlooking the Havelock marina.

Getting There & Away
The weekdays Blenheim-Nelson service with Delta Coachlines runs through Havelock. Newmans also have a Blenheim-Nelson service through Havelock, usually several times daily.

There's a minibus mail service along Queen Charlotte Drive between Picton and Havelock. Check with the tea rooms at the Havelock end.

SOUTH TO CHRISTCHURCH
Many travellers head off west or north-west from Picton, to the walking tracks or the West Coast glaciers. There are also a number of points of interest along the straight-forward route south to Christchurch.

KAIKOURA
Kaikoura or 'crayfish food' in Maori is noted for its fishing and its fine setting, on a bay backed by the steeply rising foothills of the Kaikoura Range. There are some caves and if you walk out to the end of the peninsula there is a seal and seabird colony and a small aquarium, plus you pass some historic buildings on the way. Good walks in the area include Mt Fyffe and tracks in the State Forest.

Shortly south of Kaikoura the road splits, SH 1 continuing along the coast while SH 70 branches off inland and later merges with SH 7 crossing over from the West Coast.

Places to Stay
The *Maui Youth Hostel* (tel 5931) is a modern hostel on the esplanade about two km south of the centre. Ask bus drivers if they will drop you off closer to the hostel. Nightly cost is $11. The *Kaikoura Holiday Camp* (tel 207) is on Beach Rd next to the railway station but there are quite a few other campsites, hotels and motels.

Places to Eat
In season crayfish are often featured in Kaikoura restaurants, you even find it in local takeaways and travellers report that it's a good enough reason for making a stop here! The *Craypot Restaurant* has excellent seafood and other dishes.

KAIAPOI
SH 7 and SH 1 merge again at Waipara and 19 km before Christchurch you reach Kaiapoi, noted for its wool mills. The Kaiapoi Museum in the Old Courthouse on Williams St has exhibits on local history. It's open Sundays and Thursdays 2 to 4 pm, entry 50c.

From Kaiapoi you can make trips on the *MV Tuhoe* which sails most Sundays to Kairaki and back. The round trip costs $6 (children $3) and takes 1½ to two hours. You can reach Kaiapoi from Christchurch on a 1R, 1T, 1V, 4R or 4V bus.

WAIMAKARIRI RIVER
Shortly after Kaiapoi the road crosses the Waimakariri River. This is another popular river for jet-boating, and day trips to the Waimakariri Gorge can easily be made from Christchurch. Longer rafting trips are also made on this river – contact Rafting Tours (tel 60-419) in Christchurch.

Nelson

Population 44,000
Nelson's a pleasant, bright and active town. The Nelson area is noted for having some of the finest beaches in New Zealand and more sunshine than any other part of the country so it's not surprising that it's a popular holiday area. Apart from beaches and bays, Nelson is noted for its fruit-growing industry and its very energetic local arts and crafts activity.

History

The Maoris began to migrate to the South Island during the 16th century and among the first to arrive in Nelson were the Ngati-tumatakokiri. By 1550 this tribe occupied most of the province as Abel Tasman was to find out to his cost when he turned up at the place he later named Murderers' Bay.

Other tribes followed the Tumatakokiri, settling at the mouth of the Waimea River. The Tumatakokiri remained supreme in Tasman Bay until the 18th century when the Ngati-apa from Wanganui and Ngati-tahu – the largest tribe in the South Island – got together in a devastating attack on the Tumatakokiri who virtually ceased to exist as an independent tribe after 1800. But the Ngati-apa's victory was short-lived for between 1828 and 1830 they were practically annihilated by armed tribes from Taranaki and Wellington who sailed into the bay in the largest fleet of canoes ever assembled in New Zealand.

By the time the immigrants arrived there were no Maoris living at Te Wakatu – the nearest pa being at Motueka – and the population was so decimated, those that remained put up no resistance. The first white settlers sailed in response to advertisements by the New Zealand Company which was set up by Edward Gibbon Wakefield to colonise the country systematically. In theory the idea was to transplant a complete slice of English life from all social classes – a grandiose scheme – in reality 'too few gentlemen with too little money' took up the challenge and the new colony almost foundered in its first few years from lack of money. Only the later arrival of hardworking German immigrants saved the region from economic ruin.

The settlement was planned to comprise small but workable farms grouped around central towns. However, the New Zealand Company's entitlement to the land was disputed and it was almost a year before this problem was sorted out. This meant that while the land around the town had been distributed early, the farmland was not available for such a long time that landowners and labourers forced to live in town had whittled away their capital in survival. The Wairau disaster – read about it in the Marlborough Sounds section – which resulted in the deaths of 22 of Nelson's most able citizens, including Captain Wakefield whose leadership was irreplaceable, plunged the colony into deep gloom. To make matters worse the

1	California Guest House
2	Air New Zealand
3	Information Centre
4	Automobile Association
5	CPO
6	Hotel Naumai
7	YMCA
8	Suburban Bus Company
9	Pizza My Heart
10	Colonial Restaurant
11	Hitching Post Pizza
12	Royal Hotel
13	Hotel Wakatu, Cobb & Co
14	Riverside Pool
15	Suter Art Gallery
16	Public Library
17	Newmans Bus Station
18	Chez Eelco
19	Traffers
20	Cultured Cow Yoghurt
21	City Lights Cafe
22	NZR Travel Office
23	South St Gallery
24	Cathedral
25	Bishop School

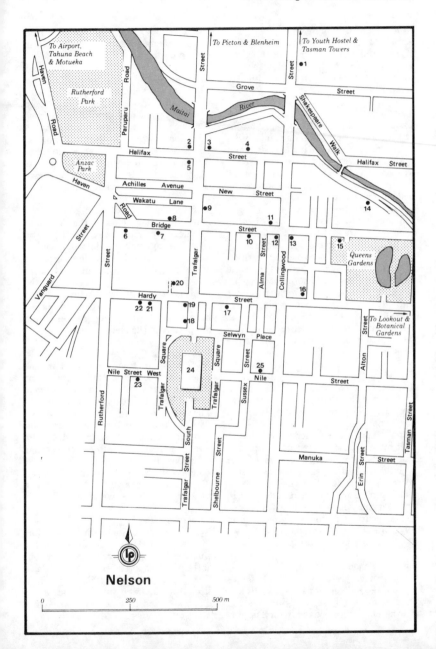

Nelson

0   250   500 m

New Zealand Company went bankrupt in April 1844 and since nearly three-quarters of the population were dependent on it in some way or another, particularly for sustenance, the situation was so grim as to be near famine.

Information

The Public Relations Office (tel 82-304) is on the corner of Trafalgar and Halifax Sts and is open 8.30 am to 5 pm weekdays and during the Christmas holidays also on weekends. Trafalgar St, which crosses the river just before the information centre and runs straight up to the cathedral, is the main street in Nelson.

The Riverside Pool is walking distance from the centre and costs $1.30 (children 70c). If you are on a working holiday there's fruit and tobacco picking in season (February to May) and there may be some casual daily work at fisheries at the port. Contact the Labour Department or individual growers about picking work. WWOOF, Willing Workers on Organic Farms, are based in Nelson – see the introductory information in Facts for the Visitor under farm visits.

Cathedral

The focal point of Nelson is its cathedral, at the top of Trafalgar St. It's open 8 am to 4 pm daily. The present building has had a somewhat chequered career. The foundation stone for the cathedral was laid in 1925 but construction dragged on for many years and in the '50s arguments raged over whether the building should be completed to its original design. Eventually construction recommenced to a modified design in the '60s and was completed in '67. When the cathedral was finally consecrated in 1972 no less than 47 years had passed since the foundation stone was laid!

Bishop's School

For about 90 years from 1840, Bishop's School served Nelson as a school. It's in Nile St East and it's open Sundays and during holiday periods only on Tuesday

and Thursday, 2 to 4 pm. You can read some of the notes and textbooks used in the old days.

Galleries

The Suter Art Gallery adjoins Queen's Gardens in Bridge St and is open from 10.30 am to 4.30 pm. Entry is $1, children 20c. As well as having a permanent art collection it provides for theatrical, musical and dance performances, art exhibitions, films and craft displays. The gallery takes it's name from Bishop Suter, who formed the Bishopdale Sketching Club back in 1889.

If you're interested in pottery, visit the South St Gallery, close to the Cathedral on Nile St West. It's open 10 am to 5 pm on weekdays, to 9 pm on Fridays and 11 am to 4 pm on weekends. There are numerous other galleries in the area. Nelson's artistic reputation is partly due to the local clay which attracted many potters to the town. The Nelson Potters Association have a guide leaflet showing where to find the potters in the Nelson area.

Museums

At 87 Atawhai Drive, Founders Park is a collection of the Nelson buildings, reflecting the town's early history. It's open 10 am to 4.30 pm daily and entry is $4 (children $2). The Nelson Provincial Museum is at Isel Park in Stoke and has an important photographic collection and exhibits on local and Maori history. It's open Tuesday to Friday 10 am to 4 pm, Saturdays, Sundays and holidays 2 to 5 pm. There's a 50c admission charge on weekends and holidays but it's free weekdays.

Gardens & Walks

Nelson has some fine gardens including the beautiful Botanic Gardens and the Queens Gardens. There's a good lookout at the top of Botanical Hill in the gardens. The riverside footpath makes a pleasant stroll through the city and there are many fine walks and tramps around the city. The Matai Valley is a particularly restful and beautiful area and the Maungatapu Track leads from here across to the Pelorus.

Beaches

The best known beach in Nelson is Tahuna, five km from the city centre. At Ruby Bay, 35 km north-west of Nelson, a rock concert is held in March each year. The best beach in the area is Kaiteriteri, 64 km to the north-west, although the dreaded katipo, New Zealand's only poisonous spider, is reputed to lurk in driftwood on this beach.

Tours

There are various tours available from Nelson. Contact the Public Relations Office for details.

Places to Stay

Hostels Nelson has a YHA hostel and a private hostel, close to each other on Weka St about a km to the north of the centre. The neat, clean and friendly *Nelson Youth Hostel* (tel 88-817) is at 42 Weka St and has room for 32 people at $11 a night. The hostel is housed in one of Nelson's original homesteads and there's an overflow hostel to cope with peak season crowds. The hostel operates a free bus service to Motueka Hostel every day at 8 pm.

Tasman Towers (tel 87-950) is at 10 Weka St and is a brand new purpose-built hostel. Rooms are mainly for two, three or four and there are plenty of doubles for couples. Nightly cost is $12 and there are good kitchen and lounge facilities. The people who operate it are ex-YHA and have made a real effort to cater for travellers' needs.

Only three km from the city centre Cedric and Isabel Hockey's *Pavlova Farm House* (tel 89-906) at 328 Brook St is a farm hostel. It's unusual in that this 40 hectare farm is actually within the city boundaries. Nightly cost is $12 and apart from the farm animals they also have bicycles to borrow, camping equipment to rent if you're off tramping, lots of

tramping advice and they'll pick you up from Nelson. The pavlovas are pretty good too!

Right in the centre of town at 8 Bridge Rd the *Naumai Private Hotel* (tel 83-287) has some regular rooms at $40/50 but also some rooms with four or six two-tier bunks. These cost $12 per person on a share basis.

Camping & Cabins There are plenty of campsites around Nelson including, near the airport and Tahuna Beach, the *Tahuna Beach Holiday Park* (tel 85-158) which is the largest in New Zealand. There are lots of camping places at around $12 for two, cabins and lodges from $20 to $30, tourist flats at $32 to $40. The site is five km from the city centre and just a couple of minutes from the beach.

The *Brook Reservoir Motor Camp* (tel 80-399) in the upper Brook Valley is situated in a superb position near a stream and surrounded by rolling pastures and forested hills. It's about the same distance from the centre as Tahuna, but rather smaller and more personal. Camping costs from $5 per person, slightly more with power. There are cabins from very basic four-bunk ones at $13 for two up to more luxurious ones at around $16 to $22. The camp is a long way uphill if you're walking. The *Maitai Reserve Motor Camp* (tel 81-059) is operated by the city council and is on the riverbank, six km from the centre. Sites are $9 for two people, $6 per person with power. They also have some cabins at $13.

Nelson Cabins & Caravan Park (tel 81-445) at 230 Vanguard St has cabins which are supplied with cutlery and cooking utensils – but you need a sleeping bag – for $26 and tourist flats from around $35. It's very central but there are no tent sites, powered sites are $12.

Other sites in the area include the *Richmond Holiday Park* (tel RD 7323), which is 13 km out at Richmond, and the *Waimea Town & Country Club Caravan Park* (tel RD 6476), also in Richmond.

The *Mapua Leisure Park* (tel Mapua 666) at Mapua, 33 km from Nelson and near Motueka, claims to be 'New Zealand's first dress optional leisure park'. They have sites for tents and caravans, a bunk house, on-site caravans, cabins and tourist flats.

Guest Houses Nelson has plenty of bed and breakfast places, but you still might have difficulty finding somewhere to stay in the high season. Best known and probably most expensive is *California House* (tel 84-173) at 29 Collingwood St, just across the river heading towards the two hostels. It's run by Carol Glen, who is (would you believe it) a Californian, and provides a real 'Californian' breakfast that might include orange juice, fresh berries and cream, ham and sour cream omelettes, apricot nut bread, apple and cheese blintzes, pancakes with maple syrup and coffee. Cost is $60 to $80 for a couple including that hearty breakfast. There are only double rooms, if you're by yourself it's going to cost $45 but you do get a double bed. California gets lots of recommendations but it's only open from October through May.

California is definitely upper class bed & breakfast but there are various other more conventional places in Nelson, all of which include breakfast in their tariff. *Palm Grove* (tel 84-645) at 52 Cambria St costs $23 per person. The *Alpha Inn Private Hotel* (tel 86-077) at 25 Muritai St has doubles at around $42. *Abbey Lodge* (tel 88-816) at 84 Grove St is $25 per person. *Hunts Home Hosts* (tel 80-123) at 15 Riverside is $29/50 for singles/doubles. There are several others including the *Naumai Private Hotel*, listed under hostels above.

For real Kiwi hospitality stay with *Kay and Roger Morrison* (tel 87-993) at 81 Cleveland Terrace. They have a self-contained two-bed unit, four at a squeeze, which they rent out for $15 per person. They've done a lot of travelling themselves, are very friendly and an excellent source

of information on local doings, farm work, etc. They're very friendly people but there is just the one room so please phone ahead. It's up a steep hill on the west side of town, great views but a tough walk!

Hotels There are plenty of regular hotels around Nelson. They include the *Dominion* (tel 84-984) at 2 Nile St West where singles are $22 to $25, doubles $33 to $37. Or the *Metropolitan* (tel 81-485) at 131 Bridge St where singles/doubles are $44/60. Also on Bridge St at number 152 the *Royal Hotel* (tel 83-190) has rooms at $30/46 including breakfast.

The more expensive *Quality Inn Nelson* (tel 82-299) is on Trafalgar St and has everything from a sauna and swimming pool to a spa and gym. Rooms cost from around $100 although there are discounts on the weekend.

Motels There are a great number of motels in Nelson, many of them near the airport at Tahunanui. Motels that are both fairly central and reasonably priced include the *Lynton Lodge Motel* (tel 87-112) at 25 Examiner St with room at $46 to $54. The *Riverlodge Motel* (tel 83-094) is at 31 Collingwood St on the corner with Grove St and rooms here are $54 to $58. The *Trafalgar Lodge Motel* (tel 83-980) at 46 Trafalgar St has singles/doubles at $50/55.

Right in the centre of town at 218 Trafalgar St the *Mid City Motel* (tel 83-595) has rooms at $60/70. By the river at 8 Ajax Avenue the *AA Nelson Motel* (tel 88-213) is very conveniently located but more expensive with rooms around $60 to $65.

Places to Eat

Takeaways & Fast Food There are plenty of sandwich specialists around the centre and, a little further out, a *Pizza Hut* and a *Kentucky Fried Chicken*.

At 147 Trafalgar St, down at the river and CPO end, *Pizza my Heart* does takeaway pizzas by the slice from $2 to $2.50 – or by the whole pizza of course. The *Pegasus Coffee Bar* on Hardy St at the entrance to Newmans is a good place for sandwiches and snacks. For a more expensive but pleasant lunch the cafe at the *Suter Art Gallery* is worth considering – good food in a pleasant setting.

Pub Food There's a *Cobb & Co* in the Wakatu Hotel on the corner of Collingwood St and Bridge Rd. The usual Cobb & Co menu and the usual 7.30 am to 10 pm opening hours. *Traffers*, on the corner of Trafalgar St and Hardy St, also has a fairly standard pub-style menu with main courses at around $12 to $14 and also a children's menu at $4.

Other hotels with pub food include the *Royal Hotel* with its Dixies Restaurant across the road from the Cobb & Co on the corner of Collingwood St and Bridge Rd. The *Metropolitan Hotel* on Bridge Rd also has a low-priced bistro menu with most things at $5 to $6. It's open for lunch and dinner daily.

Restaurants The popular *Hitching Post* at 145 Bridge St does good pizzas from around $5.50 for small ones, from $7.50 for mediums and from $14.50 for large ones. The menu goes much further, however, with main courses around $7 to $10, serve yourself salads for $3, drinks, desserts and so on. If the weather's good they also have an open air courtyard out back.

Across the road is the *Colonial Restaurant* at 114 Bridge Rd which does, despite the name, Mexican food. It's a little hole-in-the-wall place with main courses at $11 to $13. Also on Bridge Rd, *Papa Gino's* has all the Italian regulars.

Chez Eelco, directly below the cathedral at 296 Trafalgar St, is a Nelson institution. It's a relaxed coffee bar cum restaurant which goes from 6 am to 11 pm seven days a week. Apart from those wonderful hours it also has tables and chairs out on the widewalk which makes it one of the few (if not only) sidewalk cafes in NZ. They serve up everything from strong coffee to croissants, sandwiches to fruit juices, with regular restaurant meals

thrown in for good measure. It's a popular meeting place and the front window is an equally popular local noticeboard. Give it a try.

Just round the corner at 142 Hardy St is *City Lights*, a glossy modern restaurant with a decidedly international menu with Greek, Californian, Mexican, Chinese, you-name-it influences. Main course are $12 to $20 and it's open seven nights a week.

Entertainment
Nelson's 'not to be missed' highlight of the year is the New Year Mardi Gras which can get very active after midnight. Various pubs have entertainment including the *Turf Hotel* at Stoke or the *Ocean Lodge Hotel* at Tahunanui, both with discos. The glossy new *Traffers* in the central city puts on light entertainment at the weekends too.

Wherever you're drinking in Nelson make it a point to try a Mac's beer. Nelson's own beer is brewed by the last independent brewery left in the whole country and it's not bad.

Getting There & Away
Air Air New Zealand (tel 82-329) is on the corner of Trafalgar and Halifax Sts, by the river and right across from the CPO and PRO. They have direct flights to Wellington ($92), Auckland ($185) and Christchurch ($116, $126 via Wellington). The great majority of connections, even to Auckland and Christchurch, go via Wellington.

Eagle Air (tel 75-110) flies between Nelson and Palmerston North ($106), Auckland ($164) and Hamilton ($148) and also have connections from Palmerston North to other North Island centres. Air Nelson (tel 76-066) flies between Nelson and Wellington. Their fares vary from $45 to $73 depending on what flight you take. These are essentially business commuter flights for people going to Wellington for the day. People willing to fly at other times get a big discount. Pacifica Air were scheduled to commence a Wellington-Nelson-Christchurch service.

Road Delta Coachlines (80-285) operate from Skyline Travel on Achilles Avenue. They have a weekday service from Blenheim to Nelson which takes about two hours and Skyline Travel take over from there to Motueka. Delta have a daily service from Picton to Greymouth. Nelson Lakes Service operate from Nelson to St Arnaud, a two-hour trip, connecting with the Picton-Greymouth bus there.

Newmans (tel 88-369) have a terminal at 220 Hardy St, quite close to the cathedral. They have a variety of services running through Nelson including a direct Picton-Havelock-Nelson service, a Picton-Blenheim-Havelock-Nelson and a Blenheim-Havelock-Nelson service. From Blenheim they then have connections south to Christchurch or there is a direct Nelson-Christchurch service via the Lewis Pass, Monday to Saturday.

Beyond Nelson, Newmans have a Monday to Saturday service to Westport and Greymouth or up to three times daily during the week (but only one on Saturday and none on Sunday) from Nelson to Motueka. Monday to Saturday one of the services continues to Takaka where another bus connects with the Newmans bus to take you to Collingwood, starting point for the Heaphy Track. Newmans fares to or from Nelson include Blenheim $19, Christchurch $57, Picton $23 and Takaka $18.

Although NZRRS don't run through Nelson they have a travel centre on Hardy St. It's open Monday to Friday from 8.30 am to 4.30 pm.

There are a number of alternatives for transport into the Abel Tasman and North-West Nelson parks. Abel Tasman Connection (tel 80-686) have a minibus from Nelson to points in the park for around $25 per person.

Hitching Getting out of Nelson is not easy as the city sprawls so far. It's best to take a bus out to the outskirts. Hitching to the west coast can be hard going, take a bus as far as Tapawere.

Getting Around
Airport Transport A taxi to the airport costs about $8.

Local Transport The Suburban Bus Company operates local services from its terminal in the city on Lower Bridge St. They run out to Richmond via Tahuna.

Bicycle Rental Bikes can be hired from Winns (tel 83-877) at 101 Bridge St or Stewart Cycles (tel 84-344) at 126 Hardy St.

Around Nelson

Nelson Lakes National Park
The Nelson Lakes park is 118 km southwest of Nelson. There's good tramping, walking, lake scenery and skiing in winter. In St Arnaud the *Yellow House Guest House* (tel 36-850) has hostel-style accommodation at $12 a night, $5 extra for bedding. There are daily bus connections between St Arnaud and Nelson, Blenheim and Picton.

Wakefield
South of Nelson, at Pigeon Valley, Wakefield, is the Waimea Steam Museum, which has an interesting collection of vintage steam-driven machinery. It's open daily from 9 am to 4.30 pm.

Moutere Eels
On the back road route along Wilson's Rd to Motueka are the tame eels of the Anatoki River. They're about 11 km from Upper Moutere village, look out for the signpost. Patient feeding over the years has made them so tame that they'll actually slither out of the water to take bits of meat from your hand. It's an unusual sight! Entry is $2 (children 50c) and supposedly feeding time is 10 am to 12 noon and 1 to 4 pm but they're fairly flexible. The eels hibernate over winter, from just after the May school holidays until just before the August ones!

Wineries

There are a number of vineyards on the Nelson Wine Trail which you can follow by doing a loop from Nelson through Richmond to Motueka, following the SH 60 coast road in one direction and the inland Moutere River road in the other. Wineries which are open for visitors include Korepo Wines, Neudorf Vineyards, Weingut Seifried, Redwood Cellars, Ranzau Winery, Robinson Brothers and Laska Cellars.

MOTUEKA

Motueka is the centre for a tobacco, hops and fruit-growing area. People often come here for the summer picking work and it's also a popular transit point for trampers en route to the walks in the Abel Tasman park and the Heaphy Track walk.

Information

Motueka is essentially one long main street, High St. The Information Centre is being relocated to a combined museum and gallery in the old Motueka District High School on High St.

Places to Stay

Hostels There's a YHA summer *Youth Hostel* (tel 88-962) at Motueka High School on Whakarewa St. It's just a few hundred metres from the centre of town but it's only open for a very short time – from mid-December to late January – check for specific dates at other hostels. Nightly cost is $9.

The *YMCA* (tel 88-652) has a hostel at 500 High St, on the Nelson side of town. Nightly cost in this pleasant and modern hostel is $9 per night plus a $5 key deposit.

Seven km out of Motueka on the back road route to Nelson is the *Riverside Community*, a well-organised community established about 40 years ago. Anyone can stay here for $6 a day which includes accommodation and vegetables picked from the garden. There's no difficulty in finding it – all the locals know it and there's a sign on the road.

Camping & Cabins *Vineyard Tourist Units* (tel 88-550) are at 328 High St, not far from the centre of town. They have a variety of cabins and flats and they're simple but good value. Small cabins which can sleep up to four are $20 for two, the tourist units with their own toilet facilities are $29 or there are proper motel units with attached bathroom and with bedding provided for $42.

Campsites are *Fearon's Bush Motor Camp* (tel 87-189) at the north end of town, the *Motueka Beach Reserve Camp* (tel 87-169) at Port Motueka and the *Marahau Beach Camp* (tel 78-176) which is 18 km north. The Motueka Beach camp is camping or caravans only, the other two also have cabins.

Guest Houses *White's Guest House* (tel 87-318) at 430 High St is a friendly bed & breakfast place in what used to be a nunnery! All rooms have a washbasin and there's a lounge with pleasant views, tea and coffee-making equipment and a fridge plus a laundry. Nightly cost is $25 per person and the breakfast is a substantial one. You can get dinner here for another $14.

Hotels & Motels The *Post Office Hotel* (tel 89-890) is right in the middle of town and has rooms at $25/45. Other alternatives include the *Abel Tasman Motor Inn* (tel 87-699) at 43 High St with rooms at $45/55 or the *Motueka Garden Motel* (tel 89-299) near the clocktower at 71 King Edward St with rooms from $50.

Places to Eat

Takeaways & Pub Food There's the usual string of takeaways and sandwich bars along Motueka's endless main street including, right across from the post office, the *Wheelhouse*, a three part operation with takeaways at one end, fish & chips at the other and a sit-down-and-eat-it-there space in the middle. They have Chinese food as well as burgers and they're open every day of the week until at least 8.30 pm and on Fridays and Saturdays until 12 midnight. For sandwiches and snacks try the *Silver Spoon Bakery* at 105 High St or the fancier *Sandwiched Eaterie* at 219 High St.

Opposite the post office, next to the Wheelhouse, is the *Post Office Hotel* which is open seven days a week, till 10 pm on Saturdays, till 9 pm on other days. The menu is the pub regular with prices around the $10 or $11 mark for main courses. The other two hotels – the *Motueka Hotel* and the *Swan Hotel* – also have food but the Post Office Hotel is the most serious about it.

Restaurants Motueka's most interesting food question, however, is how did a little Kiwi country town end up with two such interesting restaurants. At the Nelson end of the shopping area at 265 High St there's *Mottandoor* where the menu features an incredibly diverse array of Asian dishes. You can try a Burmese or Malay curry, an Indonesian satay or a Thai fried rice. Or, of course, Indian dishes prepared in the tandoor oven. Starters are $7, main courses $13, desserts (also from all over Asia) are $5.50.

At the other end of the central area at 98 High St is *The Place* where the decor is rustic (ie the chairs and tables don't match) and the menu basically Italian with some flair. Main courses here are in the $11 to $16 bracket and include some good vegetarian dishes. They also have pizzas at $8.50. Either of these restaurants would be an asset to most small NZ towns, Motueka's lucky to have them both.

Getting There & Away
Air Motueka Air (tel 88-772) operate a daily services connecting Motueka with Wellington ($60) and Takaka.

Road Newmans operate from Nelson through Motueka to Takaka from where a connecting bus goes to Collingwood. Their office is on High St at the Takaka end of town. The Skyline Travel bus station (tel 88-850) is on Wallace St and they also have a Nelson-Motueka service for $5.50.

Getting Around
Stanton's Service Station on Greenwood St rent bicycles.

MOTUEKA TO TAKAKA
From Motueka, Highway 60 continues on over Takaka Hill to Takaka and Collingwood. Before ascending Takaka Hill you pass a turn-off on your right to Kaiteriteri and the southern end of Abel Tasman National Park, then a turn-off on your left to Riwaka Valley, a good area for picnicking, swimming in river pools, and walks. You can walk to the spring that is the source of the Riwaka River.

On top of Takaka Hill at Marble Mountain are the Ngarua Caves where you can see moa bones. The caves are open daily but closed from mid-June through August. As you cross the crest of the pass there are fine views down the valley to Takaka from the Harwood Lookout. There's an interesting explanation of the geography and geology of the area at the lookout. Near Takaka are the Pupu Springs, one of the largest freshwater springs in the world.

Abel Tasman National Park
The coastal Abel Tasman National Park is a popular tramping area and the various walks includes one around the coast (but beware of the sandflies!). The park is at the northern end of a range of marble and limestone extending up from North-West Nelson Forest Park, and the interior is honeycombed with caves and potholes. See the introductory Tramping section for more information on the park.

Abel Tasman National Park Enterprises have a four-day guided walk through the park. Tom's Kayak Hire rents kayaks over the summer months for around $10 an hour and also does half day kayak trips to Fisherman's Island in the park for $25.

Top: Post Office, The Square, Christchurch (TW)
Left: The Wizard invoking his acolytes (MC)
Right: Scott Monument, Christchurch (TW)

Top: Antigua Boathouse, Christchurch (TW)
Bottom: Airforce Museum, Christchurch (TW)

Abel Tasman National Park

Getting There & Away From Motueka in the summer Skyline Bus Services (tel 88-850) operate a daily service to Marahau, the start of the Abel Tasman walk, and a twice daily service to the beach resort of Kaiteriteri. Motueka Taxis (tel 87-900) also have a daily service to Marahau.

Over the summer months the *MV Waingaro, MV Ponui* and *MV Matangi* operate a coastal service around the park, going from Kaiteriteri to Torrent Bay, Tonga Bay, Bark Bay, Totoranui or Awaroa with fares from around $12 to $25. Phone Motueka 87-801 for details.

TAKAKA

The small centre of Takaka is the last town of any size as you head towards the north-west corner of the South Island. It's the main centre for the beautiful Golden Bay area. Pohara Beach is a popular summer resort near the town. Takaka has a museum (entry $1, children 50c) which is open daily. Near Takaka there are more tame eels in the Anatoki River.

Information

There's a Department of Conservation office with a great deal of tramping information. It's open Monday to Friday from 9 am to 12 noon and 1 to 5 pm. Also on the Motueka side of town there's a very helpful Information Centre open seven days a week from 9 am to 5 pm in summer, 10 am to 4 pm in winter.

Crafts

There are many craftspeople working in the Golden Bay area – painters, potters, blacksmiths, screenprinters, silversmiths, knitwear designers and so on. There's a *Golden Bay Craft Trail* leaflet with directions to galleries and workshops in the area.

Places to Stay

Hostels The *Takaka Summer Hostel* (tel 59-067) is in the Golden Bay High School on Meihana St. It's only open over the Christmas-January period and costs $9 a night.

Camping & Cabins There are sites at *Pohara Beach Camp* (tel 59-500 which is 10 km from Takaka, the *Golden Bay Holiday Park* (tel 59-742) which is 18 km from Takaka and eight km from Collingwood, or the *Totaranui Beach* site at Totaranui which is 33 km from Takaka in the Abel Tasman National Park.

Hotels & Motels The *Junction Hotel* (tel 59-207) and *Telegraph Hotel* (tel 59-308) are both in Takaka and have rooms at around $25 per person. A few km on the Motueka side the *Upper Takaka Hotel* (tel 59-411) is better known as the Rat Trap! Nightly cost including breakfast is $33.

There are a number of motels in or around Takaka, particularly at Pohara Beach.

Places to Eat

The *Wholemeal Trading Company* does health food or there's *Milliways* (the restaurant at the end of the universe for Douglas Adam fans) with main courses at $15 to $18.

Getting There & Away

Air Motueka Air fly between Motueka and Takaka.

Road Newmans service from Nelson through Motueka terminates at Takaka. There's a connecting service by Collingwood Bus Services to Collingwood. Newmans' fares include Motueka $12 and Nelson $18.

COLLINGWOOD

The tiny township of Collingwood is the end of the line, which is really why people come here. For most it's simply the jumping-off point to the Heaphy Track. You can head south-west to more caves and the Heaphy Track in the North-West Nelson State Forest Park, or north-east to Farewell Spit, the huge sandspit which is also a wildlife sanctuary. Collingwood Motors organises safaris to the spit with a tour of the Farewell Spit Lighthouse. The trip takes about five hours and covers 120 km. Collingwood has a small museum.

Places to Stay

Camping & Cabins Right by the centre of the tiny township the *Collingwood Motor Camp* (tel Takaka 48-149) has sites at $9 for two or slightly more with power. They also have cabins and tourist flats. The *Pakawau Beach Motor Camp* (tel Takaka 48-327) is 13 km north of Collingwood which means it's even more at the end of the road.

Other *Collingwood Vacations* (tel Takaka 48-112) has bed & breakfast at $22 per person and also self-contained units at $30 for two, you have to supply bedding. The *Collingwood Motel* (tel Takaka 48-224) is $37/42 a night.

Places to Eat

If you're not fixing your own food there's only the pub across from the post office or the *Country Style Tearooms*, which are closed on Mondays and all Baha'i holidays since the owners are followers of that faith.

Getting There & Away

Collingwood Bus Services (tel 48-188) are right behind the post office in Collingwood and they're the key to all local transport questions. Twice daily from Monday to Saturday they operate a service which connects with Newmans buses terminating at or starting from Takaka. The Collingwood-Takaka fare is $5. They also have a mail run service to Pakawau and Puponga ($15), a Cobb Valley Tour ($30) and will arrange transport to or from the Heaphy Track, 35 km from Collingwood, for $50 for the minibus or $10 a head if there are more than five people.

Christchurch

Population 289,000

Since I was born outside Christchurch, England, I find it rather curious that New Zealand's Christchurch isn't named after the English one and the fact that the River Avon flows through both cities is also unconnected. The rivers are remarkably similar – placid and picturesque – but the down-under Avon is named after a Scottish Avon not the English one. The name Christchurch comes from Christ Church College at Oxford University – one of the leaders of the early settlers was educated there.

The first Europeans to arrive in Christchurch began building huts along the Avon in 1851 but it was not until March 1862 that it was incorporated as a city. Situated at the base of the hills of Banks Peninsula, Christchurch is often described as the most English of New Zealand's cities. True or not it's a lovely city, relaxed, picturesque and with that pretty-as-a-postcard river winding its way right through the centre.

Information & Orientation

The Cathedral Square (just look for the spire) is very much the centre of town. Climb up to the top to get your orientation. The NZTP and the Central Post Office are both on the Square. Christchurch is a pleasantly compact city and walking is a pleasure but finding your way around is slightly complicated by the river which twists and winds through the centre and seems to cross your path in disconcertingly varied directions.

Colombo St, running north-south through the Square, is one of the main shopping streets.

Information The NZTP is right on the Square in the Government Life Building. If you march down Worcester St from the Square you'll come to the Information Centre (tel 799-629) by the riverside, on the corner of Oxford Terrace. It's open Monday to Friday 8.30 am to 5 pm and on Saturdays and Sundays from 9 am to 4 pm.

The New Zealand YHA headquarters are in Christchurch. The office (tel 799-970) is at 28 Worcester St in the Arts Centre. It handles YHA membership, takes passport photographs, sells camping equipment, packs, clothes and books and also makes travel reservations.

There are left luggage facilities at Rent-a-Bike on Gloucester St. Christchurch has numerous bookshops including the Government Book Shop at 159 Hereford St.

Airlines

Airline offices are generally close to the Square, Qantas and Air New Zealand are right on the Square.

Air New Zealand
    BNZ Building, Cathedral Square (tel 588-039)
Ansett New Zealand
    530-544 Memorial Avenue (tel 791-300)
Mt Cook Airlines
    91 Worcester St (tel 790-690)
Qantas
    CML Building, Cathedral Square (tel 793-100)
Singapore Airlines
    AMP Building, Cathedral Square (tel 68-099)

Consulates

Denmark (tel 899-099)
Finland (tel 60-709)
France (tel 484-059)
Japan (tel 65-680)
Netherlands (tel 69-280)
Sweden (tel 798-600)
UK (tel 63-143)
USA (tel 790-040)

Cathedral Square

Christchurch is a calm, orderly city – and pancake flat so it's a good place to explore

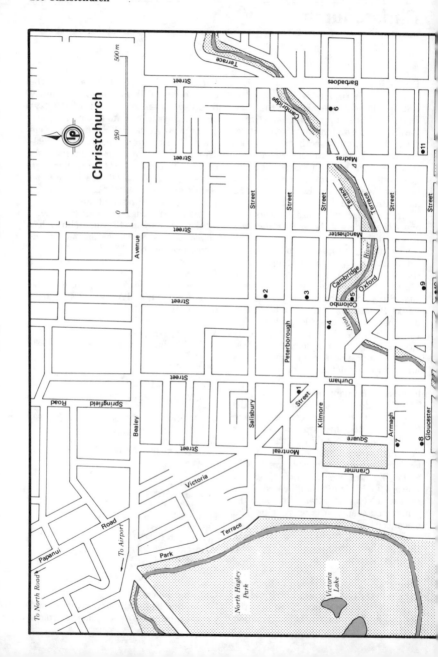

Christchurch

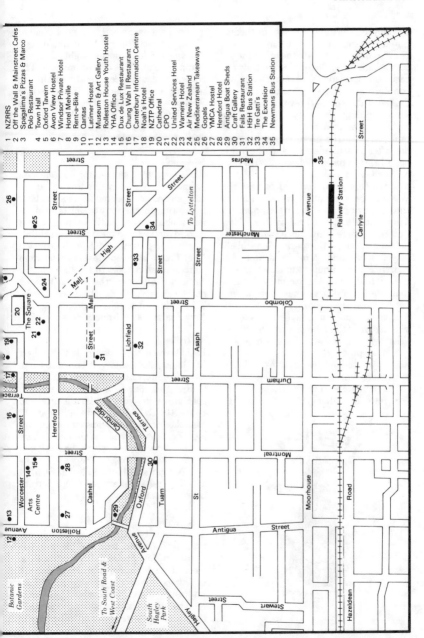

1 NZRRS
2 Off the Wall & Mainstreet Cafes
3 Spagalima's Pizzas & Marco
  Polo Restaurant
4 Town Hall
5 Oxford Tavern
6 Avon View Hostel
7 Windsor Private Hotel
8 Hotel Melville
9 Rent-a-Bike
10 Qantas
11 Latimer Hostel
12 Museum & Art Gallery
13 Rolleston House Youth Hostel
14 YHA Office
15 Dux de Lux Restaurant
16 Chung Wah II Restaurant
17 Canterbury Information Centre
18 Noah's Hotel
19 NZTP Office
20 Cathedral
21 CPO
22 United Services Hotel
23 Warners Hotel
24 Air New Zealand
25 Mediterranean Takeaways
26 Gopals
27 YMCA Hostel
28 Hereford Hotel
29 Antigua Boat Sheds
30 Craft Gallery
31 Fails Restaurant
32 H&H Bus Station
33 Tre Gatti's
34 The Excelsior
35 Newmans Bus Station

by bicycle. Start from the Cathedral Square where, for $1 (children 50c), you can climb up 139 steps to the top of the 63-metre-high spire. There you can study the cathedral bells and look around while you contemplate that earthquakes have damaged the spire on several occasions, once toppling the very top into the Square! The pointed stone top was replaced with the green copper-skinned one after that incident. The cathedral is open 9 am to 4 pm weekdays, 12.30 to 4 pm on Sunday afternoons.

Make sure you're around to hear the Wizard – he attempts to conquer gravity through levity – spouting in the Square at 1 pm from Monday to Friday. One of New Zealand's more amusing eccentrics, he not only dresses the part – long black velvet robes and cape in winter and chartreuse green outfits in summer – he plays it to the hilt. An extremely eloquent man, the Wizard has a line of glib patter – pet subjects to have a go at are bureaucracy and feminism – and a skilful way of playing with the hecklers in the crowd. Whether you like what he has to say or not, it's a production you shouldn't miss and trying to spot his acolytes makes it even more fun.

Unfortunately in early '87 the Wizard got into a minor dispute with the government over whether or not he had to fill in a census form. He claimed he'd disappeared on census night and not reappeared until the census was over. The government disagreed and fined him for refusing to fill in the form. In protest the Wizard went on strike. If he's not back on the job (the job of being the Wizard that is) you can probably sign a protest form at the Information Centre.

Museum

Christchurch's fine museum on Rolleston Avenue is open every day from 10 am to 4.30 pm and admission is free. Particularly interesting are the early colonists' exhibits featuring a century old Christchurch street reconstruction, and the Antarctic exhibit. Christchurch is the HQ for 'Operation Deep Freeze' and supplies are ferried from Christchurch Airport to US bases in the Antarctic although the US is making noises about shifting the operation to Tasmania in Australia in protest against New Zealand's anti-nuclear stance.

Art Galleries

Right behind the museum is the Robert McDougall Art Gallery. It's open 10 am to 4.30 pm daily. Other galleries are the CSA Gallery at 66 Gloucester St which specialises in New Zealand's arts and crafts, the Brooke/Gifford Gallery at 112 Manchester St which has contemporary New Zealand art and the Gingko Gallery in the Arts Centre which has original prints and drawings. There's also the GEFN Crafts Co-Op on Cashel St Mall and the Crafts Gallery on Oxford Terrace near the boat sheds.

Arts Centre

The University of Canterbury town site has been transformed into the biggest Arts Centre in New Zealand. It's worth a look, even if just to see the beautiful old buildings – there's usually something interesting there. New Zealand has a lot of good handicraft centres making some really fine pottery, jewellery and other crafts

and Christchurch is particularly well represented. The Arts Centre has everything from galleries to hand-made toys to Maori carvings. The complex also has a couple of good restaurants and you'll find the New Zealand YHA headquarters there. There's an arts, crafts and antiques market held here over the summer weekends.

There are some beautiful old (by New Zealand standards, anyway) stone buildings around Christchurch, especially around the Arts Centre.

Botanic Gardens

Beside the museum off Rolleston Avenue the Botanic Gardens are open 7 am to sunset. It has 30 hectares of greenery with the Avon River burbling gently by on one side. The electric 'toast rack' operates tours of the gardens from outside the cafe between 11 am and 4 pm when the weather is fine.

Town Hall

Christchurch citizens are justly proud of their modern town hall on the riverbank (see map). Visitors are welcome from 9 am to 5 pm weekdays, 1 to 5 pm weekends and holidays and there are guided tours every half hour. Outside is a fountain by the same designer as Sydney's Kings Cross el Alamein Fountain. It goes two better by having three dandelions.

Avon River

That invitingly calm Avon River obviously requires canoes so head to the Antigua Boatsheds by the footbridge at the bottom of Rolleston Avenue. Here you can hire one-person canoes for $2.50 an hour, two-person canoes for $5 an hour. They also have paddle boats for $5 a half hour. The boatshed is open 9.30 am to 5 pm daily and there's a good sandwich bar right by it.

If paddling a canoe sounds like too much effort you can be punted along the river for $5 per person for 20 minutes – the Christchurch Punting Company operates from beside the Thomas Edmonds Restaurant on Cambridge Terrace!

Air Force Museum

Opened in 1987 the RNZAF Museum is exceptionally well presented. There are a variety of aircraft used by the RNZAF over the years, convincingly displayed with figures and background scenery. Antarctic aircraft sit in the snow, aircraft are serviced, a Canberra bomber of the '50s taxis out at night, a WW II fighter is hidden in the jungle. There are also displays of air force memorabilia and many exceptionally good models.

The museum is at the Wigram airport, quite close to the centre, and can be reached by a No 25 Hornby bus from the Cathedral Square. It's open Monday to Saturday from 10 am to 4 pm, Sunday 1 to 4 pm. Entry is $5 (children $2).

Other Museums

South-east of the centre the Ferrymead Historic Park at 269 Bridle Path Rd, Heathcote, is a Museum with trams, railway engines, cars and machinery of all types. It's open 10 am to 4.30 pm daily and you can get there on a No 3 Sumner Bus. Entry is $6 (children $2) including a ride on a steam train or tram.

The Yaldhurst Transport Museum opposite the Yaldhurst Hotel on the Main West Rd, is open daily between 10 am and 5 pm. Displayed in the grounds of an attractive old homestead – built in 1876 – is some of New Zealand's earliest transport.

Orana Park Wildlife Trust

The Orana Park lion reserve, the first one in New Zealand, also has tigers, camels, water buffalo and recently a kiwi house has been added. Feeding times are 2.30 pm on week days and 11.30 am on weekends and holidays. It's open 10 am to 5 pm daily and entry is $6 (children $3). It's on McLeans Island Rd, Harewood, which is beyond the airport.

Willowbank Wildlife Reserve

This reserve also has exotic and local animals including a variety of domestic animals. There's also a pre-European

Maori village model. The reserve is open daily from 10 am to 6 pm and entry is $4 (children $2).

Other Attractions

There's an aquarium and zoo at 155 Beach Rd, North Beach. It's open daily from 10 am to 5 pm, admission is $2.50 (children $1) and you can get there on a 19M, 29M or 10N bus.

Just over the Ferrymead Bridge on the main road to Sumner, Cob Cottage is a restored sod hut originally built in the 1860s. Deans Bush and Homestead on Kauri St was built in 1843, it's the oldest building in the province and is now a private museum. The grounds of Mona Vale, an Elizabethan-style homestead now used as a reception centre, are open every day. It's less than two km from the city centre beside the river.

The Nga-Hau-e-Wha National Marae at 250 Pages Rd, Aranui is a national Maori cultural centre with a meeting house with carved gateway.

Beaches

The closest beaches to the city are North Beach (10 km, bus No 19), South Brighton (10 km, bus No 5S), Sumner (11 km, bus No 3), Waimairi (10 km, bus No 19), New Brighton (eight km, bus No 5) and Taylors Mistake – a pleasant sheltered beach further out from Sumner, popular for surfing. All bus numbers refer to Christchurch Transport Board buses.

Walks

There are lots of walks around Christchurch worth considering, see the Information Centre for details and leaflets. There's also a leaflet available from the transport information centre on bus access to the various walks.

Starting in the city is the Riverside Walk – the leaflet on this is packed with information. From the *Sign of the Takahe* there is a walkway up to the *Sign of the Kiwi* through Victoria Park, and then along near the Summit Rd to Scott

Reserve – good views from many points. The walk is accessible by bus from Victoria Square (near the Town Hall).

How about walking one way to Lyttelton on the Bridle Path? It leads from Heathcote Valley to Lyttelton and takes one to 1½ hours at a reasonably easy pace. The Godley Head Walkway is a two-hour round-trip from Taylors Mistake, crossing then recrossing Summit Rd – beautiful views on a clear day. It is part of a planned Crater Rim walkway around Lyttelton Harbour. The Rapaki track is an excellent walk taking just a couple of hours – fine views of the whole city and of Lyttelton.

Tours & Trips

Bus Tours There are a variety of bus tours around Christchurch and the surrounding country. The Christchurch Transport Board have three Red Bus Tours which are good value. There's a 10 am two-hour tour of the city which costs $10 (children $5), a three-hour afternoon tour of the hills, coast and harbour including a short harbour cruise and a stop for tea at the *Sign of the Takahe*. This one costs $12 (children $6), tea extra! Finally there's a three days a week (daily during school holidays) wildlife tour to the Orana Park reserve. Cost is $12 ($6 for children) including admission to the reserve. Bookings can be made at the Bus Information Centre in the Square.

Other Tours Canterbury Scenic Tours (tel 69-660) have half day city tours ($22) and day tours further afield to Akaroa ($75) or Hanmer Springs ($75). Mt Cook/H&H (tel 799-120) have a daily 1½ hour city tour and a 2½ hour tour of the surrounding area.

Geocraft Tours (tel 61-937) operate an interesting all-day tour exploring the interesting geology of the Christchurch area and visiting local craftspeople. The tour costs $66 including lunch. There are also day trips out to rivers in the Canterbury area for jet-boat trips.

Places to Stay

Christchurch is the major city and the only international arrival point on the South Island. As a result it has far more accommodation in every category than you might expect – there are lots of hostels, campsites, guest houses, hotels, motels, you name it.

Hostels Christchurch is well equipped with hostels including two youth hostels and some popular private ones. *Rolleston House Youth Hostel* (tel 66-564) at 5 Worcester St is close to the museum and only 700 metres from the centre so its very conveniently located. There are 48 beds at $13 a night.

The other hostel, *Cora Wilding* (tel 899-199), is five km from the centre at 9 Eveleyn Couzins Avenue and has 40 beds. To get there catch a 10 bus from the Square to Tweed St. Costs here are also $11 a night.

The exceptionally popular *Avon View* (tel 69-720) is at 208 Kilmore St near the Madras St end. It's a straightforward travellers' hostel (no children or groups their card announces) and it's relatively small and pleasant. You may have trouble getting a bed here so phone ahead. There's a very pleasant little garden out back, the usual kitchen and laundry facilities and a bed costs $11 a night. The rooms are for two to five, the rooms for two cost $23 as a double. It's run by ex-YHA people who are very au fait with what travellers want and need.

The *Latimer Hostel* (tel 798-429) on the corner of Madras and Gloucester Sts used to be a YWCA hostel and has a variety of rooms as well as bunkroom accommodation. In the bunkrooms a bed costs $12 or the rooms are $22/32 for singles/doubles. This is a larger, less personal place but crowded and popular for all that. There are the usual kitchen and laundry facilities, a games room with a pool table and other distractions and a TV room with an amazingly eclectic mixture of chairs.

Similar in style with a mixture of bunkroom accommodation and regular rooms is the *Hereford Private Hotel* (tel 799-536) at 36 Hereford St. It's opposite the Arts Centre and very close to the YMCA and youth hostel. Bunkroom accommodation is $11, singles $17, doubles or twins $25. It's very plain and straightforward but excellent value, especially for its single and double rooms. There are kitchens and laundry facilities for guests' use and this place has had strong recommendations from a number of travellers.

The *YMCA* (tel 60-689) is at 12 Hereford St, only a few steps from the Botanic Gardens, the Rolleston Avenue Youth Hostel and the Hereford Hotel. Accommodation here is almost all in single rooms and although much of it is given over to permanents there's usually room for casual visitors. It takes men or women and costs $18 a night or $22 with breakfast, $28 with breakfast and dinner. By the week it costs $99 including breakfast and dinner. The rooms are spartan and straightforward and there's a snack bar in the front of the building which is open Monday to Friday from 7 am to 9 pm and on Saturday from 8 am to 4.30 pm.

As in other major cities it may be possible to find accommodation at the university during student vacations. You can call the student association on 487-069.

Camping & Cabins There are plenty of campsites in and around Christchurch with a number of them very conveniently located. *Addington Showground Camp* (tel 389-770), at 47-51 Whiteleigh Rd off Lincoln Rd, is only three km from the centre. It has camping at $10 for two people, cabins for as little as $22 for two or $36 with attached shower and toilet. There's a $1.20 one-night surcharge. It's conveniently located, comfortable and cheap – but closed for two weeks during the show in early November.

Riccarton Park Motor Camp (tel 485-690) at 19 Main South Rd, Upper Riccarton is six km from the centre. Tent sites are $7.50 per night. Cabins for two are $18 to $22 per night. *Meadow Park Motor Camp* (tel 529-176), at 39 Meadow St off the Main North Rd, is five km out. Camping costs $7.50 for one person, $12 for two. There are cabins from around $25 to $40. The camp has a pool and bicycles for hire. Get there on a No 1 bus (Northcote).

Russley Park Motor Camp (tel 427-021) is at 372 Yaldhurst Rd, opposite Riccarton Racecourse about 10 km from the Square or five km from the airport. At this pleasant camp tent sites cost $12 for two people. The camp also has on-site vans at $24 to $29 for two, chalet cabins from $24 to $34 for two and some fancier tourist flats from $42.

South New Brighton Park (tel 889-844), in Halsey St off Estuary Rd, is another pleasant park and also 10 km out. Caravan sites cost $7 for one, $14 for two or there are a few on-site caravans at $18 plus the site charges.

Amber Park (tel 483-327) is conveniently located at 308 Blenheim Rd, only five km south of the centre. There are no camping sites here, caravan sites cost $7 for each adult. Tourist flats, which share the camp kitchen facilities but have their own showers and toilets, cost $36 to $40 a night.

Guest Houses The *Windsor Private Hotel* (tel 61-503) at 52 Armagh St is just five to 10 minutes' walk from the city centre. It's meticulously clean and orderly and rooms cost $42/60 for singles/doubles including a traditional cooked breakfast.

There are a number of other places within a stone's throw of the Windsor, such as the *Hotel Melville* (tel 798-956) at 49 Gloucester St. It's not quite as neat and tidy as the Windsor but most of the rooms have washbasins, unlike the Windsor. Bed and breakfast at the Melville costs $30/50 for singles/doubles in the more basic detached rooms out back. In the main building rooms are $40/60. The Melville also provides a 9 pm supper and may offer additional discounts for YHA or student card holders. The Melville may be opening a hostel in the building next door.

There are a couple of centrally located guest houses which offer rock bottom prices and some hostel-style bunkroom accommodation as well as regular rooms. See the Latimer Hostel and Hereford Private Hotel, both very popular with travellers and covered in the Hostels section.

Two km north-west of the Square the *Wolseley Lodge* (tel 556-202) at 107 Papanui Rd is a pleasantly old fashioned place in a pleasantly quiet setting with bed & breakfast at $27 single, $38 double. A few doors down the road at 121 the *Highway Lodge* (tel 555-418) has singles at $25 to $36, doubles at $36 to $42. It's also a pleasantly olde worlde place and you can get to both these places on a No 1 bus. In the same direction at 69 Bealey Avenue the *Bealey Lodge* (tel 66-770) offers bed & breakfast at $28/44.

The *Ambassadors Hotel* (tel 67-808) at 19 Manchester St is south of the centre and very close to the railway station and Newmans bus depot. Bed & breakfast is $36/55. The *New City Hotel* (tel 60-769) is in the same area at 527 Colombo St and offers rooms including breakfast at $35/55, more for rooms with attached bathrooms.

Further out is the *Aarangi Guest House* (tel 483-584) at 15 Riccarton Rd with rooms at $30/50 including breakfast. At the junction of Riccarton and Yaldhurst Rds, at 21 Main South Rd, the *Thistle Guest House* (tel 481-499) has bed & breakfast at $30 per person.

Hotels *Warners Hotel* (tel 65-159), is an old landmark right in the Square. Singles/doubles cost $40/60 with a washbasin but not an attached bathroom, with facilities a double is $80. Warners is noted for its 'hearty English-style breakfasts'.

Also on the Square, the old but very grand *United Services Hotel* (tel 791-060) is right beside the post office. You certainly couldn't get more central than this, even at Warners you have to cross the street to the Square. Rooms are $55/72 but they may have an off-season rate if you specifically ask at quiet times of year.

Top bracket Christchurch hotels include the *Avon Hotel* (tel 791-180) at 356 Oxford Terrace, the *Chateau Regency* (tel 488-999) on the corner of Deans Avenue and Kilmarnock St, *Noahs* (tel 794-700) on the corner of Worcester St and Oxford Terrace, and out at the airport the *Christchurch Airport Travelodge* (tel 583-139). At all of these hotels doubles are in the $120 and up range, a long way up at Noahs.

Motels Christchurch is equally as well equipped with motels as in the other categories. Most of them start from around $60 for a double. As in other towns there are bargains to be found at the campsites, which often have motels, tourist flats and cabins as well as sites for camping or campervans.

Some of the better priced motels include:

Adorian Motel (tel 67-626), 47 Worcester St, singles $46-50, doubles $60 to $65.
Avon City Motel (tel 526-079), 402 Main North Rd, doubles $52 to $55, one night surcharge.
Bucklands Motel (tel 889-442), 525 Pages Rd, near New Brighton, swimming pool, singles/doubles $38/44.
Canterbury Court Motel (tel 388-351), 140 Lincoln Rd, swimming pool, doubles $50.
Cashel Court Motel (tel 892-768), 457 Cashel St, swimming pool, doubles $48 to $52.
City Court Motels (tel 69-099), 850 Colombo St, centrally located at corner of Salisbury St, doubles $42.
Colombo Travel Lodge (tel 63-029), 965 Colombo St, one km north of the Square, singles/doubles $45/50.
Fairlane Court (tel 894-943), 69 Linwood Avenue, doubles $40, one night surcharge.
Hillvue Court Motel (tel 385-112), 37 Hillier Place, singles/doubles $42/55.
Holiday Lodge Motel (tel 66-584), 862 Colombo St, doubles $45.
Middle Park Kowhai Lodge (tel 487-320), 120 Main South Rd, Upper Riccarton, doubles $50.
Riccarton Motel (tel 487-126), 92 Main South Rd, Upper Riccarton, doubles $48, one night surcharge.
Salisbury Motel (tel 68-713), 206 Salisbury St, centrally located, singles/doubles $42/48.

Places to Eat

Opening hours in Christchurch have considerably improved in recent years. No longer are the weekends a fasting time and you can also get something late at night. There are a number of restaurants, luncheon places and takeaways around and near Cathedral Square and the two block stretch of Colombo St just north of the river has a number of interesting restaurants.

Fast Food & Takeaways There are various places around the Square, including *Warners*, a takeaway bar right behind Warners Hotel, in the north-east corner. It's open all night. *Leo Coffee Lounge* near the Square is open seven days a week until late.

Apart from the usual sandwich places there are some more exotic takeaways to be found around the Square. Try *Zorros* for takeaway tacos or other Mexican food. It's in the arcade off the north-east corner of the Square through to Gloucester St. It's open late seven nights a week. Or only a block from the Square at 176A Manchester St there's the *Mediterranean Take Away* with that eastern Med blend of Turkish/Greek/Lebanese food including doner kebabs. It's a good place for a lunch to take and eat in the Square.

The *Coffee Pot* at 16 New Regent St is another lunchtime possibility although it's moderately expensive with fancy sandwiches at $6 or $7. The *Victoria Coffee Gallery* on the corner of Oxford Terrace and Montreal St by the river is also good for lunch. There's an economically priced snack bar at the *YMCA*, across from the Arts Centre on Hereford St.

Vegetarian Food Vegetarians are well catered for in Christchurch with good vegetarian food in all price categories. *Gopals* at 143 Worcester St is another of the excellent Hare Krishna-run vegetarian restaurants. It's open for lunch weekdays and on Friday evenings.

Rather more expensive but exceptionally good vegetarian food can be found at the

Mainstreet Cafe on Colombo St by the corner with Salisbury St, in those restaurant blocks north of the river. Mainstreet is a pleasantly relaxed and very popular place with an open-air courtyard out back. Imaginative main courses are around $13 or you could have bread and salad for $5. The salads are good and the desserts, particularly their varied selection of cheesecakes, are mouthwatering. It's open for lunch Monday to Friday and for dinner from 5.30 to 11 pm every night of the week.

Dux de Lux is another well known Christchurch restaurant for gourmet taste treats. In fact it can be so popular that booking may be a wise idea. Dux de Lux is in the Art Centre, on Montreal St near Hereford St. Again there's a pleasantly green outdoor courtyard and it's open seven days for lunch and dinner. Starters are in the $5 to $7 range, main courses $14 to $16 and desserts $5 to $6 so it's not cheap. At lunch time there are lighter meals in the $6.50 to $7.50 range. Dux de Lux is licensed.

Pub Food On Colombo St right by the river the *Oxford Tavern* has a family restaurant dubbed the Major Bunbury. It's open every day of the week from 11 am to either 9 or 10 pm. Main courses, which span the pub-food universe from chicken schnitzel to T-bone steaks, are in the $6.50 to $9 range and there's also a children's menu at $3.50. It's conveniently located but unfortunately this is distinctly second-rate pub food.

Upstairs in the *United Services Hotel* on the Cathedral Square the Mr Pickwick Restaurant has most main courses in the $9 to $11 range. It's open from 5 to 10 pm every night and on Sunday's there's an all-you-can-eat smorgasbord at $17.50 (half price for children). Other places with pub food include the *Excelsior* on the corner of High and Manchester Sts with main courses again in the $9 to $11 range and again it's open for lunch and dinner seven days a week. It's a real pleasure,

Lunch — Seven Days 11.30 to 2.30
Evening — Seven Days 5.30 to 11.00
Colombo Salisbury Cnr
Fine Vegetarian Food

these days, to report how many places in Christchurch are in operation seven nights a week.

There are a couple of *Cobb & Co's* in Christchurch, one at the *Caledonian Hotel*, 101 Caledonian Rd, north of the Square, the other south of the Square at the *Bush Inn Courts*, 364 Riccarton Rd. Cobb & Co's are all open seven days a week until 10 pm at night and have a standard and highly consistent pub food menu.

Other pub food possibilities include the *Carlton Hotel* on the corner of Papanui Rd and Bealey Avenue and the *Clarendon Hotel* on the corner of Worcester and Oxford Sts.

Restaurants The *Gardens Restaurant* in Christchurch's wonderful Botanic Gardens is renowned for its excellent smorgasbord which costs $9 including coffee. It's served 12 noon to 2 pm daily and also from 5.30 to 7.30 pm during the summer. The restaurant is open from 10 am for snacks and other light meals.

The riverside setting of the *Town Hall Restaurant* makes it a popular place to eat. There's a daily lunchtime smorgasbord for $15, Sunday lunch or dinner for $16 and also a regular menu for dinner or later supper.

Right across from the Botanic Gardens at the Rolleston Avenue end of the Botanic Gardens is *Jambalay* a new, in '87, restaurant serving New Orleans cajun food. At lunch time main courses are in the $6 to $9 range.

Those restaurant blocks of Colombo St, just north of the river, offer several good dining possibilities. At the river end try *Spagalima's Italian Pizza Restaurant* at number 798. It's a very popular place with takeaways as well. Pizzas range from $3 to $5 for the little ones up to $11 for the fanciest large pizza. It's open Tuesday through Sunday until 9.30 pm through to 12 midnight, depending on the day.

Other possibilities in the same few blocks include the Oxford Tavern just south of the river (see Pub Food) and Mainstreet further north (see Vegetarian). Or try *Marco Polo's* at 812 with an interesting mix of Indonesian and Indian dishes. At 834 the *Off the Wall Cafe* is a trendy looking place with expensive starters at $7.50 to $9.50 and main courses at $8 to $11.

Fail's seafood restaurant, in the pedestrian mall at 82 Cashel St, near the river, is a Christchurch institution and must be one of the longest running restaurants in the city. Recently, however, it's gone through a major renovation and it's now considerably glossier and (of course) much more expensive. Still, if seafood is what you're after Fail's certainly has it. Main courses are in the $13 to $20 range and it's open 6 to 10 pm every night and for lunch as well on Wednesday through Friday.

At 76 Lichfield St, just south of the centre, *Tre Gatti's* has pretty reasonable standard Italian dishes and is open commendably late at night. There are plenty of Chinese restaurants around Christchurch although the Chung Wah, probably the best known of the bunch, closed in '87. The imposing *Chung Wah II* is at 61-63 Worcester St. *Kim's* at 805 Colombo St is a lower key Chinese place.

Expensive Restaurants The riverside *Thomas Edmonds Restaurant* is housed in what used to be a band rotunda right by the riverside on Cambridge Terrace. It's a great position and you can complement the romantic atmosphere by arriving for dinner by punt! The restaurant has a number of punts (and punters) to transport diners to the restaurant. Count on up towards $100 for two.

New Zealand's first Maori restaurant is *Te Waka O Maui* in Carlton Courts on the corner of Papanui Rd and Bealey Avenue. The menu features a variety of Maori fish dishes, including raw fish. Out of the city the *Sign of the Takahe* at Cashmere Hills has fine views of the city, a great setting, careful service and high prices to go with it.

Entertainment

Pub Music There are quite a few pubs with rock music at night, particularly on the weekends. Popular ones include the *Bush Inn Courts* at 364 Riccarton Rd which has a small cover charge. The *Carlton*, corner Bealey Avenue and Papanui Rd, also has weekend entertainment. Or there's the *Star & Garter* at 332 Oxford Terrace, the *Imperial* on the corner of St Asaphs and Barbados Sts, the *Ferrymead Tavern*, the *Bishopdale Tavern*, the *Lancaster Park Hotel* and plenty of others.

Other There's rock all week at *The Playroom* on the corner of Cuffs Rd and Pages Rd. The *Firehouse* at 293 Colombo St in the centre is a nightclub. Other Christchurch nightclubs are the *Palladium* on Gloucester St and *Romanov's* on Manchester St. *Warners*, in the Square, has folk music.

Getting There & Away

Air Christchurch is the only international arrival and departure point on the South Island. Qantas, Air New Zealand and Singapore Airlines all fly here. Safeair fly between Christchurch and the Chatham Islands.

Air New Zealand have their Christchurch office (tel 795-200) right in the Cathedral Square. There are connections between Christchurch and most destinations in the North and South Islands including Auckland (1½ hours, $218), Dunedin (45 minutes, $131), Hokitika (45 minutes, $95), Invercargill (1 hour, $159), Wellington (45 minutes, $125).

There are as many as eight to 10 flights daily to Auckland or Wellington. Hokitika is 40 km south of Greymouth on the west coast of the South Island and there are connecting buses.

Ansett New Zealand (tel 791-300) and Mt Cook Airlines (tel 790-690) both fly into and out of Christchurch as well. Ansett have flights to Auckland ($210), Mt Cook ($138), Queenstown ($219), Rotorua ($191), Te Anau ($222) and Wanaka ($221). Mt Cook fly between Christchurch and Auckland, Mt Cook, Queenstown, Rotorua and Te Anau at similar fares to Ansett.

Smaller airlines operating out of Christchurch include Associated Air (tel 488-929) who fly to Blenheim and on to Paraparaumu near Wellington on the North Island. Wairarapa Airlines (tel 488-929) fly between Christchurch and Nelson or Masterton on the North Island.

Road NZRRS buses (tel 794-040) depart from their station on Victoria St, north of the Square. Newmans buses (tel 795-641) leave from 347 Moorhouse Avenue near the railway station. H&H buses (tel 799-120) go from 40 Lichfield St, quite close to the Cathedral Square. Mt Cook (tel 790-690) operate from Shands Rd. Since Mt Cook has taken over H&H it's possible their offices may be merged.

Christchurch-Picton is about six hours and the fare is $42. NZRRS, Newmans and Mt Cook/H&H all do this route. All three also operate south to Dunedin – about 5½ hours at a fare of $29. NZRRS and Mt Cook/H&H continue south from Dunedin to Invercargill, another three hours with a fare from Christchurch of $51.

Newmans have a Christchurch-Nelson service with connections through to Westport and Greymouth on the west coast. NZRRS have more direct services to the west coast from both the north and south and also to Mt Cook and Queenstown. Their fares include Fox Glacier $65, Franz Josef $62, Greymouth $38, Queenstown $71, Westport $46. The trip to the glaciers via Arthurs Pass is a stunningly beautiful journey, not to be missed. Mt Cook also have bus services between Christchurch and Mt Cook or Queenstown.

Driving From Christchurch it's 340 km north to Picton, 362 km south to Dunedin. About four or five hours' drive in either direction. Westbound it's 248 km to Greymouth, 331 to Mt Cook or 486 to Queenstown.

Hitching Christchurch-Dunedin can be a long day's hitch. Generally it gets harder the further south you go, then easier as you approach Dunedin, but it's pretty good hitching on the whole. Catch a Templeton bus (No 22) to get out of the city. It's also possible to hitch between Christchurch and Picton in a day although there can be long waits in some places. If you're hitching northwards take a Christchurch bus to Belfast to get you on your way.

Hitching west get a No 8F (Riccarton) bus – then keep your fingers crossed; it can be a long hard haul west, say a two-day trip. Pick up the train somewhere along the way if you become despondent. The first part of this trip is easily hitched, but once you leave Highway 1 it gets steadily harder.

Rail The railway station is quite a long walk south of the Square and as in the

North Island services are being contracted and may contract further. Meanwhile there are daily services each way between Christchurch and Picton, a Monday to Saturday service each way between Christchurch and Invercargill via Dunedin and a daily service (twice on Fridays) between Christchurch and Greymouth. Crossing over to the west coast at Greymouth the section of railway through the Waimakariri Gorge (above Springfield) has interesting scenery, but the road follows a different and even more spectacular route.

Fares to or from Christchurch are Dunedin $28, Greymouth $29, Invercargill $48, Picton $38. Reservations can be made in Christchurch by phoning 794-040.

Getting Around
Airport Transport The bus service to the airport is operated by the city transport board from outside the Avon Picture Theatre on Worcester St, just off the Square. The 11-km trip costs $1.50 from 9 am to 4 pm on weekdays, $3 at any other time. Going out to the airport it's bus No 24, coming in it's bus No 28. Buses go about every half hour from around 6 am to nearly 6 pm then less frequently until 9.45 pm on weekdays but they're less frequent on Saturdays and even worse on Sundays.

A taxi to or from the airport will cost about $10 to $13 depending on the time you go. The airport is modern and has an information centre. There are luggage lockers available for up to 24 hours for 50c. Ask about storing luggage for longer periods. Don't forget your $2 departure tax on international flights.

Bus Most city buses are operated by the Christchurch Transport Board and run from the Square. Christchurch has a good, cheap and well-organised bus service, unlike most New Zealand cities. There's a bus info office (tel 794-600) in the Square, it's open daily but variable hours. Fares start at 50c and step up 50c at a time to $2.50. You can buy 10-ride (or more) concession

tickets. Note the Christchurch tradition of hanging baby strollers and pushchairs off the back of the buses.

Taxis There are plenty of taxis in Christchurch but, as with other places in New Zealand, they don't cruise. You have to find them on taxi ranks or phone for them.

Rent-a-Cars The major operators all have offices in Christchurch as do numerous smaller local companies. With the smaller operators unlimited km rates start from around $45 a day plus $7 to $10 insurance per day for rentals of five days or more.

Avis
    94 Gloucester St (tel 793-840)
Avon Rent-a-Car
    407 Ferry Rd (tel 891-350)
Budget Rent-a-Car
    corner Oxford Terrace & Lichfield St (tel 60-072)
Hertz
    44-46 Lichfield St (tel 60-549)
Letz Rent-a-Car
    40 Oxford Terrace (tel 796-880)
Percy Rent-a-Car
    154 Durham St (tel 793-466)
Renny Rent-a-Car
    113 Tuam St (tel 66-790)
Southern Cross Rental Group
    105-107 Victoria St (tel 794-547)
Thrifty Car Rental
    136-138 St Asaph St (tel 67-097)

Campervan companies operating from Christchurch include:

Horizon
    530-544 Memorial Avenue (tel 535-600)
Johnston's Motor Homes
    132 Kilmore St (tel 50-707)
Maui Campavans
    23 Sheffield Crescent (tel 584-159)
Mt Cook Line Motorhomes
    47 Riccarton Rd (tel 482-099)
Newmans
    530-544 Memorial Avenue (tel 535-800)

Bicycle Rental You can rent motorcycles or bicycles in Christchurch. Bicycles are ideal for Christchurch as it is nice and flat. There are cycling lanes on many roads and Hagley Park, which encompasses the Botanical Gardens, has many cycling paths. You can pedal away from Rent-a- Bike (tel 64-409) in the Avon Carpark Building, 139 Gloucester St (open 7 days a week, till late) for $1 an hour, $5 a day, or $25 a week. Ten-speed touring bikes are $3/10/60 and tandems $4/$10/$50. Theft insurance is an optional $1 a day and children's seats can be hired for $1 per hire.

Bicycles can also be hired from the Outdoor Recreation Information Centre (tel 799-395) in the Arts Centre Complex near the Botanical Gardens. The centre is open 10 am to 4 pm and hourly/daily rates are $3/10 for regular bikes, $5/15 for tandems. Garden City Cycle Tours operate two-hour guided bike tours from the Arts Centre bike hire place. They go from 2 to 4 pm and cost $12.50 per person (children $6.25).

Discount Cycles (tel 485-811) at 81A Riccarton Rd has 10-speed mountain bikes at $4 an hour, $16 a day or $77 a week. Insurance is $1.50 a day. Contact the Recreational Cycling Club if you'd like to join the club's Sunday tours.

Motorcycle Rental Renta Scoota (tel 64-409) operates from the same address as Rent-a-Bike (see above) and rents mopeds at $20 a day, $100 a week plus $5 per day insurance. Helmets are an extra $1 per hire and there's a $75 refundable security deposit. All you need is a car licence to rent a moped but if you're 21 (minimum age) to 25 there's an insurance excess of $200.

LYTTELTON

To the south-east are the hills, and behind them Lyttelton Harbour, Christchurch's port. Like Wellington Harbour it is the drowned crater of a long extinct volcano.

Harbour Trips

There are all sorts of boat trips on Lyttelton Harbour, starting from as low as $2 for the one-way trip to Diamond Harbour and Quail Island. The turn-of-

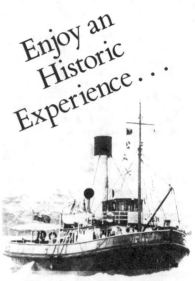

Enjoy an Historic Experience . . .

Steam Tug Lyttelton, built 1907

the-century steam tug *Lyttelton* does two-hour harbour cruises every Sunday at 2 pm, possibly more frequently in summer. They depart from No 2 Wharf and cost $8 (children $3). There are also cruises every day at 2 pm from Jetty B to Ripapa Island Historic Reserve.

Museum

The Lyttelton Museum has displays on colonial Lyttelton, a maritime gallery and an Antarctic gallery. It's in the centre of Lyttelton on Gladstone Quay and is open weekends from 2 to 4 pm.

Timeball Station

In Reserve Terrace, Lyttelton, is the Timeball Station, one of the few remaining in the world. Built in 1876, it once fulfilled an important maritime duty as all ships sailing from Lyttelton Harbour relied on it to set their chronometers. It's open daily from 10 am to dusk and entry is $1.50 (children 50c).

Getting There & Away

Bus No 28G or 28H from the Square takes

Top: Shantytown, Greymouth (TW)
Bottom: Punakaiki (Pancake Rocks), South Island (MC)

Top: Olveston, Dunedin (TW)
Bottom: Lake Te Anau (VB)

you to Lyttelton. From Christchurch there are three roads to Lyttelton. The quickest way to get there is through the road tunnel (12 km). Alternatively, you can go via Sumner and Evans Pass (19 km) or head straight down Colombo St from the Square, and continue up over Dyers Pass (22 km). The Dyers Pass route passes the *Sign of the Takahe*, an impressive stone building, built in the Gothic style, now housing an olde-English-style tea house, a popular stop for the bus tours – bus No 2 goes to the hills. There is also a road along the summit of the hills.

AKAROA

Akaroa on the Banks Peninsula, the site of the only French colony in New Zealand, is good value for day trips – there are boats for rent, horseback riding and 'the best fish & chips in NZ'. The Summit road back to the city is amazingly winding. Daily cruises are operated on the harbour

on the *Charmaine*. There's still some French flavour in the town, particularly in the French street names.

Places to Stay

Hostels The small *Kukupa Hostel* (tel Pigeon Bay 825) at Pigeon Bay has had rave reviews and is a good base for exploring Banks Peninsula. Set in magnificent bush land, it's the oldest youth hostel in New Zealand and costs $9 a night. Pigeon Bay is about 20 km from Akaroa and very remote, you can get there on the mail bus service but check with the YHA office in Christchurch about connection times before you set off.

Also in Akaroa is Jeff Hamilton and Trish Hatfield's *Farm Hostel* right on the bay on a 400 hectare sheep farm. Recognise it by the anti-nuclear sign on the roof! It's a friendly and relaxed place with a good library. Nightly costs are $6 to $10.

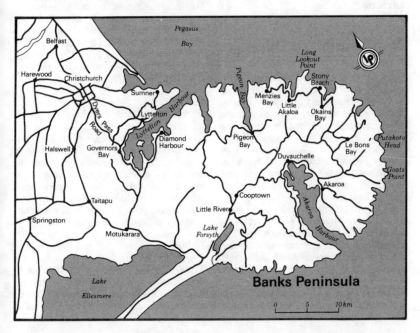

Banks Peninsula

Camping & Cabins The *Akaroa Holiday Park* (tel 471) has sites at $15 for two and also on-site caravans for $24. It's on Morgans Rd off Old Coach Rd.

Hotels & Motels The *Grand Hotel* (tel 11) on Rue Lavaud has rooms at $20 per person. The *Mt Vernon Lodge & Stables* (tel 180) at Rue Balgueri has rooms from $40. The rooms have a mezzanine floor over the main area and there are share-kitchen facilities. Cheaper motels include *La Rive Motel* (tel 281) at 1 Rue Lavaudhas with rooms from $48. Or there's the *Wai-iti Motel* (tel 292) at 64 Rue Jolie (pretty street) with rooms from the same price.

Getting There & Away

Akaroa is only 80 km from Christchurch and there are regular buses as well as daily NZRRS day excursions. The NZRRS depot in Akaroa is on Aubrey St close to the centre.

Christchurch to Dunedin

Highway 1, south of Christchurch, is generally very flat and boring for many km as you cross the Canterbury Plains. There are long straight stretches and one town looks much like another. Being in a truck, or even a bus, makes all the difference to your view, allowing you to see over the nearby hedges and obstructions. In clear weather there are some magnificent views of the Southern Alps and their foothills in the distance.

South of Christchurch you drive through man-made forests that were flattened by a storm some years ago. The remnants of these forests are still being picked through, though much has merely been bulldozed into long mounds and new trees planted.

There are many wide, glacial-fed rivers that have to be crossed – quite a sight in flood, though you don't see much water at other times. The Rakaia River Bridge is about two km long and this river is popular for jet boating – contact White Water Jets (tel Glenroy 898) in Rakaia or Windwhistle Jets (tel Glenroy 850) in Darfield. Salmon fishing is popular in South Canterbury.

METHVEN

Inland from Ashburton below Mt Hutt is Methven, a good centre for the Canterbury Plains or the mountains.

Places to Stay

There's hostel-style accommodation from $12 at *Mt Hutt Accommodation* (tel 28-508 or 585) at 32 Lampard St. The YHA has the *Methven Winter Hostel* (tel 28-590) at the Methven Trotting Club with beds at $11. It's open over the winter skiing season.

Aorangi Lodge (tel 28-482) is at 38 Spaxton St and has rooms from $32/55. *Mt Hutt Homestead* (tel 28-130) is part of a high country sheep and deer station just outside Methven. It's not cheap at $90/150 for dinner, bed and breakfast but the food is excellent and it's an interesting place to stay. There are other motels, hotels and campsites.

GERALDINE

Off the main Christchurch-Timaru road on the road inland to Mt Cook is Geraldine, a picturesque town with an interesting Vintage Car & Machinery Museum. The museum has a couple of dozen cars a single aircraft and a large amount of rather rusty agricultural machinery including more than 60 tractors. It's open 10.30 am to 12 noon and 1.30 to 4 pm daily and entry is $2.

TIMARU

Population 29,000

Timaru doesn't have much to offer, but it does have a reasonable choice of accommodation if you want to stopover. If you are around this area during the 'silly season' the Christmas Carnival at

Caroline Bay is superb. If you've always wondered whether spaghetti grows on trees you can visit the only spaghetti and macaroni factory in New Zealand at Timaru and find out. On weekdays you can make tours of the DB Brewery.

Places to Stay
Hostels The *Timaru Youth Hostel* (tel 84-685) at 14-16 Elizabeth St is quite a grand one which sleeps 20 and charges $11 a night.

Camping & Cabins The *Selwyn Holiday Park* (tel 47-690) is in Selwyn St, two km north of the centre. It has sites from $5 per person and also cabins (from $15) or cottages (from $21). There's also the *Timaru Showground Camp* (tel 44-463), north of the centre at Smithfield on the main highway, or the *Glenmark Motor Camp* (tel 43-682), on Beaconsfield Rd south of the centre.

Guest Houses & Hotels *Jan's Place* (tel 84-589) at 4A Rose St offers bed & breakfast at $22. Or there's the *Kiwi Guest House* (tel 43-127) at 67 King St which is similarly priced.

The *Dominion Hotel* (tel 86-189) on Stafford St North has rooms at $26, breakfast is also available. On the same street the *Grand Hotel* (tel 47-059) is somewhat grander, rooms are $30/40 or with attached bathroom they're $46/50. The *Grosvenor Hotel* (tel 83-129) on Cains Terrace is more expensive still with rooms from $65.

Motels Timaru has numerous motels, almost all of them from around $55 a night. The *Anchor Motel* (tel 45-067 at 42 Evans St is marginally cheaper.

Places to Eat
Pub food is available at the *Richard Pearse Restaurant* in *The Tavern* on Le Cren St. There's also a *Cobb & Co* at 4 Latter St. Near the railway station *The Kitchen* at 5 George St has health food

and good salads but it's open Monday to Friday until 5 pm only

Getting There & Away
Air Air New Zealand have direct flights from Timaru to Oamaru and Wellington with connections to other centres.

Road There is absolutely no shortage of bus services to and from Timaru. NZRRS have buses through Timaru on their Christchurch-Dunedin-Invercargill services. Mt Cook/H&H run through Timaru on their Picton-Christchurch-Dunedin-Invercargill service. Newmans also go through Timaru but only as far as Dunedin southbound. Mt Cook Line have a Timaru-Christchurch service and also connect Timaru with Queenstown and Mt Cook. Fares include Christchurch $14, Dunedin $18. It takes about three hours Christchurch-Timaru or a bit more Timaru-Dunedin.

For hitching north get a Grants Rd bus to Jellicoe St and save yourself a walk.

Rail Timaru is on the Christchurch-Dunedin-Invercargill railway route. Fares to or from Timaru include Christchurch $15, Dunedin $18 and Invercargill $37.

Getting Around
A taxi to Timaru airport costs about $16.

OAMARU
Population 15,000
Oamaru is a quiet, rural sort of town but the beaches are interesting and in the town you can visit the Forrester Art Gallery and the museum. The monument on the hill on the left just after you leave Oamaru is to the man who shipped the first refrigerated meat from New Zealand.

Places to Stay
Hostels The Oamaru *Red Kettle Youth Hostel* (tel 45-008) is a seasonal hostel open from late October through to late April. It's on the corner of Reed and Cross Sts and the nightly cost is $11.

Camping & Cabins The *AA (North Otago* Motor Camp (tel 47-666) has sites for $6.50 and cabins from $20 to $35.

Guest Houses The *Anne Mieke Travel Hotel* (tel 48-051) at 47 Tees St has bed & breakfast at $24 per person. At the *Nevada Guest House* (tel 48-668) at 24 Coquet St bed & breakfast is $26. Other places are the *Totara Lodge* (tel 48-332) at 299 Thames St at $26 including breakfast and the very cheap *White Stone Lodge* (tel 71-493) at 296 Thames Highway where singles are less than $20.

Motels The *Thames Court Motel* (tel 46-963) at 252 Thames St has rooms at $50, at the *Avenue Motel* (tel 70-091) at 473 Thames St rooms are $44 to $55.

Getting There & Away
Air Air New Zealand fly from Oamaru to Timaru with connections on from there to other centres.

Road The NZRRS, Mt Cook/H&H and Newmans services between Christchurch and Dunedin all run through Oamaru. Fares include Timaru $9, Christchurch $21 and Dunedin $11.

Rail The Christchurch-Dunedin-Invercargill rail services also goes through Oamaru. It's $21 to Christchurch, $12 to Dunedin.

Getting Around
A taxi to Oamaru airport costs about $20.

MOERAKI & SOUTH
At Moeraki, 30 km south of Oamaru, you will notice some extraordinary spherical boulders that look rather like giant marbles. There are others further south at Kaitiki and Shag Point. There's a seasonal *Youth Hostel* at Waikouati. It's open late October to late April and costs $9 a night. You'll need to take all your food with you as the nearest shop is at Palmerston, 10 km away. The motor camp at Moeraki, less than an hour's walk to the boulders, is run by very friendly and helpful people.

Once past Shag Point you'll see a high, pointed hill with a phallic-shaped symbol on top, a monument to Sir John MacKenzie, the MP who was responsible for splitting up large farms into smaller holdings, farms that are now being bought up again. The hill, near Palmerston, is called Puketapu and there's a track to the top signposted from the northern end of Palmerston. Every Labour Weekend there is a race up the hill (19 minutes is the record), known as 'Kelly's Canter' because, during the war, Kelly, the local policeman, had to climb it every day to keep an eye out for shipping.

As you approach Dunedin it gets hillier. You pass over the Kilmog, then the Northern Motorway hill, and you're in Dunedin.

West Coast & Glaciers

The two glaciers, the Fox and the Franz Josef, are the major west coast attractions but the whole stretch of the coast is worth exploring. The road hugs the coastline most of the way from Westport in the north to Hokitika, then runs inland until it finally joins the coast again for the last stretch, before turning east and heading over the Haast Pass. Not far inland from the coast, but a long way by road, is Mt Cook with the Tasman Glacier.

Weather

Westland could equally aptly be 'Wetland'. It rains a lot on the west coast, five metres (200 inches) or more a year. A poetically inspired visitor to Hokitika earlier this century summed up the Westland weather situation pretty well:

It rained and rained and rained
The average fall was well maintained
And when the tracks were simply bogs
It started raining cats and dogs
After a drought of half an hour
We had a most refreshing shower
And then the most curious thing of all
A gentle rain began to fall
Next day also was fairly dry
Save for a deluge from the sky
Which wetted the party to the skin
And after that the rain set in

Glaciers

Some glacial terminology for visitors to the Fox or Franz Josef Glaciers or the glaciers of the Mt Cook Region:

Accumulation Zone – where the snow collects
Ablation Zone – where the glacier melts
Bergschrund – large crevasse in the ice near the headwall or starting point of the glacier
Blue Ice – as the accumulation zone or névé snow is compressed by subsequent snowfalls it becomes firn and then blue ice
Crevasses – as the glacial ice moves down the mountain it bends and cracks open in crevasses as it crosses irregularities
Dead Ice – as a glacier retreats isolated chunks of ice may be left behind. Sometimes these can remain for many years
Firn – partly compressed snow on the way to becoming glacial ice
Glacial Flour – the river of melted ice that flows off glaciers is a milky colour from the suspension of finely ground rocks
Icefall – when a glacier descends so steeply that the upper ice breaks up in a jumble of iceblocks
Kettle Lake – lake formed by the melt of an area of isolated dead ice
Lateral Moraine – walls formed at the sides of the glacier

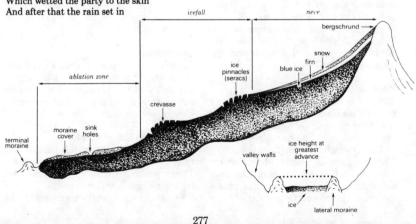

Névé – snowfield area where firn is formed

Seracs – ice pinnacles formed, like crevasses, by the glacier bending over irregularities

Terminal – the final ice face at the end of the glacier

Terminal Moraine – mass of boulders and rocks marking the end point of the glacier, its final push down the valley

Westland

You can approach the north end of the west coast from three directions – coming south from Nelson or the two crossings from Christchurch, the northern one passing close to Hanmer Springs while the southern one runs through Arthur's Pass.

NELSON TO THE COAST

The road across from Nelson in the north to the coast is quite an interesting and scenic one. The Buller area is still scarred from the 1929 Murchison and 1968 Inangahua earthquakes. From Inangahua junction you can head through the Lower Buller Gorge to the coast, or you can go on to Greymouth via Reefton on the inland route. The coastal route has more to offer but is a fair bit longer.

HANMER SPRINGS

About 10 km off SH 7, the route that crosses over to the west coast, Hanmer Springs is the main thermal resort on the South Island and is popular for a variety of outdoor activities including fishing and walking.

Places to Stay

Camping & Cabins There are cabins at a couple of the Hanmer Springs campsites but not at the *Hanmer Domain Camp*. There are also cabins at *Hanmer Alpine Village* (tel 7111) which is six km from the centre. They cost from $30 a night. *Mountainview Holiday Park* (tel 7113) is on the town outskirts and has camping sites plus a variety of cabins and tourist flats.

Guest Houses & Motels

The *Shining Cuckoo Guest House* (tel 7095) at 6 Cheltenham St has rooms at $25/45 and is conveniently close to the centre. There are numerous motels – the *Willowbank Motel* (tel 7211) on Argelins Rd has rooms from $40 to $50. *The Lodge* (tel 7021) is a fine old place right in the centre of town with rooms at $40/60.

Places to Eat

The *Alpine Restaurant*, around the corner from the post office, is good for basic takeaways.

Getting There & Away

NZRRS have services to Hanmer Springs or a connecting bus from the main road junction for their services which simply pass straight by. Buses run here from Christchurch and Greymouth. Newmans buses, on the other hand, just drop you at the junction and you have to make your own way into the town.

ARTHUR'S PASS

The small settlement of Arthur's Pass is four km from the pass of the same name, discovered by Arthur Dobson in 1864. The 924-metre pass was on the route used by the Maoris to reach the Westland.

The town is a fine base for the walks, climbs, views and winter-time skiing of Arthur's Pass National Park and you can day-trip there from Greymouth or Christchurch.

Information

There's a National Park Visitor Centre in the town. They have information on all the park walks and can also offer valuable advice on the park's often savagely changeable weather conditions.

Arthur's Pass National Park

There are day-walks in the park which offer 360° views of snow-capped peaks. Thirty peaks are over 1800 metres, the highest being Mt Rolleston at 2271 metres. The park has huts on the tramping tracks

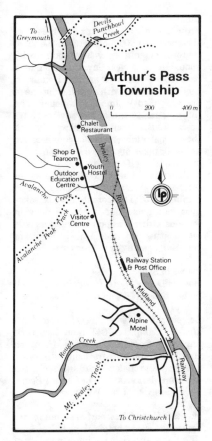

Arthur's Pass Township

The *Alpine Motel* (tel 583) on the main road through town has rooms at $55 and some simpler rooms from $38.

You can eat in the *Arthur's Pass Store & Tearoom* or in the *Chalet Restaurant* which has a cheaper coffee bar beyond its restaurant area.

Getting There & Away
You can get to Arthur's Pass by road or rail. The road goes over the top of the pass, rather more spectacular than the rail route which goes through a tunnel.

WESTPORT
Westport is the major town at the north end of Westland. Its prosperity is based on coal mining although the mining activity takes place some distance from the town.

Information
Palmerston St is the main street of Westport. There's an information centre in the Westport Motor Hotel on Palmerston St. It's open weekdays and although it may move at some time in the future it is likely to still be located on Palmerston St.

Coaltown
Coaltown on Queen St is a well laid out museum reconstructing aspects of coal-mining life. It's open 8.30 am to 4.30 pm every day, admission is $3 (children $1.50), which includes audio-visual presentations.

Seal Colony
At Tauranga Bay, 12 km from Westport, there's a seal colony. To get there follow the signposted road to Carters Beach. You can approach the seals very closely but take care not to get between them and the sea. The seal colony is on the Cape Foulwind Walkway which follows the coastline for four km from Cape Foulwind to Tauranga Bay. The walk takes one to 1½ hours and a brochure describing the walk is available from the information centre in Westport.

and also several areas suitable for camping although there are no special camping facilities. The day walks leaflet available from the information centre lists half day walks of one to four hours and day walks of five to eight hours. The two-hour (one-way) walk to Temple Basin provides superb views of the surrounding peaks.

Places to Stay & Eat
The *Arthur's Pass Youth Hostel* (tel 528) is close to the town centre and has bunkroom accommodation at $9 a night.

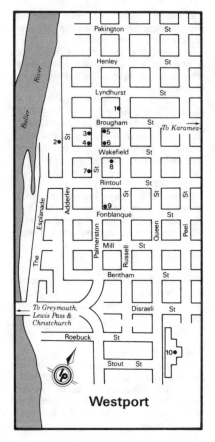

Westport

1	Youth Hostel
2	NZRRS Depot
3	Black & White Hotel
4	Bonanza Takeaways
5	Post Office
6	Cunningham's Coaches
7	Newmans Coachlines
8	Cristy's Restaurant
9	Information Centre, DB Westport Motor Hotel
10	Coaltown Museum

Other

From Denniston, 27 km north-east of Westport and 600 metres up in the hills, there are magnificent views if you're lucky enough to get a clear day. Coal from here used to be taken down the Denniston Incline, a railway with a gradient of one in one (yes!), to Waimangaroa below. The information centre has a brochure describing the Denniston Walkway through the old coal mining area. The complete five km walk takes about two hours downhill or three hours if you do it uphill.

Charming Creek Walk is another interesting Westport walk through a mining area. The complete walk takes over four hours but it can be done in sections. Other Westport activities include jet boating on the Buller River or tramping, caving or fishing trips.

Places to Stay

Hostels *Dale's Youth Hostel* at 56 Russell St has beds at $11 including breakfast.

Camping & Cabins The *Howard Park Holiday Camp* (tel 7043) is on Domett St only a km from the post office. Camping costs $10 for two, an extra dollar with power. There are also chalets at $18 and bunkroom accommodation at $8. The *Carters Beach Camp* is six km from Westport.

Hotels & Motels Westport has a number of centrally located hotels along Palmerston St plus a surprisingly large number of motels from around $50 a night. Try the *A1 Motel* (tel 808) at 63 Queen St with rooms at $45 to $55 for two.

Places to Eat

There are a number of takeaways and sandwich places along Palmerston St including the *Bonanza Takeaway* near the Wakefield St corner. There's pub food at several of the hotels including the *Black & White* on Palmerston St or the *Wagon Wheel Restaurant* in Larsens Tavern. Up market *Cristy's* on Wakefield St is Westport's flashy licensed restaurant.

Getting There & Away

Air Air New Zealand have direct flights between Westport and Hokitika ($84) or Christchurch ($110).

Road NZRRS services connect Westport with Christchurch (nine hours, $46), Greymouth (three to 3½ hours, $23) and on down the coast to the glaciers. Heading north to Karamea for the Heaphy Track, Cunningham have buses daily from Monday to Friday for $15.

Newmans have a Nelson-Westport-Greymouth service Monday to Saturday. From Nelson there are connections to Motueka and Takaka, to Picton or to Christchurch.

Getting Around

Air New Zealand have a bus service for their flights. The fare is $2 (children $1). You can rent bicycles from Beckers Cycles & Sports on Palmerston St.

NORTH OF WESTPORT

From Waimangaroa, Highway 67 continues north to Karamea near the end of the Heaphy Track and other tramps. There are lots of beautiful beaches around here but the only drawback is millions of sandflies. A long-running local joke is that 'sandflies work in pairs – one pulls back the sheets, while the other eats you alive'.

WESTPORT TO GREYMOUTH

The coast road has some most unusual bridges – not only are they one-lane, so traffic can only pass in one direction at a time, but they also share the bridge with the railway line. It's best to give way to trains!

Punakaiki

About 60 km south of Westport is Punakaiki, better known as the Pancake Rocks. These limestone rocks have formed into what look like stacks of pancakes just waiting for a hungry sea giant. If there's a good sea running here, the water surges into caverns below the rocks and squirts out in impressive geysers. There's a walk from the road, around the rocks and geyser, and back again. It's best to go at high tide when the blowholes really perform.

Just north of the rocks you can rent canoes on the Pororari River. The area inland in this vicinity has numerous bush tracks and is riddled with caves. You need to know what you're doing though – in some caves the water rises so fast after rain that you'd drown before you had a chance to get out. There has been pressure to declare this area a national park, but to no avail – the New Zealand Forest Service is determined to continue logging in the area.

Places to Stay & Eat There's a motor camp with cabins at Punakaiki so this could be an interesting place to pause for a day. *Cliff and Elaine Lawrence* (tel Barrytown 852) have a pleasant little bed & breakfast operation with a room at $15 per person and some motel units at $50 for two.

There's a cafe across from the rocks and also the very pleasant *Nikau Palms Cafe* which may be closed in the winter.

GREYMOUTH

Population 12,000

It's another 44 km to Greymouth, a town with a long gold mining history and still a bit of gold town flavour today. It's the largest town on the west coast despite its small population.

Information

There's an information office in the Regent Theatre at the bottom of Mackay St, the main street. It's open 8.30 am to 5 pm on weekdays.

Shantytown

Greymouth's major tourist attraction is just eight km south of the town and then three km inland from the main road. Shantytown is a fine reproduction of west coast life in the gold rush days. You'll find all the buildings a town of that era would have had and a few it certainly wouldn't! For many the prime attraction will be the

1897 steam locomotive which will take you out for a short trip into the bush (not running in winter). You can also have a go at gold panning there.

Shantytown is open 8.30 am to 5 pm daily and entry is $3 (children 50c). A train ride will cost you another $1. There's an NZRRS bus to Shantytown at 11 am, returning at 1.35 pm. It costs $5 return. At Paroa, the turn-off for Shantytown, there's a wildlife park with many species of local wildlife. Entry is $2.50 (children $1) and it's open 9 am to dusk.

If you continue 17 km inland from Shantytown through Marsden and Dunganville you come to the interesting Woods Creek Track, an easy one-km loop walk through an old gold mining area. There are a number of tunnels which you can enter if you have a torch (flashlight).

Other Attractions

You can take jet boat trips on the Grey River for $25 (children $20) for 1½ hour trips. Horse treks and fishing safaris are other Greymouth activities. The information centre has a leaflet produced by the Greymouth Lions Club with details of walks in and around the town. There are some fine walks around Blackball, an old mining town 25 km north-east of Greymouth. The Croesus Track is a day walk from Blackball north to Barrytown, on the coast south of Punakaiki.

Places to Stay

Hostels The *Greymouth Youth Hostel* (tel 4951) is on Cowper St a km or so from the centre and sleeps 48. Cost is $11 a night and bicycles are available for hire. If you take the evening train from Christchurch

Shantytown, Greymouth

you may arrive too late to be admitted as the hostel closes at 10.30 pm.

Right across the road from the information centre on the corner of Mackay St and Boundary Rd the *Golden Eagle Hotel* offers bunkroom accommodation at $10 per person.

North of Greymouth at Blackball on the road to Reefton the *Blackball Hilton* (tel Ngahere 705) offers dormitory accommodation at $9 and rooms at $14. Blackball is an interesting old coal-mining town and the 'hilton' is an equally interesting place to stay. There's a TV lounge and a sauna and spa pool.

Camping & Cabins *Greymouth Seaside Motor Camp* (tel 6618) is 2½ km south of the centre on Chesterfield St. Camping charges for two people are $11 or with power $12.50. Cabins cost $20, on-site vans $25, tourist cabins $27 and tourist flats $40. It's right beside Greymouth's grey and cold looking beach and right at the end of the airport runway.

The *South Beach Motel* also has a camp site, about five km south of Greymouth.

Guest Houses There are two guest houses close to the centre. *West Haven Tourist Lodge* (tel 5605) is at 62 Albert St beside the railway line. Nightly cost in this pretty basic sort of place is $15 per person or $20 with breakfast.

Golden Coast Guest House (tel 7839) is

at 10 Smith St overlooking the river and is a bit up-market from the West Haven with rooms at $30/50 for singles/doubles including breakfast.

Hotels That gold mining history shows in the number of hotels you'll find around central Greymouth. None of them are particularly special. You could try the *Duke of Edinburgh*, the *Cobden Hotel* or the *Australasian Hotel*. Rooms cost from around $30 for one, $35 for two.

Revington's (tel 7055) on Tainui St has a Cobb & Co Restaurant and rooms at $30/60 or with attached bathroom at $60/70. *Kings' Motor Hotel* (tel 5085) on Mawhera Quay is the town's top hotel with a wide variety of rooms from around $60 at a minimum to well over $100.

Motels There are plenty of motels in Greymouth but there's hardly anything under $50 a night. The *Ace Tourist Motel* (tel 6884) is on Omoto Rd, two km from

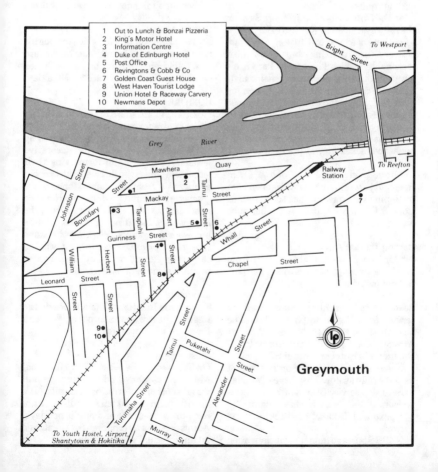

1   Out to Lunch & Bonzai Pizzeria
2   King's Motor Hotel
3   Information Centre
4   Duke of Edinburgh Hotel
5   Post Office
6   Revingtons & Cobb & Co
7   Golden Coast Guest House
8   West Haven Tourist Lodge
9   Union Hotel & Raceway Carvery
10 Newmans Depot

Greymouth

the centre. Rooms are $50 for two. Others are the *South Beach Motel* (tel 26-768) at 318 Main South Rd and the *Greymouth Motel* (tel 6090) at 195 High St.

Places to Eat

There's the usual selection of cafes and sandwich places around the centre. You could try the *Hideaway (Tea & Coffee House)* on Albert St or the *Out to Lunch* sandwich bar on Mackay St. The *Bonzai Pizzeria* at 29 Mackay St is a pleasant little place that's open reasonable hours and has quite good pizzas.

At the *Union Hotel* on Herbert St near the railway tracks the *Raceway Carvery* is something of a local institution. The front is very unpromising but it's quite reasonable inside. The accent here is on low prices and big quantities, cuisine high lights are a definite second. It's open for breakfast, lunch and dinner daily. Dinner is served from around 5 to 8 pm Monday to Thursday, to 9 pm Friday to Sunday. The menu has all the pub regulars from T-bones to chicken kiev at prices around $7 to $10.

Alternatively there's a *Cobb & Co* in Revington's on Tainui St which is open 7 am to 10 pm every day and has the standard Cobb & Co menu. Quite a few other pubs offer food.

Getting There & Away

Air Air New Zealand flights operate from Hokitika although there is a small airport in Greymouth.

Road Delta Coachlines have a daily service from Picton to Greymouth. The fare all the way to Picton is $50, to St Arnaud it's $33. Tickets are sold at Revington's Hotel on Tainui St.

Newmans (tel 6118) are on Herbert St near the railway line. They have a Monday to Saturday service Greymouth-Westport-Nelson. From Nelson they operate to Motueka and Takaka, Christchurch and Picton.

NZRRS buses go from the railway station and they have services to and from Christchurch, north to Westport and south down the coast to the glaciers. Travel times and fares are Christchurch (seven hours, $38), Westport (three to 3½ hours, $23), Franz Josef Glacier (3½ hours, $29) and Fox Glacier (four hours, $32).

Rail The Trans-Alpine Express operates between Christchurch and Greymouth daily and twice on Fridays. The trip takes about five hours and costs $29. Between Arthur's Pass and Greymouth the road and railway line take quite different routes.

Getting Around

Air New Zealand provide a bus service for their flights to and from Hokitika, the fare is $4 (children $1). Kitchingham's Cycles on Mackay St rents bicycles for $10 a day.

HOKITIKA

Hokitika, 40 km south of Greymouth, is a major centre for greenstone. Historically, greenstone or jade was much treasured by the Maoris who used it for decorative jewellery – *tikis* – and for carving their lethal weapons – the flat war clubs known as *meres* – from the hard stone. Since greenstone is found predominantly on the west coast, expeditions undertaken by the Maoris to collect it not only took months but were dangerous. Working the stone with their primitive equipment was no easy task either, but they managed to produce some exquisite items.

Information

The Public Relations Office is beside the Regent Theatre on the corner of Weld and Revell Sts. It's open on weekdays.

Museum

On Tancred St the West Coast Historical Museum has many gold-mining relics and various other interesting exhibits. It's open 9.30 am to 4.30 pm weekdays, 10 am to 4 pm on weekends and public holidays. Admission is $2.50 (children 50c) including an audio-visual presentation.

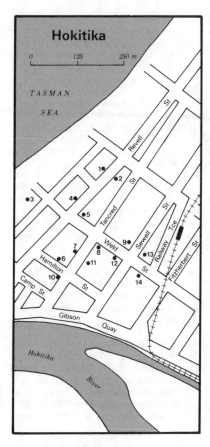

Hokitika

0   125   250 m

TASMAN
SEA

Hokitika

River

1   Club Hotel
2   Free Form Glass Blowing
3   Tasman View Restaurant
4   Southland Hotel
5   Westland Hotel
6   Central Guest House
7   Hokitika Craft Gallery
8   PRO
9   Railway Hotel
10 West Coast Historical Museum
11 Westland Greenstone
12 Fowlers' Tearoom
13 Post Office
14 NZRRS Depot

Crafts

You can buy jewellery, tikis of course, and other greenstone ornaments from Westland Greenstone on Tancred St. It's open every day 8 am to 5 pm. Whether you're buying or not you can visit the workshop and see it being cut and carved. Even with modern tools and electric power, working greenstone is not simple and good greenstone pieces will not be cheap.

There are several other craft outlets in Hokitika including the Hokitika Craft Gallery across the road from Westland Greenstone and open 8.30 am to 5 pm daily. A block over on Revell St is the Coastline Gallery and Genesis Creations, further up the same street you can see, on weekdays, glass blowing at Free Form Glass Blowing

Other Attractions

There's a glow-worm dell right beside the road on the northern edge of the town. Hokitika has a number of historically interesting old buildings and the information centre or the museum has a leaflet describing a historic walk. Back in 1866 Revell St had no less than 84 hotels! Only three are left.

Places to Stay

The *Hokitika Holiday Park* (tel 172) is on the corner of SH 6 and Livingstone St and has camping facilities and cabins. There are a number of motels, all from around $50 a night. There are also several hotels around the centre of town. The big *Westland Hotel* (tel 411), on the corner of Weld and Revell Sts, has rooms with attached bathroom at $40/52. The *Club Hotel* (tel 170) and the *Southland Hotel* (tel 344), both on Revell St, are cheaper.

Right in the centre the pleasant *Central Guest House* (tel 1232) at 20 Hamilton St is a cosy place with rooms at $21/35 for singles/doubles. Meals are extra but $3 gets you a big continental breakfast complete with muesli and juice or for $6 you can have a full cooked breakfast.

Places to Eat

For snacks and sandwiches you can try the *Preston Bakery & Tearoom* on Revell St or *Fowlers Tearoom & Restaurant* on Weld St has good pies and light meals. Next to the NZRRS depot, across from the post office, the *Seafood Shop* does fish & chips.

In the pub food category the *Westland Hotel* has a carvery for lunch and dinner or across from the post office on Sawell St *Chez Pierre* is in the Railway Hotel and has main courses for $12 to $16. Overlooking Hokitika's windswept and grey beach is the *Tasman View* restaurant.

Getting There & Away

Air Air New Zealand connect Hokitika with Christchurch ($88) and Westport ($84).

Road The NZRRS services down the coast run through Hokitika and you can make round-trip excursions to various places from Hokitika. It's $10 return to Ross, $33 to the Franz Josef Glacier, $11 to Shantytown near Greymouth or $38 to Arthur's Pass.

Getting Around

Air New Zealand operate a bus service to Hokitika airport and from the airport to Greymouth. The fare between Hokitika and the airport is $2 (children $1).

SOUTH FROM HOKITIKA

It's about 140 km south from Hokitika to the Franz Josef Glacier but you can make a few stops on the way.

Ross

Ross, 30 km south of Hokitika, has a small, but unusual, museum of stuffed animals and goldfield equipment on the main street. It may be closed in the winter. Also centrally located is a display of old gold mining equipment and buildings and you can make the Jones Flat Walk, also known as the Ross Goldfield Walkway, a two km walk around the old goldrush area. The walk takes one to 1½ hours.

Places to Stay & Eat Ross has a campsite, a motel and a couple of hotels. The *Empire Hotel* has bar meals at lunch and dinner time. Or there's the *Nicada Tearooms & Restaurant* on the main street.

Okarito

From Ross it's another 109 km to Franz Josef, but there are plenty of bush tracks and lakes along the way if you want to break the journey and can stand the sandflies.

When you reach The Forks, you're almost there, but if you turn off here you will find peaceful Okarito, 10 km away on the coast. This is the breeding ground for the white heron (kotuku) but you need permission to go and see them. It's a good place for watching all kinds of birds in their natural habitat including kiwis. There are lots of walks along the coast from here – get hold of leaflets from the New Zealand Forest Service in Hokitika or Harihari. Soon after The Forks you reach Franz Josef, Westland National Park and the magnificent peaks of the Southern Alps.

Places to Stay The small *Okarito Youth Hostel* (tel Whataroa 734) is 25 km north of the Franz Josef Glacier. It's a shelter hostel – no electricity, spartan facilities, just $3.50 a night and room only for 10. It was originally the old school, built in the 1870s when Okarito was a a thriving gold town.

The Glaciers

The two glaciers of the Westland National Park – the Fox and the Franz Josef, 25 km to the north – are amongst the most interesting sights in New Zealand. Nowhere else in the world, at this latitude, do glaciers approach so close to the sea. Unlike the Tasman Glacier, on the other side of the dividing range in Mt Cook National Park, these two are just what glaciers should be – mighty rivers of ice, tumbling down a valley towards the sea.

From many viewpoints you can admire them from lookouts fringed with sub-tropical vegetation. There are visitors' centres at both townships with maps, leaflets, evening slide shows and much useful information.

The reason for the glaciers' unusual development is three-fold. The wet west coast weather means there's a lot of snow on the mountain slopes. Secondly the zone where the ice accumulates on the glaciers is very large, so there's a lot of ice to push down the valley. Finally, they're very steep glaciers – the ice can get a long way before it finally melts. The rate of descent is staggering – a plane that crashed on the Franz Josef in 1943, 3½ km from the terminal face, made it down to the bottom 6½ years later – a speed of 1½ metres a day. At times the glacier can move at up to five metres a day, over 10 times as fast as glaciers in the Swiss Alps. More usually it moves a metre a day.

Advance & Retreat

Glaciers always advance, they never really retreat. The word 'retreat', with its image of the glacier pulling back up the valley, is rather a misnomer. The ice is always advancing, it's just that sometimes it melts even faster than it advances. And in that case the terminal or end face of the glacier moves back up the mountain.

Glacial ice, pushed by gravity, always advances downhill, but at the same time it melts. When advance exceeds melt the whole length of the glacier increases, when melt exceeds advance the length decreases. The great mass of ice higher up the mountain pushes the ice down the Fox and Franz Josef valleys at prodigious speeds but like most glaciers in the world this past century has been a story of steady retreat and only the odd short advance.

The last great ice age of 15,000 to 20,000 years ago saw the glaciers reach right down to the sea. Then warmer weather came and they may have retreated even further back than their current position. In the 14th century a new 'mini ice age' started and for centuries the glaciers advanced, reaching their greatest extent around 1750. At both the Fox and Franz Josef the terminal moraines from that last major advance can be clearly seen. In the nearly 250 years since then the glaciers have steadily retreated and the terminal face is now several km back from it's first recorded position in the late 19th century or even from its position in the 1930s.

From 1965 to 1968 the Fox and Franz Josef Glaciers made brief advances of about 180 metres but in 1985 they once again started to advance and moved forward steadily through '86 and then fairly dramatically in the latter part of '86 and early '87. Nobody is quite sure why this advance is taking place. It could be cooler or more overcast summers or it could be the result of heavy snowfalls 10 or 15 years ago which are now working their way down to the bottom of the glacier. It's a pity this interesting natural phenomenon is not being more carefully chronicled. An advance of up to 20 metres a month would make a fascinating photographic subject simply by taking the same photo daily or weekly from the same spot.

FRANZ JOSEF GLACIER

The Franz Josef was first explored in 1865 by Austrian Julius Haast, who named it after the Austrian emperor. Apart from short advances from 1907-09, 1921-34, 1946-59 and 1965-67 the glacier has generally been in retreat since that time although in 1985 it started advancing again and in '87 it was still moving down. It had progressed about 1000 metres although it is still several km back from the terminal point Haast first recorded.

Information

The Westland National Park Information Centre is open 8 am to 5 pm daily. They have educational and interesting evening slide shows during the summer and during holiday periods. The centre also has leaflets on the short walks around the glacier. In the summer, a free programme of guided walks and evening lectures operates from park HQ.

Walks

There are many walks to do around the glacier. Ask at the visitors' centre for their excellent walk leaflets. There are several good glacier viewpoints close to the road up to the glacier car park – including one from where the first photo of the glacier was taken, with a reproduction of that

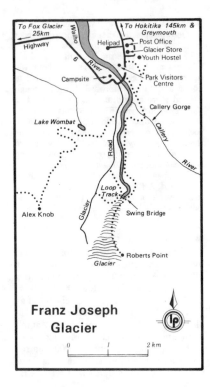

To Fox Glacier 25km
Highway
Waiho River
To Hokitika 145km & Greymouth
Helipad
Post Office
Glacier Store
Youth Hostel
Park Visitors Centre
Campsite
Callery Gorge
Lake Wombat
Callery River
Road
Loop Track
Alex Knob
Glacier
Swing Bridge
Roberts Point
Glacier

Franz Joseph Glacier

0   1   2 km

Terrace Track, which starts on the old Callery Track, scene of much gold mining activity in earlier days, and leads up onto a terrace at the back of the village, giving pleasant views down the Waiho River.

Flights
Mt Cook Airlines (tel 714) have skiplane flights over both glaciers. You can fly over both glaciers for $70 (children $53), land on one of them for $85 ($64), visit the Tasman Glacier on the other side as well for $191 ($143) including a landing or make that same grand circle route but without the landing for $143 ($107). The Helicopter Line (tel 767) flies from Franz Josef and has glacier flights from $45 up to $66 for a snow landing, $110 for both glaciers and a landing on one or $145 for the full circuit across the divide and a landing. Flights up and over the glaciers are expensive but they're a superb experience, it's money well spent. You can also make helihikes with a flight up to the glacier and then a guided walk across the ice.

Keas
There's plenty of opportunity to observe these large, cheeky parrots at the Fox and Franz Josef Glaciers. At the car park at the terminal of the Fox Glacier they hang around waiting for tourist handouts. Signs warn you of their destructive tendencies and they make concerted assaults on campervan roof hatches as soon as the passengers have wandered off. Or they ride nonchalantly on the spinning roof ventilators on tourist buses.

Down at the Franz Josef motor camp one evening we watched two keas methodically moving through the park, knocking each bin over in turn and plundering the contents.

Places to Stay
Hostels The *Franz Josef Youth Hostel* (tel 754) is at 2-4 Cron St, just back from the main road. It's a pleasant and fairly new hostel and costs $11 a night. It can be a bit chilly in winter. The motor camp has some bunkroom accommodation. Okarito (see above) with it's small shelter hostel, is only 25 km north but some walk from the main road.

historic photo there, so you can check how things have changed. You can walk to the glacier from the car park, or you may find it worthwhile to fork out $20 (children $12) for a guided walk on the glacier ice with an experienced guide. In season the walks depart twice daily from the THC hotel and equipment, including boots, is included.

Other walks require a little, worthwhile footslogging. The loop track is a short 15-minute stroll by the terminal moraine from the 1750 advance and Peter's Pool – a small 'kettle lake' formed by the melting of ice buried and left by a retreating glacier. It's a longer walk (3½ hours) to Robert's Point, overlooking and quite close to the terminal face. There is a pleasant one-hour round trip around the

Top: Glacier landing, Fox Glacier (TW)
Bottom: Fox Glacier Walk (TW)

Top: Lake Tekapo (TW)
Left: Mt Cook (TW)
Right: Copeland River (VB)

CARE FOR KEAS

Issued by the New Zealand Wildlife Service, Dept. of Internal Affairs

Camping & Cabins The *Franz Josef Motor Camp* (tel 766) is a km or so south of the township, right beside the river. Tent sites are $5 per person, sites with power are $7 for one or $12 for two. There are cabins at $10/16 or cottages from $25 plus motel accommodation at $50. The camp was supposed to have had a rather overdue renovation by late '87. The smaller *Forks Motor Camp* is 16 km north of Franz Josef.

Guest House Next to the hostel the *Callery Lodge* (tel 738) has rooms at $25/35 for singles/doubles without private facilities or $45/50 with bathroom.

Hotels & Motels There are a half dozen motels in Franz Josef, most of them with rooms from around $50 a night. The *Westland Motor Inn* is rather more expensive as is the *THC Franz Josef* (tel 719) which is about a km north of the township and has rooms at around $100.

Places to Eat

The shops at Franz Josef have a good selection of food supplies. You can eat at the *Glacier Store & Tearoom* or at *DA's Restaurant & Tearoom*. Curiously at DA's the cafe and takeaway section offers much the same menu as the proper restaurant side but at higher prices! In the restaurant there's a standard pub-style menu from chicken kiev to ham steak at around $10.50 to $12.50 including serve-yourself salads. Main courses in the coffee shop at the *THC Franz Josef* are in the $12 to $20 range.

Entertainment

There's a bar at the *Franz Josef Hotel* but it's some distance from the centre.

Getting There & Away

The NZRRS bus services northbound and southbound overlap between the two glaciers. See the Fox Glacier section below for rough travel times and frequency details. Fares from Franz Josef include Christchurch $62, Greymouth $30, Hokitika $29, Queenstown $71 and Wanaka $53. The connections are such that Nelson to Queenstown (or vice versa) by bus along the west coast takes a minimum of three days. In the peak summer season buses along the coast can be heavily booked, plan well ahead or be prepared to wait until there's space.

Hitching along the west coast can be very bleak. If you're lucky you might do Greymouth to Queenstown in three days – if you're not you could well stand on the same spot for three days.

FOX GLACIER

If time is short seeing one glacier may be enough but if you have the time it's nice to see both. Basically the same activities are offered at both glaciers – walks, glacier walks, flights and so on. Like the Franz Josef the Fox Glacier has, despite the consistent retreat throughout this century, been on the advance since 1985. In 1987 it had moved forward something like 1000 metres.

Information

The Visitors Centre is open 8 am to 5 pm daily. In the summer and at holiday periods there are evening slide shows and sometimes there'll be a quick walk down to the glow-worm grotto organised

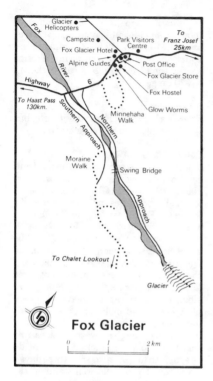

Glacier Helicopters
Campsite ●
Fox Glacier Hotel ●
Park Visitors Centre ●
To Franz Josef 25km
Alpine Guides ●
Post Office
Fox Glacier Store
Fox Hostel
Glow Worms
Highway
Fox River
6
To Haast Pass 130km.
Southern Approach
Northern Approach
Minnehaha Walk
Moraine Walk
Swing Bridge
Approach
To Chalet Lookout
Glacier

Fox Glacier

0   1   2 km

lake and at the far end you'll get a spectacular view of the mountains and their reflection in the lake. An almost equally famous viewpoint can be found by making the short climb up to Cone Rock, overlooking the glacier from a green and leafy lookout point, or the easier walk to Chalet lookout. Mt Fox is another excellent viewpoint – a three-hour walk one way.

There are many other interesting walks around the glacier including the short moraine walk over the advance of 200 years ago or forest walks on the Ngai Tahu Track, the short Minnehaha Walk or the River Walk. A particularly interesting walk is the 1½ or two-hour coastal walk to the seal colony at Gillespies Beach. Up to 1500 seals can be seen here and the walk also passes an old miners' cemetery and the remains of gold dredges from the gold mining days.

As at the Franz Josef you can make guided walks up on to the glacier ice with Alpine Guides. They leave at 9.30 am and 2 pm daily and boots and other equipment are included in the $20 (children $10) cost. Of course you can just follow the marked track to the glacier from the car park although they officially disapprove of unguided walkers going up on the ice.

Alpine Guides also have half day and full day helihikes (from $85) and an overnight trip to Chancellor Hut. The overnight trip includes hut fees, food and the flight up for $225 each for three people, $270 each for two. You walk back. If you want to cross the Copland Pass to Mt Cook, Alpine Guides will organise that for you at a cost of $500 for one person, $270 each for two, $200 each for three.

afterwards. The centre has leaflets on a number of interesting short walks around the glacier.

Walks

The shortest and most popular walk at the Fox Glacier is the couple of minutes stroll from the centre to the glow-worm grotto. It's close to the roadside just across from the garage. See the Waitomo section in the North Island for more information on glow-worms.

Head towards the coast from the township to a viewpoint with superb views of the glacier and the whole mountain range. Before this viewpoint is the turn-off to Lake Matheson and one of the most famous views in New Zealand. It's an hour's walk around the flat calm of the

Flights

Mt Cook Airlines (tel 812) have the same flights from Fox Glacier as they do from Franz Josef – see the Franz Josef section for details. Glacier Helicopters (tel 803) have short flights up to the glacier for $45 (children $40) or with a landing near the glacier for $70 (children $60). A flight over both glaciers including a landing is $100 (children $90). As at the Franz Josef Glacier these helicopter trips up to the glacier are expensive but a superb experience with quite amazing views.

Places to Stay

Hostels At the Fox Glacier the *Private Hostel* (tel 838) has bunk accommodation for $12. Some people report it's not the friendliest of hostels. The motor camp has bunkroom accommodation for $8 in the peak season only.

Camping & Cabins The *Fox Glacier Motor Park* (tel 821) is down the Lake Matheson road from the centre. Tent sites are $6 for one, $12 for two. Sites with power are $10 for one, $13 for two. Or there are very basic standard cabins at $12/$20, tourist cabins at $28/35 and motel rooms at the associated Alpine View Motel.

Hotels & Motels At the *Alpine View Motel* (tel 821) in the motor camp rooms are $44/50. The small *Halseys Motel* (tel 833) is right in the township and a little cheaper. There are a couple of other more expensive motels and the elderly *Fox Glacier Hotel* (tel 839) which has rooms with facilities for $70 plus a smaller number of cheaper rooms without attached bathrooms.

Places to Eat

The shop has a reasonable selection of essentials although not as wide a choice as you'll find at the Franz Josef Glacier. You can eat at the *Fox Glacier Restaurant & Tearoom* or there are pretty good sandwiches and light meals at the *Hobnail Coffee Shop* in the Alpine Guides building. At the *Fox Glacier Hotel* there's a bar and dinner is available for $20, breakfast for $9.

Entertainment

Unlike at the Franz Josef Glacier the *Fox Hotel* is wonderfully central and you can sit with a jug of beer and talk about where you've been during the day.

Getting There & Away

The NZRRS bus services overlap – southbound services from Christchurch and Westport start and finish at the Fox, northbound ones from Queenstown continue to the Franz Josef. There are one or two services daily to and from Westport (nine hours) or Greymouth (four hours, $32), a Monday to Saturday service to and from Christchurch (10 hours, $65) and also to and from Queenstown (9½ hours, $67). Other fares are Hokitika $28 and Wanaka $50.

See the Franz Josef section for the sad news on hitch-hiking and a warning about the heavily booked bus services.

Getting Around

Bicycles can be hired from Alpine Guides for $12 a half day or $20 a full day. They organise a back-country cycle tour which costs $60.

HAAST PASS

South of the glaciers the road eventually departs from the coast and climbs over the Haast Pass and on down to Queenstown. It's a longish, all day drive, but the Haast Pass isn't as amazing as New Zealanders like to think it is. It was only opened in 1965, prior to that there was no southern link to the west coast.

Aspiring Air make flights from Haast to Mt Aspiring, Mt Cook and Milford Sound.

Mt Cook

The Mt Cook National Park is almost 700 square km in size and one of the most spectacular parks in a country famed for them. Encompassed by the main divide, the Two Thumb, Liebig and Ben Ohau Ranges, more than one third of the park is in permanent snow and glacial ice.

Of the 27 New Zealand mountains over 3050 metres, 22 are in this park including the mighty Mt Cook – at 3764 metres the highest peak in New Zealand and Australasia. Known to the Maoris as Aorangi – cloud piercer – the tent-shaped Mt Cook was named by Captain Stokes of the survey ship *HMS Acheron* after James Cook. It was first climbed on Christmas Day 1894 and many famous climbers (including Sir Edmund Hillary) learnt how on this formidable peak. It towers over the park and provides a fine view from the famed Hermitage Hotel.

Information

The Park Visitors' Centre, open daily from 8 am to 5 pm, will advise you on what guided tours are available and on tramping routes. For information before you arrive write to: The Chief Ranger, PO Box 5, Mt Cook. There's a post office at Mt Cook and travellers' cheques can be cashed at the Hermitage.

Alpine Guides Mountain Shop sells skiing and mountaineering equipment or you can rent a variety of equipment from here – boots, parkas, ice axes, crampons, packs, rain pants, day packs and gaiters at around $20 per item. It's usually open from 8.30 am to 5.30 pm.

Alpine Guides have ski-touring and mountaineering courses but the costs are almost as steep as Mt Cook itself. A week-long Mountain Experience course is $1200, a 12-day Technical Mountaineering Course $1950, other courses and expeditions range around $2000. Want a private guide for the day? Well by yourself that will be $220, between four of you it comes down to $85 each. Heliskiing on the glacier? $300 to $400 please.

The Hermitage

Skiing on the Tasman Glacier (see Skiing) and the Copland Pass Walk (see Tramping) over the main divide to Westland National Park are two of the energetic attractions of the park but one of the park's chief attractions is rather more sedentary. The *Hermitage* is the most famous hotel in New Zealand – principally for its location and the fantastic views out

to Mt Cook. Originally constructed in 1884, when travel up here from Christchurch took several days, the first hotel was destroyed in a flash flood in 1913. You can see the foundations about a km from the current Hermitage. Rebuilt, it survived until 1957 when it was totally burnt out and the present Hermitage was built on the same site.

Tasman Glacier

Higher up, the Tasman is a spectacular sweep of ice just like a glacier should be, but further down it's ugly. Glaciers in New Zealand (and elsewhere in the world) have generally been retreating all this century. Normally as a glacier retreats it melts back up the mountain but the Tasman is unusual because its last few km are almost horizontal. In the process of melting over the last 75-or-so years it has contracted vertically rather than horizontally: the stones, rocks and boulders it carried down the mountain are left on top as the ice around them melts. So the Tasman in its 'ablation zone' (the region it melts in) is covered in a more-or-less solid mass of debris – which slows down its melting rate and makes it look pretty unpleasant.

Despite this considerable melt the ice by the site of the old Ball Hut is still estimated to be over 600 metres thick. In its last major advance, 17,000 years ago, the glacier crept right down to Pukaki, carving out Lake Pukaki in the process.

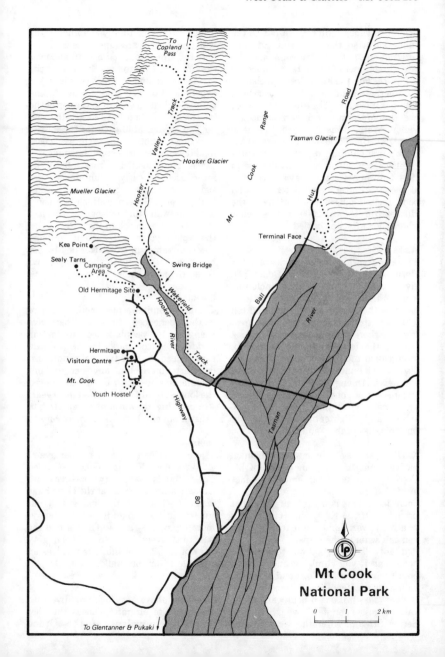

Mt Cook
National Park

0   1   2 km

A later advance didn't reach out to the valley sides so the Ball Hut Rd runs between the outer valley walls and the lateral moraines of this later advance.

Like the Fox and Franz Josef Glaciers on the other side of the divide the glaciers from Mt Cook move fast. The Alpine Memorial, near the old Hermitage Site on the Hooker Valley Walk, illustrates the glaciers' speed. The memorial commemorates Mt Cook's first climbing disaster when three climbers were killed by an avalanche in 1914. Only one of the bodies was recovered at the time but 12 years later a second body melted out of the bottom of the Hochstetter Icefall, 2000 metres below where the party was buried.

Walks

There are various easy walks from the Hermitage area. The Visitors Centre can give you all the info on them including leaflets that list the main attractions, describe the degree of difficulty and tell you about the flora and fauna in the area. If you're there in the summer keep a look out for the large mountain buttercup, often called the Mt Cook lily. There are also lots of mountain daisies, gentians and edelweiss. Among the animals you may see are the thar, one of the goat family and an excellent climber, the chamois, smaller and of lighter build than the thar but an agile climber, and red deer.

Kea Point An easy 1½ hour walk with much native plant life and fine views of Mt Cook, the Hooker Valley and the ice face at Mt Sefton.

Sealy Tarns This is a 2½ hour walk that branches off the Kea Point track. If the weather is warm and you're feeling brave you can swim in the tarns.

Red Tarns This is a good way to spend 1½ hours and if you climb for another half hour the views of Mt Cook and along the valley are spectacular.

Hooker Valley It is a two-hour walk up the valley across a couple of swing bridges to Sefton Stream. After the second swing bridge Mt Cook totally dominates the valley and there are superb views. From here the alpine route climbs up and over the Copland Pass to the other side of the divide but crossing this high pass is for the experienced or well-guided only. Alpine Guides will guide you up to the top of the pass for $300 if you're by yourself, $190 each for two of you, $140 each for three. The walk down the other side to the west coast road doesn't require expert assistance.

Others The Wakefield Track follows the route used by early mountaineers and sightseers then returns by the Hooker Valley track. Governors Bush is a short one-hour walk through one of the last stands of silver beech in the park.

Overnight If you're well enough equipped you can tramp up to Hooker or Mueller hut, the closest hut to the village, and spend the night there.

Climbing

There is unlimited scope for climbing here for the experienced, but beware, there have been over 100 people killed in climbing accidents in the park. Unless you are experienced in these types of conditions, don't attempt to climb anywhere without a guide. In mid-87 Mt Cook had enjoyed the longest fatality free period in 10 years – in part due, the authorities reported, to 'Australian climbers taking more care'!

Tours

The interesting (but rather expensive at $25) 2¼ hour Tasman Glacier Guided Coach Tour is operated two or three times a day in season – check at the Hermitage or Glencoe Lodge about bookings and tour times. The rocky road follows the lateral moraines of the Tasman Glacier and the bus stops several times to see this mighty river of ice. Part of the tour involves an optional 15-minute walk.

Flights

The skies above Mt Cook are alive with the sound of aircraft. This is the New Zealand equivalent of the Grand

Canyon in the US although fortunately the skies are not yet that crowded. Well, the views are superb and glacier landings are a great experience.

Flightseeing trips are operated by Mt Cook Airlines from Mt Cook or by Air Safari and the Helicopter Line from Glentanner. Air Safari operates the same trips at the same fare from Tekapo.

The Mt Cook skiplane flights are most expensive – depending on the length of the flight and the route they cost $96 (children $72) through $134 ($101) up to $191 ($143) for the full 'land on the glacier' operation.

The Helicopter Line has short flights for $35 to $60 or the big flight up over the Tasman Glacier and by Mt Cook with a glacier landing for $140. These flights go from Glentanner Park as do the Air Safari flights which are probably the best value although they do not actually land on the glacier. Air Safari's 'Grand Traverse' takes you up the Tasman Glacier, over the upper part of the Fox and Franz Josef Glaciers, by Mt Cook and Mt Tasman and generally gives you your fill of mountain scenery for $80 (children $60). Transport is available to Glentanner Park from Mt Cook village.

Other Activities

There are lots of other things to do – all expensive in keeping with Mt Cook's reputation – including rafting, horse trekking and motorbike trekking. From the Glentanner camp you can go on horse treks from $10 for half an hour to $80 for a full day. Or four-wheel drive trips for $20 and up. Or rent trail motorcycles. There are also rafting trips on the Tasman River.

Places to Stay

Mt Cook is a resort and priced accordingly. Despite the prices, demand has been running ahead of supply so it's wise to book in advance, particularly during the summer high season. Apart from the Youth Hostel all the places are operated by the government-run THC.

Hostels The excellent and friendly new *Mt Cook Youth Hostel* (tel 820) has lots more room than the small old one. Nevertheless it can still get crowded in the high season, so book ahead if you can. It's well equipped, conveniently located, open in the day and costs $14 a night. Ask about using the Hermitage's sauna.

Camping & Cabins Camping is allowed in the park but around the village and roads in the Tasman and Hooker Valley it is restricted to the 'Picnic Areas'. Up at the old Hermitage site, starting point for the Hooker Valley track, there's running water and toilets but no electricity, showers or the other sorts of luxuries you find at motor camps.

The nearest motor camp to the park is 23 km down the valley on the shores of Lake Pukaki at *Glentanner Park*. Facilities are good and camping costs $6 per person. Or there are on-site vans at $26 for two, basic cabins at $28 for two, deluxe cabins at $48 for two. Note that the camp store here is only open from 8 am to 5 pm. The only other store is up at Mt Cook so if you're going to arrive late bring supplies with you, or prepare to starve!

If you are hiking or mountaineering there are a lot of huts scattered around the park, but some of them are only accessible to the experienced climber. The Information Centre can tell you where they are as well as advise on good walks. Hut fees are generally $3, $7 or $11 a night.

Chalets, Motels & Hotels Everything else is run by the THC and is booked by phoning Mt Cook 809 or Wellington 72-9179. At the bottom of their price range are the *Mt Cook Chalets* which cost $72 for two, then $18 for each extra adult. They have two mini-bedrooms and a fold-down double bed-sofa, so between six of you they can be reasonably economical. Well-equipped kitchens and a dining table add to the convenience. They may be closed in the winter season though. The *Mt Cook Motels* which are operated by the Glencoe

Lodge cost the same and are also equipped with kitchens.

Beyond this, the prices start to get expensive. The *Glencoe Lodge* costs $130/145 for singles/doubles including breakfast. The *Hermitage* (well it is nice to stay there) has prices in line with its fame – about $190 for a single or double, $240 for a suite.

Places to Eat

The only way to eat economically at Mt Cook is to fix your own food. There's a small, but well stocked, store and prices aren't too out of line, although you'll save a bit by bringing food up with you. The Glentanner motor camp also has a small store and their cafe probably has the best low-priced food around.

Otherwise you have three choices at the Hermitage and one at the Glencoe Lodge. The Hermitage base line is their *coffee shop* which is usually open 9 am to 8 pm but sometimes closes earlier. It does very unexciting sandwiches and pies. By the end of the day they can look very tired and even more unexciting than they did at the beginning of the day!

Otherwise there's the *Alpine Room* where main courses are around $17 to $22 and desserts $6 to $8 although you can get things like mushrooms on toast for $15! Still, $17 for roast lamb gets you a filling meal. Breakfast in the Alpine Room ranges from $7 (tea and toast!) to $14 (buffet and cooked breakfast). The Glencoe Lodge has a similarly priced restaurant. Finally there's the Hermitage's *Panorama Room* where for two people you can count on spending well over $100 – starters are $15 to $18, main courses $25 to $40, desserts $7 to $10.

Entertainment

You can drink at the bar, sit around and talk or there's a disco at *Glencoe Lodge* on Friday and Saturday evenings during the busy season. The Hermitage has a resident pianist.

Getting There & Away

Air Mt Cook Airlines fly to Mt Cook from Queenstown, Christchurch and Rotorua. Ansett New Zealand fly in to Glentanner, 23 km down the valley. Fares are Christchurch $138, Queenstown $126, Rotorua $329. The Mt Cook bus to the Mt Cook airport is $4. Mt Cook reservations and enquiries are made by calling 849, Ansett New Zealand's number is 855.

There's no scheduled air service to Fox or Franz Josef but you can fly over one-way if you like. It's a way of combining transport with a scenic flight and means you can avoid the difficult Haast route if hitching. But you can't rely on the weather and may get held up at Mt Cook for quite a while waiting for suitable conditions to get across.

Road There's a daily bus service to both Queenstown and Christchurch for $42 by Mt Cook (the tourist company – Mt Cook is the name of a mountain, the village beneath it and the bus and plane operating tourist company).

It's over five hours drive from Christchurch or Queenstown. Hitching is hard – expect long waits once you leave Highway 1 if coming from Christchurch or Dunedin and long waits all the way if coming from Queenstown. Hardest of all, though, is simply getting out of Mt Cook itself since the road is a dead end. It's worth considering the $11 bus ride down to Twizel, where there's much more traffic.

MacKenzie Country

The high country from which the Mt Cook park rises is known as MacKenzie country after a legendary sheep rustler, Jock MacKenzie, who ran his stolen flocks in that uninhabited region about 1843. When he was finally caught other settlers realised the potential of the land and followed in his footsteps. The first people to traverse the MacKenzie were the

Maoris who used to trek across the country from Banks Peninsula to Otago hundreds of years ago.

TEKAPO

At the southern end of Lake Tekapo the small settlement of Tekapo is a popular rest stop for buses heading to or from Mt Cook or Queenstown. There's a little cluster of businesses up by the main road from where there are sweeping views across the lake with the hills and mountains as a backdrop. Walks, the lake itself and, in winter, skiing are the Lake Tekapo attractions.

Church of the Good Shepherd

The picturesque little church beside the lake was built of stone and oak in 1935. Further along from the church is a statue of a collie dog, a tribute to the sheep dogs which made the development of the MacKenzie country possible.

Walks

It's an hour's walk to the top of Mt John and you can continue on to Lakes Alexandrina and McGregor, an all day walk. Other walks are along the east side of the lake to the ski field road, the one hour return walk to the Tekapo lookout or 1½ hours to the power station.

Flights

Air Safari (tel 880) operate flights from Tekapo over Mt Cook and its glaciers. The flights don't actually land on the glacier but Air Safari's 'Grand Traverse' takes you up the Tasman glacier, over the upper part of the Fox and Franz Josef Glaciers, and by Mt Cook and Mt Tasman. Air Safari operates the same tour from Glentanner for the same price ($80, children $60), but YHA members can get a discount from Tekapo (not available from Glentanner). They are much cheaper than similar flights offered by other airlines from Mt Cook.

Lake Tekapo

Other Activities

October to May you can tour the Mt John observatory, phone 813 for details. It's also possible to tour the hydro-power station. Fishing and boating are other summer activities, see the Skiing section for details on skiing at Round Hill or Mt Dobson.

Places to Stay

Hostels The *Lake Tekapo Youth Hostel* (tel 857) is just beyond the post office, restaurants and shops on the Mt Cook side of town. There are great views across the lake (this is the hostel with the 'million dollar view') and the nightly cost is $11.

Camping & Cabins Besides the lake the *Tekapo Camp* (tel 825) has sites from $6 per person, cabins and on-site caravans from $14, cottages with cooking facilities and motel units from $50.

Hotels & Motels The *Lake Tekapo Motel* (tel 808) has rooms at $30/55 for singles/doubles or motels units for $55. The *Lake Tekapo Alpine Inn* (tel 848) is much more expensive with rooms from around $70 to $110.

Places to Eat

There are a number of takeaways and cafes as well as a bakery in the business centre by the main road.

Getting There & Away

The Mt Cook southbound service to Queenstown ($39), Wanaka ($39) and Mt Cook ($15) comes through every day, as does the northbound service to Timaru ($13) and Christchurch ($28). Book at the petrol station. Hitching in or out of Tekapo can sometimes be difficult as there is not much traffic. Once you've got a ride it will probably be going a fair way though.

TWIZEL

Slightly south of Lake Pukaki, Twizel is a conveniently central location for the whole area. By car it's only a half hour from Mt Cook and nearby Lake Ruataniwha has an international rowing centre.

Information

The Twizel Information Centre (tel 497) is on Wairepo Rd and is open every day from 9 am to 5 pm.

Places to Stay

The *Basil Lodge* (tel 671) has all sorts of accommodation starting with hostel-style bunks (only two beds to a room, though) at $12, singles at $27, twins or doubles at $39.

On the edge of town the *MacKenzie Country Inn* (tel 869) has rooms at $60/72. Or right beside the lake, four km out of town, the *Ruataniwha Motor Camp* (tel 613) has sites at $6 per person and some cheap although fairly basic cabins at $11 per person.

Places to Eat

The *Basil Lodge* serves breakfast ($5 to $8), lunch ($8) and dinner ($10). In the small shopping centre the *Black Stilt Cafe* is a plain and straightforward cafe offering takeaways, burgers at $2 to $3 and meals at $6 to $8. For higher class dining there's the restaurant at the *MacKenzie Country Inn*.

Queenstown

Close to what many say is the finest skiing in New Zealand, situated on a beautiful lake with a variety of summer cruises, handy to some of the best walking country, with a good vintage car museum and some exciting shoot-the-rapids expeditions thrown in for good measure – it's no wonder Queenstown is one of the most popular vacation areas in the country. If it sounds like a tourist trap, it is, but if you want to have a good time, this is a great place to be.

It's extremely easy to get through a lot of money here but Queenstown is a 'doing' place and sometimes you just have to forget the cost and 'do' it. So relax and enjoy the fantastic setting, there's lots to do, a large and friendly transient work population and more nightlife than most places in New Zealand.

History
There is evidence that Queenstown was once the site of a Maori settlement. However, when the whites began arriving in the mid-1850s the region was deserted. The first Europeans to settle the area were sheep farmers, but in 1862 two shearers, Thomas Arthur and Harry Redfern, discovered gold on the banks of the Shotover which caused a rush of prospectors to the area. Queenstown quickly developed into a mining town and by early 1863 streets had been laid out and permanent buildings established. Then the gold petered out and by 1900 the population had dropped from several thousand to a mere 190 people.

During this era the lake was the principal means of communication and at the height of the mining boom there were four paddle steamers and about 30 other craft plying the waters. One of those early steamers, still in use today, was the *TSS Earnslaw*, which was prefabricated in Dunedin, carted overland in sections, and rebuilt at Kingston in 1912. The highway edging the lake between Queenstown and Glenorchy was only completed in 1962, the centenary of the founding of the township. There are several theories on how Queenstown got its name, but the most popular is that it commemorates the town of the same name on Great Island in Cork Harbour, Ireland, probably because the majority of the diggers were Irish.

Information & Orientation
Queenstown is a tiny, compact township fronting on to beautiful Lake Wakatipu, and backed by equally beautiful hills. The main street is the pedestrians-only Mall.

Tourist Information The NZTP (tel 28-238) is at 49 Shotover St, across from the Mountaineer. It does local tour bookings and has plenty of local information although the staff are not all as knowledgeable as they should be. The office is open 8.30 am to 5 pm.

Across the road is the Queenstown Tourist Centre (tel 29-708) at the Bay Centre. The Lands & Surveys Information Centre is on the corner of Ballarat and Stanley Sts, a block behind the post office. It's open from about 8.30 am to 5 pm from Monday to Friday.

Tour Agents There are plenty of places to book Queenstown's plethora of activities. You can try the NZTP office or Queenstown centre mentioned above or there's Fiordland Travel and the NZRRS office by the *Earnslaw* wharf, Mt Cook Travel at the end of the Mall and plenty of others. The Newmans office is on Church St across from the Mt Cook Landlines depot.

Telephones Queenstown has recently been

changing lots of phone numbers which may continue to cause some confusion. Queenstown phone boxes seem to be completely devoid of phone directories – I did see an Invercargill directory in one box, but never a Queenstown one. Despite this Queenstown's notoriously bad-tempered telephone operators abuse you for not looking up the number if you ring directory enquiries!

Other There's a useful notice stand right in the middle of the Mall. If you've got plenty of dirty clothes and nowhere to wash them head for the Alpine Laundrette on Shotover St just above the Athol St junction. You can leave washing in at 4 Brecon St, just off Shotover St and next to Queenstown Electrical. For tramping and camping gear try Alp Sports in the Skyline Arcade, off the Mall.

Views

Try starting at the top of the town. Catch the gondola lift to the summit of the hill overlooking the town for incredible views over the lake – well worth the $6 (children $2). There's a licensed cafe up at the top which is not bad and also a more expensive restaurant for dinner. In mid-87 the terminals went through a major renovation and new gondola equipment was installed permitting a much greater passenger flow.

If you're more energetic you can walk up the vehicle track to Skyline from Lomond Crescent, but the ride is worth experiencing. The lift operates from 10 am daily.

What really makes Queenstown's setting is the Remarkables. A written description can hardly do them justice, but you can easily spend a day just watching the constant changes in their appearance in different lights. They're especially beautiful capped with snow, at sunrise or in the after-glow of dusk. If you're super fit it's a long, hard, steep climb to the top, 2000 metres above the lake level – very energy sapping in the hot Central Otago sun.

Queenstown Motor Museum

The motor museum is just below the Skyline Gondola lower terminal and has a fine collection of cars, all of them well restored and in running order. There's also a motorcycle collection upstairs and a fine old Tiger Moth flying overhead. The museum is open 9 am to 5.30 pm daily and admission is $3.50 (children $1.50).

Kiwi & Birdlife Park

Right below the gondola terminal is the kiwi house and birdlife park. It has what is becoming a New Zealand standard – the nocturnal kiwi house. Keas and a variety of other birds can also be seen in the pleasant park. The park is open 9 am to 5 pm daily and admission is $4 (children $2.50).

Between the kiwi park and the motor museum there's a maze but in mid-87 it seemed to be out of operation.

Waterworld

On the pier right at the end of the Mall in the centre of Queenstown is waterworld, a submerged observation gallery where you can look out and see eels and trout in the clear waters of Lake Wakatipu. The agile little scaup or 'diving' ducks also make periodic appearances outside the windows. Regular feedings, you can add to them for 50c, attract the fish and eels. Waterworld is open 9 am to 5.30 pm daily and entry is $3 (children $1.50).

The Earnslaw

The stately old coal-burning steamer the *TSS Earnslaw* is the most famous of Queenstown's many lake cruise boats. There's a daily three-hour cruise at 2 pm which goes out to the Mt Nicholas sheep station and back. On the way you can sip a beer, watch the activity in the immaculate engine room or sing along with a pianist. At the station you see a sheep dog demonstration and sheep shearing. Cost is $25 ($10).

The *Earnslaw* also operates a short lunchtime cruise at 12.30 pm which costs $15 (children $7.50), not including lunch.

And there's an evening dinner cruise at 6 pm. In winter months the expensive-to-run *Earnslaw* used to be parked in favour of a smaller modern boat but these days Queenstown may be busy enough to operate the Earnslaw year round.

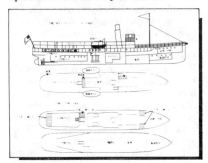

The TSS (Twin Screw Steamer) *Earnslaw* is steel hulled and weighs 330 tons. At full speed she churns across the lake at 13 knots, burning a ton of coal an hour. She measures 51 metres in length and 7.3 metres across the beam. The *Earnslaw* is licensed to carry 810 passengers and at one time was the major means of transport on the lake. The development of modern roads ended her career with New Zealand Railways and she has been used for lake cruises since 1969.

Other Lake Cruises

There are various other lake cruises to choose from including an hourly half-hour zip round the lake by hydrofoil for $20. It departs from the pier at the end of the Mall.

The Cecil Peak cruise is similar to the *Earnslaw* operation with a cruise across the lake to a station, sheep dogs in action, sheep shearing and tea and scones to complete the picture. Cost for the 2½ hour cruises from 9.30 am or 2.15 pm is $25 (children $6). There's also a Walter Peak cruise – also twice daily lasting three hours – which costs $24 (children $12).

Jet Boat Trips

Hurtling up the rivers around Quenstown in jet boats or hurtling down them in inflatable rafts is another popular activity. The Shotover and the Kawarau are the popular jet-boat rivers. Trips either depart straight from Queenstown or go by minibus to the river and then by boat. The trips generally take about an hour and cost around $40 to $45.

The Shotover Jet is one of the most popular; the narrow and shallow Shotover is particularly exciting for jet-boating. Be prepared to get wet but it's great fun. The Twin Rivers Jet operates on the Upper Kawarau and Lower Shotover Rivers but I've got to give them a thumbs down. Their ticket warns you that they may cancel their trips without prior warning but fails to add that they may not bother to tell you that they've cancelled.

The Goldstream Jet departs from the town wharf and crosses the lake to the Kawarau River, this trip is $28. For people who really want to do everything you can combine helicopter and jetboat rides (from $65 to $85) or helicopters, jetboats and raft rides (from $100).

Raft Trips

So much for jet boating up the rivers, they're equally good for rafting down.

Again the Shotover and Kawarau Rivers are the locations. Rivers are graded, for rafting purposes, from 1 to 6 with 6 being rated as 'unraftable'. The upper canyon of the Shotover is rated 2+, the lower canyon 4+, the Kawarau River 4, the Tucker Beach section of the Shotover as 2. On the rougher stretches there's usually a minimum age limit of 12 or 13 years. The rafting companies supply wetsuits and life jackets. Trips typically take from two hours (adults $25, children $12.50) to a whole day ($90 to $120) or even longer. If you opt to helicopter in rather than go by minibus you can pay even more.

Rafting companies include Challenge Rafting (Shotover 4½ hours, Kawarau three hours), Kon Tiki (lower Shotover two hours), Danes (Shotover four or six hours, Tuckers Beach two hours, Kawarau three hours, Landborough three days) and Kawarau Raft Expeditions (Kawarau 3½ hours, Shotover five hours or full day) and Value Tours (Kawarau three hours, Shotover five hours). An alternative to the raft trips are two-hour canoe safaris on the lower Shotover for $25.

Cattledrome

The Cattledrome is a 'cattle stage show' at Arthur's Point. There are two shows a day at 9.30 am and 2.30 pm for $5 (children

$1.50). If you're suddenly overcome with a desire to be practical you can learn how to milk a cow and get a certificate which proves it!

Arrowtown

Near Queenstown, Arrowtown is a restored early gold-mining settlement, you can still find gold in the river there. The Lake District Centennial Museum at Arrowtown has displays on gold mining and local history. It's open from 9 am to 5 pm and admission is $2 (children 50c).

Bus Trips

There are all sorts of bus trips from Queenstown:

Close to Town You can take a one-hour Queenstown tour for $14 (children $7) or a 4½ hour trip to the head of the lake for $55 (children $35). Or visit the ski slopes of Coronet Peak for $10 (children $6) for the bus, plus $8 (children $4) for the chairlift in the summer season. At Coronet Peak you can then ride the metal 'cresta slide' for $3.50. Trips out to Cattledrome cost $21 (children $10.50) including admission or you can visit Cattledrome and Arrowtown for $31 (children $15.50).

Skippers Canyon There's a twice daily 3½ hour trip up the winding road above the Shotover River. The scenery is spectacular, the road hair-raising and it's full of historical interest as well. Cost is $40 (children $20). Another tour, lasting an hour longer, goes further up the canyon – $45 (children $25).

Milford Sound & Elsewhere Day trips via Te Anau to Milford Sound are operated by Fiordland, Mt Cook/H&H and NZRRS. They take 12 to 13 hours and cost $80 to $90 (children about half price) including a launch cruise on the sound. All the way from Queenstown this is a very long day, if you're going to Te Anau it makes a lot more sense to go from there. Ditto for trips to Doubtful Sound which cost $110 (children \$55) from Queenstown. H&H have day trips to the Routeburn or Greenstone Valleys.

Flights

No possibility is ignored at Queenstown – if you can't boat up it, down it or across it, walk around it or chairlift over it then why not fly above it. There are all sorts of flights from short helicopter flights over Queenstown from \$35 to flights to Milford Sound from \$100. More expensive Milford flights include a brief landing or a one or two hour launch cruise on the sound. Mt Cook and Air Wakatipu are two of the operators.

Walks

Many of Queenstown's activities are decidedly expensive but the walks cost nothing. Stroll along the waterfront through town and keep going to the park on the peninsula. It's a peaceful place. There's now a walkway from Queenstown at the end of Peninsula St – takes about 1¼ hours each way – following the lake shore.

One of the shortest climbs around Queenstown is Queenstown Hill, overlooking the town. It's 900 metres high, and a comfortable climb with good views – two to three hours return. For a more spectacular view climb Ben Lomond (1746 metres) – it takes five hours there and back. Follow the Skyline vehicle track for half an hour until you get to a small rock cairn, which marks a turn-off on your left. When you reach the saddle head west to the top of Ben Lomond. During the summer if you leave about midnight you'll have a spectacular view of the sunrise. You can climb higher than the Skyline vehicle track.

There are many other walks in the area especially from Arthurs Point and Arrowtown, areas rich in history of the gold days – consult people who live in the area or the Lands & Survey Information Office for info. Feeding bread to the ducks and seagulls along the lakefront is another cheap form of entertainment.

Still More

Still more Queenstown activity? Well you can go fishing, charter yachts, ride horses, play squash, try a hang gliding simulator, waterbike, parafly, visit the amusement park or the nearby deer park. Over the summer season the restored steam train the Kingston Flyer makes three daily return trips between Kingston at the south end of Lake Wakatipu and Fairlight.

Places to Stay

Despite the plethora of accommodation in Queenstown you may still have trouble finding a room at peak periods. Try the NZTP or the Queenstown Information Centre if you're stuck. Prices vary with the season, they go sky high at the peak summer period or in the middle of the ski season, drop in between. I've tried to give high season prices in what follows. There's considerable overlap between accommodation types in Queenstown – a number of the guest houses and campsites also have motel rooms for example.

Hostels The *Queenstown Youth Hostel* (tel 28-413) is right by the lake at 80 Lake Esplanade. There are beds for 84 people and the nightly cost is \$13. The night time curfew at the hostel has now been extended until 12 midnight and you can also get tasty food here – a huge lasagne for \$6 for example. In the late December-January period overflow accommodation is available – check hostel noticeboards for dates and places. In winter the hostel can get hopelessly booked out due to all the skiers.

There are a couple of private hostel possibilities close to the centre of Queenstown. The *Redwood Ski Lodge* (tel 29-116) is just above the centre on Lower Malaghan St and has great views over the town and lake. It's a small place with beds at \$12, supply your own bedding as usual.

A little further from the centre is *Pinewood Lodge* (tel 28-273) at 48 Hamilton Rd. This used to offer motel-style accommodation but is now a hostel

Top: Near Queenstown (TW)
Left: Queenstown gondola (TW)
Right: Routeburn River Valley (VB)

TSS Earnslaw, Queenstown (TW)

operation with two or three rooms for two people, sharing a lounge and kitchen area and bathroom. Supply your own bedding and the nightly cost for a bed is $12. There are also some bunkrooms at $10 per person.

Right out at Frankton, which may be too far from town for most people, is the *Wakatipu Lodge* (tel 23-037) on Stewart St. The rooms are mainly for two and cost $16 per person. You can also camp here for $8. There are the usual kitchen facilities and a recreation room. They have a courtesy bus which runs into Queenstown several times a day, phone to check. A final possibility is the *Contiki Lodge* (tel 27-107) on Fernhill Rd, just a couple of km from the centre. Bunkroom accommodation there is $22 including a cooked breakfast.

Camping & Cabins There are plenty of campsites in and around Queenstown, all have cabins. Closest is *Queenstown Motor Park* (tel 27-254) which is less than a km from the centre. Camping will set you back $6 per person or $7 per person with power. There are also cabins from $35 for two, tourist lodges from $45, tourist flats from $55, motel flats from $70. As well as being so convenient the camp is very well equipped – good kitchen, coin-operated laundry, TV room and so on but it's also coldly efficient, regimented and off-hand. You may be charged a $20 refundable deposit when you check in.

Mountain View Lodge Holiday Camp (tel 28-246) is just over a km from the centre on the Frankton side. Camping here costs $5 a night, cabins are $25/40 for singles/doubles, units for two cost $60 or $75 for the fancier units with kitchen. Bedding is supplied in the cabins but you need your own cooking equipment for the communal kitchens. The camp also has a restaurant and bar.

Frankton Motor Camp (tel 27-247), is six km out. Camping here costs $7 per person, and cabins range from $20 for two in the simpler units, $25 to $35 for the fancier ones with shower and kitchen

facilities. Also in Frankton the *Kawarau Falls Holiday Camp* (tel 23-101) is about a km further on than the Frankton camp. It has a particularly attractive setting and camping is $4.50 per person but there's a one night surcharge. Lodges and cabins start from $9 per person, $22 to $30 for two in the cabins with kitchen. *Queenstown Holiday Park* (tel 29-306) is at Arthurs Point. It has camping for $12 for two or cabins for $22 for two.

Guest Houses *Melbourne House* (tel 28-431) at 35 Melbourne St offers bed & breakfast at $40/66 for single/double share facility rooms. They also have studio units at $55/73 or larger kitchen units from $66 up to $132 depending on the size. With these rooms breakfast is available for $5 (continental) or $8.50 (cooked). It's a friendly and well organised place with laundry facilities and a guest lounge and it's conveniently close to the centre.

At 69 Hallenstein St on the corner of Malaghan St, *Queenstown House* (tel 29-043) is a pleasant place with bed & breakfast at $33/50 and nice views over the town and lake from the balcony. It's also close to the centre.

Goldfields Guest House (tel 27-211) is at 41 Frankton Rd just beyond the Hyatt. Like Melbourne House it has a variety of accommodation ranging from bed & breakfast at $65 ($60 for the couple of rooms without private facilities), through some very pleasant A-line chalet rooms which cost $75 including a continental breakfast or regular motel rooms at $71 without breakfast.

Back towards the centre, between Melbourne House and Queenstown House is the wonderful old *Hulbert House* (tel 28-767) at 68 Ballarat St. This is upper class bed & breakfast, just a handful of very gracious rooms, wonderful views and a price tag of $100 to $140 a night. There is, however, just one very cheap cabin-style room separate from the main house.

Hotels Overlooking the lake at 32

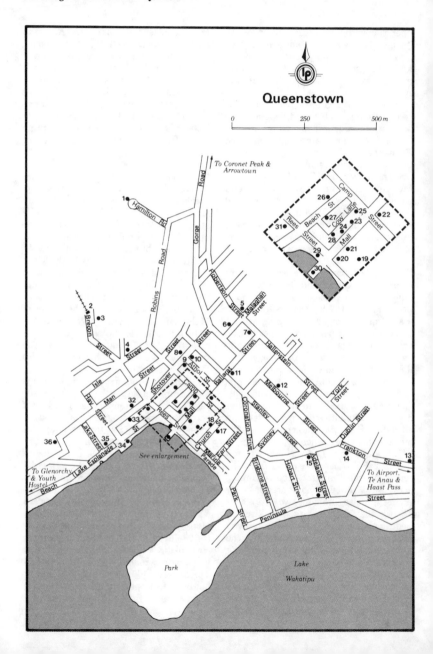

Queenstown

0   250   500 m

To Coronet Peak &
Arrowtown

To Glenorchy
& Youth
Hostel

See enlargement

To Airport,
Te Anau &
Haast Pass

Park

Lake
Wakatipu

1	Pinewood Lodge	21	Saguaro Restaurant
2	Skyline Gondola Terminal	22	Post Office
3	Kiwi House	23	Cardrona's Cafe
4	Car Museum	24	Avanti Restaurant
5	Queenstown Guest House	25	H&H Office
6	Redwood Ski Lodge	26	Down to Earth
7	Hulbert House	27	O'Connell's Hotel
8	The Bakery	28	The Cow
9	California Fried Chicken	29	Mt Cook Airline & Travel Office
10	Alpine Laundromat	30	Water World
11	Lands & Survey Information Office	31	The Mountaineer
12	Melbourne House	32	NZTP Office
13	Mountain View Lodge	33	Upstairs, Downstairs, Gourmet
14	Goldfields Guest House		Express & Queenstown Information
15	Hyatt Kingsgate Hotel		Centre
16	Hotel Esplanade	34	Wharf, NZRRS Office &
17	Mt Cook Landline Office		Fiordland Travel
18	Newmans Office	35	Travelodge
19	Jazzbar	36	Queenstown Motor Camp
20	Eichardt's Hotel		

Peninsula St *Hotel Esplanade* (tel 28-611) has rooms with bathroom at $31/62 for singles/doubles. There's also a $17 bunkroom and breakfast is available for $7 (continental) or $9 (cooked). Rooms have TVs and there's an indoor pool, it's pretty good value.

The *Mountaineer Queenstown Establishment* (tel 27-400) is on Beach St right in the centre. Rooms with private facilities are $100 or there are a handful of rooms without attached bathrooms for $40. It's convenient and the rooms have tea and coffee-making facilities.

Motels Queenstown has plenty of motels and motel flats including some at the various campsites or with the guest houses, see above for details. The *Mountain View Lodge* (tel 28-246) on Frankton Rd is a good example – there are cabins and motel-style rooms as well as the adjoining camping facilities. The main building is known as the bottle house due to the nearly 15,000 bottles (none of them beer bottles!) set into the walls. *Melbourne House* and *Goldfields Motel* also have motel rooms as well as bed & breakfast.

Other moderately priced motel rooms include those attached to *Melbourne House* and *Goldfields Guest House*, see Guest Houses above. The A-line chalet rooms at Goldfields are very pleasant. *Mountain View Lodge* (see Camping & Cabins) also has motel units.

Aroha Motel Flats (tel 27-777) is at a couple of central addresses but check at 20 Hay St where the manager resides. Units here cost from $50 for their cheapest one-bedroom unit, larger units are from $60. They're good value but there aren't many of them and they're often full – plan ahead. There are quite a few other motels around Queenstown with costs generally from around $60 or $70 a night. Prices in Queenstown are not cheap but they tend to fluctuate with the seasons.

Places to Eat
Queenstown has its share of pretentiously over-priced restaurants (well it is a ski-resort) but there are plenty of places with reasonably priced good-value food. The centre is very compact so it's no problem walking to any of these places.

Fast Food & Takeaways There is an assortment of the usual – sandwiches, fish & chips, and the like. For coffee-bar food, pancakes and light meals (breakfast, lunch and early dinner) try *Cardrona's* in the Mall where you can sit down and watch the Mall activity. Next door *Sweet Memories* is a patisserie and chocolate shop with tasty baked goods and sandwiches.

A block over at 5 Beach St *Down to Earth* has good sandwiches and excellent wholemeal munchies. Another block over in the arcade at 37 Shotover St the *Lucullus Delicatessen* is a good looking sandwich place. Up Shotover St, just beyond Camp St, is *The Bakery* with more baked goods, sandwiches and also pizzas. Round the corner on Camp St the *Town Fish Shop* is not bad for fish & chips.

Near the waterfront in the arcade at the corner of Rees St and Beach St (across from the Mountaineer), *Food for Thought* masquerades as a health food place and tries to serve up white-bread sandwiches if you don't complain!

Pizza Hut, on the corner of Camp St and Church St, is the only one of the American fast food giants to make an appearance (yet) in Queenstown. There is, however, a *Californian Fried Chicken* on the corner of Shotover and Athol Sts! It looks remarkably like its Kentucky relation. Down Shotover St towards the waterfront in the Bay Centre *Gourmet Express* looks very American and Denny-like. It's very popular from 7 am when you can get a continental breakfast for $4.50 or pancakes for $5. The menu features the fast food regulars including a variety of good-looking burgers from $3.50 to $6.50. It closes at 9 pm.

If you want a really late night snack head for the *Jazzbar* takeaway in the car park behind Eichardt's. It's not great value but after the pubs shut it's usually crowded and stays open until midnight or later most nights.

Restaurants There's a *Cobb & Co*, open the usual long hours, in the Mountaineer.

Across the road in that corner arcade the *Lakeside Café & Steakhouse* has main courses in the $14 to $18 range but also does cheaper lunchtime dishes and some tables have nice views over the lake.

The Cow in Cow Lane is something of a Queenstown institution, a tiny old stone-walled building with a roaring fire (in winter) and excellent pizzas and pastas. The pizzas are $7 to $10 for small ones, $10 to $14 for large. Either way they're substantial so bring an appetite. Spaghetti is around $10. It's an atmospheric little byo with the emphasis on little. You'll probably have to queue for a table although they do takeaways as well.

Over on the Mall *Avanti* is a plain and straightforward Italian byo with pastas in the $7 to $8 range, omelettes, osso buco and other standard dishes around $10, desserts at $4. Nothing special but good value and with a pleasant courtyard at the back.

At the bottom end of the Mall *Saguaro* has Mexican food – enchiladas, tacos, frijoles – for around $14, lunchtime specials at $8. It's open until late every night.

Expensive Restaurants There are plenty of places a notch (sometimes a big notch) up. *Westy's*, in an arcade off the Mall, is moderately expensive. Facing each other across Shotover St *Upstairs Downstairs* and *Roaring Megs* are two of Queenstown's better and pricier eating places with main courses in the $15 to $20 range. Roaring Megs is housed in an old miner's cottage. All three are byo.

Right at the top, altitude-wise at least, would have to be dinner at the *Skyline Restaurant*. Including the gondola ride to the top dinner is $35 for adults, $17.50 for children. Great views.

Entertainment

Queenstown is a small place but there's a reasonable variety of night time activities. In the Mall near the waterfront is *Eichardt's*, which has been around for a long time – during the 1879 floods, hard drinking miners are said to have paddled up to the bar in rowboats! During the Franco-Prussian war Herr Eichardt, being a good Prussian nationalist, ran the German flag up the flagpole after every German victory. Meanwhile, down the road at Monsieur Francois St Omer's bakery the tricolour flew every time the frogs won. The public bar is a popular local meeting and drinking place while upstairs you'll find activity until late at night in the *Penthouse* nightclub.

Only a block away is the *Mountaineer*, near where the bakery once was. You may also find some night time activity in this more family oriented pub. *O'Connell's Hotel* on Beach St has recently gone through a major rebuild. On Shotover St there's the *Harlequin Nightclub*. Or you can ride the gondola to the *Skyline Restaurant* where there's entertainment with the $30 dinner each night.

Getting There & Away

Air Mt Cook Airlines and Ansett New Zealand both fly into Queenstown. Fares include Auckland $348, Christchurch $138, Dunedin $109, Mt Cook $126 and Te Anau $74. A flying day trip to Milford Sound costs $175. Mt Cook (tel 27-650) are in the Mt Cook office by the wharf, Ansett New Zealand (tel 23-010) can be contacted at the airport.

Road The NZRRS depot is beside the steamship wharf and is open 7 am to 8.30 pm on weekdays, 7 am to 12 noon on Saturdays, 7 am to 5.30 pm on Sundays. H&H has its Queenstown depot in Camp St just round the corner from the Mall, while Mt Cook buses leave from the depot on Church St.

NZRRS fares from Queenstown include Christchurch $71, Dunedin $42, Fox Glacier $67, Invercargill $25, Milford Sound $51, Te Anau $27 and Wanaka $20. The West Coast service to the glaciers operates Monday to Saturday and takes 8½ hours to the Fox Glacier. If you want to continue up the coast from the glaciers you have to overnight at Franz Josef. It takes a minimum of three days (longer if you want to see anything except a bus window) to get up the West Coast to Nelson by bus. Although the bus is expensive, hitching could take forever!

To or from Dunedin there are two or three NZRRS services daily except on Sundays when there is only one. The trip takes about six hours. Invercargill (four hours) has a daily service, Milford (five to six hours) has two daily services Monday to Saturday. The Milford bus goes via Te Anau, 2½ hours from Queenstown.

The daily Mt Cook service to or from Mt Cook ($42) takes about six hours. There are also daily connections via Geraldine with Christchurch ($64), 8½ hours away. You can get to Arrowtown on the Mt Cook or Christchurch services, or hitching isn't too bad. During the ski season the Mt Cook bus service to Coronet Peak costs $16.

H&H has a bus service to Frankton ($1.25), three times a day.

It's 170 km by road between Queenstown and Te Anau but a new and interesting route should come into use about the time this book is published. Fiordland Travel intend to operate a vehicle ferry across from Wilson's Bay, 20 minutes' drive from Queenstown, to Walter Peak from where you can drive through the Walter Peak and Mt Nicholas sheep stations to Te Anau in about two to 2½ hours.

Tramping Transport H&H run buses to the start of the Greenstone and Caples walks (via Kinloch) for $22 or to the Routeburn, Rees and Dart for $18. They generally go two or three times weekly but except at peak times they may only be operating for guided walks. NZRRS also have a Routeburn bus during the tramping season and you can use their Milford service for access to the Milford, Hollyford, Routeburn and Greenstone tracks.

The Magic Bus service between Queenstown and the Routeburn walk costs $15. This is probably the most popular means of transport to the trailheads and they also have a Te Anau-Milford service.

The Glenorchy Holiday Park (tel (0294) 29-939) is conveniently near many of the walks and they offer packages of transport to their camp, overnight accommodation and transport the next morning to the walks. Glenorchy is near the start of the walks so this is a good way to make an early start. For the Routeburn or Rees/ Dart walks the cost is $20 if you're camping, $24 in their lodge. For the Greenstown/Caples walk the cost is $22 and $26. Contact Shotover Taxis at 56 Shotover St in Queenstown. The distances and straight transport costs from the camp are Routeburn (27 km, $7), Greenstone/Caples (40 km, $10), Rees/ Dart (20 km, $6), Paradise (20 km, $6).

Hitching Hitching into Queenstown is relatively easy, but getting out may require real patience. Be prepared for very long waits. It's an open question whether it's better to start hitching straight from Queenstown or take a bus to Frankton first.

Getting Around

Airport Transport Mt Cook runs a bus meeting flights at the airport which will also take people to Frankton - it can be caught from the Mt Cook airlines office by the waterfront or from various hotels. The cost is $5.

Bicycle Rental You can rent bikes on Beach St. They have single speed bikes, tandems, 10 and 12 speeds, and 12 and 18 speed mountain bikes. They start from $3 for a single speed bike for an hour or $11 a day. The 10 or 12-speed bikes are $8 for two hours, $17 for a day.

CROMWELL

On the main route between Queenstown and Wanaka this pleasant little town is a good place for a short pause. There's an information office in the new town centre on Barry Avenue with some excellent displays and slide presentations on the hydro power projects in the Clutha Valley.

The gorge between here and Queenstown is often extremely spectacular and you can pause to walk over the interesting old Kawarau suspension bridge. It was built in 1880 for access to the Wakatipu goldfields and used right up until 1963.

Places to Stay & Eat

Sunhaven Motor Camp (tel 50-164) on Alpha St has camping and cabins. It's about two km from the centre. There are also hotels and motels.

In the new shopping mall there are a number of sandwich places, *John's Restaurant* has good food or you can try the pricier *Daniel's*.

Wanaka

Just over 100 km from Queenstown at the southern end of the lake of the same name, Wanaka is well worth a stopover if you're headed for the Haast Pass. It's the gateway to New Zealand's newest national park, Mt Aspiring, and ski field, Cardrona. The first step to set aside this glacier country for a park took place in 1935, but it was not until December 1964 that around 200 hectares in north-west Otago and south Westland were earmarked. The park, named after its highest peak, 3035-metre Mt Aspiring, now extends over an area of 2900 square km along the Southern Alps between the Haast and Te Anau highways.

Information

The Wanaka Booking Centre (tel 7277 or 7930) is right across the road from the jetty on Ardmore St. The Headquarters & Visitors Centre (tel 7660) for Mt Aspiring National Park, on the corner of Ballantyne and Main Rds is open 8 am to 5 pm daily from mid-December to mid-January and from Monday to Friday for the rest of the year. Huts in Mt Aspiring Park are $5 to $7 a night per person.

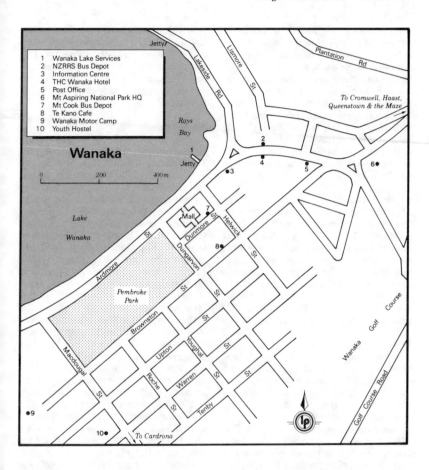

Wanaka

1   Wanaka Lake Services
2   NZRRS Bus Depot
3   Information Centre
4   THC Wanaka Hotel
5   Post Office
6   Mt Aspiring National Park HQ
7   Mt Cook Bus Depot
8   Te Kano Cafe
9   Wanaka Motor Camp
10 Youth Hostel

The Maze

Two km from Wanaka on the road to Cromwell is the maze and puzzle centre. Three-dimensional mazes have become quite a craze in New Zealand and they're now exporting them overseas but this was the original one. It's a series of fenced-off corridors and alleys with a confusing number of dead ends and further complicated by several 'bridges' that carry you from one quadrant to another.

The idea is to find your way to the towers at each corner and then back to the exit. And it's more difficult than you think. Tashi and I finally gave up after an hour, we'd found our way to three of the corners but it was starting to get dark! The maze is open 8.30 am to 5.30 pm and entry is $3 (children $2). If you're still lost when it closes you can keep on searching all night – there are emergency exits for when frustration sets in.

On the Water

Wanaka offers lots of activity on its beautiful lake. There's a hovercraft which makes trips (hovers?) over the lake twice daily – $14 for a 15 minute trip, $40 for an hour. Check with Wanaka Lake Services (tel 7495) by the waterfront. There's some local opposition to this noisy device. Or try a 1½ hour cruise for $20 on the former round-the-world yacht *City of Dunedin*. Or take lake cruises from one to four hours on the *MV Ena-De*. Trips to Pigeon Island (four hours) and Ruby Island (two hours) are popular. Alpine Safaris (tel 8446) have jet boat trips on the lake and up the Clutha River.

Kayaks & Rafts

Matatap Kayaks offer kayaking trips on the Motatapu River or more heady trips on the fast flowing Hawea or Matukituki Rivers. They also rent kayaks on the lake. Good Sports is another kayaking operator and they also offer rafting trips on the Hawea or Clutha Rivers and have windsurfers to hire on the lake. A four-hour kayak trip costs $35 (children $22) and rafting trips are similarly priced.

Walks & Tramps

You don't have to be a physical fitness freak to attempt the fairly gentle climb up Mt Iron (527 metres) near the Maze. It is 45 minutes from the road to the top and the view of the rivers, lakes and mountains is worth the effort.

More exhausting is the trek up Mt Roy (1585 metres). It will take you about three hours from the road to the top if you're fit – longer if you're the sedentary type. The track winds every step of the eight km from base to peak, but Mt Aspiring is quite a knockout from here.

There are lots of places to go tramping in Mt Aspiring National Park and Matukituki, Motatapu and Wilkin Valleys. You can get all the info you need on these walks and tramps from the Visitors Centre.

Horse Riding

South of Wanaka on the way to Cardrona are the Gin & Raspberry Stables (tel 8152) where you can make half-day or whole day horse-riding treks to the lower slopes of Mt Cardrona. Lunch is included on the day trips or you can make short rides into the Matukituki Valley. The main season is from Christmas until mid-March but special arrangements can be made at other times of the year.

Flights

Aspiring Air (tel 7942 or 3) has a variety of flights ranging from a 15-minute jaunt over Ruby Island, Glendhu Bay, Matukituki River and other local beauty spots costing $45 (children $30), to a 45-minute flight over Mt Aspiring and the glacier and alpine country for $90 (children $60). There are also flights to Mt Cook for $180 (children $110) or Milford Sound for $150 (children $100). With a launch trip as well the Milford trips costs $170 (children $115).

The Helicopter Line also has flights in the Wanaka area.

Other Activities

In the central Mall, Illusions has displays of optical illusions and holograms. It's open 9 am to 5.30 pm and entry is $2.75 (children $1.70).

Matuki Services (tel 7135) have various bus trips as well as providing access to the tramping tracks. Or try Aspiring Detours (tel 7872) for four-wheel drive trips in the area. They have trips from around $30 up to $100. Both Lakes Wanaka and Hawea – about 16 km from Wanaka – are good for trout and salmon fishing.

Wanaka is close to two ski fields – Treble Cone and Cardrona – and Cardrona has the longest skiing season in New Zealand. See the skiing section for more details. This is also a great area for heli-skiing.

Places to Stay

Hostels The *Wanaka Youth Hostel* (tel 7405) is at 181 Upton St and costs $11 a night. It has a homey, friendly atmosphere.

Camping & Cabins The *Wanaka Motor Camp* (tel 7883) is on Brownston St, about a km from the centre. Camping costs $7 per person with power point. There are cabins at $25 for two and tourist flats at $50.

Three km from Wanaka the *Pleasant Lodge Caravan Park* (tel 7360) on Mt Aspiring Rd is similarly priced. There are also cabins here ($25 for two) and tourist flats ($35 to $45 for two).

Adjacent to Lake Wanaka – 13 km out of town on the Treble Cone road – is the *Glendhu Bay Camp* (tel 7243), again with camping and cabins. Finally *Penrith Park* (tel 7009) is at Beacon Point and has camping facilities, cabins and a bunkroom.

Guest Houses The info centre has a list of small bed & breakfasts in Wanaka. *Wanaka Lodge* (tel 7837) at 117 Lakeside Rd is pleasantly situated right beside the lake but it may be going through some changes. Meanwhile it has rooms for $28 per person. Add on $8.50 for breakfast or $20 for a smorgasbord dinner.

The small *Creekside Guest House* (tel 7834) at 84 Helwick St has just three rooms with prices at around $27/54 for singles/doubles with breakfast. The *Te Kano Cafe* (tel 7028), see the restaurant section below, has one room available at a bargain $16 per person.

Hotels & Motels There are plenty of places in this category in Wanaka and you can also find accommodation at the campsites. Cheaper motels include the *All Seasons Motel* (tel 7530), five km from town on the Haast Highway. Rooms here are $45 for two. More centrally located is the similarly priced *Wunderview Motel* (tel 7480) on Brownston St.

Top of the market is the *THC Wanaka Hotel* (tel 7826) on Ardmore St. Rooms here cost $80 to $110.

Places to Eat

Snacks & Takeaways On Ardmore St by the Mall the *Snack Shack* does pizzas and the usual takeaway stuff. In the Mall there's the *Coffee Shop* which is open from reasonably early for breakfast plus the *Doughbin* for bread and baked goods.

Aspiring Takeaways is on Ardmore St next to the NZRRS depot and has hamburgers, toasted sandwiches and the like. Or try the *Wanaka Fast Food & Fish Supply*, Helwick St, which has fresh fish, seafood, hamburgers and sandwiches.

Restaurants Wanaka is surprisingly well equipped with restaurants including the superb *Te Kano Cafe* on Brownston St. This atmospheric little cottage has wonderful vegetarian food – well prepared, imaginative, filling and delicious. While updating this edition of this book this was the best meal I had in either island! Soup is $3.50, starters around $6, main courses $9 to $12. In winter they have gluhwein – hot spiced red wine.

In the Mall the up-market *Ripples Restaurant* offers al fresco dining on the verandah with good views of the lakes and mountains. The food here also has a good reputation. *Cappricio* is an Italian restaurant, also in the Mall, which sometimes has intriguingly un-Italian 'Chinese nights'! The menu mainly features pastas at $13 to $15. Or there's the *First Cafe* on Ardmore St which has takeaways as well as regular meals. The menu ranges from BLTs through spaghettis, dishes with an Indonesian or Chinese flavour and on to steaks.

The *THC Wanaka Hotel* has a bistro restaurant with pub-style meals. Finally there's the well restored *Cardrona Restaurant* (tel 8153) in the Cardrona Valley. This is a place for splurges – it's licensed and 30 km from town.

Getting There & Away

Road The depot for NZRRS is at the Biao Gift Shop at the bottom end of Ardmore St, right across from the THC Wanaka Hotel. NZRRS have twice daily services to Dunedin (five to six hours, $41) on weekdays. In August and September only there's a Wanaka-Dunedin service on

Sundays, but not in the other direction. The Monday to Saturday service between the west coast glaciers and Queenstown goes through Wanaka. It's about 2½ hours between Queenstown and Wanaka ($20) and six hours between the Fox Glacier and Wanaka ($50).

Mt Cook operate from the Wanaka Travel Agency on Dunmore St in the centre. They have a daily service to Christchurch for $63. H&H also operate from Wanaka and have a Monday to Friday bus to Invercargill. For access to tramping tracks or trips along the back road via Cardrona to Queenstown check with Matuki Services (tel 7135). They depart from the information centre and will take you to Cameron Flat for $11, to the road end for $13 or on a scenic return trip for $18. Wanaka Taxis (tel 7804 or 8565) also offer trampers transport (Raspberry Hut in the Matukituki Valley costs $82 for up to five passengers), local scenic trips, airport transport ($16) and in the winter ski-field transport.

On the map the Cardrona road to Queenstown looks much shorter than the route via Cromwell. It is much shorter but it's a winding, twisting, climbing, unsealed mountain road so travel time is likely to be no shorter. And officially rental cars and campervans are banned from using it.

Hitching If you're heading out of Queenstown to the Haast Pass and glacier country you could try hitching to Wanaka, but you will have to be very patient. Hitching out of Queenstown is difficult and hitching through the Haast Pass to Fox or Franz Josef almost impossible because of the light traffic although once you're offered a lift you're more than likely to get one going the whole way. The Haast Pass road branches off the Cromwell road a couple of km out of Wanaka, just beyond the maze. Hitch-hikers have written the sorry stories of their long waits on stones by the roadside.

Getting Around
You can hire bicycles from Wanaka Lake Services by the lake.

Te Anau & Fiordland

Te Anau is the jumping-off point for visits to the Fiordland National Park and for some of New Zealand's most famous walks, including the best known of the lot, the Milford Track. Information on that walk can be found in the chapter on Tramping & Skiing. The two main towns in the area are Te Anau and, a little to the south, Manapouri on Lake Manapouri.

Annoying Weather & Wildlife
Once you leave Te Anau, you hit two of the menaces of Fiordland: rain and sandflies. Some definitions might be in order. Rain, for those Australians who haven't come across it, is water falling from the sky – Milford gets over 6 metres (20 feet) per annum! Sandflies, for those who haven't met them, are nasty little biting insects, smaller than mosquitoes with a similar bite – you will see clouds of them at Milford. Don't be put off sightseeing by rain, the masses of water hurtling down the sheer walls of Milford Sound are an incredible sight and rain tends to keep the sandflies away. For walking and tramping it is a different story, causing flooded rivers and poor visibility.

TE ANAU
Beautifully situated on the shores of Lake Te Anau, the town of Te Anau is like a smaller, lower key version of Queenstown. Like Queenstown there are all manner of activities and trips to keep you busy although for many visitors the town is just a jumping-off point for the Milford Track.

Information
The Fiordland National Park Visitors Centre is on Te Anau Terrace beside the lake. You can get all your information on tramping or shorter walks here – they're open 8 am to 12 noon and 1 to 5 pm daily.

As well as the Milford Track, Te Anau is also the jumping-off point for walking the Greenstone, Caples, Routeburn or Hollyford Track so this is a very popular walking locale. The walks are covered in the introductory Tramping section.

Fiordland Travel, the company that operates the lake cruises and tours, is also on the lakeside, where the Milford Rd intersects it. If you're going on more than one of their trips check the discounts they offer for multiple bookings. YHA members are also eligible for discounts. Mt Cook Airlines Travel Office is on the other side of the road.

You can rent row boats, outboard motors, pedal boats, catamarans or canoes from Lakeland Boat Hire.

Cruises & Trips

There are all manner of cruises and trips from Te Anau. See the following section on Milford Sound for details of trips to the Sound.

Cruises on Lake Te Anau, the largest lake in the South Island – 53 km long and

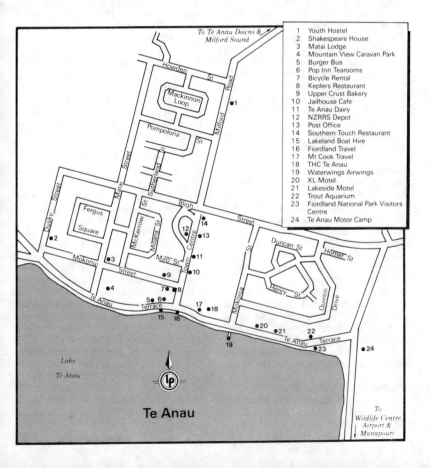

1	Youth Hostel
2	Shakespeare House
3	Matai Lodge
4	Mountain View Caravan Park
5	Burger Bus
6	Pop Inn Tearooms
7	Bicycle Rental
8	Keplers Restaurant
9	Upper Crust Bakery
10	Jailhouse Cafe
11	Te Anau Dairy
12	NZRRS Depot
13	Post Office
14	Southern Touch Restaurant
15	Lakeland Boat Hire
16	Fiordland Travel
17	Mt Cook Travel
18	THC Te Anau
19	Waterwings Airwings
20	XL Motel
21	Lakeside Motel
22	Trout Aquarium
23	Fiordland National Park Visitors Centre
24	Te Anau Motor Camp

Te Anau

10 km across at its widest point, are very popular. One of the cheaper trips goes to the unique Te Anau-au Caves (caves of swirling waters), which were rediscovered in 1948. On the shores of the lake and accessible only by boat, these caves are magical with their waterfalls, whirlpools and glow-worm grotto. It's $21 (children $8) for the two-hour trip.

You can also go to Glade House, the starting point for the Milford track. Unfortunately, for most of the track season the Glade House trip operates directly up and back not allowing any stopover at Glade House. During the very beginning and very end of the season (October and April respectively), before and after daylight saving, it is possible to go up in the morning and return in the afternoon, with about a six-hour stopover. The return boat trip costs $28 (children $8) but the boat leaves from Te Anau Downs. There's a connecting NZRRS bus to the boat.

Yacht charters and cruises on the lake are also made by Sindbad Cruises.

Flights
There are lots of flightseeing opportunities from Te Anau. Air Fiordland (tel 7505) have flights to Milford Sound for $99, to Doubtful Sound for $65, over Fiordland National Park for $145 or a short 'Fiordland Look Around' for $33. The flight to the sound goes over the Milford track with views of the amazing drop of the Sutherland Falls.

Waterwings Floatplanes (tel 7405) have flights from right off Te Anau Terrace in the centre. There's a quick zip around the area for $25, a flight to Doubtful Sound for $75 or the longer trip to Milford Sound for $115. Southern Lakes Helicopters (tel 7167) also has flights around the area.

Wildlife Centre & Trout Stream
Just outside Te Anau towards Manapouri is the small Te Anau Wildlife Centre which concentrates on native birds. It's free, compact, nicely laid-out and

worthwhile taking time out if only to see the rare takahe, one of New Zealand's species of flightless birds, considered to be extinct until a colony was discovered in 1948. There are still less than 200 in the wild in the Murchison Mountains but the ones here are so tame that you won't have to wait long to see them. The centre has a variety of other New Zealand birds both common and rare. Beside the keas a sign warns trampers that keas:

enjoy the following sports: ripping tents, flys and sleeping bags, trying on tramping boots (if they don't fit they usually cut a bit off here and there), eating your supplies, criticising alpine landscape artists . . .

There's also a salmon hatchery at the centre. In the town, opposite the national park centre on Te Anau Terrace, is an underground trout aquarium. Admission is $1. Between Te Anau and Manapouri there's a wildlife park with wapiti, red deer and a few fallow deer.

Places to Stay
Hostels The *Te Anau Youth Hostel* (tel 7847) is about 1½ km out of town on the Milford Rd and has room for 40 people plus there's a summer overflow hostel to cope with the busy peak periods. The nightly charge is $11 and you can leave gear here while you're away tramping.

Camping & Cabins The *Te Anau Motor Camp* (tel 7457) is just a km from the town and has sites at $6 per person or slightly more with power. There are also cabins from $24 for two, tourist flats from $35 and motel-style units from $55. They also have a bunkhouse where a bed costs $10. It's a large camp, in attractive surroundings and has a nice atmosphere.

The *Mountain View Park* (tel 7462) on Mokonui Rd has cabins and on-site caravans from $22 but has no facilities for tent campers. Powered sites are $6 per person.

Guest Houses Te Anau has a couple of well kept bed & breakfast places. At 10 Dusky St, *Shakespeare House* (tel 7349) offers bed & breakfast accommodation 'as you like it'. They're quiet and pleasant rooms off a bright, covered-in verandah and the breakfast is a substantial one, you're fixed up for the day! Costs are $45 single and $55 to $60 for doubles in the December to March season. Out of season prices drop about $5.

Matai Lodge (tel 7360) on the corner of Mati and Mokonui Sts has bed & breakfast at $50/55 for singles/doubles in season. Out of season prices drop to around $30/45.

Motels & Hotels At 52 Te Anau Terrace the *XL Motel* (tel 7258) has rooms at $50 to $60 per night. There's a small one-night surcharge and lower off-season rates. At 36 Te Anau Terrace the *Lakeside Motel* (tel 7435) is slightly more expensive with rooms in the $60 to $65 range.

Other moderately priced motels include the *Anchorage* (tel 7256) at 47 Quintin Drive. There are numerous other motels at similar or higher prices. If you're aiming for the top the *THC Te Anau Hotel* (tel 7411) is on Te Anau Terrace right in the centre and rooms start from close to $200.

Places to Eat

Takeaways & Fast Food Close to Fiordland Travel near the lakefront the *Pop Inn Tearoom* has light snacks and sandwiches and a pleasant outdoor eating area looking out over the lake. Nearby the *Burger Bus* appears at night to dispense hamburgers and other fast food.

There are several places along Milford Rd in the centre with snacks and takeaways – try the *Jailhouse Cafe* which has nice sandwiches, the popular *Te Anau Dairy* or for baked goods there's the *Upper Crust Bakery*.

If you're going to Milford take some supplies with you, there's not much available in the cheap eats department.

Pub Food & Restaurants In the *THC Te Anau Hotel* there's *Henry's Restaurant & Bar* with main courses at $13 to $20. *Kepler's* on Milford Rd features venison and seafood on its menu with main courses from $15 to $20. Up at the Milford end of the centre there's the *Southern Touch Steakhouse*.

Getting There & Away

Air Ansett and Mt Cook Airlines fly to Te Anau with costs of Queenstown $72, Mt Cook $153 and Christchurch $222.

Road NZRRS has bus services to and from Te Anau with fares of Christchurch $67, Dunedin $38, Invercargill $22, Queenstown $27. Buses depart from the Fiordland Travel office by the lake and ticketing is also done there. The Milford buses will pick up from or drop off at the Youth Hostel, out of town on the Milford road.

Hitching in and out is a bit easier than to Milford, though still fairly hard. Hitching between Manapouri and Te Anau is good if you go there for a day trip.

It's 170 km by road between Queenstown and Te Anau but a new and interesting route should come into use about the time this book is published. Fiordland Travel intend to operate a vehicle ferry across from Wilson's Bay, 20 minutes' drive from Queenstown, to Walter Peak from where you can drive through the Walter Peak and Mt Nicholas sheep stations to Te Anau in about two to 2½ hours.

Getting Around
You can hire bikes from the miniature golf course just off the main street for $3 an hour. They also have tandems.

MANAPOURI
If Te Anau is a low-key version of Queenstown then Manapouri is a low-key version of Te Anau. Just 19 km south of Te Anau, on the shores of Lake Manapouri, it's also a popular centre for trips, cruises and walking expeditions.

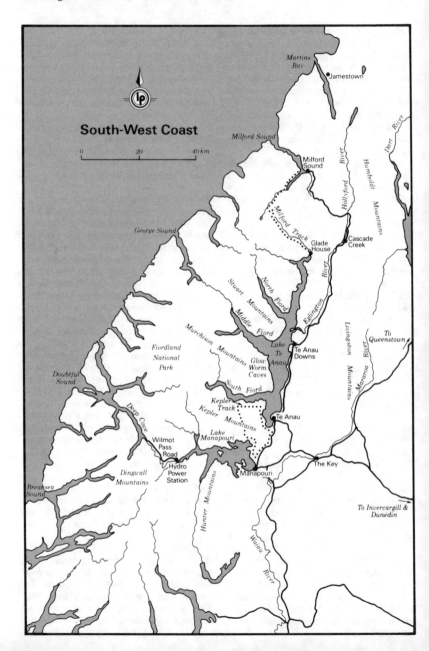

Information

Fiordland Travel (tel 7416) is the main information and tour centre – their office at the waterfront organises most of the trips. Although the Manapouri Power Station and Doubtful Sound trips depart from Manapouri there are connecting buses from Te Anau for these trips.

Cruises & Trips

There are two popular cruises from Manapouri with Fiordland Travel. One takes you across the lake to visit the power station at West Arm. The Doubtful Sound trip follows the power station visit with a drive over Wilmot Pass to Deep Cove on Doubtful Sound and then a cruise on Doubtful Sound up Hall Arm.

The hydro-power station at West Arm was built primarily to provide power for the Comalco aluminium smelter near Bluff. It generates 760,000 kw and discharge five million gallons of water a minute from Lake Manapouri into Doubtful Sound. Not surprisingly the whole project was the focus for intense environmental battles. At one time it was planned to considerably raise the level of the lake but this plan was defeated by the Save Manapouri Petition – the longest petition in New Zealand's history. When you see the beauty of what has been described as 'New Zealand's loveliest lake' it's hard to imagine that anyone would want to destroy it. Lake Manapouri is the second deepest lake in New Zealand with a greatest depth of 443 metres.

The cruise across the lake from Manapouri is followed by a bus trip down a two km spiral tunnel to the power station machine hall. This underground powerhouse is 213 metres underground (a long way!) and from here the water is passed through a 10-km long tail-race to Deep Cove in Doubtful Sound. During the construction of the powerhouse a road was built from West Arm over the Wilmot Pass to Doubtful Sound, a stretch of road totally isolated from the rest of the New Zealand road system.

The power station visit takes nearly four hours and the cost is $31 (children $8). If you want to continue on to Deep Cove by bus the trip then costs $59 (children $30). Or if you want to do the whole eight hour 'triple trip' including the cruise on Doubtful Sound then you're looking at $88 (children $33). Fiordland give you a 20% discount on this trip if you've also been on one of various other trips from Te Anau or Queenstown. You can order lunch on the trip when you book or take your own.

Walks

The National Parks office has a leaflet on short Manapouri walks ranging from one to four hours. They're all across the Lower Waiau River from Manapouri, so you to row across to the starting point.

Places to Stay

Camping & Cabins The *Manapouri Holiday Camp* (tel 624) is a km from the post office on the Te Anau road and has sites for $12 for two plus cabins from $22. The site has a sauna and spa pool.

On a stunning site, adjacent to the river and lake, is the *Manapouri Glade Caravan Park* (tel 623) with sites at $12 per night, cabins at $18 and on-site caravans at $28.

Guest Houses & Motels The fine old *Murrell's Grand View* (tel 642), built in 1889, has singles at $35, meals are also available.

There are motels by both camps – the *Lakeview Motel* (tel 624) has units at $57 while at the *Manapouri Glade Motel* (tel 623) units are $50.

Places to Eat

The coffee lounge under Fiordland Travel does good sandwiches for 80c and other snacks. If you're going on a daytrip it's probably better putting something together here rather than laying out $6 for a Fiordland Travel lunch pack. Meals are available at *Murrell's Grand View*.

Getting There & Away

NZRRS have services from Manapouri through Te Anau to Milford or from Manapouri to Invercargill, Queenstown or Dunedin. Some of their bus services only call into Manapouri if requested in advance. Fiordland Travel have lots of people going from Manapouri to Te Anau to hook up on their Te Anau trips and vice versa so they operate a Te Anau-Manapouri bus service which costs $4 (children $2) one-way.

Getting Around

You can rent row boats from Manapouri Stores for $7 a half day. Just to row across the river costs $3.

MILFORD SOUND

Whether or not you walk the Milford Track you should make a visit to Milford Sound, the 22-km-long fiord that marks the end of the walk and beside which rises the beautiful, 1695-metre-high Mitre Peak. The fiord is really breathtaking. The water, usually calm, mirrors the sheer peaks that rise all around.

Cruises & Trips

Boat cruises on Milford Sound are very popular so it's a good idea to book a few days ahead. The Fiordland Travel cruise costs $20 (children $8) on the *MV Milford Haven*. The catamaran for $23 is faster, smoother and bigger. The wharf is only a few hundred metres from the hotel, but if you don't want to walk there's a free shuttle bus 15 minutes before launch departure time. Lunch is available on board the lunchtime cruises for $11 or you can get a snack lunch for $5. You'll do better bringing your own lunch from Te Anau.

Places to Stay

Milford Sound Not only is accommodation at Milford Sound expensive it's also limited, book ahead if you want to stay there. Much of the accommodation is reserved for THC walkers on the Milford Track. At the *THC Milford Hotel* even the 'economy' rooms are up towards $100 and the regular rooms are in the $150 to $200 range. The hotel is very attractively situated and has great views.

The hostel-style *Milford Lodge*, formerly

operated by the THC, is now looked after by the park headquarters and you can get a bed there for $15. You have to supply your own bedding and cooking utensils but the store does have basic supplies. Unlike the hotel the lodge has no special situation or great views.

Along the Road There are a number of camping areas along the Milford road between Te Anau and the Eglinton Valley – check with the park HQ. You can camp at *Gunn's Camp* in the Hollyford Valley for $3 and they also have primitive cabins (a mattress and wood burning stove, you supply the rest) for $10 for a single, $16 for two. There's an interesting little museum there. A few km up the road from Milford there's a very basic little campsite.

Places to Eat
The *THC Hotel* has a restaurant and a cheaper cafeteria nearby.

Getting There & Away
You can reach the Sound by three methods, all interesting. The walk has already been mentioned. Probably the most spectacular way to go is to fly there – flights operate from Queenstown, Te Anau and other centres. A good combination trip is to go to Milford by bus and return by air.

Or you can do the round trip by bus from Te Anau or further afield. Making the round trip from Queenstown in one day involves a lot of bus travel so Te Anau is a better jumping-off point. A day trip from Queenstown means about 10 hours of bus travel, from Te Anau it's only about five hours. The 121 km trip by road is spectacular and both NZRRS and Fiordland Travel run regular bus services from Te Anau for $27 one way or $40 return. The one-day Fiordland Travel excursion leaves Te Anau at 8.15 am, returns at 5 pm and costs $70 (children $35). From Queenstown the trips depart at 7.15 am and return at 7.45 pm. NZRRS also have an excursion trip which includes a boat cruise on the sound. It's essential to

book in advance for this trip during the season.

The trekker's Magic Bus also goes to Milford for $15 or to the Divide (for the Routeburn walk) for $10. Between the Divide and Milford costs $5. It departs from the Te Anau Motorcamp, the Mountain View Caravan Park and the Youth Hostel.

The tunnel which made the road possible was started in 1935 as a major depression works project but proved too big a task and was not opened to vehicles until 1953. Until recently the tunnel was only one-way. Now it has been widened and sealed and you no longer need to plan your trip to arrive at the tunnel at the right time to be able to go straight through without waiting. The road is now normally open all year, but may occasionally be closed due to heavy snow and avalanches in the winter. If you do go by car make sure you allow time to stop off on the way, especially if you're planning to take photographs.

Hitching on the Milford road is possible but hard going. There's little traffic and nearly all of it is tourist traffic which is unlikely to stop. There are walks off the Milford road including walks close to both ends of the tunnel and also walks off the Lower Hollyford road which branches off the Milford road.

Dunedin

Population 105,000
There's a distinct Scottish feeling about Dunedin – not surprising considering the name is Celtic for Edinburgh. It's a solid, no nonsense sort of place – second city of the South Island, home of New Zealand's first university and at one time (during the gold rush days) the largest city in New Zealand.

The city itself is situated in a kind of natural amphitheatre at the head of

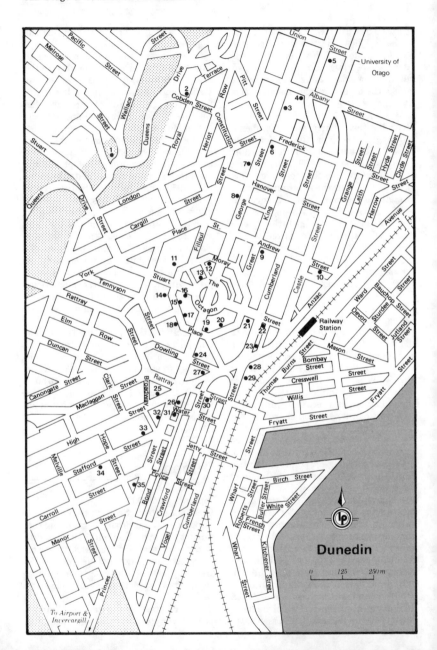

Dunedin

0   125   250 m

To Airport &
Invercargill

1	Moana Swimming Pool
2	Olveston
3	Blades, Governors & Epi d'Or
4	Captain Cook Hotel
5	Otago Museum
6	Robbie Burns & The Larder
7	Partners & Ritchies
8	Upper Crust
9	H&H Bus Terminal
10	Newmans Bus Terminal
11	Quality Inn
12	Library
13	Visitors Centre
14	Stage Left Cafe & YWCA
15	Carnegie Centre & Terrace Cafe
16	Friendship Centre & Los Gatos
17	YMCA
18	Ma Cuisine
19	Sidewalk Cafe
20	Automobile Association
21	Potpourri
22	Law Courts Establishment
23	Leviathan Hotel
24	NZTP Office
25	Southern Cross Hotel
26	Air New Zealand
27	Palms Cafe
28	Early Settlers' Museum
29	NZRRS Bus Terminal
30	Doug's Diner
31	CPO
32	Wains Hotel
33	Provincial Hotel
34	Youth Hostel
35	Prince of Wales Hotel & Carnarvon Station Restaurant

Otago Harbour, a long fiord-like inlet. It is the gateway to Otago with its many lakes and mountain resorts.

History

The first Europeans arrived at Port Chalmers in March 1848, six years after the plan for a Presbyterian settlement on the east coast of the South Island was initially mooted. Not long after the settlers' arrival in Dunedin gold was discovered in Otago and the province quickly became the richest and most influential in the colony.

Information & Orientation

The eight-sided Octagon is really more of a circle but whatever, it marks the centre of Dunedin. The main street runs through it, changing name from Princes St on the south side to George St on the north.

Being very much a university town, Dunedin becomes rather dead (or peaceful, depending on your viewpoint) during university vacations.

Tourist Information You'll find the NZTP at 123 Princes St and it's open 8.30 am to 5 pm, Monday to Friday but this is another NZTP office which is essentially a travel agent.

The Dunedin Visitors Centre (tel 774-176) is at 48 The Octagon and they're very organised and extremely helpful. The office is open weekdays 8.30 am to 5.30 pm, weekends 9 am to 5 pm. Apart from a great deal of information and advice they also book tours.

The AA is at 450 Moray Place, just down from Princes St on the left – open Monday to Friday, 8.30 am to 5 pm. The Lands & Survey Department is on the 5th (maps) and 6th floors of John Wickliffe House in Princes St – the Air New Zealand office is on the ground floor. By now the sign may say Department of Conservation but in any case most information they have is also available from the Visitors Centre.

You can only leave luggage at the railway station or NZRRS depot if you are travelling that day and you check it in. The helpful Visitors Centre will also look after left luggage.

Around the City

Various *Know the City* and *Know the Region* brochures at around 50c each help you to explore on foot or by car. Walk No 1 takes you from the Octagon, that marks Dunedin's centre, by the many old buildings close to the centre, past the port, by many elderly churches, the fine old railway station, a plaque marking the landing place of the first settlers and back to your starting point. There are many other old churches worth a look. The new library at the back of the Octagon is quite impressive.

Olveston

Olveston is a fine old turn-of-the-century house at 42 Royal Terrace, preserved as it was when lived in by a wealthy and cultured family of the early 1900s. The guided tour is a real education. Admission is $3 (children $1) and there are five tours a day from Monday to Saturday, the first one at 9.30 am and the last at 4 pm. On Sunday there are only three tours: 1.30, 2.45 and 4 pm. It's an idea to phone Olveston (tel 773-320) and reserve yourself a place on the tour.

Cadbury Chocolate

A tour of the Cadbury's chocolate factory is a major attraction – in fact it's so popular that you have to book well in advance and you can give up all hope during school vacations! The one hour tours are twice daily from Monday to Thursday and can be booked at the Visitors Centre or by phoning 741-126. The entrance to the factory is on Cumberland St.

Speight's Brewery

When you've overdosed on chocolate you can head to Speight's Brewery for their tour. It operates Monday to Friday at 10.30 am and costs $2.50 (children free). You must book in advance by phoning 779-480. Tours start from the visitors centre in Rattray St. The brewery is one of the smallest in the country and the 1½ hour tour costs $2 and concludes with a glass of beer in the company board room!

Early Settlers Museum

The Early Settlers Museum at 220 Cumberland St, between the Railway Station and NZRRS depot, has a fine collection relating to the early settlement of the region. At the railway station end of the museum there are a couple of old steam locomotives displayed in glassed-in showrooms. It's open weekdays from 8.30 am to 4.30 pm, Saturday 10.30 am to 4.30 pm, Sunday 1.30 to 4.30 pm. Admission is $3, children 50c. A horse-drawn tram operates from the museum.

Other Museums & Galleries

The Art Gallery is at Logan Park, at the end of Anzac Avenue heading out from the city – open weekdays 10 am to 4.30 pm, weekends 2 to 5 pm. It's the oldest art gallery in New Zealand and has an extensive international collection. The Carnegie Centre at 110 Moray Place is a complex of craft shops and galleries including an interesting toy shop and the excellent Press Gallery which specialises in original prints by local New Zealand artists.

The Otago Museum on the corner of Great King and Union St, houses Maori and South Sea exhibits. Admission is free and it's open weekdays 10 am to 5 pm, Saturday 1 to 5 pm, Sunday 2 to 5 pm.

The Otago Military Museum is at the Army headquarters Drill Hall in Bridgman St. Admission free, weekdays 8.30 am to 4.30 pm, but not Wednesday afternoons. Ask at the 4th Otago/Southland orderly room. The Transport & Technology Museum on Russell St in Seacliff is open on Sundays from 11 am to 5 pm or by arrangement if you phone 757-775. Out on the peninsula the Otago Peninsula Museum & Historical Society at Portobello is open on Sundays from 1.30 to 4.30 pm and admission is $2. Phone 780-294 for details.

University of Otago

The Geology Museum of the University of Otago has displays illustrating mineral types and New Zealand fossils. Admission is free and it's open 9 am to 5 pm weekdays during term time. Phone 771-640 out of term time.

The university itself is worth a walk around. It was founded in 1869, 25 years after the settlement of Otago, with 81 students. Today it has 7000; more than two-thirds from outside Otago. A wide variety of old and new styles of architecture contrast on the campus. Dunedin, more than any other New Zealand city, is a university town.

Parks & Pools

Dunedin has plenty of parks, including the Botanical Gardens at the north end of the city on the lower slopes of Signal Hill. The hothouse there is open from 10 am to 4.30 pm. Rhododendron Week, the third week in October, is a big deal at the gardens. The gardens also have an aviary with keas and other native birds.

In Upper Stuart St is a fine Olympic swimming pool, Moana Pool (tel 776-206), heated to 27°C. There's a hydroslide maze associated with the pool. It's best to phone first to check on hours as they're rather complex and further complicated by the fact that some of the time it's open only for school or university parties, not the public. Entry is $1.50 (children 75c), the hydroslide costs $5.50 (children $4).

Other Attractions

In the centre of the Octagon the musical Star Fountain plays at 12.30, 6, 7.30 and 9 pm daily. If the night is clear and you've made prior arrangements it's possible to do a little star gazing at the Beverly Begg Observatory, in the Robin Hood Ground. Phone 774-213 or 738-101.

Tours & Cruises

H&H (tel 740-674) have tours departing the Visitors Centre at 9.30 am and returning at 12 noon. Twilight Tours (tel 774-176) have tours of the city and peninsula from $10 to $30. Dunedin Unlimited (tel 774-176 or 740-198 after hours) does two-hour guided walking tours of the city.

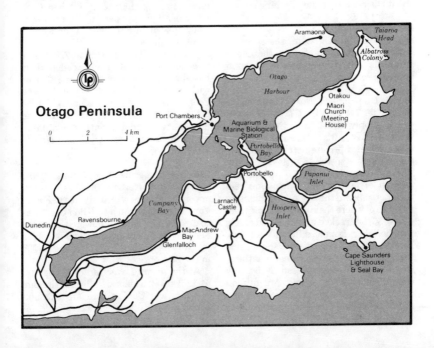

You can make 2½ to four-hour boat trips with Otago Harbour Cruises (tel 774-215) on the *MV Monarch*. They have various trips from Rattray St Wharf including the cruise out along Otago Harbour passing seal, shag and gull colonies and the royal albatross colony at Taiaroa Head. This half-day cruise costs $20 (children $11). Or you can make a hovercraft trip with Harbour Cruises Dunedin (tel 740-924) from the hoverport at Kitchener St. They have 'flights' ranging from 15 minutes ($15, children $10) to one hour ($40, children $26). Train excursions through the Taieri River Gorge and scenic flights are other possibilities.

Newton's Tours (tel 52-199) have tours to the peninsula. Further afield Silverpeaks Tours (tel Mosgiel 6167) has jet-boating and whitewater rafting trips on the Taieri River. Or enquire at the Otago Tramping & Mountaineering Club - they meet on Tuesday at 7.30 pm at 261 Stuart St - about their walking and climbing trips.

Places to Stay

Apart from in Dunedin there are a handful of places to stay on the Otago Peninsula. See the following Around Dunedin section.

Hostels Dunedin's *Stafford Gables Youth Hostel* (tel 741-919) is at 71 Stafford St, which is only about five minutes' walk from the CPO. It's a nice old building, once used as a private hotel before being converted to a hostel. Nightly cost is $13. There's room here for 62 including a number of family and twin rooms. On their noticeboard they've got a fascinating analysis of where their visitors came from - in 85/86 they racked up 12,652 bed nights with hostellers from 52 different countries. In order of nights stayed Australians came first, Americans second, Canadians third, British fourth. I wondered if by any chance one of the dozen or so Argentinian visitors happened to stay there the same night as some Brits and their solitary Falkland Islander!

There's a new private hostel called *Elm Lodge* (tel 741-872), recently opened at 74 Elm Rd, 10 minutes uphill (five going back down) from the Octagon. Run by an ex-YHA manager it has dorm beds and double rooms at $12 per person and despite its central location it has great harbour views.

Kinnaird House (tel 776-781) is in the YWCA building at 97 Moray Place (the outer circle of the Octagon) and offers bed & breakfast accommodation at $30 single or $40 twin. It takes men and women and it's a large very centrally situated building although it can suffer a bit from street noise. The breakfast is a 'light' one and the cafeteria offers a cooked lunch for $3 or dinner for $7.

The new *YMCA* (tel 779-555) is at 54 Moray Place. They generally cater for permanents, but will take casuals when they have room. It's shared accommodation - six people to a flat in single and double rooms, sharing a lounge and kitchen. Cost is $15 per night per person, $70 per week. They take men and women, and don't segregate them.

Phone the *Oasis Hostel* on 730-260 or after hours on 877-108 to check about their hostel-style accommodation for $12.50 or with meals for $18. It's run by the Pentecostal Church and is on Gladstone Rd in North Dunedin. There may be university accommodation available during their holidays - try *Arana Hall* at 770 778.

Camping & Cabins The *Tahuna Park Seaside Camp* (tel 54-690) is by the beach and near the showgrounds at St Kilda. You can get there on a St Kilda bus. Sites cost $5.50 per person, powered sites are $11 for two. There are a variety of cabins from $14 for two in the simplest ones to $38 in the best ones.

At the *Aaron Lodge Motor Camp* (tel 64-725) at 162 Kaikorai Valley Rd sites are $12 for two. Cabins here are $22 and blankets and utensils are available for hire. You can get there on a Bradford bus or on some runs the Brockville bus also goes nearby.

The *Leith Valley Touring Park* (tel 741-936) is a new site at 103 Malvern St, Woodhaugh. Sites are $7 per person and there are sometimes on-site caravans available.

Guest Houses The *Sahara Guesthouse & Motel* (tel 776-662) is at 619 George St, just off the north end of the map and quite close to the university. They mysteriously claim that 'all rooms hot and cold' and also have some motel units. Singles/doubles are $28/48 including breakfast or the motel units are $40 to $50.

Magnolia House (tel 771-999) on Grindon St is a Victorian villa where bed & breakfast accommodation is available for $30 single or $55 double. It's a really pleasant place but all bookings must be made by phone, don't just turn up, and it's strictly non-smoking.

Hotels Cheaper hotels in Dunedin include the small *Hotel Branson* (tel 778-411) at 91 St Andrews St. Rooms are typically $35 to $60 although they may sometimes have special deals. Cheap bistro meals are also available here. The *Wharf Hotel* (tel 771-233) at 25 Fryatt St offers bed & breakfast from $25.

The *Beach Hotel* (tel 54-642), on the corner of Prince Albert and Victoria Rds at St Kilda, has rooms with private facilities for $36/46. *Wains* (tel 779-283) at 310 Princes St is a great looking old place close to the centre and has rooms at $42/52. Out at Port Chalmers, *Chicks Hotel* (tel 8736) at 2 Mount St is a classic old stone building with rooms at $55.

The solid, reliable, old fashioned and centrally located *Leviathan Hotel* (tel 773-160), on the corner of Cumberland and High Sts across from the railway station, is a Dunedin landmark. Singles/doubles are $60/70 and all rooms have attached bathrooms. The Leviathan is tourist licensed (ie for guests only) unlike the other fully licensed hotels.

Also centrally located, the *Law Courts Establishment* (tel 778-036) on the corner of Stuart and Cumberland Sts has rooms at $75/85.

Right up at the top of the Dunedin hotel list are the *Quality Inn* (tel 776-784) on Upper Moray Place and the *Southern Cross* (tel 770-752) at 118 High St. Both start from the wrong side of $100 and both are centrally located.

Motels There are a number of moderately priced motels along Musselburgh Rise, on the Otago Peninsula side of town. They include the *Arcadian Motel* (tel 42-000) at 85-89, the *Chequers Motel* (tel 45-244) at 119 and the *Bayfield Motel* (tel 45-648) at 210. Doubles are around $50 at each of these places.

Others to try include the *Aaron Motel* (see Camping & Cabins above) and the *Sahara Motel* (see Guest Houses above). The *Dunedin Motel* (tel 777-692) at 624 George St has doubles from $50. Or on the corner of Duke and George Sts the *Argyle Court Motel* (tel 779-803) is in the same price range. The *St Kilda Motel* (tel 51-151) on the corner of Victoria Rd and Queen's Drive is marginally cheaper. There are plenty of other motels.

Places to Eat

Dunedin's a surprisingly good place for eating out in just about all categories. In fact there are so many dining out possibilities there's even a guide to *Eating Out in Dunedin*, it's available from the Visitors' Centre. They also have free leaflets on restaurants and on places which are open on Sundays.

Takeaways & Cafes Dunedin has an excellent selection of places for a sandwich or for lunch. There are lots along George St and around Moray Place. If the weather's lousy and you need a place to eat your sandwiches head for the *Friendship Centre* at the Central Methodist Mission, just up Stuart St from the Octagon. It's a very considerate public service and they'll also supply tea and biscuits for 60c or a bowl of soup for 50c. The centre is open 10 am to 3 pm daily.

There are several excellent places around Moray Place for lunch. At number 45 *Ma Cuisine* is a wholefood cafe with quiches, spinach pies, sandwiches and so on. A mixed salad costs $3.50, rolls are $1.50, vegetarian pizza $3 - good value. Only a few steps further round Moray Place the spacious *Stage Left Cafe* is equally well priced and is another pleasantly relaxed place to sit and eat.

Or try the *Sidewalk Cafe* at 480. It's open lunchtimes Monday to Friday and on Fridays it's also open to 9 pm. Sometimes they may be open on weekend evenings as well. They have an excellent selection of sandwiches and light meals and it's a popular and pleasant place to eat them. Continue a little further round Moray Place and turn right into Stuart St where *Potpourri* at number 97 is another nice wholefood place open for lunch Monday to Saturday and for dinner from 5 to 8 pm from Monday to Friday. They have salads at around $6, tacos at $4.50, quiche at $4 and other light meals.

Head down George St and there are several other sandwich or light lunch possibilities. There are good salads and sandwiches at the *Upper Crust*, 263 George St. It's open for lunch Monday to Saturday and provides salads, sandwiches and baked goods. A bit further down at 351 is *Partners* which is a bit more expensive than some of the other lunchtime cafes but the food is excellent. For $3.50 you can have a big bowl of excellent soup with French bread or there are open sandwiches at $2, larger meals at $7 and diet-blowing (but superb looking) cakes for $3.

Dunedin, unlike some New Zealand towns, has plenty of places for healthy snacks and sandwiches but *Ritchies Restaurant* at 339 George St is definitely trad. Mince on toast, roast lamb with mint sauce, followed by rhubarb crumble, that sort of thing!

Still on George St, *The Larder* at 388 has a big selection of takeaway sandwiches or at 430 there's the French bakery *Epi d'Or*. Back by the Octagon the *YWCA* takes casual diners for straightforward but low-priced meals. *Stewarts Coffee House*, downstairs at 12 Lower Octagon, has cheap sandwiches and excellent coffee. The *Bakers Dozen* at 11 Lower Octagon is a good, big bakery. Good food is also available in the *Botanic Gardens Restaurant* - open 10 am to 4 pm daily.

Finally *Doug's Diner* at 116 Lower Rattray St is a straightforward place for grilled food and takeaways but it's open early and closes late. If you want to start the day with bacon and eggs and finish it with a late night burger then this is the place.

Pub Food Near the Youth Hostel at 474 Princes St in the *Prince of Wales Hotel* the *Carnarvon Station Restaurant* is quite something. The hotel looks pretty ordinary but when you finally wend your way back to the restaurant area there's a complete steam locomotive and a series of railway carriages in which you can eat. Getting this distinctly heavyweight equipment inside must have been quite a feat. The food is just the standard pub regulars, nothing unusual, and rather expensive at $15 to $17 for main courses. It's open for lunch Monday to Friday, for dinner every night. There's a cheaper Italian restaurant section in the hotel.

Also near the Youth Hostel at 6 Stafford St the *Provincial Hotel* has its *Rhumbline* bistro open for lunch or dinner with burgers at $2.50, light meals at $5 to $6, main courses at $8 to $10. Or there's *Zouga Ballantynes* at 71 Frederick St with its African decor. It's open for lunch Monday to Saturday, for dinner Friday to Sunday.

There's a *Cobb & Co* in the *Law Courts Establishment* on the corner of Stuart and Cumberland Sts. It has the standard Cobb & Co menu and is open their commendably generous hours.

Well up George St at number 370 the *Robbie Burns Hotel* has *Foxy's Cafe* with the pub food regulars from $12 to $15, or cheaper dishes like curried lamb or pastas. At the same address *Zapatas* does tacos, pastas, enchiladas, quiches and other varied but definitely un-Dunedin-like food! Round the corner at the Albany St and Great Kings St intersection the *Captain Cook* is a popular student pub and has good food upstairs – if you can get in the door.

Restaurants The *Palms Cafe* on the corner of Dowling and High St is a very pleasant and deservedly popular place open 6 to 9 pm from Wednesday to Sunday. They have nice salads, pastas at $5 to $6, main courses at $8 to $12 and desserts around $4.

Near the Friendship Centre, just off the Octagon at 199 Stuart St, *Los Gatos* is said to have some of the most authentic Mexican food in New Zealand. It's reasonably priced too but it's also so popular that unless you book you may not get a table. Round the corner at 118 Moray Place the *Terrace Cafe* is also very popular. Here the menu is an imaginative blend of cuisines as diverse as Italian and Indian. Main courses are $12 to $14 and they have some interesting vegetarian dishes.

If you're looking for an expensive night out at the best Dunedin has to offer then two places to try are *Blades*, way up George St at number 450, or *95 Filleul*, at 95 Filleul St. *Yopes* at 401 Moray Place does Indonesian food with dishes around $13 to $15 or rijstaffel for two from $35 to $40.

Entertainment

Pubs Dunedin's a drinkers' town and there are plenty of places to slake that thirst. They include several of the places already mentioned above under Pub Food – like the *Prince of Wales*, the *Provincial*, or the *Law Courts Establishment*.

On the corner of Albany and Great Kings St near the university the *Captain Cook* is a very popular student pub, so crowded you can hardly get in the door sometimes. If there is room there's a very pleasant garden bar which is great in summer.

Pubs with music, particularly in the evenings, include the *Beach Hotel* at St Kilda, *Hotel Branson*, *The Provincial*, *Foxy's Cafe* at the Robbie Burns and a great many others. Check the *Otago Daily Times* on Sunday for what's on. The *Sands* bar at the *Beach Hotel* is popular for its satellite dish reception of US TV stations, something of a rarity in New Zealand.

Other *Sammy's* and the *Tai-Pei Cabaret* are nightclubs. Dunedin has a number of theatres including the professional *Fortune Theatre* and several amateur companies. The *New Edinburgh Folk Club* meets at 6 Carroll St at 8.30 pm on Friday nights.

Getting There & Away

Air Air New Zealand's office (tel 775-769) is in John Wickliffe House at 263 Princes St. There are direct flights to Auckland ($272), Christchurch ($131), Invercargill ($95) and Wellington ($186) and connections to other centres. Air New Zealand are the agents for Mt Cook Airlines who fly from Dunedin to Queenstown with connections to Te Anau, Milford, Mt Cook and other centres.

Road The NZRRS bus station on Cumberland St is only a couple of blocks from the Octagon and a hundred or so metres from the railway station. It's a fine example of art deco architecture. They have services north to Christchurch, south to Invercargill and west to Queenstown, Wanaka, the west coast and other centres. There are several services daily to Invercargill. Fares from Dunedin include Christchurch $29, Fox Glacier $89, Invercargill $24, Queenstown $42, Te Anau $38 and Wanaka $41.

Mt Cook/H&H Coachlines are at 67

Great King St (tel 740-674). They have daily services up and down the east coast of the South Island, all the way from Picton to Invercargill via Dunedin. It takes 16 hours from end to end, Dunedin is just over three hours north of Invercargill, just over 12 hours south of Picton.

Newmans (tel 773-476) are at 205 St Andrew St. They have a twice daily service on weekdays and a daily service on weekends between Dunedin and Christchurch with connections from Christchurch to Picton or Nelson.

Hitching To hitch north you can get a Pinehill bus to the beginning of the motorway, or a Normandy bus to the Gardens from the Octagon, or walk it – about 30 to 40 minutes. You can get an NZRRS Cherry Farm bus to Waitati and avoid the city and the motorway. Hitching south, you can take an Otago Road Services bus from Lower High St (opposite Queen's Gardens) to Fairfield. Alternatively take an NZRRS bus to Mosgiel, alighting at the turn-off or, if it's a long distance bus, at East Taieri.

Rail Stuart St, which runs through the Octagon, continues down to the railway station on Anzac Avenue. Monday to Saturday the Christchurch-Invercargill train passes through in both directions. To Christchurch takes about six hours for $28, to Invercargill about 3½ hours for $24. The railway station is a local landmark, an example of Dunedin architecture at it's most imposing and confident.

Getting Around

Airport Transport There is a bus service out to the airport operated by Richie Southern Services (tel 779-239). It operates from the Visitors Centre and also stops opposite the Southern Cross Hotel, High St, nearer to the Youth Hostel. The 31-km trip takes 40 minutes and costs $7. The restaurant at the airport is better than most.

Local Transport City buses leave from the Octagon or from the intersection of High and Princes Sts. The local buses are operated by the Dunedin City Council and are generally expensive and infrequent.

Bicycle Rental You can rent bicycles (tel 741-211) for $8 a half day or $12 a full day from 77 Lower Stuart St. Bikes can be taken with you by bus from $1.50.

AROUND DUNEDIN

You can spend a pleasant afternoon or longer tripping around the Otago Peninsula. Stops can be made at Glenfalloch Woodland Gardens, the Portobello Aquarium and Marine Biological Station (closed Fridays), and Otakou where there's a Maori church and meeting house with a small museum.

Glenfalloch Woodland Gardens

About nine km out of Dunedin the gardens are noted for their rare rhododendrons and azaleas and for the peacocks and domestic birds which wander freely in the grounds. They are open 9 am to 5 pm daily and entry is $2.50. You can get there on a Portobello bus.

Larnach's Castle

Highlight of the peninsula is probably Larnach's Castle (tel 761-302) on the hilltop of the peninsula and open to the public from 9 am to 5 pm (or longer from December to May). Built by J W M Larnach in 1871, it is said to be the most expensive house in the southern hemisphere – construction cost over $10 million by today's standards. A conglomeration of architectural styles and fantasies, its owner, an able politician, committed suicide in a Parliament House committee room in 1898.

You can get to Larnach's Castle, 15 km from central Dunedin, by taking the Peninsula bus to Company Bay. From here it's a four-km uphill walk. Entry is $6 (children $3) and the cafe at the castle does Devonshire teas or light lunches.

Taiaroa Head & the Albatrosses

At the end of the peninsula is Taiaroa Head where the only royal albatross colony in the world close to human habitation can be seen. Public access is allowed only by purchasing a permit ($7) from the NZTP office or the Visitors Centre in Dunedin, which entitles you to a one-hour conducted visit. Visiting hours are at 2.30 pm Monday, Wednesday, Thursday and Saturday.

To get to the albatross colony catch a Ritchie's Peninsula bus to Portobello then you've got 11 km to walk or hitch through beautiful scenery to the colony. There is talk about an albatross shuttle bus service starting. There is an element of chance in what you will see – in calm weather it's unlikely you'll see an albatross flying. The later you get there the more likely you are to see them fly as there's usually more wind later in the day.

The royal albatross is the largest sea bird in the world with a wingspan which can exceed three metres. Because of their great size they nest only where there are the high winds and favourable updraughts which they need in order to get airborne. The birds mate in October, the chicks hatch out in January and remain at the colony until December. Between March and September the chicks are left alone at the colony while their parents collect food for them. It's possible the Wildlife Service may close the colony from time to time.

Penguins and seals are also to be found on the peninsula. To visit the penguin and seal colony you have to get a key from McGrouther's farm down Harrington Point Rd on the Otago Peninsula. You can't miss it – there's a big sign for the 'Penguin Place'. The penguins can be hard to see, late in the afternoon is the best time. It costs $3 plus a $4 deposit for the key.

Ocean Beach Railway

During the week you can sometimes see restoration work in progress at the Ocean Beach Railway (tel 52-798). On Sundays

from 2 to 5 pm you can have a ride but phone and check what's going on before you go out. Catch the St Kilda bus from John Wickliffe House in town, to its terminus.

Beaches & Walks

On the headland at the end of St Clair Beach is a heated outdoor saltwater pool. It's open only in the summer – catch bus No 7. St Clair and St Kilda are also good beaches to walk along or if you happen to be there on the Shortest Day (ie middle of the winter) you can join the famous swim (in the sea not the heated pool!).

You can walk to the remnants of Cargills Castle from St Clair. There is hope that there will be a walkway from here to Tunnel Beach one day, but at present it is overgrown private property. You can walk to Tunnel Beach another way, but this is also across private property, so phone Mr Walker (tel 878-481) first for permission. Then catch a Corstorphine bus from the Octagon to Stenhope Crescent and walk along Blackhead Rd till you reach a 'no exit' road leading towards the coast. Head towards the triangular promontory, where you'll find a hand-carved stone tunnel leading towards a secluded beach. It's best to have a 50-metre rope to get down as wave erosion has worn down the steps. For more information see the Visitors Centre.

If you catch a Dunedin City Council Normandy bus to the start of Norwood

Rd, you can walk up it to the Mt Cargill-Bethunes Gully Walkway. It takes two hours uphill, 1½ down. The highlight is the view from Mt Cargill (accessible by car). Take warm clothes as it gets very windy at the top. The walkway is extended from Mt Cargill to the Organ Pipes.

Up behind Dunedin is the Pineapple Flagstaff Walk, which is not accessible by public transport. You can get leaflets on these walks from the Visitors Centre.

Places to Stay

There are a few places where you can stay on the peninsula. You you can camp at the *Portobello Domain* (tel 780-899) – the nightly cost is $2.50 per person but there's no power although there is a facilities block. At *McGrouther's Farm*, near the penguins, you can stay in an old army barracks, the minimal cost is just to cover the electricity.

The only other place to stay on the peninsula is the *Larnach Castle Lodge* (tel 761-302) where there are cabins at $26 for two and a handful of campervan positions. The castle also has some hotel-style rooms at $38 or with private facilities at $50.

Invercargill

Population 54,000

The southernmost city in New Zealand, Invercargill is very much a farming servicing community, with a surprising amount of wealth (you notice more Jags here than anywhere else in New Zealand). To most travellers coming here it's just a jumping-off point for the tramping tracks of Stewart Island. Invercargill is surprisingly far south although relative to South America it's at the north end of Patagonia rather than the south.

History

When the Chief Surveyor of Otago, J T Thomson, travelled south to settle on a site for Invercargill the region was uninhabited and covered in a dense forest, known as Taurakitewaru Wood, which stretched from the Otepuni Stream (then known as the Otarewa) in the south to the Waihopai River in the north. Realising that ships of 500 tons could sail up the estuary to the mouth of the Otepuni Stream, Thomson chose Taurakitewaru Wood as the best site for the new town. It was laid out over 'a mile square' with four reserves just inside its boundaries and a fifth one running down the banks of the Otepuni Stream. Originally, Queens Park was just over the northern boundary and 200 acres (around 80 hectares) of forest was set aside for it. Today the only part of the forest that remains is a small area known as Thomsons Bush.

Information & Orientation

The locals staunchly defend their city, despite snide comments from the rest of the country about its backwardness. There are minor variations in speech and language throughout New Zealand, but in Southland the difference is most marked. Watch for the 'Southland drawl', with its rolled 'r's' – more pronounced in the more isolated rural areas.

The two major streets are Tay St, which is the main road in from Dunedin from the east, and Dee St which meets Tay St at right angles and heads north for Queenstown. The shopping centre is between them, north of Tay and east of Dee St. Invercargill really sprawls – they had lots of room to build it and they used it all!

Tourist Information There's a Visitors Information Service (tel 86-091) at 82 Dee St. It's open weekdays only. The CPO, with its strange purple and white colour scheme, is at the bottom of Dee St, but postal services are separate from the main post office on Spey St between Dee and Leven Sts.

The AA (Southland) (tel 89-033) is at 47 Gala St and the Lands & Survey

Department (tel 87-334) is in Menzies Building, Esk St, opposite the railway station. If you're going to Stewart Island it's a good idea to drop into Lands & Survey to pick up all the info on walks.

Museum & Art Gallery

Invercargill's main attraction is the Southland Museum & Art Gallery, near the entrance to Queens Park in Gala St, one of its claims to fame being some live tuatara, the ancient and fairly rare New Zealand reptile. The technology section upstairs is good too.

There's also an observatory here, open from 7 to 9 pm on Wednesday nights during the winter – good fun on a starry night. Museum hours are from 10 am to 4.30 pm Monday to Friday, 1 to 5 pm on Saturday and Sunday. While you are there, the 80-hectare Queens Park itself is worth a quiet wander. You can pick up a town walking-tour leaflet from the museum.

There is another Art Gallery (tel 57-432) at Andersons Park, seven km north on the main road to Queenstown. It's open 2 to 4.30 pm daily except Monday and Friday.

Beaches & Pools

There are two warm water indoor swimming pools in Invercargill, one on Conon St, just off Tay St, and one on Queen's Drive at the end of Queen's Park.

Invercargill's beach is Oreti, 9½ km west of the city. It's a long sweeping beach and the water is much milder than most South Island beaches because a warm current sweeps across from Australia. You can collect toheroa shellfish from this beach during the season, but the number is strictly limited.

Riverton, 38 km west, is considered to be one of the oldest settlements in New Zealand, dating from the sealing and whaling days. It's quite interesting and the nearby Riverton Rocks area is a popular local beach and holiday resort.

Bluff

Invercargill's port, and the departure point for the Stewart Island ferry, is Bluff, 27 km to the south. There's an observation point at the top of Bluff Hill (265 metres) – you can walk it in half an hour or so – from which you can see the Island Harbour, Foveaux Strait, Stewart Island and the Tiwai Point aluminium smelter. Hills being quite a rare physical feature in this area, it's one of the better vantage spots.

Across the harbour from Bluff is the Tiwai Aluminium Smelter, eighth largest in the world. Overseas owned, it was attracted to Bluff by promises of cheap power; the Manapouri Power Scheme was built to feed it, and if there hadn't been such a public outcry Lake Manapouri would have been raised and destroyed to cater for the hunger for electricity. The smelter is now a major source of employment for Invercargill's citizens – around 1600 jobs – and they get mighty sensitive to any hint of criticism about it. Free tours can be arranged by phoning 85-999 in advance.

For safety reasons you need clothing covering the arms and legs, and heavy footwear. No watches or cameras are allowed. The tours are twice weekly, or daily in holiday periods, but you need your own transport to get out there.

Walks

The main attraction is Foveaux Walk, a 6.6 km walkway from the southern end of State Highway 1 to Ocean Beach where it emerges at a bus stop – takes about 2½ hours. Don't be misled by the name 'Ocean Beach' – what you will find there is a smelly freezing works. Another track (Glory Track) leaves from Gunpot Rd and passes through Bluff Hill's only remaining stand of native bush, connecting with the main walkway (35 minutes). Waihopai Walkway is only 10 minutes from the Youth Hostel. There are several other walks, details of which are obtainable from the Visitors Information Centre or the Lands & Survey Department.

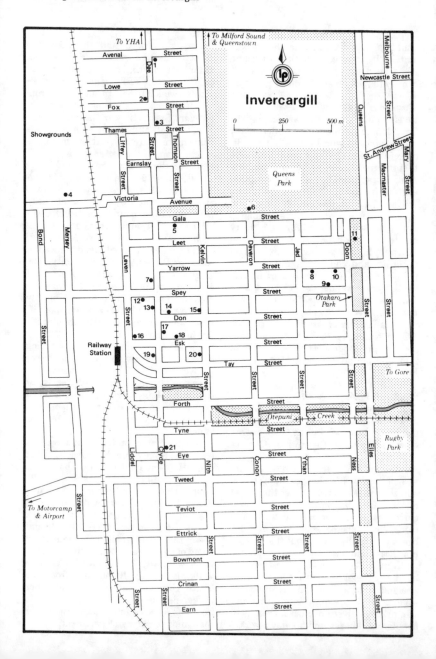

Invercargill

0   250   500 m

To YHA

To Milford Sound
& Queenstown

Avenal Street
Dee Street
1

Lowe Street
2

Fox Street
3 Thomson Street

Thames Street
Liffey Street

Earnslay Street

Showgrounds

4

Victoria Avenue

6 Street

Gala Street
5

Leet Street

Kelvin Street
Deveron Street
Jed Street
Doon Street

11

Yarrow Street

8   10
9

Spey Street

Otakaro
Park

12
13 14   15

Don Street

17
16   18

Esk Street

19   20

Tay Street

To Gore

Forth Street

Otepuni   Creek

Tyne Street

Rugby
Park

21 Eye Street

Tweed Street

Teviot Street

Ettrick Street

Bowmont Street

Crinan Street

Earn Street

Queens Park

Melbourne Street

Newcastle Street

Queens Street

St Andrew Street
Macmaster Street
Mary Street

Railway
Station

Bond Street
Mersey Street
Leven Street
7

To Motorcamp
& Airport

Liddel Street
Clyde Street
Nith Street
Conon Street
Ythan Street
Ness Street
Ellis Street

1	Avenal Homestead
2	Pizza Hut
3	Kentucky Fried Chicken
4	Showground Motor Camp
5	Automobile Association
6	Southland Museum
7	Moa's Restaurant, Joy's Gourmet Kitchen & Fresh Sea Food
8	Aachen Hotel
9	Montecillo Travel Hotel
10	Yarrow Motel
11	Water Tower
12	Postal Services
13	Southland Information Centre & Grand Hotel
14	Tillerman's Restaurant
15	H&H Bus Station
16	Railway Hotel
17	Nobles
18	Air New Zealand
19	Grand Hotel
20	Kelvin Hotel
21	Clyde Tavern

Other Attractions

If you want to go horse riding contact the Otatara Riding Centre (tel 331-127) on Oreti Rd. It's open every day, but bookings are essential. The curious water tower at the bottom of Leet St was built in 1889.

Tours

H&H (tel 82-419) offers a city sights tour from Monday to Friday at 1.15 pm. It takes a couple of hours and you get a running commentary on all the historical, cultural and beauty spots of Invercargill. The tour leaves from the terminal on the corner of Don and Kelvin Sts. Blue Star Taxis (tel 86-079) offer tours for smaller groups. Southern Scenic Tours (tel 397-155) offer trips further afield including farm visits, jet boating, fishing and so on.

Places to Stay

Hostels The world's southernmost *Youth Hostel* (tel 59-344) is at 122 North Rd, Waikiwi, about three km from the town centre. The nightly costs are $11 and it sleeps 44. See the warden about private youth hostel accommodation on Stewart Island. There is also a *YMCA* (tel 82-989) on Tay St but it doesn't have any accommodation although it does have squash courts.

Camping & Cabins The *Invercargill Caravan Park* (tel 88-787) is at the A&P Showgrounds on Victoria Avenue off Dee St, only a km from the centre. It's closed during showtime but the rest of the year tent sites are only $5 per person, power sites are slightly more. There are also some very cheap cabins.

At 705 Tay St the *Coachman's Caravan Park* (tel 76-046) has sites at $11 or a dollar or so more with power. There are also cabins here, costing from $24 for two people. Out towards Oreti Beach, eight km from the centre, the *Beach Road Motor Camp* (tel 330-400) has sites at $6.50 per person and cabins from $12 per person plus some recently constructed units.

Hotels & Motels The *Montecillo Travel Hotel & Motel* (tel 82-503), 234-240 Spey St, is a friendly place with hotel and motel rooms. Including breakfast the hotel rooms are $50/60 or $35/55 for the rooms without private facilities. The motel units cost $47/53 but without breakfast. The Montecillo is a straightforward but well kept place and conveniently close to the centre. There are numerous other motels, typically from around $60.

Gerrard's Private Railway Hotel (tel 83-406), is on the corner of Esk and Leven Sts, right across the road from the railway station. It's a deliciously ornate 1896 (with additions in 1907) building which has recently been through a major renovation and also houses one of the town's best restaurants. Singles cost $40 to $49 (the more expensive rooms have attached bathrooms), doubles or twins are $54.

On Dee St opposite the end of Don St

the imposing old *Grand Hotel* (tel 88-059) has singles from $40 to $56 depending on their size. Doubles or twins are $68. The restaurant here is open seven days a week. On Kelvin St in the centre the *Kelvin Hotel* (tel 82-829) is the largest hotel in town, it's well kept but bland and costs a fairly hefty $84/94 for singles/doubles although there are also a handful of singles without attached bathrooms for $55.

Places to Eat

Being at the centre of an important fishing area there's lots of fish for sale – particularly crayfish, cod and the superb Bluff oysters for less than $5 a dozen. Also this is the home of mutton birds. The local Maoris have a season when they are allowed to collect them from small islands off Stewart Island. They keep the best ones and sell the rest through the shops. But make sure you know how to cook them or they'll taste revolting!

Takeaways & Fast Food Particularly along Dee St and around the centre there's the usual collection of fast food places and a number of sandwich places. *Nobles* at 47 Dee St has pretty reasonable sandwiches and comfortable surroundings. It's open Monday to Friday for lunch and until 8 pm on Fridays.

Joy's Kitchen at 122 Dee St has a good selection of salads and wholemeal goodies plus sandwiches (from $1.20), quiches (from $2) and pizzas (from $1.50 a slice). The best vegetarian/wholemeal/healthfood place in Invercargill is *Tillerman's*, upstairs at 16 Don St. It's quite a gathering spot locally and is open 10 am to 3 pm Monday to Friday. Friday it also opens from 5 to 7 pm and then from 9.15 pm until late for coffees/teas and snacks.

Moa's Restaurant is something of a local institution and is open commendably long hours. It's at 130 Dee St and serves up straightforward food in large quantities – this is the sort of place where the plate disappears under the steak and chips. Grills are around $8 to $10. Lighter meals (egg and chips, that sort of thing) will cost you $6 or $7. Opening hours are Monday and Tuesday 9 am to 4 pm, Wednesday and Thursday 9 am to 11 pm, Friday 9 am to 1 am, Saturday 11 am to 1 am and Sunday from 11 am to 2 pm and then from 4.30 to 10 pm.

There's the usual selection of fish & chipperies including, a couple of door's from Moa's, *Fresh Sea Foods* at 136 Dee St. It's open 9 am to 11 pm weekdays, and 11 am to 8 pm weekends. The food here is straightforward and good value. Further north up Dee St, about half way to the YHA, there's a *Pizza Hut* and a *Kentucky Fried Chicken* plus several other big drive-in takeaways. *Enter the Dragon* at 107 Tay St is a Chinese takeaway although in Invercargill they do burgers too.

Pub Food Like Dunedin there are plenty of pubs here and most of them serve up food as well. If you're just back from tramping around Stewart Island and have brought a horrendous appetite with you then you could do worse than try the *Kelvin Carvery* in the Kelvin Hotel on Kelvin St. Depending on the day lunch costs $12.50 to $14.50, dinner $16 to $17.50 and for that price you can eat yourself silly. You get soup, various meats from the carvery, a wide assortment of salads and vegetables, plus desserts, tea or coffee. It's good, solid, simple food (the salads are excellent) in a 'frozen-in-the-50s' dining room. At night there's live muzak from an organist who drones away in the background and all in all this is a slice of forgotten NZ that's worth experiencing.

North up Dee St on the corner of Avenal St is the *Avenal Homestead* with the usual bars plus a good restaurant very much out of the Cobb & Co mould. It's a modern, pleasant place with the standard pub-food menu at $10 to $14. Still further north on Dee St, at Gimblett St, very close to the Youth Hostel, the *Galaxy Family*

Restaurant at the *Waikiwi Tavern* is even more modern with its shiny/blinking-light space-age setting. The food, however, is more down to earth. All the regular pub fare is on the menu with prices in the $9 to $11 bracket. Down the other end of Dee St, where it becomes Clyde St, the *Clyde Tavern* does cheap bistro lunches.

Restaurants Most of the restaurants in Invercargill are pretty mundane. You could try the *Ainos Steak House* at the Waikiwi Shopping Centre, on Dee St seven blocks north of the Youth Hostel. It's simple, straightforward and open Monday to Saturday.

Back in the centre *Gerrard's* at the Station Hotel, right across from the railway station, is one local restaurant which does seem to have a good reputation. It's open every night of the week and if you need a really flashy night out in Invercargill this could be the place.

Entertainment
There's not much of this in the centre of town, which seems to close with a clang after 9 pm. You really need to get out to the suburbs to find anything happening at all, apart from the movies.

The weekend editions of the *Southland Times* will tell you what's on. The *Rafters Bar* at the Whitehouse Hotel is possibly the best to go to, but it's right out at Lorneville, eight km north of Waikiwi. There's a cover charge. The *Waikiwi Tavern* is at least handy to the Youth Hostel. Other pubs with entertainment include the *Ascot Park Motor Hotel* at the corner of Tay St and Racecourse Rd or the *Southland Hotel* on Elles Rd.

Getting There & Away
Air Air New Zealand (tel 44-737) have their office at 46 Esk St. There are direct flights to Dunedin ($95), Christchurch ($159), Auckland ($300) and Wellington ($220) although not all flights to Auckland and Wellington go direct.

Flights to Stewart Island are made with Southern Air (tel 89-129). Air New Zealand and NZRRS are both agents for Southern Air. See the Stewart Island section below for details.

Road The Railway Station (including NZRRS) is behind the CPO in Leven St. They have bus services from Invercargill to Te Anau ($38), Queenstown ($42), Dunedin ($24) and other centres. Te Anau and Queenstown are daily, Dunedin more frequently.

The Mt Cook/H&H depot (tel 82-419) is on the corner of Don and Kelvin Sts. This is their head office and apart from the daily service up the coast through Dunedin (three hours), Christchurch (10 hours) and on to Picton (16 hours) they also have a number of local services to Bluff and other centres further afield in Southland. See the following Getting Around section.

If you've got your own transport and you're travelling between Dunedin and Invercargill consider taking the coastal route. The distance is pretty similar although it's somewhat slower since some of the road is unsealed. There are some interesting reserves on the way.

Hitching Hitching between Dunedin and Invercargill is usually fairly simple and should only take about half a day. If you're on your way to Queenstown or Te Anau it gets steadily harder the further you go and many people get stuck overnight in Lumsden. Without transport the coastal route between Dunedin and Invercargill is pretty hard – public transport is almost non-existent and there's little traffic for hitching.

Rail The Southerner operates Christchurch-Dunedin-Invercargill from Monday to Saturday. Fares are Christchurch $48 and Dunedin $24.

Getting Around

Airport Transport The airport is only 2.5 km from the centre and you can get there by the H&H bus service which connects with arrivals and departures or by taxi. The bus fare is $2.50.

In 1984 Invercargill had bad floods which caused immense destruction throughout the region, isolating it from the rest of New Zealand - and the world - for several weeks. The airport was completely flooded and there's a high water marker two metres above floor level in the terminal building. Despite extensive flood prevention measures there was a repeat performance in 1987 and again the airport was inundated, although this time only a metre or so. Air New Zealand flights were halted for weeks but flights for Stewart Island operated from the local race course.

Local Transport The Invercargill City Council Transport Department (tel 87-108) puts out a timetable with a colour-coded map of bus routes. You can get hold of a copy from the Visitors Information Centre. Local bus services cost 65c.

H&H operate a regular daily service to Bluff including connections with the Stewart Island ferry. They also have a variety of other local services to Gore, Riverton and other centres and to places further afield in Southland such as Te Anau, Wanaka or Queenstown.

Stewart Island

Population 450

New Zealand is generally thought of as just two big islands - but actually there are lots of little-uns and one other fair size one slung right off the southern end of Invercargill. A sort of Tierra del Fuego of New Zealand? Actually Stewart Island is not as inhospitable as that, but it most definitely is a get-away-from-it-all type of place. The miniscule population is congregated together, except for a few households on the west side of the island at Mason's Bay. It's 64 km long and 40 km across, has less than 15 km of roads and its rocky coastline is incised by numerous inlets, the largest of these being Paterson. The highest point on the island is Mt Anglem at 980 metres.

History

There is all sorts of evidence that parts of Stewart Island were occupied by moa-hunters as early as the 13th century. According to Polynesian mythology New Zealand was hauled up from the depths of the South Pacific Ocean by Maui who said 'Let us go out of sight of land and when we have quite lost sight of it, then let the anchor be dropped; but let it be very far off - quite out in the open sea'. One interpretation of this myth is that the North Island was a great flat fish caught by Maui; the South Island his canoe and Stewart Island the anchor - Te Punga o te Waka a Maui being the legendary name for the latter. Much later the Maoris called it Rakiura - the island of the glowing sky.

The first Pakeha to come across Stewart Island was good old Captain Cook in 1770, who sailed around the eastern, southern and western coasts but could not make up his mind whether it was an island or a peninsula. Deciding it was part of the South Island mainland he called it Cape South. Several decades later this theory was disproved when under the command of Captain Chase, the sealing vessel *Pegasus* - presumed the first European ship to do so - circumnavigated Stewart Island. The island was named after William Stewart, first officer of the *Pegasus*, who charted the southern coast of the island in detail.

In June 1864 Stewart and the adjacent islands were bought from the Maoris for the sum of £6000. Early industries consisted of sealing, timber milling, fish curing and ship building. The discovery of gold and tin towards the end of the 19th century also led to an increase in settlement but the rush didn't last long and today the island's economy is based on fishing – crays and cod – and tourism. The principal settlement is Oban around Halfmoon Bay, with roads extending only a few km further out from here. All electricity is generated by private plant – nearly every house has its own small diesel generator and in the evening Halfmoon Bay hums with them. Cooking and heating is usually with wood stoves.

The people are hardy, independent, insular and suspicious of mainlanders,

the law and bureaucracy. The weather is incredibly changeable – brilliant sunshine one minute, pouring rain the next. Conditions can be very muddy underfoot and you will need boots and waterproof clothing but the temperature is much milder than you would expect.

Flora & Fauna

If you know anything about trees the first thing you'll notice is that, unlike the North and South Islands, there is no beech forest on Stewart Island. The predominant lowland vegetation is hard-

wood but there are also lots of tree ferns and a variety of ground ferns as well as several different kinds of orchid, including three species of lady's slipper, two of earina and a number of spider orchids. Along the coast the vegetation consists of muttonbird scrub, grass tree, tree daisies, jack vine and leatherwood. You need a trusty machete to hack through the last two if there are no defined tramping tracks! You are warned, however, not to go tramping off the beaten track.

Stewart Island is an ornithologist's delight. Apart from the numerous sea birds that breed here, bush birds such as tuis, parakeets, kakas, bellbirds, fernbirds, robins – the last two are found near Freshwater Flats – dottrels and kiwis abound – much rarer are the kokako, kakapo and weka but they're around if you look.

Bluebird Songster

Two species of deer were introduced to the island early in the 20th century. They are the red deer found mainly around Mt Anglem, Freshwater and Rakeahua Valleys and at Toi Toi Flat in the south-east and the Virginia (whitetail) deer which inhabit the coastal areas of the

island. Also introduced were brush-tailed possums, which are particularly numerous in the northern half of the island and rather destructive on the native bush. Stewart Island also has lots of seals.

Information

There is a post office where you can cash travellers' cheques. It's on Elgin Terrace, Halfmoon Bay, about five minutes' walk from the wharf. The telephone exchange is manual and is open from 6 am to 12 midnight from Monday to Saturday and from 6 am to 10 pm on Sunday.

For information on tracks and tramping contact the Lands & Survey Department (tel 87-334), Menzies Building, opposite the railway station in Invercargill, before you take off for the island, or the senior ranger on the island, Dundee St, Halfmoon Bay. The New Zealand Forest Service on Main Rd, just past the deer park, also has lots of useful info and displays on flora, fauna and walks, etc including several low-priced publications – *Get Out & Walk – A Guide to Walking Tracks in Southland, Stewart Island, Stewart Island – Day Track & General Information* and *Stewart Island – Track & Hut Information*. You can store gear there while you're walking.

There are two general stores in Halfmoon Bay but as all food and commodities – this includes coal, meat and bread – have to be imported from the South Island, prices are high. Hours are 9 am to 5 pm during the week and 10 am until 12 noon on Saturdays and Sundays. Make sure you order bread, milk, eggs and newspapers in advance if you want them because supplies are limited.

Walks

If you want to visit Stewart Island plan on spending a few days there so you can enjoy the beaches, seals, rare bird and plant life. There are many walks on the island but although some take only a couple of hours there and back, a day trip to Stewart Island is hardly worthwhile as it's a tramper's paradise. You can spend weeks tramping here.

There is a good network of tracks and huts in the northern part of the island, but the southern part is undeveloped and can be very desolate and isolated. Visit the ranger from the Department of Lands & Survey or the New Zealand Forest Service and get hold of their booklets before you set off. They have detailed information on the walks, the time they take, when to go and accommodation facilities.

You are advised not to go off on your own – particularly from the established walks – unless you have discussed your itinerary with someone beforehand. Foam rubber mattresses, camp ovens and billies are provided at each hut but you need to take food, sleeping bags, ground sheets, eating and cooking utensils, first aid equipment and so on with you and, if you have them, a tent and primus may be useful as the huts can get packed out at certain times of the year. The first huts are about four to 5½ hours from Halfmoon Bay and a lot of people just take the north-west circuit to here. The track's well-defined and it's an easy walk, the major drawback being that it gets very crowded in the summer. There's a maximum stay of two nights in a hut (no charge). Further away from Halfmoon Bay the tracks can be very muddy and quite steep in places.

Museum & Other Attractions
The Rakiura Museum on Ayr St is no Victoria & Albert but it's worth a visit if you're interested in the history of the island. Opening hours are limited to 10.30 am to 1.30 pm each Monday, Wednesday and Friday – the three days a week the boat comes in.

Also on Ayr St is a library which is open for even less hours a week; from 2 to 3 pm on Wednesdays and 11 am to 12 noon on Fridays. On your way to the NZ Forest Service, drop into the deer park and check out the difference between red and whitetail deer. It's not far along Main Rd.

Tours
In summer there are minibus tours around Paterson Inlet, Halfmoon Bay and various other places. They're zippy little trips – only take about an hour – because there really isn't very far you can drive on Stewart Island! There are also boat trips to Ulva Island – great bird sanctuary, Ocean Beach, Port Adventure, Port William and Euchre Creek. Check the noticeboards next to the store for more detailed information.

Places to Stay
Apart from the free forestry huts if you're tramping, accommodation is generally expensive. Some caravans may be available by private arrangement, but don't expect anything fancy. YHA members can find accommodation in private homes and holidays houses are often available by private arrangement. The Invercargill Youth Hostel may also have information on these. Whatever you are offered check the location first, you could find yourself way out in the sticks. Make sure you're reasonably accessible to Oban/Halfmoon Bay.

Matches, a torch (flashlight) and candles are important equipment on Stewart Island. Water, hot or cold, is scarce – don't expect hot showers.

Hostels The Youth Hostel in Invercargill can give you names of people who offer private hostel-style accommodation on the island, usually for $8 a night.

Camping & Cabins There is a free campsite at Apple Bridge, Fern Tree Gully but it's definitely basic, comprising a fireplace, wood and water supply and pit toilets only. It's about a half-hour walk from the wharf along Main Rd.

Four km from Halfmoon Bay, *Horseshoe Haven* (tel 156K) has all the essentials and the sites cost $7 per person. An A-frame unit in which bedding, pots, pans and crockery are provided costs $38. They also have a bunkroom lodge at $13 per person, the power is turned off at 10.30 pm.

Ferndale Caravan Park (tel 52M) in Halfmoon Bay has on-site caravans at $42 for two people – all you have to supply are towels but here too the power goes off at 10.30 pm.

Hotels & Motels *Rakiura Motel* (tel 27S) is 1.5 km from the township and costs $55 for doubles. Close to the wharf is the *South Sea Hotel* (tel 6) which costs $35 per person, room only. The *Stewart Island Lodge* (tel 25) is much more expensive, its four rooms all have private facilities and cost about $150 per person including all meals.

Places to Eat
There's not much choice of where to eat on Stewart Island. It comes down to the *Travel Inn* tearoom or the *South Sea Hotel* where meals are available by prior arrangement. You should expect prices to be higher than the mainland due to freight costs. Apart from these, you can get basic necessities from the general store, buy fresh fish and crays from the locals (it's the main industry of the island so there should be no shortage), catch your own fish or bring food across from Invercargill and prepare meals yourself.

Entertainment
The only place to go for any nightlife here is the pub. The action will consist of bending the elbow, darts, eight-ball and maybe a brawl. Every now and again the fishermen get stuck into each other just for the hell of it.

Getting There & Away
Air Southern Air (tel 89-129) fly Invercargill to Stewart Island for $48 one-way (children $24). They have a student/YHA stand-by fare of $24. They like you to be at the airport 30 minutes before departure to see if there are any seats. Flights supposedly go three or four times a day and take 20 minutes to hop over the

narrow strait but in actual fact they put on as many flights as necessary. Sometimes they shuttle back and forth all day.

If you're staying at the Youth Hostel one of the pilots lives just down the road and will even pick you up and give you a ride to the airport! The bus from the airstrip to 'town' on Stewart Island is included. The free baggage allowance is only 15 kg per person, very little if you're carrying camping and/or tramping gear.

Ferry Catch an H&H bus (tel 82-419) from the corner of Don and Kelvin Sts, Invercargill, to Bluff then the ferry out to the island. The cost is $32 one way or $18 stand-by.

Usually departures are three times a week but over the summer they go every day Monday to Friday and over the Christmas holiday peak period they go daily. There are often extra sailings on public holidays but it's always wise to book well ahead. Phone Bluff 37-8376 for details.

Sometimes the regular boat is taken off the run for surveys or for trips to Campbell Island to deliver fuel, stores, mail and so on. There's another boat which takes over when that happens. The crossing takes two to 2½ hours across Foveaux Strait, noted for its often stormy weather – it can be a rough trip, so take some seasickness pills with you. You'll see a lot of seabirds on the crossing.

Chatham Islands

Population 750

Way out in the Pacific, about 800 km due east of Christchurch, the Chatham Islands are one of the most remote parts of New Zealand. There are 10 islands in the group but apart from the 50 or so people on Pitt Island only Chatham Island is populated. It's a wild and attractive place, and very much off the beaten track.

History

Chatham is renowned for being the last home of the Moriori, the pre-Maori or first Maori settlers depending who you read. They are thought to have been here from the time of the first settlement of New Zealand but with the arrival of Europeans things rapidly began to go wrong.

A British expedition first arrived at the island in 1791 and even that initial visit resulted in a clash, at aptly named Skirmish Bay. In the 1820s and 1830s European and American whalers began to arrive and then, in 1835, a Maori tribe was resettled in the Chathams. The impact on the peaceable Moriois was dramatic and their population crashed from around 2000 at the time of the first European arrival in 1791 to only about 100 in the 1860s. By the beginning of this century there were just 12 full-blooded Moriois left and the last one died in 1933.

Information

Waitangi is the only town on the islands. There are a couple of shops and a post office with savings bank facilities. The free *Chatham Island News & Views* carries the local news.

Things to See & Do

The islands have plenty of fine beaches and it's a popular place for fishing and particularly for catching crayfish. Crayfish are a major industry in the Chathams, they're exported to North America. Birdwatching is another popular activity for visitors, there are numerous rare and unusual birds to be seen. Scuba divers can explore the shipwrecks around the islands while trampers will also find interesting country to explore, particularly at the southern end of Chatham Island itself. Finally there's a small museum with Moriori artefacts in the council offices.

Places to Stay & Eat

The *Hotel Chathams* and the *Tuanui Motel* are the two accommodation possibilities. Both have rates including all meals but the motel also has a communal kitchen available for guests' use. It's also possible to stay with local people.

Getting There & Away

Apart from a freight-only cargo ship every four or five weeks the only transport to the islands is the Safe Air Argosy flight every five days or so from either Wellington or Christchurch. The flight takes three hours and since only 30 seats are available, try to book well ahead with Air New Zealand.

Getting Around

Outside of Waitangi most roads are unsealed and there is no public transport. Chatham Motors has a car and a couple of Land-Rovers to rent and it's also fairly easy to hitch. To other islands, in particular Pitt Island, Mt Hutt Aviation fly a three-seat light aircraft. You may be able to hitch a ride across with fishermen but the seas can be very rough.

Index

344

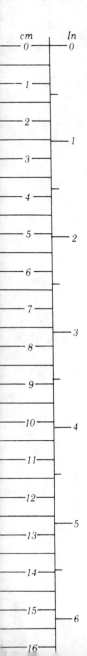

Temperature

To convert °C to °F multiply by 1.8 and add 32

To convert °F to °C subtract 32 and multiply by ·55

Length, Distance & Area

	multiply by
inches to centimetres	2.54
centimetres to inches	0.39
feet to metres	0.30
metres to feet	3.28
yards to metres	0.91
metres to yards	1.09
miles to kilometres	1.61
kilometres to miles	0.62
acres to hectares	0.40
hectares to acres	2.47

Weight

	multiply by
ounces to grams	28.35
grams to ounces	0.035
pounds to kilograms	0.45
kilograms to pounds	2.21
British tons to kilograms	1016
US tons to kilograms	907

A British ton is 2240 lbs, a US ton is 2000 lbs

Volume

	multiply by
Imperial gallons to litres	4.55
litres to imperial gallons	0.22
US gallons to litres	3.79
litres to US gallons	0.26

5 imperial gallons equals 6 US gallons
a litre is slightly more than a US quart, slightly less
than a British one

Dear traveller

Prices go up, good places go bad, bad places go bankrupt ... and every guide book is inevitably outdated in places. Fortunately, many travellers write to us about their experiences, telling us when things have changed. If we reprint a book between editions, we try to include as much of this information as possible in a Stop Press section. Most of this information has not been verified by our own writers.

We really enjoy hearing from people out on the road, and apart from guaranteeing that others will benefit from your good and bad experiences, we're prepared to bribe you with the offer of a free book for sending us substantial useful information.

Thank you to everyone who has written, and to those who haven't, I hope you do find this book useful – and that you let us know when it isn't.

Tony Wheeler

New Zealand's political arena has seen the resignation of Prime Minister Lange after a confrontation with one of his ministers.

In YHA Hostels it is possible to pay three ways; pay as you go, getting your card stamped and every 13th, 19th and 20th night will be free; or pay A$98 for eight nights (valid for 30 days); or A$230 for twenty nights (valid for 60 days).

Auckland Airport apart from the Airport Shuttle service also has a mini-bus which will take you for the same price of NZ$8 from the airport to a number of hostels and backpacker places. In Wellington there is also a freight ferry to the South Island that departs from the same area as the Cook Straight ferry between 11.30 am and 2.30 pm. There is no specified time of departure, but it usually departs around noon. The cost is the same as for the passenger ferry, NZ$30 per person.

The information in this Stop Press was compiled from letters sent to us by the following travellers: Joe Doherty (Ire), Richard Herlick (C), Lysbett M Innes (UK), & Paul Johnson (USA).

Money & Costs

The New Zealand economy is still suffering from its many woes. The inflation rate has been brought down to a manageable 4.5 per cent, but unemployment has risen. Currently, the exchange rate is around US$1 to NZ$1.67. The departure tax has increased to NZ$15.

Travellers' Tips & Comments

For those visiting Waitomo Caves, who don't mind a little different (wet) look at those crazy glow worms, should try the Black Water Rafting. You sit in an inner tube wearing a wetsuit, with a miner's lamp and float through the caves. Further information and tickets are available from the Information Centre in the Museum. The cost is NZ$35 per person and includes free entry to the Museum and tea with toast after the tour.

Paul Johnson – USA

Queenstown offers one of the craziest stunts around – bungy jumping. It costs NZ$75 (of which NZ$25 is for restoration of Queenstown's historic railway bridge) to jump 43 metres above a river from an old abandoned railway bridge. There is a catch. You have a giant rubber band which is attached to your ankles. This prevents you from a total free fall. The cost also includes a certificate and a T-shirt. It's organised by the New Action Sports, who are about 15 km outside of Queenstown. All the locals know where the 'crazies' do it, just ask in town, look for the T-shirts and listen to the stories of the participants.

Paul Johnson – USA

Lonely Planet Guidebooks

Lonely Planet guidebooks cover virtually every accessible part of Asia as well as Australia, the Pacific, Central and South America, Africa, the Middle East and parts of North America. There are four main series: 'travel survival kits', covering a single country for a range of budgets; 'shoestring' guides with compact information for low-budget travel in a major region; trekking guides; and 'phrasebooks'.

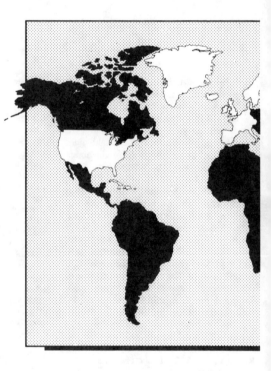